Binding Them All:
Interdisciplinary Perspectives
on JRR Tolkien and His Works

Binding Them All:
Interdisciplinary Perspectives on
J.R.R. Tolkien and His Works

edited by
Monika Kirner-Ludwig, Stephan Köser
& Sebastian Streitberger

2017

Cormarë Series No. 37

Series Editors: Peter Buchs • Thomas Honegger • Andrew Moglestue • Johanna Schön

Series Editor responsible for this volume: Thomas Honegger

Library of Congress Cataloging-in-Publication Data

Monika Kirner-Ludwig, Stephan Köser & Sebastian Streitberger (eds.):
Binding Them All: Interdisciplinary Perspectives on J.R.R. Tolkien and His Works
ISBN 978-3-905703-37-5

Subject headings:
Tolkien, J.R.R. (John Ronald Reuel), 1892-1973
Interdisciplinary Perspectives
Middle-earth
The Lord of the Rings
The Hobbit
The Silmarillion

Cormarë Series No. 37

First published 2017

© Walking Tree Publishers, Zurich and Jena, 2017

All rights reserved. No portion of this book may be reproduced, by any process or technique, without the express written consent of the publisher

Set in Adobe Garamond Pro and Shannon by Walking Tree Publishers
Printed by Lightning Source in the United Kingdom and United States

Cover by Sebastian 'Warhol' Streitberger

Board of Advisors

Academic Advisors

Douglas A. Anderson (independent scholar)

Dieter Bachmann (Universität Zürich)

Patrick Curry (independent scholar)

Michael D.C. Drout (Wheaton College)

Vincent Ferré (Université de Paris-Est Créteil UPEC)

Dimitra Fimi (Cardiff Metropolitan University)

Verlyn Flieger (University of Maryland)

Thomas Fornet-Ponse (Rheinische Friedrich-Wilhelms-Universität Bonn)

Christopher Garbowski (University of Lublin, Poland)

Mark T. Hooker (Indiana University)

Andrew James Johnston (Freie Universität Berlin)

Rainer Nagel (Johannes Gutenberg-Universität Mainz)

Helmut W. Pesch (independent scholar)

Tom Shippey (University of Winchester)

Allan Turner (Friedrich-Schiller-Universität Jena)

Frank Weinreich (independent scholar)

General Readers

Johan Boots

Jean Chausse

Friedhelm Schneidewind

Isaac Juan Tomas

Patrick Van den hole

Johan Vanhecke (Letterenhuis, Antwerp)

Acknowledgments

Many thanks to all those who worked with us to make this volume possible – most prominently, of course, the editors and contributors!

A great 'thank you' also to Larissa Zoller, Sophia Mehlhausen, and Maryna Tymoshchuk who helped with the layouting and proofreading of the text. Also I want to thank my colleagues at Walking Tree Publishers, Andrew Moglestue, Peter Buchs, and Johanna Schön, who did a great job with the quality management of the layout, helped with the editing of the tables and pictures, and made sure that the quality of the (colour) printing meets our standards.

Jena, August 2017
Thomas Honegger, Series Editor

Contents

Stephan Köser (with Monika Kirner-Ludwig & Sebastian Streitberger)
The Tolkien Journey at the University of Augsburg ... 1

Thomas Honegger
"Meet the Professor" –
A Present-day Colleague's View of Tolkien's Academic Life and Work ... 17

Monika Kirner-Ludwig
A Meta-pragmatic and Discourse-analytical Approach to Tolkien's "*Beowulf*:
The Monsters and the Critics": A Deliberate Look at its Edges, not its Center ... 39

Heike Krebs
"One trailer to bring them all and in the darkness bind them?" –
The Lord of the Rings Trailers and their Communicative Functions ... 71

Birgit Schwan
Searching "For a Better Rhythm, or a Better Word or Phrase":
J.R.R. Tolkien's Re-Telling of the Legend of King Arthur in Alliterative Metre ... 111

Heike Schwarz
Wounds That Can(not) Be Wholly Cured: Ecopsychology, Solastalgia
and Mental Substainability in J.R.R. Tolkien's *The Lord of the Rings* ... 139

Magdalena Spachmann
Ethereal Elvish and Horrid Orkish: An Attempt to Capture J.R.R. Tolkien's
Controversial Theory of Linguistic Aesthetics and Phonetic Fitness ... 169

Sebastian Streitberger
Concepts of Space in Middle-earth's Landscapes
or the Potential of Fantasy and Film for School Geography ... 193

Sabine Timpf
Insights into Mapping the Imagined World of J.R.R. Tolkien ... 231

Carolin Tober
How J.R.R. Tolkien Used Kennings to Make
The Lord of the Rings into a Medieval Epic for the 20th Century ... 253

Oliver M. Traxel
Exploring the Linguistic Past through the Work(s) of J.R.R. Tolkien:
Some Points of Orientation from English Language History ... 279

Christine Vogt-William
Tolkien's Green Man: The Racialised Cultural Other
Within and Green Spaces in *The Lord of the Rings* ... 305

Stephan Köser

(with Monika Kirner-Ludwig and Sebastian Streitberger)

The Tolkien Journey at the University of Augsburg

> "It's a dangerous business, Frodo, going out of your door," he used to say. "You step into the Road, and if you don't keep your feet, there is no knowing where you might be swept off to."
>
> J.R.R. Tolkien, *The Fellowship of the Ring*

Truth be told, this widely quoted passage from the first installment of *The Lord of the Rings* was not in our minds as we set out on our journey to bring J.R.R. Tolkien and his works to the lecture halls of the University of Augsburg. Little did we know that it would become the subliminal central theme of our ambitions.

When we first discussed the possibility of incorporating the literary writings of Professor Tolkien, we imagined him to bring two fields of study together which have – so it seems – forcefully been kept apart too often: linguistics and literature. We sought to view and study Tolkien and his brilliant intertwining of both language and narrative writing from both these fields of study so to have them profit from each other, as millions of fans around the globe have done from his tales. But how is one to sell an idea like ours, especially within the university frame which traditionally justifies and administers the autonomy of Linguistics on the one hand and Literature on the other? After all, far into the 1990s Tolkien's seemingly unconventional works had been frowned upon by colleagues and critics alike (cf. Wilson, Thompson, Inglis, Griffin), often only judging him by his fictional writing as his scholarly output was only limited.[1] Only since scholars such as Tom Shippey, Chris Upton, Thomas Honegger, Verlyn Flieger, Alan Turner and Jane Chance has he gained acceptance and acknowledgement as an author. While this "identity" as a fantasy literature

---

[1] Concerning his academic career, Tolkien is primarily recognized for his lectures "A Secret Vice"(1930), "Beowulf: The Monsters and the Critics"(1936), "On Fairy-Stories"(1939) and "English and Welsh"(1955).

author seems to have risen far beyond his scholarly one due to his major fantasy novel *The Lord of the Rings*, first published in 1954/55. The release of the movie adaptation of *The Lord of the Rings* (2001-03) and *The Hobbit* (2012-14) renewed the global hype around *The Lord of the Rings* and the fantasy genre and we thought it would be too limited an approach to have the focus of our lecture series solely on these two works, as it did not do the author nor his works any justice.

With our minds set on launching an interdisciplinary lecture series revolving around J.R.R. Tolkien's narrative and scholarly works in 2014 we began our journey with recruiting a fellowship to accompany us on our way. One of the major questions we were asked back then was: "Why Tolkien?" And our response was as simple and straightforward as: *applicability*! Anyone who has dedicated their time to some of the works of the literary worldbuilder Tolkien – for many this will have been *The Lord of the Rings* – will agree with Patrick Curry, who observed that Tolkien incorporated "fundamental themes of human existence" into his writings (Curry 10:20-10:30). He created languages that provide rich source materials for linguistic analysis and invented stories taking up and continuing older legends – with the effect that his stories have been in turn adapted by later authors. He designed worlds that enable geographers to apply their field of expertise. Through his tales, he gathered a fan base, which is – up to this day – one of the largest in the world, providing possibilities for social studies to study the influence of his books, while his complex characters have been scrutinized by experts of psychology. And indirectly he even developed the source material for some of the most successful movies of all times, already having gained the status of being classic examples in media sciences.

Keeping this in mind, Shippey however explained how fans often swing between two extremes when it comes to trying to understand Tolkien: On the one hand, people tend to expect too much of him and his works, meaning that through the incorporation of central themes of human lives such as death and immortality, ethics, religion, justice and love they expect answers to questions he most likely never meant to pose in the first place. After all, in his foreword to *The Lord of the Rings*, Tolkien points out that "[a]s for any inner meaning or 'message', it has in the intention of the author none. It is neither allegorical nor topical." On the other hand, readers have been oversimplifying the book's contents. It is a well-known fact that Tolkien warily viewed the comparison made between Germany under the Nazi-regime and the rise of Sauron in Mordor, which had become something like the central form of interpretation already in Tolkien's own days, especially during the first years after the publication of *The Lord of the Rings* (Garth 309-310). Tolkien himself maintained the following in reference to such an allegorical interpretation of his work:

> [...] I cordially dislike allegory in all its manifestations, and always have done so since I grew old and wary enough to detect its presence. I much prefer history, true or feigned, with its varied applicability to the thought and experience of readers. I think that many confuse 'applicability' with 'allegory'; but the one resides in the freedom of the reader, and the other in the purposed domination of the author. (Tolkien, "Preface" *Fellowship* xi)

Taking Tolkien's statement into account, it had never been his intention to provide a one-to-one transference between the stories – they were first and foremost an outgrowth of his fantastic worlds created to give context to the many languages he invented – and actual history or recent events. Neither did he intend for his readers to find in them the answers to the problems of the world surrounding them.

Thus, when we maintain that Tolkien is applicable to a university context, this is due to his endeavors to create worlds of absolute and minute detail. Through his incomparable gift of imagination and creativity, he has allowed generations of new readers – almost in a Roland-Barthes-*Death-of-the-Author* kind of way – to relate and apply ideas, theories and events of their lives to the tales of his writings.

Tolkien's works are interdisciplinarily applicable, which manifests itself in the academic backgrounds of my two co-editors and myself: we represent synchronic and diachronic Linguistics, Geography, History and Educational Sciences and have been continuously inspired by the fact that Tolkien offers an immense melting pot of ideas on language and linguistic principles, geographical concepts, and a huge potential for applying his storylines to factual history.

While the interwovenness of the linguistic threads will be discussed by several papers in this volume (Kirner-Ludwig, Tober, Spachmann, Traxel), let me briefly point out the geographical dimensions of Tolkien's fantasy works, as these may not be as conspicuous at first glance, but can in fact be brought into relation on a global scale. When considering the problems posed by the unchecked growth of human population – especially since the Industrial Revolution – and the needs and demands the people have, there is probably not one month that goes by without the essential discussion of climate change and climate protection measures. Although there have been several resolutions in the past 20 years, like the Kyoto-Protocol or the most recent Paris Agreement, more often than not nature has had to give way to hte so-called progress of civilization and technology. Tolkien loved nature and it must have been torture for him to see "the city creeping up the hill" from the window of his study, as Chris Upton explained (Curry 21:36-21:39). He admired cities like Venice, which was "almost free of the cursed disease of the internal combustion engine of which all the world is dying" (Arduini 299). He despised the excessive industry in the cities and rejected it wholeheartedly (Colebatch 85). Certainly, images from the *Two Towers* come to mind, where Saruman's actions mimic the fast-spreading developments of the Industrial Revolution: Saruman turns the grove of Isengard into a factory, with smelting fires and armories and after he has run dry of fuel for his machines, he starts to exploit the groves of Fangorn Forest. What Tolkien could not do or hope for in reality, he seems to have implemented in his book: nature fighting back and winning over man-made industry. Inspired by an earlier childhood experience when watching a performance of *Macbeth*, he created the Ents as the personification of nature's strength and its will to fight back. Saruman's final and in the end futile attempt to take over the Shire, finally costs him his life and trees return both to Isengard and the Shire in the end.

In lack of an individual contribution of my own to this volume, allow me a short excursion into my own field of expertise, i.e. modern history in particular, so to elaborate on its interdisciplinary relevance and the many relations and connections this academic dimension sparks. The following line of argumentation and the contents to be presented derive from my personal interpretation of Tolkien's concept of "applicability".

As we are still in a period of remembrance of the Great War of 1914-1918, let us look back 100 years, to a conflict defined by and large by the imperialistic zeitgeist Tolkien himself was affected by as a then young soldier of the Royal

British armed forces. Due to the impact of the Industrial Revolution and the improvement of medical care as a result thereof, the European nations had outgrown the confines of their countries' borders through ever increasing populations. Although the European continent had had much to offer in terms of historic events throughout the centuries, an abundance of territory cannot be considered one of these advantages. Being the center of many a conflict through the ages, the new nationalistic movements provided political, cultural and social motion in the second half of the 19th century. The compulsion of the powers of Europe to uphold their hegemony on the continent as well as the colonies, primarily in Africa, would bring the world close to a total collapse.

Even though Tolkien claimed that he did not in fact intend any allegorical references to these ongoing events, Sauron's ambitions to regain the One Ring and to plunge Middle-earth, as Gandalf puts it, into "a second darkness" (*Fellowship* 60), is a fitting parallel to draw. From his core region of Mordor, the (second) Dark Lord[2] seeks to continually increase his influence and dictatorial rule over the adjacent territories. In the beginning of the tale, his attentions are aimed towards the South and the East, where he recruits the legions of the Haradrim and the Easterlings respectively, and finally marches them to the gates of Minas Tirith. This scenario reminds me of the British Empire having their colonial troops fight on the front lines of the battle fields during World War I. Sauron had been the first to employ such tactics, even before Númenor was in its prime; the great lords of the land had sailed East as they were forbidden by the ban of the Valar to go west to Valinor (*Silmarilllion* 262). The "Akallabêth" states that first the great seafarers came as teachers and healers, but after the reign of the 14th King of Númenor Tar-Ancalimon, the Dúnedain started to build great cities by the coasts of Middle-earth and henceforth acted as masters and lords demanding tributes from the peoples (*Silmarillion* 266. Similar to the situation that European powers such as Great Britain, France and Germany, saw themselves confronted with Númenor had become too small for the aspiring kingdom, ending in Ar-Pharazôn's futile attempt to take the West by force and provoking the complete destruction of the island realm as a whole (*Silmarilllion* 269-282).

---

2 The first and true Dark Lord being the Valar Melkor.

Even if Tolkien denied that his book were an allegory of World War II and the Nazi-regime of the 1930s and 1940s, I claim that the reader may and even should recognise parallels to the narrative – if only to stay aware of history as being ever self-repeating. The "political" course of the Third Reich was characterized largely by unfathomable hate against certain cultural groups, the persecution of the people belonging to those and the attempted systematic annihilation of an entire ethnic group. Saruman's storyline does have strong correlations with certain aspects of the national-socialist movement. While his betrayal and expulsion from the Order of the Istari through Gandalf may be related to a deeply theological sector branding him as the fallen angel, as discussed in fan-fora and books alike (cf. McAvan, Rutledge, Fielding, lotrplaza.com, thetolkienforum.com) – his systematic actions against the Rohirrim could be read as the oppression of the Jewish or even the Sinti and Roma populations – the latter had been a horse-based culture for centuries (cf. Acton and Mundy). In the beginning, Saruman tries to control the thoughts of the king of Rohan and through him the convictions of his people though Gríma Wormtongue, spreading false claims against old friends of the kingdom – such as Gandalf Stormcrow – while overemphasizing the friendship that has always come from the Tower of Orthanc. However, after Gandalf's unexpected intervention at Meduseld,[3] Saruman goes into open and frontal confrontation with Rohan. When he finally releases his army of Uruk-Hai for the battle at Helm's Deep, Jackson has him utter the words "there will be no dawn for men" (Jackson, *The Two Towers*, 2:05:42-2:05:45). Even more so than the explanation of Tolkien in the books concerning the insignia displayed by the Uruk-Hai, Jackson, when he shows the battle-ready force stationed at Isengard, alludes to images familiar from the Reichsparteitag (Nazi Party rally grounds) in Nuremberg. The white hand of Saruman on the shields and standards evoke strong allusions to the swastika of the Third

---

3 Gandalf returns as Gandalf the White after his battle with the Balrog in Moria. He is accompanied by Aragorn, Legolas and Gimli as he rides for the capital of the Kingdom of Rohan. With his newfound powers, he brakes the psychological holds that Saruman has over King Theoden.

Reich. Interestingly, this symbol is one of the very few and probably the most prominent, unifying insignium of the whole tale.[4]

The conflict between East and West in Tolkien's tales is hard to miss. It is fair to assume that he drew – maybe even subconsciously – on patterns from history, potentially from a central European or even more specifically from a British-Isle-perspective: from that stance, the threats and the enemy would always have come from the east: be it the Huns and Goths at the time of the Roman Empire (410 A.D.), the Vikings in the early Middle Ages (ca. 9th century), or the Hungarians threatening the Holy Roman Empire (10th century). It really does not come as a surprise then that the enemy most often come from the west, while the antagonists were settled in the east.

In general, the pro-western bias of the book cannot be dismissed: the lingua franca of Middle-earth is called "Westron", the chief-Valar Manwë is named the "Lord of the West", primarily because Valinor lies in the West, and Aragorn, who carries a sword referred to as "Flame of the West", addresses his fellow soldiers as "Stand, Men of the West!" In contrast to this, the threat of Mordor lies to the east, the legions of "evil men" pledging themselves to Sauron are in part called "easterlings" and the two blue wizards of the Istari are also lost in the east. From a pro-western perspective, one could argue that there are great parallels to the Cold War of the post-World War II era. Like this conflict, the struggle between east and west in *The Lord of the Rings* smolders with almost no open skirmishes from the time of the last alliance up to the events in the Red Book. With a sideways glance at the developments between the United States and the Russian Federation in the last ten years, one cannot help but wonder if the differences between them may be bigger than they might seem.

***

This small excursus of mine has been an attempt to uncover threads linking Prof. Tolkien's works to historic and recent events – I have sought to

---

4 It may seem as that I am trying to contradict Tolkien with these examples. This is not my intention. Through these subjective examples, I am rather trying to show my own way of applying Tolkien's work. Even though he may not have written an allegory of the Second World War, his allegory of the ever-reoccurring history is clearly identifiable. Applicability goes hand in hand with the postmodern literary approach of the death of the author by Roland Barthes that I have mentioned before.

demonstrate his interdisciplinary applicability to a modern university and scholarly framework. But what do we mean by "interdisciplinary"? For the sake of creating a volume which would be as interdisciplinarily accessible and intriguing as possible, we have been working with a suitably broad definition of interdisciplinarity: We were not constrained by wanting to allure academics of different disciplines to work together on one presentation; on the contrary, our call for papers stated explicitly that we left it up to lecturers and students alike to present Tolkien and his works from their individual point of view, from their specific field(s) of study, and in connection with their very own interests. We embraced the fact that most participants had been educated in traditional disciplines that would differ extensively in their basic methodologies and perspectives. By providing them with a common topic or focal point, it was our contributors to the lecture series who made our project one of the most interdisciplinary approaches our campus had seen for a long time.

Within the first year of our Tolkien project at the University of Augsburg, we had ample opportunities to reach out to an increasing audience: we were invited to give lectures at schools across Augsburg, giving high school students the opportunity to not only listen to lectures about a subject prominent in their personal out-of-school lives, but also to get to know different fields of study in one fell swoop. We offered those young people, most of whom are considering to pursue a university degree, some first insights into several disciplines they may wish to study one day. In addition, we were able to organize a showing of all three movies of Peter Jackson's *Lord of the Rings* in combination with selected lectures, giving the audience a chance to rethink the films in accordance with related scholarly ideas and theses. We concluded this subproject by giving a lecture at *CineUni*, a project of the University of Augsburg in cooperation with the German cinema company *CinemaxX*, linking Peter Jackson's *The Hobbit* with Bilbo and the dwarves, considering the concepts of change, crusades and inheritance/heritage.[5]

---

[5] The original title of the lecture was "Wandel, Kreuzzug, Erbe – Inhaltliche Perspektiven auf Bilbo und die Zwerge."

The contributions gathered in this volume present a selection of papers originally given as lectures – all in all 22 in two semesters. The studies included here do not only show the educational and academic diversity of our fellowship, but also represent the combined effort of professors, lecturers and students alike, without which this project would have been pointless, aimless, and lacking the astonishing echo we received. For a junior lecturer and researcher at the beginnings of his career, it is amongst my greatest achievements that we have been able to produce a book which brings together established scholars, junior scholars and students under one topical roof.

Before presenting in short those student and scholar contributions that have been incorporated in this volume, I wish to draw attention to those presentations which are not included here but nonetheless deserve acknowledgement as they significantly added to the broad and in-depth views on Tolkien and his works. Prof. Georg Langenhorst and Christina Renczes (now Heidler) offered an overview of the religious aspects of the book in reference to a quote by Tolkien that reads: "*The Lord of the Rings* is of course a fundamentally religious and Catholic work; unconsciously so at first, but consciously in the revision." (*Letters of J.R.R. Tolkien* 172). Two junior colleagues from the German department, Katja Schneider and Julian Werlitz, analyzed Tolkien's *Letters to Father Christmas* (first published 1976), and Prof. Freimut Löser, Chair of German Medieval Language and Literature, ventured into a comparison between some of the most prominent wizards of our time: Gandalf, Dumbledore and Harry Potter in light of medieval traditions and the texts of the Middle Ages. Michael Sauter (American Studies) outlined the "storyworld of Middle-earth" from a literary point of view, and Elizabeth Fritz (English Linguistics) gave an overview of the typology and writing systems of the fictional languages incorporated in Tolkien's *The Lord of the Rings*. Annika McPherson, Junior Professor of New English Literatures and Cultural Studies, lectured on "Tolkien and the Empire", whilst taking into account the notions (Pseudo-) Medievalism, Victorian culture and the legacies of the British Empire in Tolkien's cosmos. The genesis and selected linguistic aspects of *The Hobbit* were taken into consideration by Hedwig Gwosdek, making her the only one of the lecture series to take an in-depth view at Bilbo and the dwarves. Robert Bauernfeind (Art History and Pictorial Sciences) focused on the movie adaptions of *The Lord of the Rings*, emphasizing Peter Jackson's pictorial language and imagery in combination with the aesthetics of the 18th century, the landscape depiction as a reflection of emotions and the modern popularization of natural phenomena. In addition to contributing to this book, Prof. Sabine Timpf offered a seminar and workshop on the Geographic Information System (GIS) and mapping methods of fictional places. Similarly, Monika Kirner-Ludwig offered an advanced seminar on "Tolkien: Linguist and Literary Scholar", prompting several students to write their bachelor and master's theses on this very subject.[6]

An average of 200 students attended the lectures. They came from Augsburg, Jena, Albany, Paderborn, Würzburg, Münster, Berlin, and Oldenburg, spanning across eleven different fields of study.

This volume approaches Tolkien from two different directions: There are those that have taken Tolkien as the starting point and thence explored the countless possibilities of applicability to various fields of study. Others saw their own disciplines, areas of interests and research as their springboard and applied it to the works of J.R.R. Tolkien, demonstrating that, even though it might not have been Tolkien's original intention, his concept of applicability "resides in the freedom of [his] reader" ("Preface" *Fellowship* xi) is inherently true.

We commence our volume with a contribution by Prof. Thomas Honegger (University of Jena), one of the most distinguished Tolkien experts in Europe. In his paper, Thomas Honegger introduces the reader to the works and life of Tolkien, giving us a selective view of some of his academic papers and studies as well as focusing on Prof. Tolkien's academic career and his duties and responsibilities associated with this position. It is – as Honegger puts it – a "colleague's view" on the linguist and literary scholar Tolkien.

Being the passionate historical linguist she is, Monika Kirner-Ludwig focuses on Tolkien's famous lecture "Beowulf: The Monster and the Critics" in her contribution. She takes a closer look at the meta-pragmatic layers of the lecture delivered to the British Academy in 1936, trying to put some of the statements made by other scholars about this controversial piece into perspective. This she

---

6 The papers by both Kirner-Ludwig and Timpf focus on the topic of their lecture-series presentations, not on the topic of the course.

does by working out the strategies used by Tolkien to make his points, such as referencing and debunking the arguments of the critics by showing their shortcomings.

Heike Krebs's contribution covers trailers a very important part of *The Lord of the Rings* franchise in dealing with Peter Jackson's movie adaption. She takes into consideration the evolution of *The Lord of the Rings* trailers and the necessity for their development from before the release of *The Fellowship of the Ring* to the forthcoming of the extended and Blue-Ray versions. She uses Bateman and Schmidt's trailer theory and analysis from media science by Maier as a basis for reflecting upon the techniques used by Jackson and his team.

Birgit Schwan is the perfect example for the wide outreach that this project had: Her paper compares Tolkien's *The Fall of Arthur* with his sources, mainly Thomas Malory's *Le Morte Darthur* (1485). She lays bare the methods of the author in creating a text entailing modern and medieval devices that will appeal to a modern recipient's eye and ear. She shows how Tolkien influenced the reception of Malory's work and not only contributed to the ongoing recycling of the Arthurian legend, but also opened the door for new and modern interpretations.

With her focus on eco-psychological elements in *The Lord of the Rings*, Heike Schwarz discusses one of the youngest fields of interest and debate pertaining to Tolkienian contexts: ecocriticism. Through the presentation of the importance of characters being embedded in an undamaged and well-balanced setting in respect to their mental health, Schwarz shows that Tolkien was an ecocritical writer at the core. Her paper illustrates the importance of a dichotomous balance – good vs. evil, machine vs. nature, etc. – thereby exemplifying the influence of the abstract space on the characters in *The Lord of the Rings*.

Magdalena Spachmann addresses one of the most important aspects of Tolkien's processes in inventing his wide variety of fantasy languages: linguistic aesthetics and phonetic fitness. J.R.R. himself said that he liked certain words in English and some languages as a whole more than others, simply due to the pleasing effect their sound had on him personally. Going forth from the "pleasurable cellar door" and the Welsh language, Spachmann extracts key issues of Tolkien's controversial theory of linguistic aesthetics. Her paper works out the problems he was faced with in regard to the theory of arbitrariness and how his fictitious languages are counter examples thereof.

Sebastian Streitberger brings together his two primary fields of study and expertise: didactics and geography. The main focus of this contribution is to assess the usefulness of integrating fictitious – that is to say, fantastic – spaces into high school geography students' instruction. Laying the groundwork by discussing the notions of place and space, Streitberger emphasizes the possibilities and potentials of using both space/place descriptions from *The Lord of the Rings* and images from the movie adaptations to construct a geography lesson sequence at the high school level.

The second geographer in our ranks is Sabine Timpf, Professor of Geoinformatics at the University of Augsburg. Her study combines her field of study and her great interest in fantasy and science-fiction literature and discusses the idea of mapping fictional places. After giving lectures in the past about this topic in cooperation with Prof. Katja Sarkowsky (American Studies, University of Münster), Timpf has shifted her focus to Tolkien's *The Lord of the Rings*. Her paper discusses different styles of maps, their functions in a fantasy context and Tolkien's awareness of the need of such an object as a guidance for the reader in contrast to his inability of producing a coherent atlas of Middle-earth himself. Furthermore, Timpf emphasizes the importance of Middle-earthian maps in the process of reader immersion into this particular storyworld.

Carolin Tober's paper and Prof. Oliver Traxel's contribution both cover the common ground of historical linguistics. Carolin Tober discusses the kenning as a stylistic device, a phenomenon that has seen relatively little research in the past decades, but is a key element in creating a quasi-medieval epic as seen in *The Lord of the Rings*. After creating common ground by comparing established definitions and extracting her own from them, she discusses the use and occurence of kenning in Tolkien's writings, paying particular attention to the differences between kennings proper and only seemingly accurate formations.

By drawing on a source of similar examples, Oliver Traxel demonstrates that names in Tolkien's works are multilevel items. For J.R.R. Tolkien, the name of a place, a thing, or a person would generally come before the story these would be featuring in. The naming of characters and locations in the *The Lord of the Rings* is heavily influenced by Old and Middle English, which Tolkien was (and Traxel is) an expert in. Traxel makes it clear that Tolkien created, named or described nothing at random, pointing out that characters like Éomer could only be of a horse-based culture and vice versa: cultures like Rohan's, which is interconnected to horsemanship, will essentially bring forth names for men and women that reflect upon this defining part of their culture.

This volume is rounded off by an eloquent and significantly meaningful contribution by Prof. Christine Vogt-William. She presents us with an analysis of the cultural Other in Tolkien's works, using the figure of the Green Man as her main focus of reflection. The paper, written from her postcolonial expert's point of view, focuses on the topics of realizations, decolonization, citizenship, and Englishness and proposes a critical examination of the role of Elves, Men, Ents, and the Drúedain.

With this short outlook on what the reader may expect to find in this volume, we leave you to immerse yourself into a hopefully new and somewhat different Tolkien experience. Speaking for the team of editors, we hope that the Tolkien Project at the University of Augsburg will inspire others to incorporate ideas like these into their research and teaching at their respective universities and may encourage you to visit or participate in one of our upcoming and ongoing lecture series.

About the Author

STEPHAN KÖSER studied English linguistics and literary studies, history and social studies at the University of Augsburg. After graduating with a BA in 2013, he continued his studies and was awarded his MA degree in 2017.

He is one of the initiators of the interdisciplinary lecture series on Tolkien titled "Einmal Tolkien und wieder zurück" and "J.R.R. Tolkien: fantastische Welten, viele Perspektiven", which were held at the University of Augsburg in 2014 and 2015/16 and featured speakers from more than ten departments and faculties.

Bibliography

ACTON, Thomas Alan und Gary MUNDY, eds. *Romani Culture and Gypsy Identity*, Hatfield: University of Hertfordshire Press, 1997.

ARDUINI, Roberto. "Italian Language." *J.R.R. Tolkien Encyclopedia. Scholarship and Critical Assessment*. Ed. Michael D.C. DROUT. New York: Routledge, 2007. 298-299.

CARPENTER, Humphrey, ed. *The Letters of J.R.R. Tolkien*. Ed. with the assistance of Christopher Tolkien. London: George Allen & Unwin, 1981.

COLEBATCH, Hal G.P., "Capitalism", *J.R.R. Tolkien Encyclopedia. Scholarship and Critical Assessment*. Ed. Michael D.C. DROUT. New York: Routledge, 2007. 83-85.

CURRY, Patrick. "J.R.R. Tolkien – Creator of Middle-earth." *The Fellowship of the Ring: The Appendices Part One – From Book to Vision*. New Line Cinema 2001, DVD.

FIELDING, Julien R. *Discovering World Religions at 24 Frames Per Second*. Lanham: Scarecrow Press, 2008.

GARTH, John, *Tolkien and the Great War. The Threshold of Middle-earth*. Boston: Houghton Mifflin, 2003.

GRIFFIN, Roger. "Revolts against the Modern World: The Blend of Literary and Historical Fantasy in the Italian New Right." *Literature & History* 11.1 (1985): 101-123.

INGLIS, Fred. "Gentility and Powerlessness", *J.R.R. Tolkien: This Far Land*, Robert GIDDINGS (Ed.), London: Vision Press, 1983. 25-41.

JACKSON, Peter, dir. *The Lord of the Rings. The Two Towers*. New Line Cinema 2001, DVD.

MCAVAN, Emily. *The Postmodern Sacred. Popular Culture Spirituality in the Science Fiction, Fantasy and Urban Fantasy Genres*. Jefferson NC: McFarland, 2012.

RUTLEDGE, Fleming. *The Battle for Middle-earth. Tolkien's Divine Design in The Lord of the Rings*. Grand Rapids: Wm. B. Eerdmans Publishing, 2004.

THOMPSON, E.P. "America's Europe. A Hobbit among Gandalfs." *The Nation* (24th January 1981): 68-72.

TOLKIEN, J.R.R., *The Fellowship of the Ring*, London: George Allen & Unwin, 1954.

The Silmarillion. Ed. Christopher Tolkien. London: George Allen & Unwin, 1977.

WILSON, Edmund "Oo, THOSE AWFUL ORCS! A review of *The Fellowship of the Ring.*" *The Nation*, (14th April 1956): 326-332.

Websites (all accessed 11 Feb. 2017)

<http://lotrplaza.com/showthread.php?78330-Saruman-in-the-Role-of-Lucifer>
<http://www.thetolkienforum.com/index.php?threads/the-valar.13385/>

Thomas Honegger

"Meet the Professor" – A Present-day Colleague's View of Tolkien's Academic Life and Work

Abstract

J.R.R. Tolkien saw himself primarily as an academic, a researcher in and teacher of medieval literature(s) and languages. Literary fame came relatively late – *The Lord of the Rings* was published in 1954-55 when Tolkien was approaching retirement. This late success as an author of fiction did not fundamentally change Tolkien's self-perception as (primarily) an academic. A closer look at his academic work is therefore crucial for a deeper understanding and appreciation of his literary works.

1 Introduction

Humphrey Carpenter, in his chapter "Oxford Life" of the official Tolkien biography (*Bio* 119-126),[1] accompanies Tolkien "through a typical (though entirely imaginary) day in the early nineteen-thirties" (*Bio* 120). This little exercise is very useful since it makes the reader realize that Tolkien's life was busy with many duties and obligations and that work on his legendarium[2] was only one part – and hardly ever a privileged one. This changed somewhat with the success of *The Lord of the Rings* and his retirement, so that Tolkien could focus more on his fictional writings and work on the development of the elvish (and other) languages.

I can imagine that Tolkien must have felt a bit irritated, at first at least, at being no longer primarily perceived as an academic and professional philologist. In

---

1 Most of the more recent biographies are simple re-tellings of Carpenter's study. This is partly due to the fact that Carpenter was one of the few researchers who had access to Tolkien's private papers and diaries. The best of the recent Tolkien-biographies is Raymond Edwards' *Tolkien*. Although Edwards had to rely on Carpenter concerning most of the information on Tolkien's private life, he has taken into account and incorporated the plethora of posthumous publications that appeared since Carpenter's study in 1977. Edward's book could be seen as the long awaited, updated and revised "new edition" of Carpenter's classic.
2 I use "legendarium" as the accepted term to refer to Tolkien's published and unpublished writings and drafts connected to Middle-earth.

a letter to Deborah Webster in 1958, i.e. some four years after the publication of the first volume of *The Lord of the Rings*, he objects to the "contemporary trend in criticism, with its excessive interest in the details of the lives of authors and artists" (*L* 213), only to proceed with a differentiation into significant and insignificant biographical facts. In addition to mentioning such undoubtedly important aspects as his Catholicism and his early years in "the Shire" (i.e. Sarehole), Tolkien also lists his (very personal) linguistic and culinary predilections – which have often been taken at face value and as proof for his Gallophobia.[3] What he does not mention with a single word – at least in the published excerpt – is his professional work as a philologist, which, as Shippey (e.g. in his seminal *The Road to Middle-earth*) and other scholars have shown, played a crucial role in the development of his legendarium. I cannot help but feel that Tolkien was gently pulling Webster's leg by not addressing the elephant in the room but instead providing a rather eccentric mixture of relevant information and insignificant personal idiosyncrasies.

In the following I am going to ignore Tolkien's culinary taste and focus on the elephant in the living room, i.e. his career and work as an academic. I have already published a systematic and comprehensive overview and assessment of Tolkien's academic work in the context of Stuart Lee's *A Companion to J.R.R. Tolkien* (see Honegger "Academic Writings") and do not want to repeat myself. I will therefore opt for a different approach and investigate Tolkien the academic not only by means of a selective (rather than comprehensive) discussion of some of his publications and public lectures, but also consider his university teaching and thesis-supervision duties

2 Administration

Tom Shippey, in his *Author of the Century* (69), implicitly compares the council of Elrond with a rather badly chaired faculty committee meeting. Those among us

---

3 Tolkien's biographer Humphrey Carpenter, in his account of Tolkien's visit to France in summer 1913, was the first to label Tolkien's less than enthusiastic attitude towards the French as 'Gallophobia': "He loved much of Paris and enjoyed exploring the city on his own, but he disliked the Frenchmen he saw in the streets, and wrote to Edith about the 'vulgarity and the jabber and spitting and the indecency'. Long before this expedition he had conceived a dislike of France and the French, and what he now saw did not cure him of his Gallophobia" (*Bio* 75). Garth (2003: 189), however, warns: "Carpenter […] surely pays too much attention to mischievous hypberbole".

with experience in (European) university administration will get Shippey's point immediately. Participation in academic self-administration was also in Tolkien's time part of a professor's duties. It meant, and still means, among other things, attending and chairing committee meetings and writing reports[4] and is, for most academics, a necessary evil. I don't think that Tolkien was enthusiastic about administrative duties, though he would, of course, fulfil them conscientiously. The relevance of the admin-duties for the other parts of an academic life and, in Tolkien's case, for the development of his legendarium, must be formulated negatively: the more time and energy they claim, the less work is done in other fields. I have mentioned them since they often constitute a time-consuming part of academic life and, like black holes, are noticed by observers only by their negative effects.

3 University lectures, seminars, tutorials and thesis supervisions

The main task of any university teacher is, of course, his or her teaching. This fundamental truth is nowadays often forgotten due to the contemporary trend to assess the quality of a university by the number and size of its third-party-funded projects and the publication output of its members. Tolkien would not have had to worry about the former, since the phenomenon of third-party funds was, for humanities, virtually unknown in the first half of the 20th century. Publications, however, have always been regarded as important for the prestige of a university and also Tolkien would get slightly irritated by accusations of not publishing enough.[5] He would defend himself by pointing out that he had been lecturing and teaching way beyond the call of duty. My study of Tolkien's academic papers deposited at the Bodleian Library and especially his lecture notes gave me a realistic idea of how much energy and thought he had invested into this part of his academic career.

---

4 Scull and Hammond's admirably comprehensive and detailed *Chronology* documents Tolkien's committee meetings and other administrative duties and thus gives the reader an idea of how much time Tolkien must have spent on them.
5 Shippey ("Academic Reputation" 203) points out that this worry was (at least partially) behind Niggle's concern about a visit from an Inspector in "Leaf by Niggle". Tolkien was also concerned that people would think that his writing of fiction (here *The Hobbit*) had been undertaken at the cost of his research (*L* 18-19). A similar sentiment can be detected in the "Foreword to the Second Edition" where he feels the need to point out that "the composition of *The Lord of the Rings* went on at intervals during the years 1936 to 1949, a period in which I had many duties that I did not neglect" (*LotR* xxii).

Tolkien's lectures covered not only the main Old English poetic texts long and short, such as *Beowulf, Exodus, Judith, Battle of Maldon, Brunanburh, Widsith, Waldere*, etc., but he would also deal with Middle English poems such as *The Owl and the Nightingale* or *King Horn*, and Old Norse poems such as *The Völsunga saga*.[6] Some of his ideas developed in these lecture-notes would eventually find their way into his scholarly publications – as is the case in "Beowulf: The Monsters and the Critics".[7] However, as often as not he would either lack the time to prepare his ideas for publication or judge his notes as not meeting his own rigorous standards.

On the other side, Tolkien would turn the lecture hall not only into a mead hall and the stage for his dramatic performances of Old English poetry, as his former students W.H. Auden and J.I.M. Stewart vividly remember (Fry 493), but he would also use his lectures as an opportunity to discuss ideas that were too risqué to appear in print.[8] Thus, Tolkien believed himself able to spot later insertions and alterations to the Old English poem *Beowulf*. He furthermore identifies the interpolator as Cynewulf (Tolkien, *Beowulf* 311),[9] an Anglo-Saxon poet about whom we know little more than his alleged authorship of the religious poems *Christ II* (with the famous line *Eala Earendel engla beorhtast* …), *Elene, Juliana* and *The Fates of the Apostles*, and possibly of a poem in praise of St. Guthlac (*Guthlac B*). There are good reasons for thinking of "Hrothgar's sermon", as the passage under discussion is usually called, as an interpolation or at least an adaptation of an older text. However, substantiating such a claim as well as proving the identity of the interpolator would require a great deal of painstaking philological and historical research work.[10] Maybe Tolkien intended to look into the matter in greater detail at some later occasion. In his lectures, at any rate, he felt free

---

6 Title, time and place of the lectures and seminars were announced in the *Oxford University Gazette*, where the interested reader can still look them up. Scull and Hammond's *Chronology* provides a more convenient way of accessing titles and lecture-schedules.
7 See also Kirner-Ludwig in this volume.
8 He would, of course, take scholarly risks also in his publications, but they usually remained within the accepted parameters. See, for example, his dating of *Beowulf* to the "age of Bede" (AD 672-735) (*MC* 20).
9 See also Michael Drout's perspicacious observations in his review-essay ("Review" 159-161).
10 Drout ("Review" 160) is thus speaking for all *Beowulf* scholars when he writes: "It is therefore incredibly unfortunate that Tolkien did not, at least in these commentaries, make an explicit case for this interpretation of the evidence. The conclusions are mentioned without laying out the chain of reasoning by which Tolkien arrived at them, so even experienced scholars of *Beowulf* are often left bobbing in his intellectual wake, desperately struggling to understand why he thinks what he thinks."

to voice such ideas without having to back them up immediately. Yet Tolkien would not stop at placing the composition of *Beowulf* within a rather concrete time frame and, commenting on later interpolations, he would even give the anonymous and shadowy poet a name. Christopher Tolkien notes that "when lecturing on *Beowulf* at Oxford he [JRRT] sometimes gave the unknown poet a name, calling him *Heorrenda*" (*LT II* 323). Other people before and after Tolkien have had ideas about the possible identity of the *Beowulf* poet,[11] but Heorrenda is uniquely Tolkien's and is of special interest because it provides a link to his legendarium. The name Heorrenda occurs in an Old English poem called *Deor*, which is a fictional (auto-) biographical complaint by an otherwise unknown *scop* (i.e. minstrel) called Deor who lists various historical and mythological figures who also had to face adversities. Deor claims to have been the favourite *scop* of the lord of the Heodenings until a song-skilled competitor named Heorrenda occupied his place and drove him into exile. Heorrenda is not known from any other historical or literary source and although Deor's characterization of his rival as *léoðcræftig monn* ("song-skilled man") would fit the *Beowulf*-poet, this cannot be accepted as conclusive evidence and I wonder how the original audience at Oxford reacted to Tolkien's idea. What they could not know was that the name Heorrenda features in their professor's legendarium. There he is one of the sons of Eriol and together with his half-brothers Hengest and Horsa he participates in the conquest of the Lonely Isle (aka Britain) (*LT II* 323) and later compiles the Golden Book (*LT II* 291). Tolkien links his Eriol, and thus Heorrenda, with the semi-historical brothers Hengest and Horsa, the leaders of the Anglo-Saxon invasion of Britain in the 5th century. He furthermore brings Heorrenda into play as the chronicler of events (similar to Bilbo later on)[12] and by making him the author of *Beowulf*, he creates a connection between the existing Anglo-Saxon literature and his own tales.

Most of Tolkien's university lectures have little or no direct connection with his legendarium and remain within the more narrowly defined academic field. The lecture notes are a rich treasure trove for medievalists who want to gain insight into Tolkien's ideas both developed and polished or still in the

---

11 See, for example, Richard North's study *The Origins of Beowulf. From Vergil to Wiglaf*.
12 See Honegger ("Ælfwine") for a discussion of the development of Tolkien's translation conceit. See Nagy, Vanderbeke & Turner, and Cristofari concerning the constructions of authorship and narratorship in Tolkien.

making. From a modern publish-or-perish point of view, there is material for many a paper buried in these notes,[13] but Tolkien, probably wisely, refrained from churning out publications for publications' sake. Some of these notes and preliminary or half-finished studies would find their way into the public sphere posthumously, such as Tolkien's ideas on the "The Finnsburg Episode" (in the epic poem *Beowulf*) and the related fragment *The Fight at Finnsburg*, which were edited by his former student Alan J. Bliss and published as *Finn and Hengest* in 1982.

The case of Alan J. Bliss (1921-1985), Professor of Old and Middle English at University College Dublin from 1974 to 1985, may serve as an example of how Tolkien's academic teaching influenced his students and contributed indirectly to a dissemination of his ideas. Bliss, a student at Oxford in the 1940s, wrote his B.Litt. (Bachelor of Letters) thesis under the supervision of Tolkien on the Middle English poem *Sir Orfeo*.[14] Furthermore, while still a B.Litt. student, he would teach in 1947 a course on *Sir Orfeo* (Scull and Hammond 326) and eventually publish his edition of the poem in 1954 (London: Oxford University Press). It immediately became the standard edition and a revised 2nd edition appeared in 1966 (Oxford: Clarendon Press). While Bliss must rightly be given full credit for the editorial work and research into the manuscript tradition of the poem, it is very likely that Tolkien, as the supervisor of the thesis, had influenced at least some of Bliss's ideas and editorial decisions. Tolkien got to know *Sir Orfeo* at the latest in 1920 when he started preparing a glossary[15] for Kenneth Sisam's *Fourteenth Century Verse and Prose*, which printed the poem in its entire length. Tolkien was thus intimately familiar with the text and when he directed the naval cadets' course in English (January 1943 till March 1944; see Hostetter 85), he produced a new edition of *Sir Orfeo*. Tolkien's edition was then published in 1944 by the Academic Copying Office in Oxford as a 20-page booklet entitled *Sir Orfeo* (Hostetter 85), and it may well be that Bliss, when he started with his work on the poem, knew Tolkien's earlier edition. As a consequence, it is not

---

13 For example, detailed and numerous notes on the forms of address in *Sir Gawain and the Green Knight*.
14 Scull and Hammond (313) record for 22 January 1947: "Tolkien certifies the acceptance of A.J. Bliss as a full B.Litt. student. His thesis is to be *Sir Orfeo: Introduction, Text, Commentary and Glossary*, supervised by Tolkien."
15 Tolkien was, as so many times in his life, behind schedule and Sisam first published his book without the glossary in 1921. It was re-issued together with Tolkien's *A Middle English Vocabulary* in 1922.

unlikely that Tolkien's ideas on *Sir Orfeo* were communicated to a wider academic audience not directly[16] but via the work of his student and later colleague, Alan J. Bliss. Similarly it can be assumed that Tolkien's ideas and suggestions found their way, for example, into E.V. Gordon's posthumously published edition of *Pearl* (1953)[17] and into Simonne d'Ardenne's edition and study of the Middle English life of St. Juliana of Nicomedia (1936).[18]

Tutorials and the supervision of theses constituted an important and, unfortunately, often not clearly traceable way of developing and promulgating his ideas. His lectures were another, more public way of doing so. As for Tolkien's regular lectures at university, we must not imagine overflowing lecture halls with hundreds of students, as is often the case today. Numbers could vary greatly and, if the topic was rather specialised, Tolkien would find himself with only a handful of students attending.

More public, though with a limited impact, were Tolkien's lectures and talks given to societies or on special occasions.[19] The great majority of these lectures have not been published, although most of them are accessible to researchers as part of Tolkien's academic papers at the Bodleian Library. On 1 January 1938, for example, "Tolkien lectured on 'Dragons' as part of a series of lectures for children at the University Museum, Oxford" (*L*, note 19, 435). The tone of the lecture was intentionally light though not condescending and, considering the importance of dragons in Tolkien's academic and fictional work, a critical edition of this text would be most welcome. This *desideratum* has been recently fulfilled for "A Secret Vice" (Fimi & Higgins), which started out as an address to the Johnson Society, given at Pembroke College on 29 November 1931 (Fimi & Higgins xxxi). The importance of "A Secret Vice" has been recognised ever since it was first published posthumously in 1982 in *The Monsters and the*

---

[16] It is only thanks to the posthumous publication of his translation of *Sir Orfeo* in *Sir Gawain and the Green Knight, Pearl and Sir Orfeo* (1975) as well as the publication of his Middle English edition of the text by Hostetter that we can guess some of Tolkien's ideas about the poem.
[17] See Anderson ("Little Devil") for a knowledgeable discussion of Tolkien's collaboration with Gordon on this and other projects.
[18] Anderson ("D'Ardenne" 117) writes: "As d'Ardenne herself admitted, it should have been appeared [sic] under both her and Tolkien's names, in collaboration, but published under her name alone, [...]. Dedicated to Tolkien, it ironically contains more of Tolkien's own views on early Middle English and on the West Midlands dialect than Tolkien published under his own name during his lifetime."
[19] Again, I would like to refer the interested reader to Scull and Hammond's *Chronology* for information on the dates and occasions of these invited talks and lectures.

Critics. It constitutes one of the few explicit texts about Tolkien's art of inventing languages. In origin, the lecture addresses questions relevant for the very active IAL (International Auxiliary Language) movement[20] on the one hand, and, on the other, it refers to the linguistic-philological debate about the connection(s) between sound and meaning.[21] It may be argued that both these aspects are of minor relevance today and the scholarly value of Tolkien's lecture for the linguistic academic community may be negligible, which stands in contrast to the value the text has for the exploration of Tolkien's invented languages, be this Quenya, Sindarin, Black Speech, Entish or any of the other dozen languages he worked on.[22] As such it is likely to appeal to a potential audience of several hundred thousand readers and thus has become commercially attractive so much so that HarperCollins, who are usually not known for publishing arcane scholarly texts, took on the publication of the critical edition. It is not the first nor the last time that we will see how a relatively specialised text acquires new relevance when read against the backdrop of Tolkien's legendarium.

His Sir Israel Gollancz Memorial Lecture to the British Academy in 1936 ("Beowulf: The Monsters and the Critics") or the Andrew Lang Lecture in 1939 ("On Fairy-stories") are a different matter.[23] The British Academy lecture was published in the same year (1936) and is until today considered to be one of the most influential contributions to *Beowulf* scholarship.[24] Tolkien basically presents the research up to 1936 as focusing almost exclusively on the historical-realistic aspects of the text. As a logical consequence, *Beowulf* scholars censored the poet for putting non-realistic elements such as the monsters in the centre of attention. Tolkien, by contrast, argues for appreciating the poem once more as a work of art with aesthetic qualities, and not as a quarry for historical information. He further argues that the poem's structure is based on the static

---

20 The best-known representatives would be Esperanto, Volapük, and Ido.
21 See the useful discussion of this question by Fimi & Higgins in their "Introduction" to *A Secret Vice* (li-lxv).
22 There are many good books and websites dedicated to Tolkien's elvish languages. Studies giving a general overview on the approximately one dozen invented languages of Middle-earth are few and far between. Noel's booklet (dating back to 1984) still seems to be the most popular (though somewhat flawed) introduction. More accurate are the two books by Kloczko (*Dictionnaire des langues elfiques* and *Dictionnaire des langues des hobbits*).
23 The W.P. Ker Memorial Lecture on *Sir Gawain and the Green Knight*, delivered at the University of Glasgow in 1953, also belongs to this category. It was, however, published only posthumously in 1975.
24 See Drout "*Beowulf*, the Monsters and the Critics" and Shippey "Tolkien's Two Views".

contrast between the three episodes with the fights against the monsters at their centre, which depict three crucial moments in a heroic life: The first two fights against Grendel and his mother respectively are the deeds of a young warrior on the rise. The final confrontation with the dragon provides the fitting conclusion to a long, successful reign. The balance is between these elements, and Beowulf's death in his fight against the ('mythical') dragon is tragic but nevertheless much more fitting than would be an end by a ('historical') Swedish sword. Tolkien's essay constitutes, due to his persuasive and rhetorically accomplished argumentation, something of a watershed in *Beowulf* studies and there is hardly an Anglo-Saxon scholar after 1936 who, directly or indirectly, has not made reference to it.

The publication and reception history of "On Fairy-stories" is less straightforward yet all the more instructive for the impact of Tolkien's scholarly work outside the small circle of academia. "On Fairy-stories" was delivered at the University of St. Andrews on 8 March 1939 as the Andrew Lang Lecture. A summary of Tolkien's lecture with a presentation of his main ideas was given in *The Scotsman*, *The St. Andrews Times*, and, in a much longer and more detailed form, in *The St. Andrews Citizen*. Yet the full text, revised and elaborated,[25] was published only some eight years later (1947) in *Essays Presented to Charles Williams*, a memorial volume edited by C.S. Lewis and dedicated to the fellow Inkling Charles Williams (†1945). This, however, did not mean that it was widely received. To publish an essay in a festschrift[26] and to give it a title that is, to put it mildly, somewhat misleading, has always been a foolproof recipe for non-reception. I can imagine that those readers who went through the trouble of tracking down the volume in the hope of finding out more about fairy-stories proper were rather irritated and lost by Tolkien's discussion. And those who could have profited from his ideas on fantasy and secondary worlds were not

---

25 See Flieger and Anderson's critical edition of the essay. The elaborations also affected the main argument since, as Flieger and Anderson point out (135), "neither word nor concept [of *eucatastrophe*] were part of the original lecture."
26 Originally, the book was intended as a festschrift but, due to Williams's untimely death, became a memorial volume.

very likely to look for them in an essay whose title announces an investigation of fairy-stories.[27]

To make matters worse, Oxford University Press "have infuriatingly let it [i.e. the volume containing his essay] go out of print, though it [i.e. his essay] is now in demand" (*L* 220) – as Tolkien complained in a letter to Houghton Mifflin in June 1955. The "now in demand" refers, of course, to the fact that the publication of *The Lord of the Rings* had kindled the interest of a much wider audience who wanted to learn more about Tolkien's ideas on sub-creation and fantasy. However, it was not before 1964 that "On Fairy-stories" became once more available as part of *Tree and Leaf* and was widely recognized as "the template on which he shaped his idea of sub-creation, and the manifesto in which he declared his particular concept of what fantasy is and how it ought to work" (*TOFS* 9). Thus, it was more than two decades after the delivery of the original lecture that it dawned on the critics that what Tolkien was writing about was not so much Andrew Lang's fairy tales, but his own "fairy-story" (later published as *The Lord of the Rings*). Read as a discussion of traditional fairy tales, the essay is often baffling – yet read as a commentary on *The Lord of the Rings*, which he had started writing at about the same time as he worked on "On Fairy-stories" (1938), it makes perfect sense. The importance of "On Fairy-stories" lies therefore, on the one hand, in the theoretical insights it gives us into Tolkien's creative processes. On the other, it established the blueprint for the very productive tradition of analysing Tolkien's scholarly work for ideas and concepts that could be applied to and help with the interpretation of his works of fiction – a point we will discuss in more detail when dealing with Tolkien's philological publications proper in the next section.

4 Print publications

The title of this section does not want to suggest that Tolkien also published online, but rather contrast such publications of his that had their origin in a public lecture with those that were written right from the start with a readers-only

---

[27] It is tied in fairly closely to the wide interpretation of what constitutes a fairy story as can be seen in Lang's fairy books. We must remember that this is before the time of people like Propp and Bettelheim, and fantasy, with which it is most easily associated nowadays, had not yet come to be recognised as a genre.

audience in mind. What also has to be taken into account is that contributions to scholarly journals, yearbooks and similar formats were aimed primarily at a specialised readership of experts. Early in his academic career, Tolkien cut his philological teeth and demonstrated his expertise in the field with several long review articles for *The Year's Work in English Studies*, discussing and commenting on the recent publications in philology. He stopped writing public reviews soon after his appointment as the Rawlinson and Bosworth Professor of Anglo-Saxon at Oxford University in favour of publishing his own research.[28] The number of studies and papers Tolkien saw to the press, some thirty items, is not very large[29] – but then as now a professor's output, whatever its quality or quantity, is hardly ever considered sufficient. Suffice it to say that Tolkien's publications were meticulously researched and cogently argued examples of philological acumen.

Most of Tolkien's articles focus on the discussion of the etymology and exploration of the meaning of words or expressions in medieval texts – a specialisation for which he showed an extraordinary talent and which had been developed and honed during his work for the *New English Dictionary* (later *Oxford English Dictionary*) under the supervision of Henry Bradley.[30] Yet papers like "The Devil's Coach Horses" (*Review of English Studies* 1925), "Sigelwara Land" (*Medium Aevum* 1932 & 1934), and "Chaucer as a Philologist: The Reeve's Tale" (*Transactions of the Philological Society* 1934) did not limit themselves to a purely and exclusively philological treatment of the words and expressions but would try and place the findings into a wider cultural-historical context.

His two-part article (published in 1932 and 1934 in *Medium Aevum*) on the Old English word *sigelwara* is a good example of this approach. The term *sigelwara* was used in Old English times to translate the Latin *Æthiops*, "Ethiopian", yet Tolkien argues that it must have existed before literate Anglo-Saxons used it to refer to the inhabitants of Ethiopia. He regards the manuscript form as deviating from the original correct form, which he establishes as *sigelhearwan*

---

28 The only review published after 1930 is the one on E.K. Chambers's *English Literature at the Close of the Middle Ages* in the *Sunday Times* (14 April 1946).
29 See Shippey ("Academic Reputation") and Drout ("Medieval Scholarship") for an in-depth discussion of Tolkien's academic achievement. See the appendix to this essay for a comprehensive chronological list of Tolkien's academic publications.
30 See Gilliver, Marshall & Weiner for an informed account of Tolkien's involvement with the *OED*.

(nom./acc. plural of *sigelhearwa*). He then quotes a great number of textual witnesses for the use and meaning of the two forms *sigel* and *hearwa* throughout the centuries and comes to the conclusion that *sigel* meant originally both 'sun' and 'jewel', whereas *hearwa* is the Germanic form of an Indo-European root related to Latin *carbo*, 'soot'. He then argues that before the term was applied to the sun-scorched people of Africa, it had referred to "the sons of Múspell [...],[31] the ancestors of the Silhearwan with red-hot eyes that emitted sparks, with faces black as soot" (Tolkien, "Sigelwara Land [Part 2]" 110), allowing us some glimpses of a lost heathen mythology. Although Tolkien the philologist-scholar judiciously hedges his conclusions and is anxious to remain within the narrow limits of the philological method, we can, in hindsight, see that the argument had an impact on his legendarium. As Tom Shippey (*Road to Middle-earth* 42) has pointed out, his work on *sigelwara* may have provided Tolkien with a northern analogue to his Balrog on the one hand and, on the other, helped him "to create (or corroborate) the image of the *silmaril*, that fusion of 'sun' and 'jewel' in physical form." It is furthermore an example of what Tolkien, in his lecture "A Secret Vice", termed "mythology concomitant" (*MC* 210), i.e. the mythology that constitutes a necessary part of any language – whether invented, re-discovered, or living. And even when lost as a mythology, it is to some extent possible to recover some parts of it with the help of philology, i.e. the study of language.

Perceiving the importance of philology for the exploration of a people's cultural heritage in general and for his own creative work in particular, it must have irked Tolkien greatly that philology was more and more considered a nasty "pill" (*MC* 225) to be pushed down the throat of unwilling students. He lived long enough to witness (and to mourn) the fading of the great philological tradition,[32] of which he had been a typical representative in the early decades of his academic work. Considering the general trend in academia towards a greater differentiation in and focus on synchronic linguistic studies and the concomitant loss of importance for philology (especially the historical dimension of language), it comes as no surprise that Tolkien's essays in this field had only a limited impact

---

31 Múspell, also called Muspellsheimr, is one of the nine worlds in the Old Norse mythology of the *Edda*. It is the land of fire and home of the fire-giants, i.e. the "sons of Múspell", who will be led to Ragnarök by the fire-giant Surtr.
32 See Shippey ("Fighting the Long Defeat").

and are little known nowadays. His legacy to the generations after him lies not so much in his contributions to philology itself, but in the way he made it fruitful for the study and production of literature. It was Tolkien's former student John S. Ryan who, as one of the first medievalist-philologists, started to explore this aspect of the professor's scholarly work and its relevance for his fiction.[33] The break-through for this approach came in 1982 with the publication of Tom Shippey's *The Road to Middle-earth*. Shippey's scholarly training at Oxford and further career at the University of Leeds had brought him into close contact with Tolkien's academic legacy. He had furthermore developed not only a taste for reading Science Fiction and Fantasy but also for writing fiction himself, which, however, was published under a pen name. Shippey was thus uniquely qualified to note, understand and explain not only the medieval sources-and-analogues elements in Tolkien's fiction, but also the complex and intricate poetic transformational processes that gave Tolkien's legendarium its complexity and depth. It is by the hand of Shippey that the seeming 'philological dross' of Tolkien's scholarly publications has been transformed into the 'literary gold' valued by a non-scholarly readership of Tolkien's fiction. Shippey's lead has been followed, developed and expanded by many of the later Tolkien scholars such as Michael D.C. Drout, Verlyn Flieger, Jane Chance or, most recently, Mark Atherton – all of whom are medievalists at least in part. It may be no exaggeration to claim that the 'interpretatio Shippeiana' dominated the field for a considerable time and still is one of the major strands within Tolkien studies. However, the focus within that subcategory has most recently moved away from the hard-core philological papers (Shippey's core competence) to Tolkien's more general linguistic and cultural-literary essays such as "A Secret Vice", "On Fairy-stories", or "Sir Gawain and the Green Knight" respectively. Unfortunately, one of the rare texts that combines philology, literary criticism and creative writing, namely "The Homecoming of Beorhtnoth, Beorhthelm's Son", has not yet been re-edited in a critical format.[34]

---

33 Many of his essays have been collected, edited and republished in the two volumes *Tolkien's View* (2009) and *In the Nameless Wood* (2013).
34 Honegger ("Homecoming") provides a discussion of the development of Tolkien's main argument based on a study of the manuscripts and drafts.

5 Serendipity

There lies a certain irony in the fact that Tolkien's scholarly works have survived and attained posthumously a wider circulation and recognition than during his active career as a philologist. It speaks for itself that a commercially minded publisher such as HarperCollins has republished several of his philological and scholarly essays. Tolkien, due to the overwhelming success of his *The Lord of the Rings*, has become a brand and many people seem willing to buy almost any book with his name on the cover.[35] Tolkien the philologist has thus become subservient to Tolkien the author of fiction, and his scholarly works are read mainly in view of their usefulness to elucidate aspects of his literary texts. No critic would deny that the two belong together, yet their relationship is not always straightforward. I would like to end with the well-known account of how Tolkien conceived the opening sentence of what would then become *The Hobbit*.

Tolkien himself reports[36] that he was correcting School Certificate papers, an activity that, on the one hand, requires an examiner's full attention, yet, on the other, would soon become repetitive and boring. So when one of the examinees had left a page blank, Tolkien spontaneously wrote on it "In a hole in the ground there lived a hobbit".[37] At that point, Tolkien could not make sense of either "hobbit" or the sentence as a whole. Much later, Tolkien the philologist assumed a likely Anglo-Saxon root for the word in the form of *hol-bytla* = hole-builder – which resurfaces in *The Lord of the Rings* as the Rohirrim word for the hobbits. This, however, would be as far as philology went and we cannot get beyond the not very satisfactory translation of the original sentence as "In a hole in the ground there lived a hole-builder".

It was Tolkien the author of fiction who provided a solution: By combining the names of the enigmatic *Dvergatal* from the *Völuspá* with the equally baffling *hobbit*, Tolkien invented a tale that would provide not only an explanation for who they are, but also for what they did. Yet this was not the only instance of

---

35 I wonder what those readers who bought e.g. *Finn and Hengest* made of this very scholarly and densely argued philological study. Most recently, the documents and notes related to Tolkien's (in the end never concluded) work for the Clarendon Chaucer have been prepared for publication.
36 Carpenter (*Bio* 81) and *L* 215 and 219.
37 See Honegger ("There was an old woman") for a brief overview on the discussion of the possible origin(s) of the concept and the word.

a fruitful collaboration between the two aspects of Tolkien's personality. The Riders of Rohan and several elements of their culture have their origin in philological-scholarly queries and cruxes which puzzled and fascinated Tolkien the scholar, and for which Tolkien the author could provide imaginative answers.[38]

6 Conclusion

Tolkien's scholarly work is indissolubly connected with his literary writings, the one influencing and interacting with the other. However, the wider public remained ignorant of this interconnectedness for a long time. Up to the popular success of *The Lord of the Rings* in the US in the 1960s, Tolkien was perceived predominantly as an Oxford professor who had published few but important works on Old and Middle English language and literature – and written a book or two for children, which appears to be a pardonable foible of Oxford dons since Charles Lutwidge Dodgson (aka Lewis Carroll). This perception of Tolkien changed with the overwhelming success of the paperback edition(s) of *The Lord of the Rings*, since which Tolkien has been considered the father of modern fantasy, who happened to have also penned a few learned essays on medieval languages and literature. It is only since the last two decades of the preceding century that we have seen several informed attempts to re-establish a more balanced view of Tolkien as both scholar and author. The ongoing publication of critical editions of his academic essays and lectures is an encouraging sign that this development is likely to continue and that Tolkien's scholarly heritage is going to be preserved and made accessible for future generations.

About the Author

THOMAS HONEGGER holds a Ph.D. and 'Habilitation' from the University of Zurich (Switzerland) where he taught Old and Middle English. He is, since 2002, Professor for English Medieval Studies at the Friedrich-Schiller-University, Jena (Germany). Homepage: http://www.iaa.uni-jena.de/Institut/Mitarbeiter%2Ainnen/Honegger_+Thomas-p-228.html

---

38 See Shippey (*Author* 90-102), Drout ("A Mythology"), and Honegger ("The Rohirrim").

List of Abbreviations

Bio CARPENTER, Humphrey. *J.R.R. Tolkien. A Biography*. First published 1977. Paperback edition. London: HarperCollins, 1995.

L CARPENTER, Humphrey, ed. with the assistance of Christopher Tolkien. *The Letters of J.R.R. Tolkien*. London: George Allen & Unwin, 1981. Reprinted Boston: Houghton Mifflin, 2000.

LotR TOLKIEN, John Ronald Reuel. *The Lord of the Rings*. 50th Anniversary One-Volume Edition. Boston and New York: Houghton Mifflin, 2004.

LT II TOLKIEN, John Ronald Reuel. *The Book of Lost Tales 2*. The History of Middle-earth 2. Ed. Christoph Tolkien. First published 1984. London: Grafton, 1992.

MC TOLKIEN, John Ronald Reuel. *The Monsters and the Critics and Other Essays*. Ed. Christopher Tolkien. First published 1983. Paperback edition. London: HarperCollins, 1997.

TOFS FLIEGER, Verlyn and Douglas A. ANDERSON, eds. *Tolkien On Fairy-stories*. (Expanded edition, with commentary and notes). London: HarperCollins, 2008.

Bibliography

ANDERSON, Douglas A. "'An Industrious Little Devil': E.V. Gordon as a Friend and Collaborator with Tolkien." *Tolkien the Medievalist*. Ed. Jane Chance. London: Routledge, 2003. 15-25.

"D'Ardenne, S.R.T.O. (1899-1986)." *J.R.R. Tolkien Encyclopaedia. Scholarship and Critical Assessment*. Ed. Michael D.C. Drout. New York: Routledge, 2007. 117-118.

CARPENTER, Humphrey. *J.R.R. Tolkien. A Biography*. First published 1977. Paperback edition. London: HarperCollins, 1995.

ed. with the assistance of Christopher TOLKIEN. *The Letters of J.R.R. Tolkien*. London: George Allen & Unwin, 1981. Reprinted Boston: Houghton Mifflin, 2000.

CRISTOFARI, Cécile. "The Chronicle without an Author: History, Myth and Narration in Tolkien's Legendarium." *Sub-creating Middle-earth. Constructions of Authorship and the Work of J.R.R. Tolkien*. Cormarë Series 27. Ed. Judith Klinger. Zurich and Jena: Walking Tree Publishers, 2012. 173-190.

DROUT, Michael D.C. "J.R.R. Tolkien's Medieval Scholarship and its Significance." *Tolkien Studies* 4 (2007): 113-176.

"A Mythology for Anglo-Saxon England." *Tolkien and the Invention of Myth. A Reader*. Ed. Jane Chance. Lexington, Kentucky: The University Press of Kentucky, 2004. 229-247.

"*Beowulf*, the Monsters and the Critics: The Brilliant Essay that Broke *Beowulf* Studies." *Scholars' Forum* 2010. 15 August 2016 a<http://www.lotrplaza.com/forum/forum_posts.asp?TID=237825>

"Review of *Beowulf: A Translation and Commentary together with Sellic Spell*, by J.R.R. Tolkien." *Tolkien Studies* 12 (2015): 149-173.

EDWARDS, Raymond. *Tolkien*. London: Robert Hale, 2014.

FIMI, Dimitra and Andrew HIGGINS, eds. *J.R.R. Tolkien: A Secret Vice*. London: HarperCollins, 2016.

FLIEGER, Verlyn and Douglas A. ANDERSON, eds. *Tolkien On Fairy-stories*. (Expanded edition, with commentary and notes). London: HarperCollins, 2008.

FRY, Michele. "Oxford." *J.R.R. Tolkien Encyclopaedia. Scholarship and Critical Assessment*. Ed. Michael D.C. Drout. New York: Routledge, 2007. 489-499.

GARTH, John. 2003. *Tolkien and the Great War: The Threshold of Middle-earth*. London: HarperCollins.

GILLIVER, Peter, Jeremy MARSHALL, and Edmund WEINER. *The Ring of Words. Tolkien and the Oxford English Dictionary*. Oxford: Oxford University Press, 2006.

HAMMOND, Wayne G., with the assistance of Douglas ANDERSON. *J.R.R. Tolkien: A Descriptive Bibliography*. Winchester: St Paul's Bibliographies, 1993.

HONEGGER, Thomas. "'There was an old woman, lived under a hill ...' – A Proto-Hobbit Uncovered?" *Hither Shore* 2 (2005): 247-250.

"The Homecoming of Beorhtnoth: Philology and the Literary Muse." *Tolkien Studies* 4 (2007): 189-199.

"Ælfwine." *J.R.R. Tolkien Encyclopaedia. Scholarship and Critical Assessment*. Ed. Michael D.C. Drout. New York: Routledge, 2007. 4-5.

"The Rohirrim: 'Anglo-Saxons on Horseback'? An Inquiry into Tolkien's Use of Sources." *Tolkien and the Study of His Sources: Critical Essays*. Ed. Jason Fisher. Jefferson, North Carolina and London: McFarland, 2011. 116-132.

"Academic Writings." *A Companion to J.R.R. Tolkien*. Ed. Stuart Lee. Oxford: Wiley Blackwell, 2014. 27-40.

HOSTETTER, Carl F., ed. "*Sir Orfeo*: A Middle English Version by J.R.R. Tolkien." *Tolkien Studies* 1 (2004): 85-123.

KLOCZKO, Edouard. *Dictionnaire des langues elfiques*. Toulon: Tamise Production, 1995.

Dictionnaire des langues des hobbits, des nains, des orques. Argenteuil: ARDA, 2002.

LEE, Stuart D., ed. *A Companion to J.R.R. Tolkien*. Oxford: Wiley Blackwell, 2014.

NAGY, Gergely. "The Great Chain of Reading: (Inter-)Textual Relations and the Technique of Mythopoesis in the Túrin Story." *Tolkien the Medievalist*. Ed. Jane Chance. London: Routledge, 2003. 239-258.

NOEL, Ruth S. *The Languages of Tolkien's Middle-Earth: A Complete Guide to All Fourteen of the Languages Tolkien Invented*. Boston: Houghton Mifflin, 1984.

NORTH, Richard. *The Origins of Beowulf. From Vergil to Wiglaf*. Oxford: Oxford University Press, 2006.

RYAN, John S. *Tolkien's View. Windows into his World*. Cormarë Series 19. Zurich and Jena: Walking Tree Publishers, 2009.

In the Nameless Wood. Explorations in the Philological Hinterland of Tolkien's Literary Creations. Cormarë Series 30. Zurich and Jena: Walking Tree Publishers, 2013.

SCULL, Christina and Wayne G. HAMMOND. *The J.R.R. Tolkien Companion and Guide. Chronology*. Boston and New York: Houghton Mifflin, 2006.

SHIPPEY, Tom. *J.R.R. Tolkien. Author of the Century*. London: HarperCollins, 2000.

The Road to Middle-earth. Third edition. First edition 1982. Boston: Houghton Mifflin, 2003.

"Tolkien's Academic Reputation Now." *Roots and Branches: Selected Papers on Tolkien by Tom Shippey*. Cormarë Series 11. Zurich and Berne: Walking Tree Publishers, 2007. 203-212.

"Fighting the Long Defeat: Philology in Tolkien's Life and Fiction." *Roots and Branches: Selected Papers on Tolkien by Tom Shippey*. Cormarë Series 11. Zurich and Berne: Walking Tree Publishers, 2007. 139-156.

"Tolkien's Two Views of Beowulf, one hailed, one ignored: but did we get this one right?" *Scholars' Forum* 2010. 15 August 2016 <http://www.lotrplaza.com/forum/forum_posts.asp?TID=238598&PN=1>

TOLKIEN, John Ronald Reuel. *The Book of Lost Tales 2*. The History of Middle-earth 2. Ed. Christoph Tolkien. First published 1984. London: Grafton, 1992.

The Lord of the Rings. First published 1954/55. 50th Anniversary One-Volume Edition. Boston and New York: Houghton Mifflin, 2004.

The Monsters and the Critics and Other Essays. Ed. Christopher Tolkien. First published 1983. Paperback edition. London: HarperCollins, 1997.

Beowulf. A Translation and Commentary together with Sellic Spell. Ed. Christopher Tolkien. London: HarperCollins, 2014.

VANDERBEKE, Dirk and Allan TURNER. "The One or the Many? Authorship, Voice and Corpus." *Sub-creating Middle-earth. Constructions of Authorship and the Work of J.R.R. Tolkien*. Cormarë Series 27. Ed. Judith Klinger. Zurich and Jena: Walking Tree Publishers, 2012. 1-20.

Appendix

List of academic essays and other relevant academic publications by J.R.R. Tolkien (in chronological order of publication; see also Hammond and Anderson 1993)

1922   *A Middle English Vocabulary*. Oxford: At the Clarendon Press.

1924   "Philology: General Works." *The Year's Work in English Studies* IV, 1923. Eds. Sir Sidney Lee and F.S. Boas for The English Association. London: Oxford University Press, 20-37.

1925   "Some Contributions to Middle-English Lexicography." *Review of English Studies* 1.2: 210-215.

"The Devil's Coach-Horses." *Review of English Studies* 1.3: 331-336.

Sir Gawain and the Green Knight. Eds. J.R.R. Tolkien and E.V. Gordon. Oxford: At the Clarendon Press.

1926   "Philology: General Works." *The Year's Work in English Studies* V, 1924. Eds. F.S. Boas and C.H. Herford for The English Association. London: Oxford University Press, 26-65.

1927   "Philology: General Works." *The Year's Work in English Studies* VI, 1925. Eds. F.S. Boas and C.H. Herford for The English Association. London: Oxford University Press, 32-65.

1928   "Foreword." Walter E. Haigh. *A New Glossary of the Dialect of the Huddersfield District*. London: Oxford University Press, xiii-xviii.

1929   "*Ancrene Wisse* and *Hali Meiðhad*." *Essays and Studies* XIV. Ed. H.W. Garrod. London: Oxford University Press, 104-126.

1930   "The Oxford English School." *Oxford Magazine* 48.21: 778-780, 782.

1932   "Appendix I: The Name 'Nodens'." R.E.M. Wheeler and T.V. Wheeler. *Report on the Excavation of the Prehistoric, Roman, and Post-Roman Site in Lydney Park, Gloucestershire*. Oxford: Oxford University Press, 132-137. Reprinted in *Tolkien Studies* 4 (2007): 177-183.

"Sigelwara Land [Part 1]." *Medium Aevum* 1.3: 183-196.

1934   "Sigelwara Land [Part 2]." *Medium Aevum* 3.2: 95-111.

"Chaucer as a Philologist: The Reeve's Tale." *Transactions of the Philological Society*. London: David Nutt, 1-70. Reprinted in *Tolkien Studies* 5 (2008): 109-171.

1937   *Beowulf: The Monsters and the Critics*. London: Humphrey Milford.

1940 "Prefatory Remarks on Prose Translation of Beowulf." *Beowulf and the Finnesburg Fragment. A Translation into Modern English Prose.* Trans. John R. Clark Hall. London: George Allen & Unwin, viii-xli.

1947 "Iþþlen in *Sawles Warde*." Written together with S.R.T.O. d'Ardenne. *English Studies* 27.6: 168-170.

"On Fairy-Stories." *Essays Presented to Charles Williams.* Ed. C.S. Lewis. London: Oxford University Press, 38-89.

1948 "MS Bodley 34: A Re-Collation of a Collation." Written together with S.R.T.O. d'Ardenne. *Studia Neophilologica* 20.1-2: 65-72.

1953 "Middle English 'Losenger': Sketch of an Etymological and Semantic Enquiry." *Essais de philologie moderne* (1951). Paris: Les Belles Lettres, 63-76.

"The Homecoming of Beorhtnoth, Beorhthelm's Son." *Essays and Studies* N.S. 6: 1-18. London: John Murray.

1962 *Ancrene Wisse. The English Text of the Ancrene Riwle. Edited from MS. Corpus Christi College Cambridge 402.* Ed. J.R.R. Tolkien. Published for the Early English Text Society by Oxford University Press. Oxford: Oxford University Press.

1963 "English and Welsh." *Angles and Britons. O'Donnell Lectures.* Cardiff: University of Wales Press, 1-41.

1975 *Sir Gawain and the Green Knight, Pearl, and Sir Orfeo. Translated by J.R.R. Tolkien.* Ed. Christopher Tolkien. London: George Allen & Unwin.

1981 *The Old English Exodus. Text, Translation, and Commentary by J.R.R. Tolkien.* Ed. Joan Turville-Petre. Oxford: At the Clarendon Press.

1982 *Finn and Hengest. The Fragment and the Episode.* Ed. Alan Bliss. London: George Allen & Unwin.

1983 *The Monsters and the Critics and Other Essays.* Ed. Christopher Tolkien. Contains "Beowulf: The Monsters and the Critics", "On Translating *Beowulf*", "Sir Gawain and the Green Knight", "On Fairy-Stories", "English and Welsh", "A Secret Vice", and "Valedictory Address to the University of Oxford". London: George Allen & Unwin.

2002 *Beowulf and the Critics by J.R.R. Tolkien.* Ed. Michael D.C. Drout. Medieval and Renaissance Texts and Studies 248. Tempe, Arizona: Arizona Center for Medieval and Renaissance Studies.

2004 "*Sir Orfeo*: A Middle English Version by J.R.R. Tolkien." Ed. Carl F. Hostetter. *Tolkien Studies* 1: 85-123.

2008   *Tolkien On Fairy-stories. Expanded edition, with commentary and notes.* Eds. Verlyn Flieger and Douglas A. Anderson. London: HarperCollins.

2014   *Beowulf. A Translation and Commentary together with Sellic Spell.* Ed. Christopher Tolkien. London: HarperCollins.

2016   *A Secret Vice. Tolkien on Invented Languages.* Eds. Dimitra Fimi and Andrew Higgins. London: HarperCollins.

Monika Kirner-Ludwig

A Meta-pragmatic and Discourse-analytical Approach to Tolkien's "*Beowulf*: The Monsters and the Critics": A Deliberate Look at its Edges, not its Center

Abstract

Since J.R.R. Tolkien was both philologist and writer, text linguistics as the interface between linguistics and literature provides a most suitable instrument for a thorough analysis of his lecture "*Beowulf*: The Monsters and the Critics", which was given on November 25, 1936.

Surely it was Tolkien's mission to convince the audience of *Beowulf*'s complexity, literary value, and worth as Anglo-Saxon heritage and he succeeded in convincing both his audience and many critics. However, an analysis reveals that the lecture is plainly too profound, dense, and complex for aural reception, especially for a non-professional audience. This paper will argue and demonstrate on various linguistic levels that it is highly questionable that "*Beowulf*: The Monsters and the Critics" was and is indeed (meant) to be fully grasped with nothing more than "a general knowledge [of] or interest" in *Beowulf*. My second and main claim is that Tolkien wove in numerous subtle linguistic traits that allow, when carved out and exposed, for intriguing insights into more than "just" a passionate defense of *Beowulf* as the "most successful Old English poem" (BMC 126). In order to make and sustain my point, I will propose an approach to Tolkien's text which puts his very own armamentarium to the test on a metalevel, namely the very textlinguistic principles he himself would apply to compose, shape and literally "weave" his texts to perfection.

1 Introduction

It is fair to say that scholarship on Tolkien's works is bound to be inherently interdisciplinary, considering their multi-faceted contents and poly-genre nature. It has been noted by many (see e.g. Honegger) that it is mainly his posthumous audience, though, that loudly praises his "fantastic" writings and has consumed especially *The Hobbit* (1937) and *The Lord of the Rings* (1954/5) in hundreds of millions of sold copies up till today. The many reasons why these two narratives in particular (both in their written as well as their cinematographic forms) appeal to so many people have been discussed (cf. e.g. Shippey; Weinreich & Honegger; Drout, *Encyclopedia*), and the papers by Heike Krebs,

Heike Schwarz, and Carolin Tober in this very volume provide proof of the fact that neither laymen nor scholars (and the latter in particular) can fend off the fascination that radiates from these two pieces of world literature and the wealth of readings they offer.

This paper will significantly deviate from Tolkien-mainstream approaches and objects of study (without intending to minimize their values in any way), and will tend towards one of Tolkien's many but significantly less known contributions to the field of Medieval Literature and Historical Linguistics.[1] Compared to *The Hobbit* and *The Lord of the Rings*, both the academic and the layman's interest in Tolkien's scholarly works is still marginal, which is, for one, due to the fact that Tolkien's academic field of expertise, namely Medieval Literature and medieval varieties, is hardly one that seems to spark much attention (let alone ecstasy) – and this is [alas!] so much more true today than it was when Tolkien himself lectured at Oxford. Most of his editions of Middle English texts – certainly with the exception of *Sir Gawain and the Green Knight* (co-edited with E.V. Gordon, 1925, revised by Norman Davis 1967) – e.g. *Sir Orfeo* (1944), or *Ancrene Wisse* (1962), are not considered the standard editions, and neither have many scholarly papers of his had a vigorous effect on the academia at large.[2]

Two of his essays, however, have earned Tolkien a wide-ranging acknowledgement of his work as an Anglo-Saxon scholar and cannot be ignored, if one works either on *Beowulf* or *The Battle of Maldon*: Tolkien's *Homecoming of Beorhtnoth Beorhthelm's Son* (1953) and his lecture titled "*Beowulf*: The Monsters and the Critics" (henceforth abbreviated in sources as BMC). Particularly the latter may be the one academic piece of his that has been provoking and forceful enough to come to extensive fame amongst medieval scholars, philologists and beyond. In fact, his lecture has gone down in history as having "changed the course of *Beowulf* studies [...] and [...] permanently altered our understanding of the

---

[1] I am indebted to Magdalena Spachmann (also see this volume) for sharing her inspiring insights with me and for many a fruitful discussion on the topic of this paper.
[2] One of the reasons for this may simply be that most of Tolkien's academic papers are dedicated to aspects only few experts had or have been intrigued by, cf. e.g. "Some Contributions to Middle-English Lexicography" (1925), "The Devil's Coach Horses" (1925), "*Ancrene Wisse* and *Hali Meiðhad*" (1929), "Chaucer as a Philologist: The Reeve's Tale" (1934), "On Fairy-Stories" (1947), or "Middle English "Losenger": Sketch of an Etymological and Semantic Enquiry" (1953), and "English and Welsh" (1963).

Old English poem" (Chance 8). Drout goes even further in declaring Tolkien's lecture "[t]he single most important critical essay ever written about *Beowulf*, that most revered and studied of all Anglo-Saxon monuments" (*Beowulf*, 1).

While the lecture's impact and momentum will thus hardly be doubted by many, some have raised the issue of Tolkien's highly figurative and linguistic metalanguage being extraordinarily complex and difficult to decode for recipients lacking sufficient linguistic and diachronic common ground. West, for instance, calls it "too rich for brief annotation" (2) and the worldwide web holds a wealth of similar opinions, many of which can also be found in reviews of the volume titled *The Monsters and the Critics* (ed. Christopher Tolkien). Milner, for instance, states that the book

> requires a fairly extensive understanding of Tolkien's cultural context, the scholarly world he inhabited, and the ancient literature that was the focus of his professional career. For a general reader these essays are likely to seem difficult and sometimes incomprehensible [...] [BMC] is not written for a general audience. It was written for scholars who had, among other things, a knowledge of the Old English and Latin languages and a familiarity with *Beowulf* and the critical analyses it has spawned. Tolkien's language in this essay is rich and allusive. It's not a text that one can breeze through.

Such voiced impressions seem to curiously contradict what Christopher Tolkien states in his foreword to the 1983 edition of *The Monsters and the Critics*, namely that

> while all [essays in this volume] were on specific topics, literary or linguistic, the whole audience on those occasions could in no case (save perhaps that of the *Valedictory Address*) be presumed to have more than a general knowledge or interest in the subject (*MC* 1).

I shall, for one thing, argue and demonstrate on various linguistic levels that it is highly questionable that "*Beowulf*: The Monsters and the Critics" was and is indeed (meant) to be fully grasped with nothing more than "a general knowledge [of] or interest" in *Beowulf*. My second and main claim is that Tolkien wove in numerous subtle linguistic traits that allow, when carved out and exposed, for intriguing insights into more than "just" a passionate defense of *Beowulf* as the "most successful Old English poem" (BMC 126). In order to make and sustain my point, I will propose an approach to Tolkien's text that puts his very own armamentarium to the test on a metalevel, namely the very textlinguistic principles he himself would apply to compose, shape and literally "weave" his texts to perfection.³

2 Objectives, background and motivation

One would think that this paper would certainly not be the first one to make use of the tools and methods provided by text linguistics with the aim of carving out Tolkien's own take on text composition. However, while e.g. Wicher acknowledges that "Tolkien was, first of all, a linguist and an artistic writer" (82), scholarly interest in Tolkien's works has (fairly and understandably) been restricted mostly to their contents from a literary criticism stance, rather than focusing on their linguistic metalevels. Also from a literary-criticism stance, Pesch (77) states the following on approaching Tolkien on the metalevel:

> Studying Tolkien according to his own criteria, is an approach that tends to emerge from one's personal enthusiasm for his work and from one's intrinsic motivation. [...] As much as it may be a fascinating approach, it remains one that will hardly be practically applicable. Studying Tolkien from a non-literary, and particularly a theologico-ideological stance, will be continuously feasible as long as each generation may discover new aspects by doing so. Nowadays, for instance, scholars study *The Lord of the Rings* from ecological perspectives, which, although this aspect was certainly entailed, was hardly meant as a priority.⁴

The majority of studies on Tolkien's lecture and its rhetorical layers has been conducted by literary scholars (cf. e.g. Drout "The Rhetorical Evolution"; "The Brilliant Essay"; *Beowulf and the Critics*; "Seventy-Five Years Later"; Shippey, "*Beowulf*-Poet"), while the meta-linguistic level as one worth looking into has not been given nearly enough attention so far. As an exception one might mention Branchaw's paper, which does in fact deal with "what Tolkien said [about scholarly practices] and why he said it [in BMC]." She claims that "in some respects, Tolkien was successful [...] arguably beyond his intentions [namely in having] had a regrettably discouraging effect on later scholars who might elsewise have

---

3 Latin *textum*, i.e. something that is woven.
4 "Tolkien nach seinen eigenen Kriterien zu untersuchen, ist etwas, was aus persönlicher Begeisterung geboren wird und von einem gewissen intrinsischen Interesse ist. [...] Dies mag eine faszinierende Übung sein, aber sie hat nur eine recht beschränkte Nutzanwendung. Tolkien unter nichtliterarischen, insbesondere religiös-weltanschaulichen Gesichtspunkten zu betrachten, ist etwas, das kontinuierlich möglich ist, solange jede Generation neue Aspekte für sich entdecken kann. Heute zum Beispiel wird der *Herr der Ringe* vielfach unter ökologischen Gesichtspunkten gesehen, was sicher tendenziell darin enthalten ist, aber kaum Tolkiens vordringliche Absicht war."

pursued an interest in non-literary studies of *Beowulf*" (15-17). Although she is arguing that the text should be read based on an understanding of "the context of an intellectual environment he was seeing himself in" (17) – which I agree with – and takes into account some of Tolkien's rhetorical devices – which I have included in my own analysis, too – her study is still a literary, nonetheless valuable one, focusing on a different angle than this paper will.

It is principles from text linguistics and pragmatics that this study will utilize in order to gain a more profound understanding of Tolkien's linguistic strategies and his subtler goals. Text linguistics in particular lends itself so well, as it can be regarded as being at the very interface of linguistic and literary analysis, thus so appropriate and suitable for studying Tolkien's writings. After all, they were created by a philologist's hand, and thus inherently embrace this very intersection. What is more, Tolkien's "split personality", which made him look at texts from a fantasy author's as well as an academic scholar's perspective, must have equipped him with very distinctly critical, meta-analytical measures to apply to others' as well as particularly to his own texts. Le Guin puts this neatly, when she says that Tolkien, "while wearing his professorial hat [...] wrote essays about the kind of fiction he wrote" (84).

The present paper will analyze the metalinguistic levels of Tolkien's BMC lecture, putting a pragmatic focus on the dimensions of *situationality*, *intertextuality*, and *intentionality*. In doing so, I shall assess the complexities his potentially non-professional audience was and has been faced with by his lecture. In specific, I will focus on how Tolkien was in fact weaving in discursive subtleties only (meant) to be picked up by specific recipients of his text.

3 A linguistically complex lecture as the object of text-linguistic investigation

3.1 What Tolkien explicitly claims in BMC...

Before the lecture was delivered to the British Academy in November 1936, it had undergone a massive structural evolution which had taken Tolkien years to develop. We know of an earlier version A of *Beowulf and the Critics*, which was later altered and expanded to a version B of *Beowulf and the Critics*, and finally transformed into the lecture and essay "*Beowulf*: The Monsters and the Critics" (BMC; cf. Drout, *Encyclopedia* 57). As Wicher puts it, "Tolkien's principal charge against the critics of *Beowulf* is not so much that they criticize the poem incompetently, but rather that they fail to criticize it at all" (180). He states that "Tolkien's main quarrel with the Anglo-Saxonists of his day is expressed in the following statement" (180):

> It has been said of *Beowulf* that its weakness lies in placing the unimportant things in the centre and the important on the outer edges. [...] I think it profoundly untrue of the poem, but strikingly true of the literature about it. *Beowulf* has been used as a quarry of fact and fancy far more assiduously than it has been studied as a work of art. (BMC 103)

When Tolkien states that "the literature about [*Beowulf*] place[s] the unimportant things in the centre and the important on the outer edges", he in fact sets the tone for a lecture that would criticize not only *Beowulf*'s critics but just as much his own. His mentioning of and repeated coming-back to the image of "centre and edges" is an intertextual reference most of his listeners/readers would only recognize when he explicitly introduces it as a quote from Ker, who criticized *Beowulf* harshly (cf. 108). Tolkien establishes it right at the outset of his lecture (cf. sample (1)) and deepens it by explicitly referring back to it several times in the text (cf. samples (2) to (5)).

(1) It has been said of *Beowulf* itself that its weakness lies in placing the unimportant things at the centre and the important on the outer edges. This is one of the opinions [cf. Ker 252-253] that I wish specially to consider. I think it profoundly untrue of the poem, but strikingly true of the literature about it. (BMC 103)

(2) It is in *Beowulf* that a poet has devoted a whole poem to the theme [...] The particular is on the outer edge, the essential in the centre. (BMC 114f.)

(3) For in a sense it had shirked the problem precisely by not having the monsters in the centre – as they are in *Beowulf* to the astonishment of the critics. [...] It is the strength of the northern mythological imagination that it faced this problem, put the monsters in the centre. (BMC 122)

(4) These things are mainly on the outer edges or in the background because they belong there, if they are to function in this way. But in the centre we have an heroic figure of enlarged proportions. (BMC 127)

(5) We may wish to be assured of this (and the poet has assured us), without demanding that he should put such things in the centre, when they are not the centre of his thought. (BMC 128)

Drout poses eloquently that BMC "pulled *Beowulf* out of the academic ghetto in which it had been confined and allowed it to be elevated to its proper status as one of the great works of literature from England" ("Seventy-five Years Later", 6). I shall argue that there is much more to this lecture than meets the eye, when we take a look at what Tolkien placed within the lines and at the "edges" rather than the center.

3.2 ... and how pragmatics and text linguistics might be able to reveal what Tolkien claimed implicitly

The main, mind-altering message of the lecture certainly is Tolkien's voiced concern that *Beowulf* had been treated and dissected as a purely historical document without regard to its literary value and his praise of the text as a poem "by a learned man writing of old times, who looking back on heroism and sorrow feels in them something permanent and something symbolical" (BMC 123). While this primary aim of Tolkien's shall not be left out of sight in this paper, the analytical focus will be set on his applications of such criteria that render his text coherent and logically comprehensible to his broad audience.

The wealth of criteria that may fulfil such a function for this specific study are potentially endless and certainly overlapping. Schubert, for instance, proposes – mainly on the basis of de Beaugrande & Dressler – to focus on both formal and functional characteristics when aiming to determine a text's level of coherence and its communicative vigor (29). While this is certainly a valuable recommendation and shall, as such, be followed in this study's approach, I will argue that the inclusion of the pragmatic notions of common ground – both its establishment and activation – and of the pragmatic principles and functions of referring (cf. Bublitz) will further enrich an analysis by adding socio-psychological and attitudinal dimensions of Tolkien as the composer and deliverer of his lecture. Table 1 sums up the criteria to be applied in the following.

	Textual dimensions to be applied in Section 4 below	Tolkien's strategies to be tested in Section 4 below
Establishing common ground	**Situationality** comprises the relevance and appropriateness in a communicative situation (Schubert 22; cf. Biber & Conrad).	Establishing common ground with regard to audience, topic and expected pre- and shared knowledge (4.1)
Activating common ground	**Intertextuality** refers to "the ways in which the production and reception of a given text depends upon the participants' knowledge of other texts" (de Beaugrande & Dressler 182).	Referencing other texts as well as to medieval and ancient linguistic varieties (4.2)
Offering and withholding common ground	**Intentionality** refers to the attitude of the producer of the text and their communicative goals (Schubert 21).	References and allusions to his position as a criticized scholar (4.2)

Table 1: Textual dimensions and Tolkien's pragmatic strategies applied in BMC

The analysis in this paper will zoom in on Tolkien's strategical intra- and intertextual references and the pragmatic functions he has these fulfil in establishing and activating common ground in his recipients. Setting out for this analysis, I shall regard BMC as a piece of formal written academic discourse, formally and grammatically sound and cohesively well-wrought. I will thereby consider it a given that with it Tolkien produced a "continuous stretch of […] language larger than a sentence, often constituting a coherent unit such as a sermon, argument, joke, or narrative" (Crystal 25), thus also fulfilling what e.g. Schubert (ch. 3) would call the criterion of *coherence* (G *Kohärenz*).[5] The linguistic data that will be taken into account in order to test these criteria comprises all those sentences in the essay that explicitly or implicitly address (parts of) his audience. Since BMC does not seem to be available in digital form, I have worked with an electronic version of Donoghue and Heaney's 2002 edition of the lecture so to identify and extract its metalinguistic layers efficiently.

4 Measuring BMC's pragmatic vigor by assessing Tolkien's "pragmatics of referring"

4.1 Situational common ground and self-positioning through referring expressions

A key word count reveals that the most salient terms used in BMC are *poem* (66 times), *poet* (66 times), *monster* (43 times), and words containing *critic* (59), which implies that Tolkien – on the overt level of his lecture – does in fact establish lexical cohesion and thus topical coherence for his recipients.[6] References to *Beowulf* and its characters and places are numerous – Tolkien must have justly assumed his audience to be acquainted with the contents or at least the gist of the poem when he refers to e.g. Hygelac (BMC 125, 127), Heorot (BMC 123, 125, 126, 128), King Hrothgar (BMC 118, 121, 126), and, of course, the monster Grendel (BMC 114, 118, 119, 120, 122 etc.), not to mention the hero Beowulf himself (BMC 109, 113, 114, 115, 118, 124 etc.).

Tolkien seeks to embed his observations on *Beowulf* within literary contexts he assumes his recipients to know as well – although it is fair to claim that the text in fact requires a high level of broad literary knowledge from the recipient. Such intertextual references, including both quotations and allusions (cf. Kirner-Ludwig and Zimmermann 293), include numerous pointers to Latin and Greek mythology, e.g. Virgil's *Aeneid* (BMC 120, 121, 124), Homer's

---

[5] I will acknowledge that classifying a text as coherent will always be a subjective assessment, but I still will argue that Tolkien – philologist and perfectionist that he was – would certainly seek to compose any text as a coherent whole.
[6] But also note that e.g. *melancholy* occurs four times in the text.

Odyssey (BMC 121), and the Holy Scripture(s) (BMC 115, 117, 118, 122). To what extent Tolkien included references to the Bible so to do it justice from a philologist's or "a determined Catholic['s]" point of view (Shippey, *Road* 224) cannot be assessed with any certainty. Either way, it is highly likely that he and his audience shared extensive common ground and common cultural knowledge with regard to this particular piece of world literature. Further allusions to other literary works are less explicit, e.g. his reference to Lewis Carroll's poem *Jabberwocky*.[7] All upcoming references to Tolkien's "pragmatics of referring" will stem from the basic assumption that his "act[s] of referring" (Kirner-Ludwig and Zimmermann 294) are inherently pragmatic in that

(i) they were intended as references (that the audience was in fact meant or expected by Tolkien to pick up all of them must be doubted);

(ii) they were "shifted from its source context into another" (Kirner-Ludwig and Zimmermann 301) in the sense that Tolkien applied and re-functionalized them to make his own points; and

(iii) all "entail[…] an evaluation of the quoted text and the new context [Tolkien] posed [them] in" (Kirner-Ludwig and Zimmermann 301).

This study will thus go from the basic assumption that Tolkien's intertextual references are pragmatically meaningful in expressing his stance throughout the lecture. This idea will also essentially overlap with e.g. Brown & Levinson's notion of *positive face*, as I shall inherently argue that Tolkien, through his referring and self-positioning strategies in BMC, does work on his own *face* within the frame of his lecture and status as an academic.

In order to grasp Tolkien and his BMC in a more contextualized manner, it seems useful to borrow three of Biber & Conrad's notions: *participants*, *topic* and *setting*. These lend themselves well as determining factors for situationality (also cf. e.g. Schubert) to sketch out the composition and potential dynamics of the community of practice gathered in the very lecture hall together with and including Prof. Tolkien. The setting was at the British Academy on 25 November 1936, where Tolkien gave his lecture as one in a sequence of the so-called "Sir Israel Gollancz Memorial Lectures". These had been established in

---

7 Also cf. Tolkien's references to the Shakespearian characters Shylock from *The Merchant of Venice* (ca. 1596) as well as *King Lear* (1608) (BMC 109).

1924 and since then been scheduled in an irregular biennial sequence.[8] Factors that may further shape our picture of the scenario that day in 1936, may include that Tolkien was forty-four years old at the time, just having "reform[ed] the Oxford English School in his capacity as Rawlinson and Bosworth Professor of Anglo-Saxon [which he had obtained in 1925]" (Jackson 47). His listeners on the other hand were a group of a few hundred people, with possibly "nothing more than a general knowledge of or interest in the subject" (1) – the British Academy herself describes the lectures as "accessible to scholars in different disciplines and to a broader intelligent public" – with their majority very likely being composed of Tolkien's own students, and some academic colleagues, including his fellow-Inklings, who had been meeting since 1933.[9]

As alluded to above, the assessment of situationality based on taking into account the participants physically attending Tolkien's lecture, and his speech being geared towards this particular, visible audience, is not the whole picture and might even be misleading for our analysis. After all, we have to be aware of the fact that Tolkien knew that this very lecture would be published in the *Journal of the British Academy* after its oral delivery, which was the case on 1 July 1937.[10] It is thus fair to assume that he in fact wrote it just as much with his future readers as well as with his present listeners on 25 November 1936 in mind. Going on from this assumption, it seems appropriate to even neglect the oral-delivery-scenario of BMC altogether and focus on the text as a written speech after all, which allows for a more substantiated analysis altogether. While I am aware that this may seem like a somewhat delicate move, it can be justified based on the fact that the time between Tolkien's delivery of the lecture and the publication of it was very short, thus Tolkien would not have had time to revise it significantly. What is more, Drout (*Beowulf*) shows that the published text was much shorter than the two preceding versions that have survived.

---

8   Cf. http://www.britac.ac.uk/node/3534/. Note that the British Academy website does only list the lecture titles and speakers from 1960 onwards.
9   So to avoid any anachronistic wonderings on the side of this paper's readers before we venture out into the analysis, it should be explicitly pointed out that Tolkien's listeners back in the day did certainly not receive handouts including title, structure and focal aspects of Tolkien's talk (nor were they fortunate enough to follow his line of argumentation on projected slides or transparencies – the earliest photocopiers as well as overhead projectors were not available before the mid 1950s). We have to assume that Tolkien read his essay off from the notes in his hand. To what extent he would deviate from these, or even insert discourse or pragmatic markers, which would not be included in his script, cannot be more than unsatisfactorily guessed at and shall thus be excluded as a factor.
10 Note that *The Hobbit* was published in September 1937.

This approach then leads us to infer that the audience Tolkien is addressing inevitably includes any potential readers of the journal, i.e. many of whom would not be present at his lecture, and in particular any critics (of his own as well as *Beowulf's*) who may well not have attended the lecture in person, but might still have been curious enough to read the piece once published. I would argue that it is particularly the latter that BMC is addressing.[11]

Tolkien uses a number of linguistic devices to determine in- and outgroups in relation to his arguments, including deictic markers, pointers and addressing phrases. Table 2 gathers these to sustain my claim.

Pronoun and determiner types	tokens	established reference
I	122	⇨ Tolkien himself
my, myself	5	⇨ Tolkien himself
we	85	⇨ Tolkien and his recipients
us	18	⇨ Tolkien and his academic colleagues
you	3	⇨ generic, no personal reference
they	**20** [+25 quoted uses]	
	14	⇨ cohesive reference within text
	6	⇨ the critics
those	**6** [pronominal uses only]	
	4	⇨ the critics
	2	⇨ Tolkien and others excluding the critics

---

11 Pesch (69) remarks that BMC may even be regarded as the climax and terminus of Tolkien's academic work ("Höhepunkt und zugleich gewissermaßen das Ende von Tolkiens akademischem Werk"), which Tolkien himself may have been well aware of – while his readership certainly was not.

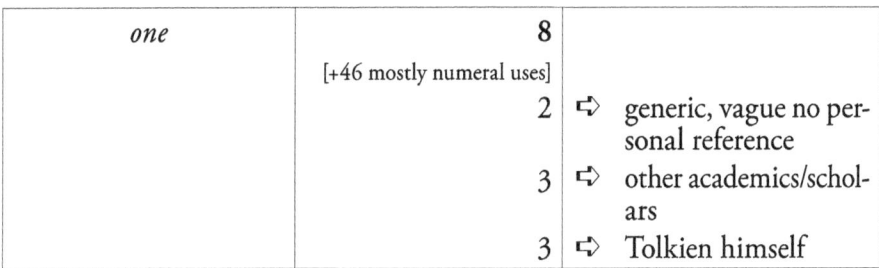

Table 2: Referring expressions in BMC

Tolkien's text demonstrates a neat balance between self-references and such that include both himself (see (6) to (11)) and his audience (see e.g. (11)). In some instances, his use of *we* and *us* seems to be even broader, extensionally referring to Tolkien as one amongst other scholars (which not necessarily all of his listeners were, but certainly all of his readers would be assumed to be), as in (12) and (13). In some other cases – in (14) in collocation with a *let-us-all* hortative, in (15) (and (11)) in a *we-must-(not)* manner – he seems to encourage his recipients to join in, while implicitly claiming that he is the only one who does not require any encouragement.

(6) I have not been a man so diligent in my special walk as duly to read all that has been printed on, or touching on, this poem. (BMC 103)

(7) I shall confine **myself** mainly to the *monsters*. (BMC 103)

(8) **my** view of [the history of the subject] (BMC 104)

(9) That is **my** concern (BMC 117)

(10) This at any rate I have always **myself** felt in reading *Beowulf*. (BMC 125)

(11) I hope I shall show that that allegory is just – even when **we** consider the more recent and more perceptive critics (whose concern is in intention with literature). To reach these **we** must pass in rapid flight over the heads of many decades of critics. As **we** do so a conflicting babel mounts up to **us**, which I can report as something after [the following] fashion (BMC 106)

(12) As for the dragon: as far as **we** know anything about these old poets, **we** know this .(BMC 113)

(13) The main interest which the poem has for **us** is thus not a purely literary interest. *Beowulf* is an important historical document. (BMC 114)

(14) Let **us** by all means esteem the old heroes: men caught in the chains of circumstance [...] dying with their backs to the wall. But *Beowulf*, I fancy, plays a larger part than is recognized in helping **us** to esteem them. [...] In these (if **we** had them) **we** could see the exaltation of undefeated will. (BMC 114)

(15) In any case **we** must not view this poem as in intention an exciting narrative or a romantic tale. (BMC 126)

It is striking that throughout his lecture Tolkien never addresses anyone – neither audience nor critics – directly. His three uses of the personal pronoun *you* are all generic (see (16) to (18))

(16) '*The Beowulf*,' they said, 'is hardly an affair of **yours**, and not in any case a protégé that **you** could be proud of [...]'. (BMC 104)

(17) We are told again that the main story of *Beowulf* is a wild folk-tale. Quite true, of course. It is true of the main story of King Lear, unless in that case **you** would prefer to substitute *silly* for *wild*. (BMC 109)

(18) Even today (despite the critics) **you** may find men not ignorant of tragic legend and history, who have heard of heroes and indeed seen them, who yet have been caught by the fascination of the worm. (BMC 113)

Tolkien's pronominal uses and variable references of *one* are worth to be mentioned as well, specifically those which in fact implicitly refer back to himself, as (19) and (20) do:

(19) There is an historical explanation of the state of *Beowulfiana* that **I** have referred to. And that explanation is important, if **one** would venture to criticize the critics. (BMC 103)

(20) There is something irritatingly odd about all this. **One** even dares to wonder if something has not gone wrong with '**our** modern judgement', supposing that it is justly represented. (BMC 110)

When it comes to Tolkien's uses of *they* in reference to the critics, these are all embedded into utterances that seem highly face-saving and respectful, but at the same time eloquently trenchant. (21), for instance, occurs in a footnote and (22) is part of Tolkien's notorious tower-allegory, in which he refers to *Beowulf*'s and his own critics by using vague and seemingly sarcastic phrasings such as "his friends", "[s]ome suspecting", "they all" and "the man's own descendants" (cf. (22)). (23) is an intratextual reference back to the allegory.

(21) It has also been favoured by the rise of 'English schools', in whose syllabuses *Beowulf* has inevitably some place […] For these cater (in fact, if not in intention) for **those** seeking knowledge about, and ready made judgements upon, works which **they** have not the time, or (often enough) the desire, to know at first hand. (BMC 111)

(22) Of the rest he took some and built a tower. But **his friends** coming perceived at once (without troubling to climb the steps) that these stones had formerly belonged to a more ancient building. So **they** pushed the tower over, with no little labour, in order to look for hidden carvings and inscriptions, or to discover whence the man's distant forefathers had obtained **their** building material. **Some suspecting** a deposit of coal under the soil began to dig for it, and forgot even the stones. **They all** said: This tower is most interesting.' But **they** also said (after pushing it over) 'What a muddle it is in!' And even **the man's own descendants**, who might have been expected to consider what he had been about, were heard to murmur: 'He is such an odd fellow! […]' (BMC 106f.)

(23) So deadly and ineluctable is the underlying thought, that **those** who in the circle of light, within the besieged hall, are absorbed in work or talk and do not look to the battlements, either do not regard it or recoil. Death comes to the feast, and **they** say He gibbers: He has no sense of proportion (BMC 115)

(24) Of none is this so true as of *The Beowulf*, as it used to be called. I have, of course, read *The Beowulf*, as have **most (but not all) of those who** have criticized it. (BMC 103)

Tolkien's pronominal uses of *those* also allow for flexible interpretations with regard to each token's reference: (21) to (24) seem to in fact refer to the critics in a self-distancing manner.

4.2 Tolkien, his audience and the critics – scholarly self-positioning by referencing others

When we move on to assess Tolkien's self-positioning and self-referencing techniques, the notions and linguistic perspectives on intentionality and intertextuality are of relevance. The latter, as defined by de Beaugrande & Dressler, pertains to "ways in which the production and reception of a given text depends upon the participants' knowledge of other texts" (182), while intentionality (together with coherence) will determine whether or to what extent a text will be successful in transmitting its message: intentionality refers to the attitude of the producer of the text and his or her communicative goals (Schubert 21).

While, as mentioned above, this study is deliberately distancing itself from making assumptions about the perceptions and common ground Tolkien's audience had or shared with him, it is highly relevant to this argumentation to consider to what extent, how and potentially why Tolkien presents intertextual references, i.e. whether he for instance includes explicit references or allusions in order to have them confirm or negate the common ground needed to understand and embed an intertextual reference or allusion.

4.2.1 Tolkien's self-positioning as a professor and anti-authoritarian educator

It is well known that Tolkien was not particularly acknowledged and respected among his literary colleagues either (cf. e.g. Faraci; Shippey, *Road*). Shippey even believes that Tolkien must have considered himself in "a losing position in the academic game" at some point (*Road* 13).[12] Such factors must have determined Tolkien's communicative goals and attitude while composing BMC. On the other hand, Drout argues that Tolkien was in fact preaching to the already converted, as his audience was not the generation of Ker and Chambers, who had been criticizing *Beowulf*, but "his own generation and his immediate superiors, [who] were happy to hear that the previous generation had been wrong and that they were right" ("Seventy-five Years Later" 16).

---

12 Also cf. Branchaw (ch. 2) for a valuable outline on Tolkien-critics.

Nevertheless, Tolkien positions himself right at the beginning of his lecture through a highly eloquent and fleshed-out *captatio benevolentiae*, quoting Oswald Cockayne[13] and his harsh critique against Joseph Bosworth. This quote is aimfully applied, as it fulfils several functions at the same time: not only does Tolkien pay his due respects to Bosworth being Tolkien's predecessor on the chair (1858–1876), and in fact one of the name-givers to the Rawlinson and Bosworth Professorship of Anglo-Saxon Tolkien had been entrusted with since 1925 (until 1945). In addition, Tolkien uses this reference to situate himself on the same level as Bosworth – as his ally in profession and fate as well as his academic role model (cf. (26)). By explicitly claiming that Cockayne's criticism and dissatisfaction (with Bosworth's dictionary) were "doubtless unfair", he sets the tone and frame for unjustified criticism against deserved scholars like himself and the need to assess such "unfair" criticism by reviewing and systematically rebuking it as unfounded (cf. e.g. (25), (27)).

(25) I have, of course, read *The Beowulf*, as have most (but not all) of those who have criticized it. (BMC 103)

(26) But I fear that, unworthy successor and beneficiary of Joseph Bosworth, I have not been a man so diligent in my special walk as duly to read all that has been printed on, or touching on, this poem. (BMC 103)

(27) It has been said of *Beowulf* itself that its weakness lies in placing the unimportant things at the centre and the important on the outer edges. This is one of the opinions that I wish specially to consider. I think it profoundly untrue of the poem, but strikingly true of the literature about it. (BMC 103)

One might argue that Tolkien's *captatio*, which, in itself is already an implicit intertextual reference to a medieval convention most of his recipients would have come across during their own studies (cf. e.g. Kirner-Ludwig and Zimmermann), is a tat too modest. This is particularly conspicuous when he refers to himself as being the "unworthy successor and beneficiary of Joseph Bosworth" (cf. (26)). But him saying so may even have suggestively affirmed some of the recipients'

---

13 According to Drout, Cockayne was "best known for his three-volume *Leechdoms, Wortcunning and Starcraft of Early England* [...and] author of *The Shrine: A Collection of Papers on Dry Subjects*" ("Seventy-five Years Later" 5).

own silent belief that he was in fact Bosworth's "unworthy successor".[14] This is also true for wordings as in (28):

(28) It is of *Beowulf*, then, as a poem that I wish to speak; and **though it may seem presumption that I should try** (BMC 103)

Throughout the lecture then, however, Tolkien takes on a confident stance of a scholarly authority, while in fact the meta-linguistic levels allow for the impression that he establishes knowledge with his audience in an overtly unimposing way. This can for instance be seen in his frequent epistemic use of modal verbs,[15] which seems to express an anti-authoritarian, very respectful and humble, non-obligatory encouragement of his recipients to reflect about his points presented (see e.g. (29) and (30)). At the same time he must have sought to implicitly remind them – in a pedagogue's manner – of a piece of information they should already know at that point (see e.g. (31)).

(29) **We may be thankful** that the product of so noble a temper has been preserved by chance (if such it be) from the dragon of destruction. (BMC 124)

(30) Great heroes, like great saints, should show themselves capable of dealing also with the ordinary things of life, even though they may do so with a strength more than ordinary. **We may wish** to be assured of this. (BMC 128)

(31) But **we may remember** that the poet of Beowulf saw clearly: the wages of heroism is death. (BMC 122)

Oftentimes Tolkien uses *may* when he admits that he cannot be sure about a translation or alleged fact, as in (32) and (33), or conditional *would* (as in (34)) in such cases where he finds his own argumentation arguably tentative.

(32) When we have read his poem, as a poem, rather than as a collection of episodes, we perceive that he who wrote *hæleð under heofenum* **may have meant** in dictionary terms 'heroes under heaven'. (BMC 115)

---

14 Note that it indeed does not seem as if Tolkien was playing modest for the deeper purposes of his lecture, but in fact expressed his humble self-awareness at other points to other recipients, e.g. in an unsent letter to Hugh Brogan: "Not being especially well read in modern English, and far more familiar with works in the ancient and "middle" idioms, my own ear is to some extent affected; so that though I could easily recollect how a modern would put this and that, what comes easiest to my mind or pen is not quite that" (Carpenter, *Letters* 225 [letter 171]).
15 I have counted 34 tokens of *may*, 31 tokens of *would*, 19 tokens of *should* and 14 tokens of *must* in BMC.

(33) But that shift is not complete in *Beowulf* – whatever **may have been true** of its period in general. (BMC 119)

(34) Any theory that will at least allow us to believe that what he did was of design, and that for that design there is a defence that may still have force, **would seem more probable**. (BMC 110f.)

For face-saving reasons presumably, Tolkien does not use either *you should* or *they should*, which would have been strong deontic choices, but instead weakens the force of his recommendations by giving them in an embedded manner in *we-should* constructions (cf. (35) and (36)).[16]

(35) Though if **we must** have a term, **we should choose** rather 'elegy'. (BMC 127)

(36) Even if Milton had done this (and he might have done worse), **we should perhaps pause** to consider whether his poetic handling had not had some effect upon the trivial theme. (BMC 110)

Even with regard to his main *Beowulf*-related arguments, Tolkien seems rather cautious and face-saving in expressing his opinions (cf. e.g. (37)), while he deliberately uses *it must*, *this must*, or *we must* only in few cases in order to mark his utterance as particularly momentous (cf. (38) to (40)).

(37) **I would suggest**, then, that the monsters are not an inexplicable blunder of taste. (BMC 115)

(38) **It must be observed** that there is a difference between the comments of the author and the things said in reported speech by his characters. (BMC 118)

(39) **We must dismiss**, of course, from mind the notion that *Beowulf* is a 'narrative poem'. (BMC 124)

(40) Indeed **this must be admitted** to be practically certain. (BMC 127)

Apart from verbal modality, Tolkien weaves in a number of other lexical devices (the list in the next (sub-)chapter, adapted from Valor (30)), does neither claim

---

[16] Note that his use of *should* in "without the first half we should miss much incidental illustration; we should miss also the dark background of the court of Heorot [...] And (most important) we should lose the direct contrast of youth and age" (BMC 126) is a display of rather unconventional or extravagant uses of *we should* in a manner of 'we would be bound to'. Quirk et al. (1985) for example do not list this particular semantic nuance of *should*.

nor aim for completeness): adverbs expressing a degree of doubt, e.g. *presumably* (BMC 125), *possibly* (BMC 108, 123), *probably* (BMC 103, 107, 112, 123, 124, 125x3); adverbs expressing conviction, e.g. *clearly* (BMC 116, 118, 121, 122, 124), *indeed* (BMC 105, 109, 110x2, 113, 124, 126, 127x2), and *undoubtedly* (BMC 122). Table 3 in the next (sub-)chapter displays the distribution of modal devices in BMC.

4.2.2 Tolkien's self-positioning strategies as an authority of Anglo-Saxon studies

While the meta-linguistic picture just sketched out might imply that Tolkien was presenting himself, his professional knowledge and his stance in an unobtrusive and modest manner, the permanent impression one gains from reading BMC is in fact a satisfyingly persuasive one, which Tolkien achieves to create by adding further meta-linguistic layers to his composition. Thus we have constructions that range from subjective to objective stance (cf. Du Bois) and from low to high force mitigation, as displayed in Table 3.

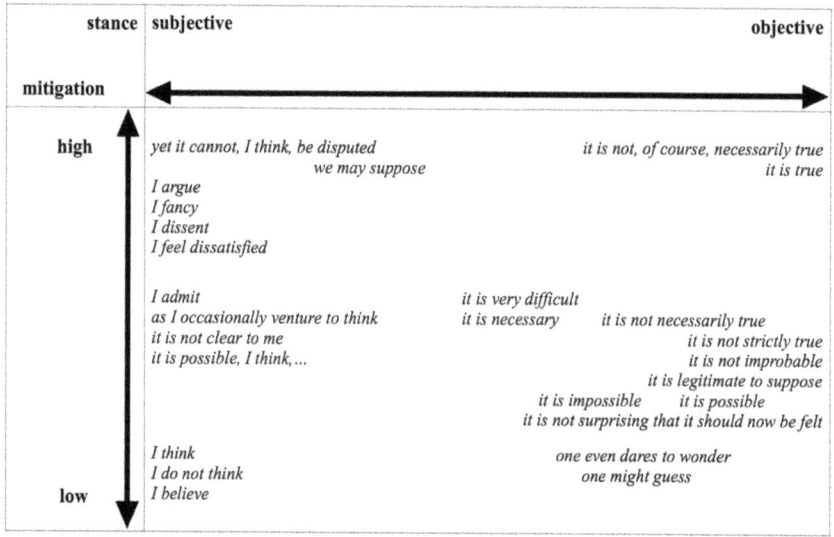

Table 3: Tolkien's self-positioning devices

The distribution of self-positioning devices shows that Tolkien's self-referring choices demonstrate a balance between subjective (*I, we*) and objective or impersonal (*it, one*). The verb phrases he selected for his argument have a relatively high tendency throughout to mitigate his claims and demands. At the same time, the lexical verbs he chose are semantically expressive (*argue, dissent*) and make his lecture strong and persuasive after all.

A second layer of complexity, which would unmistakably prove Tolkien to be the authority in medieval linguistic varieties that he was and wanted to be acknowledged as, was added by numerous Latin quotes and wordings (cf. BMC 104, 105, 114, 120), including two direct quotes from the *Aeneid* (BMC 121, 124), one Greek term (ἁμαρτία, BMC 112),[17] one Old Norse quote from *The Saga of the Volsungs* (BMC 113), two Old Norse lexemes ("*jötnar* and *álfar*", BMC 122), and eight comparably lengthy direct quotes from *Beowulf* (BMC 113, 114, 120, 121, 124, 125, 127f., 129). In nine further instances, Tolkien uses key phrases from *Beowulf*, apparently presupposing that his recipients would be well-read enough to process them as such: "*hæleð under heofenum*" ('heroes under heaven', BMC 115, 119, 124); "*gastbona*" ('demonslayer', BMC 118; cf. *Beowulf* l. 177); "Beowulf's byrne ('ringed coat of mail', BMC 119); "*eotenas* and *ylfe*" (BMC 122); "*folces hyrde*" (BMC 123; 5 times in *Beowulf*); "a young knight, who used his great gift of *mægen* to earn *dom* and *lof*" (BMC 124; cf. *Beowulf*: *mægen* 'strength' l. 1706; *dom* 'glory' l. 2147; *lof* 'praise' l. 1536); "a mere *wrecca*, an errant adventurer" (BMC 125f.; cf. *Beowulf* l. 1137); "*feond mancynnes*" (BMC 128, *Beowulf* l. 164 'foe of mankind'); "Beowulf's *geogoðfeore*" (BMC 128; cf. l. 537 *Beowulf* 'years of youth').[18]

Let us look into four instances where Tolkien even codeswitches between English, Middle English and Old English, thus demonstrating nonchalantly his remarkable skills in such varieties that are commonly just studied to be comprehended rather than being actually used:[19] firstly, (41) contains a quoted

---

17 The editor adds: "*Hamartia*, the Aristotelian term for a hero's tragic flaw".
18 In his utterance that the poet's "hearers were thinking of the *eormengrund*, the great earth, ringed with *garsecg*, the shoreless sea" (BMC 115), Tolkien provides the denotations for those Old English terms used himself. Also see footnotes on pp. 114, 115, 118 for further Old English references.
19 There are two more such code-switching instances to be mentioned in BMC, namely "the enemies of the one God, *ece Dryhten*, the eternal Captain of the new" (119; cf. e.g. "Éce Drihten wið Ahrahame spræc" *Genesis*) and "it did work with the *goðlauss viking*, without gods" (122; an adjective found in relation to Hallr goðlauss, who is e.g. mentioned in the *Landnámabók*).

section from Chaucer's *General Prologue* (cf. (42)), describing the Manciple. Samples (43) and (44) are particularly intriguing as they are pseudo-references and in fact Tolkien's inventions – the latter "patterned after Old English gnomic verse" (editor's wording, BMC 115), the former "patterned after passages in *Beowulf*" (BMC 107).

(41) It is of *Beowulf*, then, as a poem that I wish to speak; and though it may seem presumption that I should try with **swich a lewed mannes wit to pace the wisdom of an heep of lerned men**, in this department there is at least more chance for the **lewed man**. (BMC 103)

(42) Now is nat that of God a ful fair grace, / **That swich a lewed mannes wit** shal **pace / The wisdom of an heep of lerned men**? (l. 574f.)

(43) He would deserve reverence, of course, even if he still lived and had not *ellor gehworfen on Frean wære* upon a high mountain in the heart of that Europe which he loved (BMC 107, 'Turned else where into the Lord's protection.').

(44) *lif is læne: eal scæceð leoht and lif somod* (BMC 115, 'Life is transitory: all light and life departs together.')

4.2.3 Tolkien's implicit self-referencing through taking a stance for the *Beowulf*-poet

As Jackson observed, "Tolkien was talking about the poet who had written [...] *Beowulf* but his views fit his own aesthetic conception" (55). I agree with Jackson, based on my reading of BMC as not only an acknowledgement for *Beowulf* itself, but in fact for its skillful poet (see e.g. (45) – (48)):

(45) Nearly all the **censure**, and most of the praise, that has been bestowed on *The Beowulf* has been due either to the belief that it was something that it was not [...] or to **disappointment at the discovery that it was itself and not something that the scholar would have liked better**. (BMC 105)

(46) The author of *Beowulf* **cannot be held responsible** for the fact that we now have only his poem and not others. (BMC 109)

(47) It is a poem by **a learned man** writing of old times, **who looking back on the heroism and sorrow feels in them something permanent and something symbolical**. [...] He makes his minstrel sing in Heorot of the Creation of

the earth and the lights of Heaven. **So excellent is this choice** as the theme of the harp that maddened Grendel lurking joyless in the dark without that it matters little whether this is anachronistic or not. (BMC 123)

(48) **it is the poet himself who made antiquity so appealing**. His poem has more value in consequence, and is a greater contribution to early mediaeval thought than the harsh and intolerant view that consigned all the heroes to the devil. (BMC 124)

Based on wordings as in (48), I even venture to argue that Tolkien – a prolific poet himself –[20] goes beyond expressing his admiration for the 'colleague', but in fact found himself identifying with him: he rebuts the critics' points in a manner that seems to be rather personal. This can, for one thing, be argued when considering what Drout pointed to, namely that "Tolkien's audience wasn't Ker's generation [who had died in 1923], it was the next generation, his own generation and immediate superiors" ("Seventy-five Years Later" 16).[21] A good number of Tolkien's utterances demonstrate his personal emotional involvement and even offendedness by the critics, as shown in the following text excerpts (also cf. (48)):

(49) [The critics] were heard to murmur: '**He is such an odd fellow**! Imagine his using these old stones just to build a **nonsensical tower**! Why did not he restore the old house? He had no sense of proportion.' But from the top of that tower the man had been able to look out upon the sea. (BMC 105f.)

(50) There is, I think, no criticism more beside the mark than that which some have made, complaining that it is monsters in both halves that is so **disgusting**; one they could have **stomached** more easily. **That is nonsense.** [...] It would really have been **preposterous**, if the poet had recounted Beowulf's rise to fame in a 'typical' or 'commonplace' war in Frisia, [...] If the dragon is the right end for Beowulf, **and I agree**

---

20 Cf. the published poems *Goblin Feet* (1915), *Errantry* (1933), *The Adventures of Tom Bombadil* (1934) as well as e.g. *The Voyage of Earendel the Evening Star* (1914), *The Horns of Ylmir* (1914), *Kortirion among the Trees* (1915), *A Song of Aryador* (1915), *Over Old Hills and Far Away* (1916), *The Nameless Land* (1924).
21 Drout ("Seventy-five Years Later") provides an extensive discussion of the critics Tolkien explicitly and implicitly refers to, including Ker, Cockayne, Strong, Lawrence, Klaeber and Chambers.

with the author that it is, then Grendel is an eminently suitable beginning. (BMC 128)

An additional and curious lexical indicator in Tolkien's text for his identification with the *Beowulf*-poet is the adjective *sober*, which he uses three times in reference and reaction to Ker's critique of *Beowulf* (cf. (52) to (54)), who applied this adjective in the first place (cf. (51)):

(51) A reasonable view of the merit of *Beowulf* is not impossible, though rash enthusiasm may have made too much of it, while **a correct and sober taste** may have too contemptuously refused to attend to Grendel or the Fire-drake. The fault of *Beowulf* is that there is nothing much in the story. (BMC 107; quoted from Ker 252f.)

(52) This passage [i.e. referring to (53)] [...] remains, in this country at any rate, a potent influence. Yet its primary effect is to state a paradox which one feels has always strained the belief, even of those who accepted it, and has given to *Beowulf* the character of an 'enigmatic poem'. The chief virtue of the passage (not the one for which it is usually esteemed) is that it does accord some attention to the monsters, **despite correct and sober taste**. (BMC 108)

(53) He esteemed dragons, as rare as they are dire, as some do still. He liked them – as a poet, not as a **sober** zoologist; and he had good reason. (BMC 109)

(54) The proposition seems to have been passed as self-evident. **I dissent, even at the risk of being held incorrect or not sober.** (BMC 112)

Tolkien seems to fend off not only Ker's critique as a whole (i.e. in alignment of the topic of his lecture), but actually seems to specifically ridicule Ker's very peculiar lexical choice, i.e. *correct* and *sober* as supposedly antonymous to *enthusiastic* (cf. (51) again). Tolkien seems to take it personally that Ker's wording implies an arrogance towards any scholar intrigued by *Beowulf*, which is why he recontextualizes it repeatedly so to make sure his audience gets the sarcastic tone.

4.3 Tolkien: disarmingly nonchalant?

While the preceding sections of this paper have zoomed in on Tolkien's meta-linguistic stance and positioning as a scholar and professor of Anglo-Saxon, this final analytical section shall add another layer of Tolkien's rhetorical strategies that is entailed in an even more subtle manner than others: Tolkien's humorous or sarcastic submessages woven into BMC. Shippey ("Tolkien's two views") inspired this final angle when he wrote that he had once

> commented that "Tolkien's mind was one of unmatchable subtlety, not without a streak of deliberate guile". Thanks to the researches of Michael Drout, we now have an example of the "deliberate guile" better than any [Shippey himself] could have had in mind back then. We can now be sure that when he gave his famous lecture [i.e. BMC], Tolkien was, if not laughing up his sleeve at his distinguished British Academy audience, then smiling inwardly, at least at one moment, at what he knew and they didn't about what he was telling them.[22]

While by this "one moment" Shippey is referring to Tolkien's self-reference to Lewis and himself when arguing that "even today [one] may find men not ignorant of tragic legend and history, [...] who yet have been caught by the fascination of the worm" (also see above), let me show that there are in fact more situations hidden in Tolkien's lecture and the footnotes that suggest a tongue-in-cheek and rather nonchalant tone of his, hardly encountered elsewhere in his works.

Whether and to what extent Tolkien read out his footnotes during his lecture, cannot be determined with any certainty. However, there is a likeliness that he did. Either way, the recipient listening closely or taking the time to study Tolkien's 32 footnotes is in for a treat of metaphorical humor (see (55)), ranging between verbal joke (see (56)), and sarcasm (see (55) and (57)).

(55) Thus in Professor Chambers's great bibliography [...] we find a section, § 8. [...]. It is impressive, but there is no section that names Poetry. As certain of the items included show, such consideration as Poetry is accorded at all is *buried unnamed* in § 8. (BMC 104)

---

22 There are also other comments on Tolkien's subtle humor to be found, e.g. in Martinez's *Blog of Lost Talo* 2014, who states that "[y]ou never really know when J.R.R. Tolkien was joking in some subtle, philological way or if serendipity guided his choice of words".

(56) I include nothing that has not somewhere been said by someone; if not in my exact words; but I do not, of course, attempt to represent all the dicta, **wise or otherwise,** that have been uttered. (BMC 107)

(57) But we learn also at the end of his notice that: 'Those distracting allusions to things apart from the chief story make up for their want of proportion. They give the impression of reality and weight; the story is not in the air … it is part of the solid world.' **By the admission of so grave an artistic reason for the procedure of the poem Ker himself began the undermining of his own criticism of its structure.** […] Possibly it was this very thought, working in his mind, that made Ker's notice of *Beowulf* in the **small** later book, **his 'shilling shocker'**, more vague and hesitant in tone, and so **of less influence.** (BMC 108)[23]

It is well possible that Tolkien himself would follow his own main argument in inserting such humorous side remarks "on the outer edge", while placing "the essential in the centre" (114f.). There are then in fact humorous remarks he did situate within his main text, which would suggest that these were more "essential" to be made in the center rather than the margins. His reference to the Trojans, for instance, who, had they had "a Northern king and his companions" by their side against Agamemnon and Achilles,

(58) would have driven [them] into the sea, more decisively than the Greek hexameter routs the alliterative line (BMC 117),

seems to be an ironic statement that implicitly expresses Tolkien's personal preference for Nordic literature rather than Homer. He emphasizes this preference of his at several points in BMC, but his strongest justification is probably the one quoted in (58) – embracing yet another opportunity to mock *Beowulf*'s critics as well as his own for their narrow-mindedness in keeping their traditional ("to the astonishment of the critics") or media-manipulated blinders on; "under suspicion of being connected with the Government"). In order to further emphasize his indignation about this attitude, Tolkien sarcastically inserts a quote by Ker ("As a working theory absolutely impregnable"), which would certainly have been an allusion only few of his listeners would have been able to recognize.

---

23 The OED gives this phrase under *shilling*, n., C2. As follows: "shilling dreadful n. (or shilling shocker) a short sensational novel, published at a shilling."

(59) For in a sense it had shirked the problem precisely by not having the monsters in the centre – as they are in *Beowulf* **to the astonishment of the critics**. But such horrors cannot be left permanently unexplained, lurking on the outer edges and **under suspicion of being connected with the Government**. It is the strength of the northern mythological imagination that it faced this problem, put the monsters in the centre, gave them victory but no honour, and found a potent but terrible solution in naked will and courage. 'As a working theory absolutely impregnable.' (BMC 122)

Another one of Tolkien's seemingly sarcastic remarks to be mentioned as the final one in this section makes an implicit reference to his critics, who are not part of his own in-group of "intelligent living people" – certainly a main point he needed to make and a position he wished to explicitly take (also see above).

(60) Correct and sober taste may refuse to admit that there can be an interest for *us* – the proud we that includes all intelligent living people – in ogres and dragons. (BMC 112)

5 Conclusion

"One could read BMC over and over, and still discover new aspects and hidden details", as Magdalena Spachmann, a former student of mine and contributor to this volume, once claimed. As the analytical sections may have shown, it is fair to claim that the lecture was certainly so profound, dense, and complex that Tolkien's listening audience in 1936 must have missed numerous implicit layers due to what has been referred to as "information overload" (cf. e.g. Schubert 22); even though Tolkien may have well been able to assess the level of metalinguistic awareness, ability and proficiency his audience would bring to his lecture. Drout once argued that "[s]ometimes [Tolkien's] knowledge is so subtle that we can't figure out what exactly he means but that's because he assumed that his audience knew the same things he did" ("Seventy-five Years Later" 14). While I certainly agree with Drout's observation of the subtleness and refinedness of Tolkien's knowledge, I have shown and discussed extensive material from BMC which suggests that he was actually proving and establishing himself to know *much more* than his recipients. The lecture was doubtlessly not meant to be fully grasped – certainly not by anyone with nothing more than "a general knowledge or interest" (*MC* 1) and not even by such recipients who knew *Beowulf* and the secondary literature nearly as well as Tolkien did. In fact, in order to be in the position to comprehend the myriad of figurative, linguistic and referential traits in Tolkien's lecture, one would actually have had to know Tolkien well and thus what inspired him as a scholar and writer and what drove him in pursuing his own work. The chance of making some of his critics realize that they may have been wrong in criticizing him – or at least providing them with the opportunity to come to such a realization by seeking to understand Tolkien's highly implicit and rhetorically exquisite appeal to them – must have been more than an incentive for Tolkien; it must have been his private amusement.

About the Author

MONIKA KIRNER-LUDWIG is a postdoctoral associate in the Department of Educational Theory and Practice at the State University of New York at Albany, USA. She earned her Ph.D. in Historical English Linguistics and Medieval Literature from the Ludwig-Maximilians-University, Munich, Germany, in 2013, with her monograph titled *Heathens, Pagans, Misbelievers: A lexico-semantic field study and its historio-pragmatic reflections in texts from the English Middle Ages* (2015, Winter). Her teaching and research interests focus on the area of Intercultural Pragmatics, which she approaches from both synchronic and historical viewpoints. These have led to interdisciplinary and interlinguistic projects on e.g. J.R.R. Tolkien's works and language, studies into pseudo-archaisms, as well as the pragmatics of today's youth language phenomena.

List of Abbreviations

L CARPENTER, Humphrey, ed. with the assistance of Christopher Tolkien. *The Letters of J.R.R. Tolkien*. London: George Allen & Unwin, 1981. Reprinted Boston: Houghton Mifflin, 2000.

MC TOLKIEN, John Ronald Reuel. *The Monsters and the Critics and Other Essays*. Ed. Christopher Tolkien. London: George Allen & Unwin, 1983.

References

Biber, Douglas and Susan Conrad. *Register, Genre, and Style.* Cambridge: Cambridge University Press, 2009.

Branchaw, Sherrylyn. "Contextualizing the Writings of J.R.R. Tolkien on Literary Criticism." 15 January 2017 < http://scholar.valpo.edu/journaloftolkienresearch/vol1/iss1/2>

Brown, Penelope and Stephen C. Levinson. *Politeness. Some Universals in Language Usage.* Cambridge: Cambridge University Press, 1987.

British Academy Home Page. 5 December 2016 <http://www.britac.ac.uk/node/3534/>.

Bublitz, Wolfram. "Introducing Quoting as a Ubiquitous Meta-communicative Act." *The Pragmatics of Quoting Now and Then.* Eds. Jenny Arendholz, Wolfram Bublitz and Monika Kirner-Ludwig. [Topics in English Linguistics [TiEL]]. Berlin et al.: de Gruyter, 2015. 1-28.

Carpenter, Humphrey, ed. with the assistance of Christopher Tolkien. *The Letters of J.R.R. Tolkien.* Boston: Houghton Mifflin, 1981.

Chance (Nitzsche), Jane. *Tolkien's Art.* London: The MacMillan Press, 1979.

Crystal, David. *An Encyclopedic Dictionary of Language and Languages.* Cambridge, MA: Blackwell, 1992.

De Beaugrande, Robert-Alain and Wolfgang Ulrich Dressler. *Introduction to Text Linguistics.* London: Longman, 1981.

Donoghue, Daniel, ed., and Seamus Heaney, transl. *Beowulf: A Verse Translation.* (Norton Critical Editions). New York: Norton, 2002.

Drout, Michael D.C. *Beowulf and the Critics by J. R. R. Tolkien.* (Medieval and Renaissance Texts and Studies 248). Tempe, AZ: The Arizona Center for Medieval and Renaissance Studies, 2002.

"The Rhetorical Evolution of 'Beowulf: The Monsters and the Critics'." *The Lord of the Rings 1954-2004: Scholarship in Honor of Richard E. Blackwelder.* Eds. Wayne G. Hammond and Christina Scull. Marquette, WI: Marquette University Press, 2006. 183-215.

ed. *J.R.R. Tolkien Encyclopedia. Scholarship and Critical Assessment.* New York and London: Routledge, 2007.

"'*Beowulf*: The Monsters and the Critics': The Brilliant Essay that Broke *Beowulf* Studies." 2010. 20 November 2016 <http://lotrplaza.com/showthread.php?17739-Beowulf-The-Monsters-amp-the-Critics-Michael-Drout>.

"'*Beowulf*: The Monsters and the Critics' Seventy-Five Years Later." *Mythlore* 30 (2011): 5-22.

Du Bois, John W. "The Stance Triangle." *Stancetaking in Discourse: Subjectivity, Evaluation, Interaction*. Ed. Robert Englebretson. Amsterdam: Benjamins, 2007. 139-182.

Faraci, Mary. "'I Wish to Speak': Tolkien's Voice in his *Beowulf* Essay." *Tolkien the Medievalist*. Ed. Jane Chance. London and New York: Routledge, 2003. 50-62.

Honegger, Thomas. "Tolkien through the Eyes of a Medievalist." *Reconsidering Tolkien*. Ed. Thomas Honegger. Cormarë Series 8. Zurich and Berne: Walking Tree Publishers, 2005. 45-66.

Jackson, Aaron Isaac. "Authoring the Century: J.R.R. Tolkien, the Great War and Modernism." *English* 59.224 (2010): 44-69.

Ker, W. P. *The Dark Ages*. New York: Charles Scribner's Sons, 1904.

Kirner-Ludwig, Monika and Iris Zimmermann. "Quoting and Plagiarising – Searching for Concepts in Texts from the English and German Middle Ages." *The Pragmatics of Quoting Now and Then*. Eds. Jenny Arendholz, Wolfram Bublitz, and Monika Kirner-Ludwig. Berlin et al.: de Gruyter, 2015. 291-318.

Le Guin, Ursula K. 2007. "The Critics, the Monsters, and the Fantasists." 8 November 2016. Retrieved from <https://www.rc.umd.edu/sites/default/files/imported/reference/wcircle/ leguin.pdf>, 83-87.

Martinez, Michael. *A Blog of Lost Talo*. Posted 14 May 2014. 8 November 2016. <http://www.tolkiensociety.org/blog/2014/05/a-blog-of-lost-talo/>.

Milner, Liz. "J.R.R. Tolkien's *The Monsters and the Critics*." 2 January 2017. <http://thegreenmanreview.com/wordpress1/books/j-r-r-tolkiens-the-monsters-and-the-critics-2/>.

Pesch, Helmut W. "J.R.R. Tolkien. Die Hobbits und die Kritiker." *Das Licht von Mittelerde. Aufsätze und Vorträge*. Erster Deutscher Fantasy Club: Passau, 1994. 69-82. 2 November 2016 http://www.helmutwpesch.de/page4/downloads-3/files/TolkienHobbitsundKritiker.pdf.

Quirk, Randolph, Sidney Greenbaum, Geoffrey Leech, and Jan Svartvik. *A Comprehensive Grammar of the English Language*. London: Longman, 1985.

Schubert, Christoph. *Englische Textlinguistik: Eine Einführung*. Berlin: Schmidt, 2012.

Shippey, Tom. *The Road to Middle-earth*. London: HarperCollins, 2005.

"Tolkien and the *Beowulf*-Poet." *Roots and Branches: Selected Papers on Tolkien*. Cormarë Series 11. Zurich: Walking Tree Publishers, 2007. 1-18.

"Tolkien's Two Views of *Beowulf*: One hailed, one ignored. But did we get this right?" 2010. 5 December 2016 <http://lotrplaza.com/showthread.php?18483-Tolkien%27s-Two-Views-of-Beowulf-Tom-Shippey>.

SIMPSON, John and Edmund WEINER, eds. *The Oxford English Dictionary* [OED]. 20 Volumes. 2nd ed. Oxford: Clarendon Press, 1989. 15 January 2017 <http://www.oed.com/>.

TOLKIEN, John Ronald Reuel. *The Monsters and the Critics and Other Essays*. Ed. Christopher Tolkien. London: George Allen & Unwin, 1983.

VALOR, M. Lluïsa Gea. *A Pragmatic Approach to Politeness and Modality in the Book Review Articles*. [Studies in English Language and Linguistics 6]. Universitat de València: Lengua Inglesa, 2000.

WEINREICH, Frank and Thomas HONEGGER, eds. *Tolkien and Modernity*. 2 vols. Cormarë Series 9 & 10. Zurich and Berne: Walking Tree Publishers, 2006.

WEST, Richard C. *Tolkien Criticism. An Annotated Checklist*. Kent: The Kent State University Press, 1970.

WICHER, Andrzej. "What exactly does Tolkien argue for in '*Beowulf*: The Monsters and the Critics'? An attempt at a metacriticism." *'O, What a Tangled Web': Tolkien and Medieval Literature. A View from Poland*. Ed. Barbara Kowalik. Cormarë Series 29. Zurich and Jena: Walking Tree Publishers, 2013. 179-196.

Heike Krebs

"One trailer to bring them all and in the darkness bind them?" – *The Lord of the Rings* Trailers and their Communicative Functions

Abstract

Within film marketing, trailers have developed as the most effective way of advertising new films since the first days of cinema (Hediger, "Gedächtnis" 112). Setting out from a marketing perspective on film trailers, this paper combines a multimodal analysis of *The Lord of the Rings* trailers with Roman Jakobson's functions of language (*On Language*), using the latter as a framework to describe the trailers' communicative functions on their micro levels, i.e. concerning certain modes like image, speech, writing etc. as well as the interrelations of these modes.

A first comparison between twelve different film trailers shows a clear development from the very first trailer, aimed at advertising the whole trilogy, to the different trailers of the single films and the ones advertising the Blu-ray and extended edition of the trilogy. All of them must be seen in close connection to the well planned marketing strategy of the trilogy, which aimed at readers of the literary original and simultaneously needed to attract new spectators. For both purposes, certain (multi)modal patterns are used, which can be assigned to certain communicative functions.

Finally, the question of the communicative functions of trailers is considered within the contemporary context of media convergence, which has been essential for the economic success of *The Lord of the Rings* film trilogy.

1 Introduction and objectives: film trailers within the film marketing strategy

Setting out from Vinzenz Hediger's claim that film trailers are "the key element of every film advertising campaign" (*Verführung* 13, my translation, see also "Gedächtnis" 112),[1] this paper takes into scrutiny the functions that trailers can and do develop on various (textual) levels. With *The Lord of the Rings*[2] trilogy being not only a blockbuster movie (Mikos et al. 19), but also a very effectively marketed film franchise, it is a special case in several aspects,

---

1 "Der Kinotrailer ist das Schlüsselelement jeder Filmwerbekampagne."
2 Henceforth referred to as *LotR*.

which is why a closer look at two important aspects of its commercial context will be taken so to provide a frame of reference for the following trailer analysis. Both, I claim, are not only relevant for the marketing of the trilogy, but will also be discernible within modally constructed trailer functions.

Firstly, as a film adaptation of a world-famous work of fantasy literature (although not intended or labelled as such by Tolkien himself), the films and their marketing could seize the opportunity that *LotR* was considered pre-sold property (Mikos et al. 56): The literary classic by J.R.R. Tolkien being well-known, it created a high number of readers potentially interested in a film adaptation as well as a pre-existing community of fans the producers could count on (Mikos et al. 56, 65). Consequently, the *LotR* marketing strategy explicitly included leaking background information about the production of the films, giving interviews etc. for the potential audience and embraced the possibility of an independent fan culture (Shefrin 262, 266, Thompson 140-141). The fan factor had an effect not only on the films themselves, which had to comply with rather high standards of authenticity if the production was not to put off this highly lucrative fan base. Also, the producers had a tentative idea about the film audience quite early and could adapt their ways of advertising the film.

Secondly, as a film franchise,[3] *LotR* comprises not only one but three films that were released in three consecutive years. It also included other media products, from accompanying books to DVDs and video games. At the same time, the *LotR* trilogy can be assigned blockbuster status because of its economic success,[4] which in turn relies on strategic choices within production and marketing. Mikos et al. (74) attribute the success of *LotR* mainly to the well-timed utilization of pre-sold property and cross-media marketing,[5] all contributing to the aim of keeping (potential) viewers interested:

---

[3] Janet Wasko and Govind Shanadi consider the *LotR* trilogy a "nearly ideal franchise" (24) for "its already established popularity", "its appeal across demographic groups" and "its merchandise potential" (ibid.). Contrary to reducing a franchise to "mean simply sequels" (ibid. 23), or arguing against this classification because the trilogy was shot in one go (Hedling 226), which is another untypical factor from a production perspective (Mikos et al. 57), I follow Wasko and Shanadi in their definition of franchise as "a property or concept that is repeatable in multiple media platforms or outlets with merchandising and tie-in potentials" (23).

[4] For example, Iversen classifies *The Return of the King* as a blockbuster for its market share of about 60 percent (178).

[5] For a detailed list of characteristics of blockbusters see Lewis 66-68, summed up by Mikos et al. 20-21.

> Letting the fans find out enough to keep them intrigued without allowing them to divulge too much is a balancing act that Hollywood has still not fully mastered. Peter Jackson's clever handling of the problem provides a model that will surely be taken up by others (Thompson 134).

Within film advertising, trailers as well as posters and advertisements in magazines etc. count as rather classical i.e. conventional devices (Mikos et al. 70). But, considering the auditory and visual complexity of trailers, two questions arise: What can be learned from a micro analysis of trailers and how do they tie in with the macro strategy of the franchise? For an answer to either of these two questions, two aspects shall be elaborated upon in this explorative study of twelve *LotR* trailers: Applying Jakobson's functions of speech, as outlined in his *On Language*, to the functions of a trailer, (1) I argue that there are certain patterns of modes for certain communicative functions. (2) Moreover, I hypothesize that, due to the early publication of the first trailer in 2000 (Mikos et al. 70), a development from this first trailer to the final one for the extended edition Blu-ray (2011)[6] can be observed in that the multimodal structures and the functions arising from them change over time. Although different situations of watching a trailer (for example in the cinema, or on a website) can be considered, my main focus lies on the trailers themselves, i.e. their structure and functions. So, before elaborating on relevant issues of multimodality and Jakobson's model, the selection of the corpus shall be explained.

2 The Corpus: Trailers for *The Lord of the Rings*

Not only for independent movies, as Iversen has shown (188-190), but also for blockbuster movies, word-of-mouth advertising is an essential factor for the decision to see a certain film (Prommer 222). Considering the importance of pre-existing *LotR* readers, fan cultures and the fact that a satisfying film adaptation of the books had been regarded as impossible for a long time (Mikos et al. 56), the producers had to be careful not to put off their most precious target audience, but instead take their expectations into account from the very beginning (ibid. 65):

---

6 www.engadget.com

Many fans were also extremely skeptical [*sic*] about the movie. The studio and filmmakers tried to reassure these people via the Internet. Like the film itself, the Internet campaign had to both appeal to the built-in fan base and create a new, larger audience. Given that more than three years passed between New Line's acquisition of the project and the premiere of *Fellowship*, the wooing of these two publics was lengthy and convoluted. (Thompson 140)

Despite the seemingly large diversity of the examined *LotR* trailers, of which an overview is given in Table 1, they can all be assigned the main economic function of attracting viewers for the advertised film (Maier 160). Considering that the economic exploitation of filmic material does not stop after its screening in the cinemas, as marketing explicitly counts on the sale of ancillary products like DVDs and other merchandise to keep up the interest in the whole trilogy, pitching the trilogy effectively from the start seemed especially important.

	Name	Time m:ss	Source/ YouTube Channel	Release Date
Released before the trilogy				
0-1	*The Lord of the Rings* (first trailer 2000)	1:43	Alex Nuñez	7-04-2000
0-2	*The Lord of the Rings: The Fellowship of the Ring* – Trailer	1:42	Warner Movies On Demand	12-01-2001
Released prior to *The Fellowship of the Ring* (*FotR*)				
1-1	*The Lord of the Rings: The Fellowship of the Ring* (2001) Official Trailer #1 – Ian McKellen Movie HD	2:04	Warner Movies On Demand	25-06-2002
1-2	*The Lord of the Rings: The Fellowship of the Ring* (2001) Official Trailer #2 – Elijah Wood Movie HD	2:54	Movieclips Trailer Vault	24-09-2001
Released prior to *The Two Towers* (*TTT*)				
2-1	*The Lord of the Rings: The Two Towers* – Trailer	2:04	Warner Movies On Demand	25-06-2002

Name	Time m:ss	Source/ YouTube Channel	Release Date
2-2	*The Lord of the Rings: The Two Towers* (2002) Official Trailer #2 – Orlando Bloom Movie HD	3:07	Movieclips Trailer Vault	30 September 2002
Released prior to *The Return of the King* (*RotK*)				
3-1	*The Lord of the Rings: The Return of the King* (2003) – Theatrical Trailer #2	1:03	Forever Cinematic Trailers	30 July 2003
3-2	*The Lord of the Rings: The Return of the King* (2003) Official Trailer – Sean Astin Movie HD	3:00	Movieclips Trailer Vault	27 September 2003
Released after the trilogy				
4-1	*The Lord of the Rings: The Fellowship of the Ring* -Special Extended DVD Edition Trailer [HD]	3:04	Movies Fan	2002
4-2	*The Lord of the Rings* Trilogy (2001-2003) Official Blu-ray Trailer LOTR Movie HD	2:01	Movieclips Trailer Vault	March 2010
4-3	*The Lord of the Rings* Motion Picture Trilogy: Extended Edition – Trailer	2:13	Warner Bros. Home Entertainment	2011
4-4	*The Lord of the Rings* Motion Picture Trilogy: Extended Edition – Trailer 2	1:01	Warner Bros. Home Entertainment	2011

Table 1: Corpus of *LotR* trailers[7]

---

7 Henceforth, trailer references are given by stating the number of the trailer and the time, using min:sec.

As will be shown, trailers played a central part in the marketing of *LotR* as they could appeal to different audiences with different background knowledge of the literary original. However, research on the respective trailers has been wanting, with only a few exceptions.[8] This is especially striking as two trailers were even awarded a "Golden Trailer Award" (www.goldentrailer.com), which can be considered a confirmation of their quality.[9] Therefore, this study aims at incorporating a variety of trailers, from teaser trailers, that is short trailer versions, to (full) trailers of the special editions, which were released after the screenings in the cinema. With this spectrum, I hope to give a generalizable overview of the role of trailers for the *LotR* trilogy.

For this explorative study, those twelve trailers described in Table 1 will be compared: namely two trailers for the whole trilogy, and two trailers each per the three films respectively. After elaborating on emerging (multi)modal patterns within trailers and their relation to Jakobsonian functions in 3.3, in section 3.4 I will analyse the diachronic development of trailers. Considering the large time span covered (2000-2011), I hypothesize that the trailers will differ not only in their functions, but also in their form, that is modal structure. This tentative development might be especially interesting regarding a comparison with the four trailers that appeared after the films, one for the special extended edition of *The Fellowship of the Ring*[10] on DVD, one for a HD version of the trilogy on Blu-ray, and two for the extended edition on Blu-ray. All trailers were retrieved from YouTube, where they were available during the analysis (October/November 2016).

According to several sources, the first trailer (referred to as "0-1" in my analysis) was published in 2000 on the official website of the trilogy, www.lordoftherings. net, reaching 1.7 million downloads in the first 24 hours (Thompson 141, 346;[11] Mikos et al. 67, 70; www.theonering.net). As a film version of a well-known literary work, *LotR* could target a more specific audience than other trailers of

---

8 See for example Hedling, Prommer, and Thompson (133-165).
9 In 2003, a trailer for *The Two Towers* won an award for "Best Action", in 2004, a trailer for *The Return of the King* was awarded "Best Drama". There is no information as to which of the several trailers are referred to.
10 Henceforth referred to as *FotR*.
11 According to Thompson's note, and also to other sources, she must be referring to 7 April 2000 in the text (141).

new films, and was thus, at least partly, directly aimed at fans. This might be the reason for (untypically) including footage from the production of the films, especially in this first trailer, which was part of the internet campaign (Thompson 140). The second trailer for the whole trilogy ("0-2") featured more common trailer elements, like film scenes, and was released in 2001 (Mikos et al. 70). Later that year, the teaser ("1-1") and full trailer ("1-2") for *The Fellowship of the Ring* were published in May and September, respectively (www.theonering. net). A similar timeline was followed for the trailers of *The Two Towers*,[12] and *The Return of the King*,[13] each being announced by a teaser in the preceding summer and a full trailer in September. Finally, the release dates of the trailers for the trilogy editions were harder to find out as they could only be tracked online (see Table 1). On that basis, I assume the given chronological order of the trailers, beginning with the one for the DVD of *FotR* ("4-1"), then the HD Blu-ray version of the trilogy ("4-2"),[14] and finally the two trailers for the Blu-ray extended edition ("4-3" and "4-4").

3 A multimodal trailer analysis

Taking the larger frame of marketing as a starting point, this chapter seeks to shed light on the micro-level of trailers and the question of how emerging (multi)modal patterns may contribute to certain communicative functions of trailers within the marketing strategy of the whole franchise. To this aim, it is first necessary to define the concept of *multimodality*, which my analysis builds upon (3.1), in order to then apply Jakobson's six functions of language (*On Language*) in a multimodal analysis of film trailers (3.2). Jakobson's pragmatic view of language as a tool of communication (*Language* 49) and his interdisciplinary interests in music and film (Pomorska and Rudy 409) and influences, e.g. on semiotics (Waugh and Monville-Burston 41), make an adaption seem especially promising for multimodal analyses.

---

12 Henceforth referred to as *TTT*.
13 Henceforth referred to as *RotK*.
14 Although this Blu-ray set has been "distributed exclusively in Canada by Alliance Films" (4-2, 1:57), I explicitly include this trailer for reasons of comparability.

3.1 Multimodality and film trailers

According to Carmen Maier, one of the few researchers of film trailers,[15] "film trailers are multimodal texts in which several semiotic modes are combined [...] to attain a promotional purpose" (160). Thus, compared with a purely linguistic analysis, a multimodal focus provides a much more complex perspective, which not only examines one mode (e.g. language), but also the interrelation between different modes (e.g. speech, moving image and music). An agreement on the definition of mode proves difficult, however, considering that since the first appearance of the term *multimodality* in the 1990s (Jewitt, Bezemer and O'Halloran 2), at least three approaches to *multimodality* can be named, each with their own focus and methods: these are Systemic Functional Linguistics, Social Semiotics, and Conversation Analysis (ibid. 8-13).[16] Considering their differences, it becomes clear that reaching a consensus about a definition of multimodality is not easy. On the contrary,

> there are several sources of difficulty in providing definitions capable of serving as the foundation for further, more precise investigations into multimodal artefacts and how such artefacts manifest and manipulate the modes they deploy. One that is particularly tenacious has been the common linking of 'mode' with *sensory* modalities [...]. (Bateman 77)

This is the case when the classification of modes relies on the sensory channel of perception, leading to a core distinction of visual, auditory, and other, e.g. haptic or olfactory modes. John Bateman criticises that this link may lead to rash categorisations of modes, as "too often it is presumed that one knows which particular modes are operative in an artefact even prior to investigation" (ibid.). Maier (161) solves this difficulty by providing concrete elements or resources to her otherwise sensory selection of verbal, visual, and aural modes,[17] e.g. a differentiation of the verbal mode into written and oral, and further distinctions as to the source of the utterance, e.g. (non-)diegetic voice-over narrator or scenes from the film. For my purpose, I will primarily rely on Gunther Kress' widely acknowledged definition, whose degree of abstraction lies between Maier's modes and their elements:

---

15 See also Maier as well as the monographs by Lisa Kernan (*Coming Attractions*), Keith M. Johnston (*Coming Soon*) and Vinzenz Hediger (*Verführung*).
16 For further details on the difficulties of definition see Bateman 75-77.
17 She elaborates "verbal elements", "visual resources" and "auditory elements" (161).

> Mode is a socially shaped and culturally given resource for making meaning. *Image, writing, layout, music, gesture, speech, moving image, soundtrack* are examples of modes used in representation and communication. (60)

In my multimodal trailer analysis, I will focus on a selection of Kress' modes, viz. moving image, writing, speech, music and soundtrack (Figure 1). On the basis of a tabular transcription of the trailers like in Table 3, the employed modes will be assigned to Jakobson's functions and discussed accordingly. Following Hartmut Stöckl's arrangement of modes in a "hierarchically structured and networked system" (12-13), I will distinguish between modes from visual (moving image) channels on the one hand, and such from auditory channels (music and sound) on the other. This distinction in visual and auditory channels describes the sensory origin of the modes, without equating the channel with the mode itself. Channels as an additional level are a helpful way of explaining special cases like that of language, which becomes visible in Figure 1.

SENSORY CHANNEL	STÖCKL		KRESS	C. MAIER
	CORE MODES	MEDIAL VARIANTS	MODES	MODES
VISUAL	image	static / dynamic	image	visual mode
	language	static writing / animated writing / speech	writing	
				verbal mode
AUDITORY	sound		speech	
			sound	aural mode
	music	performed music / score/sheet music	music	

Figure 1: Classification of modes according to Stöckl (13), Kress (60) and Maier (161)

"The overlapping mode on both levels [channels in Stöckl's words] is that of language, which is available in written form on the visual level and as speech on the auditory levels" (Wildfeuer 34). Keeping in mind Kress' claim of the "implausibility of a mode called 'language'" (64), I will bisect language into writing and speech. A sixth mode of filmic aspects mainly describes editing, while other filmic factors like lighting, *mise-en-scène* or shot size are subsumed under the mode images.

3.2 Jakobson's functions of language in *The Lord of the Rings* trailers

While language in spoken and written form is an essential, albeit not exclusive element of meaning-making, Roman Jakobson's functions of language contribute a model that is applicable to complex multimodal structures like trailers. As I have stated elsewhere (Krebs 19-20), this is mainly because of Jakobson's interdisciplinary and functional approach to language. He focused on speech events and specified the functions of language in six "factors of the speech event" instead of describing general "factors of language" (*On Language* 72-73). Analogously, I will refer to the communication situation of watching a trailer as "trailer event". Within a speech, or trailer, event, Jakobson furthermore pointed out that language usually contains more than one function, which I assume especially relevant for trailers, too. He

> did not see the functions as absolute or exclusive but stressed that a verbal message usually fulfils several functions, which are hierarchically ordered and whose predominant function is responsible for its verbal structure (*On Language* 73, see also Waugh 58). This relative nature can also be applied to the factors themselves, so that e.g. the addresser does not necessarily have to consist of one unit, but can be subdivided further, for example in author and narrator, and even further speakers (Waugh 57-58). (Krebs 21)

This assumption of simultaneously occurring but differently weighted functions and factors of speech can be found in a trailer event, too. As mentioned above, the main function of a trailer is to advertise its film, which may be understood as a predominant *conative* function that seeks to address the recipient(s) of the message. But at the same time, trailers – or rather the producers of the film and the trailer(s) – will wish to inform the viewers about the date of the theatrical release or, sometimes, simply entertain the audience, which make up other, subordinated functions, which are constructed multimodally.

3.2.1 Factors of the trailer event

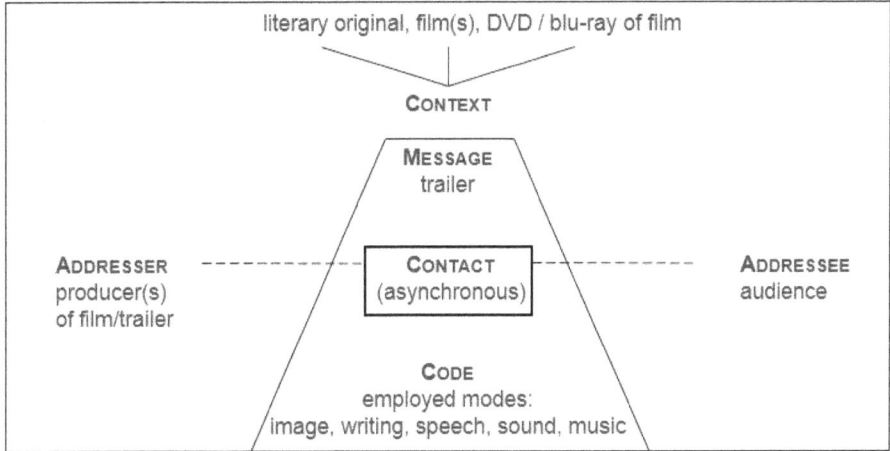

Figure 2: Factors of the trailer event, adapted version from Roman Jakobson (*On Language* 77)

The main factors in a trailer event based on Jakobson's speech event (*On Language* 77) are the *addresser*, who stands for the producers of trailer and/or film and the *addressee*, i.e. the audience of a trailer. Although film producers usually engage independent trailer production companies, Ant Farm in case of *LotR* (www.goldentrailer.com), these normally rely on the filmic material of the production company of the film, for *LotR* New Line Cinema (Internet Movie Datebase). This, additionally to the fact that the trailer is not created by one single person, makes the question of the addresser hard to pinpoint. The advertised film functions as the *context* which the trailer (*message*) refers to. As a film adaptation, *LotR* offers the original literary narrative as an additional dimension of context. Thus, in order to appeal to readers and non-readers alike, using films and books as context of the trailers was a prerequisite for an effective marketing strategy of the film, which is why, in my model of the trailer event, I divide context into film and book context. The further differentiation of the film context in film(s) and DVD / Blu-ray of film will be focussed on in 3.4.

The definition of *contact* is more complex, as the trailer event is, unlike face to face communication, asynchronous, in that addresser and addressee do not share the same time frame. Instead, the expression of the message clearly precedes its perception, offering no possibility of direct feedback by the addressee. In figure 2, the broken line between addresser and addressee signals this indirect contact. The connecting element is the message, i.e. trailer, itself. Jakobson defines *contact* as "a physical channel and psychological connection between the addresser and the addressee, enabling both of them to enter and stay in communication" (*On Language* 73, *Selected Writings* 113). While the conduit metaphor (cf. Reddy) of a physical channel underlying this idea should be considered, the (physical) comprehension of a trailer can in fact be supported or impaired by e.g. technical influences of the sound or projection system, or, when watching the trailer online, the quality of one's internet connection. Still, the relevance of the psychological connection and the aim of its extension seems more important than the physical connection, e.g. when it comes to the audience's attention. The psychological connection is foregrounded when the addresser is speaking for the sake of speaking, that is, mainly in order to stay in contact with their addressee, e.g. by prolonging the conversation. In this respect, I propose that Jakobson's idea of contact (*On Language* 73, *Selected Writings* 113) can be widened for trailer events. An attempt of the addressers to stay in touch with their addressees in case of trailers can be the presentation of the website address of the advertised film. This encourages the audience to visit the website of the film, maybe watch the trailer again, or even literally get in touch with the producers, for example by using a comment function.

Finally, "whenever the addresser or the addressee needs to check up whether they use the same code, speech is focused on the CODE" (*On Language* 75-76), entailing the use of metalanguage. Metalanguage, that is language about language, is thus often used for explanatory or comprehension purposes. In trailers, which do not dispose of language as their only code, this factor can be realised via other modes, too, which refer to any other mode on the meta level. Because of the close connection between the message and the code, both are visualised within the same trapezium (Figure 2).

3.2.2 Functions of trailers

The factors of Jakobson's communicative model fulfil certain functions, which will be described in the following by means of using examples from *LotR* trailers. After that, general modal preferences of communicative functions in *LotR* trailers will be identified.

Linguistically, the conative function "finds its purest grammatical expression in the vocative and imperative" (*On Language* 74). In the *LotR* trailers, such a direct appeal is only used for the promotion of the Blu-ray editions (4-2, 1:56; 4-3, 2:08, see Figure 3; 4-4, 0:56). The audience is rather addressed indirectly by e.g. indicating the release date of the films in writing (Figure 4), which can count as a request or an invitation for watching this film. The use of second person singular pronouns can have a similar effect (Figure 5).

Figure 3: 4-3, 2:08, Look for it on Blu-ray

Figure 4: 1-2, 2:44, release date as indirect invitation

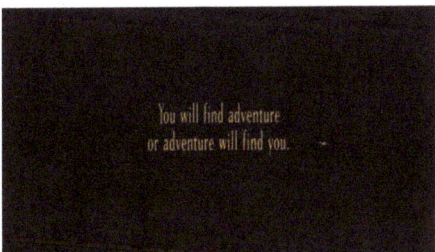

Figure 5: 0-2, 1:33, "You will find adventure or adventure will find you"

The *emotive* or *expressive* function is a „direct expression of the speaker's attitudes toward what he is speaking about" (*On Language* 73). This function can, for example, add another layer of meaning to an utterance by a certain intonation, pitch, or stress, which can even contradict the lexical meaning. In film trailers, the emotive function can be incorporated orally, for instance in rather explicit manners by superlatives like "the most extraordinary tale" (0-2, 0:39) or by other positively connotated keywords like "legend" (0-1, 0:31) or "wonder" (4-1, 1:31). In writing, the logo of the production company, here *New Line Cinema*, as well as the logos of the used sound systems (Dolby Digital, SDDS, dts) will serve as a guarantee for a certain quality (Grainge 85, 89). Visually, a positive attitude towards the advertised film is sought to be conveyed by presenting impressions of fascinating landscapes and special effects, from tracking shots of a mountain peak (0-2, 0:39) to highly dynamic fight scenes (e.g. Legolas fighting in the Battle of Helm's Deep, 2-1, 1:26).

The *referential* (also denotative or cognitive) function refers to the context of the trailer, i.e. the film that the trailer advertises. Thus, this function is carried out by the presentation of information about the plot, producers, director(s), cast or the release date of the film, be it in speech, writing, or via images. Furthermore, as *LotR* is a film adaptation, its trailers do not only refer to the upcoming films, but also back to the literary original, creating a context of another level, for example when elements of Tolkien's fantastic world are visualized for the first time, e.g. characters or fantastic creatures like "wargs" (2-2, 2:26, Figure 6)[18] or "oliphaunts" (2-2, 2:40, Figure 7).[19] Due to the connection and reference to the famous literary work, it seems plausible that, additionally to the promoted films, the first trailers also refer to Tolkien's work, whereas later trailers, which can build on knowledge of the prior films within the trilogy, also relate to the latter. This will be examined in chapter 3.4.

Figure 6: 2-2, 2:26, warg riders   Figure 7: 2-2, 2:40, oliphant

---

18 http://lotr.wikia.com/wiki/Warg_riders
19 http://lotr.wikia.com/wiki/M%C3%BBmakil

The form of the message itself is described by Jakobson's *poetic* function of language. Within trailers, a dominance of the poetic function can be assumed when there is a focus on the form of the message, which can be the case for modes like music, as far as it is used as a melodic background without denoting something. Linguistically, the poetic function in *LotR* trailers is represented by parallelisms and repetitions: these can be exclusive to the trailer such as the written messages "ALL WILL BE SACRIFICED [*sic*]" (2-2, 1:52, Figure 8), "ALL WILL BE LOST [*sic*]" (2-2, 2:02, Figure 9) or stem from the original book and film elements like the ring verse (0-1, 0:45-1:09, Figure 10; 0-2, 0:08-0:24, Figure 11), which appears in both writing and speech in the first trailer and, unless referring to the Elvish script, only orally in the trilogy. Another, non-linguistic, focus on the form of the message is conceivable in the case of the soft-lens filter used for the depiction of Arwen (2-1, 1:20, Figure 12) or other graphical elements like the red cloudy background of the Ring in the trilogy trailer with flashes of lightning (0-2, 0:08-0:24, Figure 13).

Figure 8: 2-2, 1:52

Figure 9: 2-2, 2:02

Figure 10: 0-1, 0:45, Ring verse

Figure 11: 0-2, 0:08, Ring verse

Figure 12: 2-1, 1:20, soft-lense filter   Figure 13: 0-2, 0:08-0:24

The *phatic* function is concerned with the contact between addresser and addressee. Because of the asynchronous communication situation of trailers, contact signals of face-to-face communication such as hesitation markers do not apply. Instead, there is a predominating phatic function when trailers offer a link to the official film website, www.lordoftherings.net (e.g. 0-2, 1:37, Figure 14), that is a "message [...] primarily serving to establish [or] prolong [...] communication" (*On Language* 75). The information about the website implies an extension of the communication situation of trailers by the offer to stay in touch online, which is plausible, considering that the marketing of *LotR* included online interaction with fans as a prospective audience from the beginning, for instance by providing exclusive information from the film (Shefrin 266, 274).

Figure 14: 0-2, 1:37 website of the film trilogy

As mentioned already, the phatic function is also executed by physical aspects like the volume of the soundtrack or single sounds which can "attract the attention of the interlocutor or [...] confirm his continued attention" (ibid.).[20] Consequently, the phatic function tends to sustain other functions. To this aim, a sound appearing simultaneously with the titles and release dates of the trilogy (0-2, 0:58-1:20) can for instance ensure attention for the successful communication of the referential and conative function of the writing.

Lastly, the *metalingual* function applies when Jakobson's factor "code" itself is referred to by taking up what was said, e.g. if the addresser wants to make sure they are understood or if the addressee is not sure if their perceived meaning was correct (*On Language* 76). This function can, for instance, be found when the trailer is watched online and the audience uses the commentary function in YouTube, through which viewers can discuss the use and interpretation of certain modes, suggesting the term metamodel function for the purpose of trailers.[21]

On the level of the trailer itself, the metalingual function can be further adapted to the multimodal structure of the trailer. To this aim, as an extension to Jakobson's model, I have proposed to re-label this function *intermodal*, as it relies on the interaction between different modes and, through the combination of modes, serves comprehension purposes (cf. Krebs 21-22), under which I will subsume the subfunctions of identification, narration, illustration, emphasis, and cohesion (see Table 2).

---

20 These two aspects belong to the "psychological connection" (Mathiot and Garvin 150) between addresser and addressee, which is also included in this factor.
21 See for example the discussion around the origin of the music for the trailer of *The Two Towers* (https://www.youtube.com/watch?v=LbfMDwc4azU) and the implications of its use.

Functions	Modes					Example	Possible Sub-functions
	Image	Writing	Speech	Sound	Music		
Conative		X*	X*			"Look for it on Blu-ray"	
		X				release date	
Phatic		X				URL to the website of *LotR*	contact
	X*			X*		image appearing with sound	attention
		X*		X*		release date appearing with sound	
Intermodal	X		X			introduction of names	identification, narrative function, illustration
	X	X				intertitle + following scene (elaboration)	
	X(*)			X(*)			emphasis
		X*		X*		release date appearing with sound	
		X*	X*			titles of films in Blu-ray	
					X	background music	cohesion
Poetic	X					graphical elements	
				X		melody	
	X			X		editing creating rhythm	

Functions	Modes					Example	Possible Sub-functions
	Image	Writing	Speech	Sound	Music		
Emotive			X			positive judgements about film	
		X				list of Academy Awards	
	X					landscapes	
	X*				X*	solemn orchestral music	
Referential	X					showing protagonists or fantastic animals from the books	
		X				reference to books or films (e.g. to actors as part of production)	
			X			reference to books or films	
					X	*FotR* track in trailer of *TTT*	
	X*	X*	X			interview	

Table 2, [* appearing simultaneously]

Other than in the example above, a focus on the intermodal function is primarily used on the part of the addresser. This addition to Jakobson's model seems plausible with respect to the existence of redundant signs that, according to Linda Waugh, "are those signs which inform about other signs in the text and thus cannot be said to provide independent information; they are used in a sense to ensure that the given information is provided" (*On Language* 73). In trailers, this function often includes the combination of visual and auditory modes by the oral introduction of names or characters that are subsequently presented visually (e.g. Barad-dûr in Figure 15-16, Orthanc and Saruman in 2-1, 0:30-0:35, Figure 17-18) or by two visuals (writing and image), whereas usually the writing serves as a summary that is explicated or exemplified visually by the images in the following scenes, as the example of 1-2 shows (see Table 3).

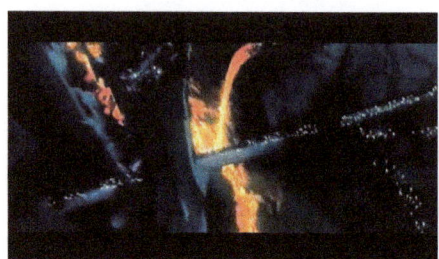

Figure 15: 2-1, 0:30, Barad-dûr1   Figure 16: 2-1, 0:30, Barad-dûr

Figure 17: 2-1, 0:32, Orthanc   Figure 18: 2-1, 0:33, Saruman

In 1-2, Frodo's utterance "I cannot do this alone" (1:02) is followed by the intertitle "A FELLOWSHIP WILL PROTECT HIM". Then, three protagonists of the Fellowship – Aragorn, Legolas and Gimli – are shown, each emphasizing their commitment orally ("You have my sword", "And you have my bow", "And my axe", 1:06-1:13).

time	(moving) image / screenshot	speech	writing	music	sound
1:01					
1:02		Frodo: I cannot do this alone.			...
1:03					
1:03			A FELLOWSHIP WILL PROTECT HIM	Drums and orchestral music	
1:05					
1:06		Aragorn: You have my sword			
1:07		Legolas: And you have my bow			
1:08		Gimli: And my axe			

Table 3: transcription of 2-1, 1:01-1:08

There are several similar examples, e.g. "THE BATTLE OF MIDDLE EARTH BEGINS" (2-1, 1:09, in writing), followed by several fighting scenes, or when after "THE FELLOWSHIP IS BROKEN" (2-2, 0:38) Frodo and Sam are shown having lost their way and, in another scene, Gandalf's defeat in his fight against the Balrog (0:41-0:48).

In contrast, the double coding by co-occurring speech and writing is not as common in the examined trailers, in fact, it only appears once for the Ring verse in 0-2 (0:08-0:24, Figure 11), when the appearance on Blu-ray (4-2, 0:19, Figure 19) or the quality of the trilogy is mentioned ("Winner of 17 Academy Awards", 4-2, 1:40, Figure 20), and for the titles of the films in the Blu-ray editions (4-2, 4-3, 4-4), given mostly at the end.

Figure 19: 4-2, 0:19   Figure 20: 4-2, 1:40

3.3 Emerging (multi)modal patterns within the functions of trailers

Before I will move on to a diachronic comparison of *LotR* trailers from a multimodal perspective in chapter 3.4, a closer look at emerging (multi)modal patterns in the communicative functions is called for. As multimodal pattern, I define the combination of certain modes in the analysed trailers. With respect to the underlying function, modal pattern refers to single recurring modes used for certain functions. Most surprisingly, the conative function is hardly tangible modally. Only in the trailers for the trilogy that appeared after the cinema screenings (4-2 to 4-4) can a direct appeal be found in writing and speech ("Look for it on Blu-ray", e.g. Figure 3). In 4-2, the direct request is given orally, accompanied by written "now available everywhere on Blu-ray" (1:56), while the modes are reversed in 4-4, a narrator commenting "available

June 28th" (0:56). Apart from that, the conative function is represented only indirectly by written elements of film titles and release dates or by additional written information like its declaration as "THE MUST SEE COMPANION [*sic*]" (4-1, 2:42, Figure 21).

Figure 21: 4-1, 2:42

Similarly, the phatic function also only draws upon two modes, one being a written link to the film website (see Figure 14, also in 0-2, 1-1, 2-1, 2-2, 3-1, 3-2) and the other one, sound, serving to attract and direct the audience's attention to a simultaneously employed mode (writing, image). Here, the parallels to the following intermodal function are obvious.

The intermodal function per se entails a combination of different modes. As to the preferred multimodal patterns, a comparison of assigned functions shows that most intermodal functions apply a combination of speech or writing with images. In combination with continuity editing, which aims at cohesion between different shots (Bordwell and Thompson 231), this can create narrative meaning in the trailer, e.g. when Frodo's question "No one knows it [the Ring]'s here, do they? [...] Do they Gandalf?" is followed by an image of the Ring wraiths tearing down and riding through a gate (1-1, 0:58-1:07).

However, combinations with the purpose of giving emphasis or ensuring comprehension are more typical. The former is often achieved by the connection of sound and image or writing, as explained already. The latter is mainly represented by combining language with images, supporting comprehension in various ways: Speech is often used to introduce new names or characters thus helping to identify them by linking them to the visual stimulus, as mentioned earlier. In trailers, which are extremely dense and usually present multimodal contents in a quick succession, these modal chains also present a useful support for the cognitive processing of information, for example when an off-screen voice announces the subsequent appearance of the respective character. The use of written language for such an identification is rather rare and only exists in the interviews in two of the trilogy trailers (0-1, Figure 22 and 4-1, Figure 23).

Figure 22: 0-1, 0:13, interview Peter Jackson / director

Figure 23: 4-1, 0:45, interview Peter Jackson, director/co-writer/producer

More frequently, images function as an elaboration or illustration of written intertitles, for instance when the writing "THE BATTLE FOR MIDDLE-EARTH BEGINS" (2-1, 1:09) is followed by Aragorn giving the order to fire. In 3-2, several intertitles are illustrated in this fashion: The fact that "THERE CAN BE NO TRIUMPH WITHOUT LOSS" (2:00) is illustrated by Gandalf walking over the battlefield after the battle, "NO VICTORY WITHOUT SUFFERING" (2:13) is depicted by a clearly suffering Arwen, who "gave away [her] life's grace" according to Elrond's off-screen voice (2:24) and "NO FREEDOM WITHOUT SACRIFICE", a more complex case, firstly by Eomer's statement "we cannot achieve victory through strength of arms", which is visualised by riders fighting an unequal battle against oliphants. The latter example additionally makes use of a visual submode: the low camera angle used for the depiction of the oliphants stresses the hopelessness of the situation, i.e. the high probability of sacrifice. Lastly, the combination of modes within the intermodal function serves the purpose of cohesion, which also adds to a better comprehension on the part of the addressee[22] and often involves the use of music joined with other modes.

---

22 An analysis of cohesive ties is not possible within the scope of this article. For detailed information see Tseng.

The poetic function is most clearly fulfilled by linguistic means, i.e. oral and written modes, e.g. the Ring verse or other poetic devices such as parallelisms ("Is it secret? Is it safe?" 1-1, 0:33; "ALL WILL BE SACRIFICED [...] ALL WILL BE LOST" 2-2, 1:51, 2:01, Figures 8-9). Still, also visual and auditory modes like graphical elements or a coordinated rhythm of music, sound and images (1-1, 1:50-2:05; *On Language* 76-79) can support the poetic function.

In order to convey a positive attitude towards the films, subsumed by the emotive function, the three main modes of speech, writing and images use different ways of representation.[23] While speech and writing can state benevolent opinions about a film, logos of technological systems (Dolby etc.) can be used as a promise for an exceptional sound (Grainge 89), it is the images that have the real potential of convincing the audience of the film's quality by showing spectacular landscapes (Conrich 119), e.g. the Fellowship walking in the snowy mountains (0-2, 0:39), or thrilling fight scenes and special effects (2-2, 2:16-2:26), usually supported by music. As a film adaptation of a fantasy story that had been considered impossible to picturize, I assume that images have at least the same importance for the emotive function as the linguistic modes (that is writing and speech), if not even more – despite speech and writing being potentially more explicit.

Finally, the subdivisions made in the trailers with regard to book and film are also reflected in the modes of the referential function. Before using this complex function as an example for the depiction of the trailer development throughout the parts of the trilogy in the next chapter, the special case of music must be mentioned. Apart from the use of writing, speech and images, which are all used to refer to Tolkien's work and the film advertised in the trailer, music is exclusive to the films and trailers and as such functions only in the filmic universe. Interestingly, however, in the trailers of *TTT*, music in the form of the theme music is used as an intertextual reference within the trilogy: To this aim, in both *TTT* trailers, the use of the track "The Ring Goes South" (Shore), which is known to the audience from *FotR*, can refer to *FotR*, thus creating the context of another film within the trilogy. This can create an effect of

---

23 Using the active voice for modes or functions is due to the complex situation of production (see 3.2.1). In fact, the application of modes obviously lies in the addresser's responsibility.

recognition for the viewers, which not only ties the trailer of the second film narratively in with the content of the first, but even more so reminds the audience of the positive experience of watching *FotR*, creating an emotive function of a second degree in turn.

3.4 *The Lord of the Rings* trailers in comparison

While the (multi)modal preferences within the communicative functions of the *LotR* trailers might be generalizable, a closer look at the referential function seems especially suitable to explain the special case of the *LotR* trilogy franchise. Thus, the connection of the micro-level of modes to the macro-level of the marketing strategy as described by various researchers can be rendered explicit.[24]

A first distinction can be made between the trailers advertising the films to be screened in the cinema and those announcing the DVDs or Blu-rays as ancillary products. In addition to the book and films, the DVDs and Blu-rays thus form a third context that trailers may refer to and which will be traced back to the employed modes in this subchapter.

Taking these three contexts as a starting point, the twelve trailers under investigation can be clustered into three groups that also correspond with slightly different target groups: The first four trailers, including both trailers for *FotR*, use the literary original as well as the films as their context, albeit with different emphases. Secondly, the trailers for *TTT* and *RotK* mostly refer to the films of the trilogy and thirdly, as mentioned already, the trailers advertising the DVD and Blu-ray editions add another context layer in that they refer explicitly to the disc versions of the films.

---

24 Most substantially, Barker and Mathijs; Mathijs; Mikos et al., and Thompson have contributed to research on the success of the franchise.

	context		
	literary original	films within trilogy	DVD / Blu-ray
trailers	0-1, 0-2, 1-1, 1-2	2-1, 2-2, 3-1, 3-2	4-1, 4-2, 4-3, 4-4
target group	special target group: readers of the books, Tokien fans	audience of *FotR*, including fans	audience of trilogy, especially fans
special (multi)modal pattern	speech (referring to the book) speech + writing + image (interview) image of box set	music	speech + writing + image (interview),

Table 4: Different contexts of *LotR* trailers

Due to *LotR* being a film adaption, the first trailers of the trilogy could target an already existing concrete audience group consisting of people who had read the books and were intrigued by the fantastic stories set in Tolkien's fictional world. Those who would even consider themselves fans were especially important because they should function as the main hubs of word-of-mouth advertising (Thompson 134-135, Mikos et al. 67). Therefore, it was not only their attention that was needed for advertising of the trilogy, but they also had to be convinced of the quality of Peter Jackson's adaptation as soon as possible so to overcome their initial scepticism (Thompson 140) towards the films, which could have had extremely negative consequences for the trilogy (Iversen 183).

This becomes apparent from the very first trailer: it starts with an off-screen male narrator saying "It has been named the greatest and most popular book of the twentieth century" (0-1, 0:02), directly followed by another voice stating that "the responsibility of bringing this world to the screen visually is obviously enormous" (0-1, 0:10). Simultaneously, the trailer uses footage from the film shoot (Figure 24). After three seconds, the second voice can be attributed to the image of Peter Jackson, who is not only shown but also identified by a written caption, as at the time, he was still quite unknown (Figure 22). After another comment by the narrator ("It introduced us to the world of fantasy", 0-1, 0:15), which is accompanied by a computer-generated image of a red ring, an on-screen testimonial by the main actor Elijah Wood draws a further explicit connection between books and films: "The thing about these books and what we're doing with the movies, it's [*sic*] they're so real you believe it really existed" (0-1, 0:22). Finally, the narrator explains that "it wasn't until now that the legend could finally come to life" (0-1, 0:29), while, in the visual mode, a flame produces the Elvish signs of the Ring verse on the Ring (Figure 25). These explicit references to the books show a clear dominance of speech directed at the prospective audience of readers in order to announce the adaptation ("Now in production", 0-1, 1:36) and raise their interest in the film. At the same time, potential viewers lacking a profound knowledge of the book are presented with information about the films' genre mostly visually, e.g. by footage of the special effects promising a thrilling experience, and orally ("fantasy" 0-1, 0:15). Furthermore, details about production information like the most famous members of the cast (0-1, 1:17) are provided in written form.

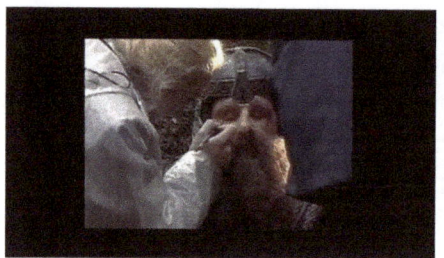 

Figure 24: 0-1, 0:10, Applying make-up at the set   Figure 25: 0-1, 0:29, Elvish ring verse

The subsequent trailers use similar methods to attract their audience: There are further spoken references to the books, like in "the most extraordinary tale ever told comes to life" (0-2, 0:39), as well as written ones, such as "The Legend comes to life" (1-2, 2:23). Meanwhile, visual modes present the advertised films as attractive to both readers and non-readers: On the one hand, they introduce the books' protagonists (0-2, 1:02) and generate potential interest in the visualization of Tolkien's fantastic creatures and scenery; on the other hand, the trailers depict the trilogy as belonging to a genre of fantasy and adventure films.[25] Thus, the trailers further emphasize the suspense of the advertised films and, not least, promise philosophical and romantic moments as referenced by Galadriel's words (e.g. 0-2, 0:49; 1-2, 1:14) and a kiss between Arwen and Aragorn (e.g. 1-2, 2:24; Hedling 232).

The trailers for the *FotR* are less oriented towards the context of the books. From 1-1 on, the voice-over narrator disappears, and the narrative content is provided by film characters instead, regularly aided by written intertitles, that is graphic written elements connecting scenes (Kernan 32)[26], which serve as a more or less abstract plot summary (Maier 167). More importantly, the mode of writing refers to the films' cinema screenings by giving their titles and release dates at the end of the trailers. As in the first trailers of the marketing campaign, images are still essential for the introduction of new characters and settings. Therefore, for instance, 2-1 starts with Éowyn standing in front of Meduseld right at the beginning of the trailer (Figure 26). 2-2, too, presents the Rohirrim in one of the first shots of the trailer (0:16, Figure 27).

Figure 26: 2-1, 0:08, Éowyn   Figure 27: 2-2, 0:16, Rohirrim

Starting with the trailers for *TTT*, the book context can be considered less important, as with *FotR*, a new context was created. Apart from presenting new information, which is central for keeping the audience interested in the new films, the trailers now also use modal means as cohesive ties to the

---

25 Giselinde Kuipers' and Jeroen de Kloet's study showed that the international audience of *LotR* ascribed diverse genres or "types of story" (137-139) to *RotK*, e.g. "Epic", "SFX film", "Fantasy" or "War" (139).
26 Historically, intertitles were used in silent film for a connection of scenes (ibid.).

other films within the trilogy. This is especially obvious when Gandalf's quote from *FotR*, "All you have to decide is what to do with the time that is given to you", is literally repeated in the *RotK* trailers (3-1, 0:50; 3-2, 2:04). A partial quote is provided by the intertitles "THE JOURNEY CONTINUES" in the *TTT* trailers, which are taken up in both trailers of *RotK* as "THE JOURNEY ENDS".

Finally, also the mode of music serves a cohesive purpose, when the trailers of *TTT* use a theme that is known from *FotR*, "The Ring Goes South", thus specifically addressing those who have seen the first film of the trilogy and conjuring up the positive memory of watching it.

In general, the modal means explained so far are also used in a similar way in the third group of trailers. But the trailers that appeared after the cinema phase of *LotR* employ additional strategies to guarantee the sale of further products such as DVDs and Blu-rays. These ancillary products make up a third context the *LotR* trailers refer to and thus foreground the referential function, strikingly presented by the recurrent image of the DVD or Blu-ray box (4-2, 4-3, 4-4). Most interestingly, the trailer for the extended version of *FotR* again uses the triple combination of speech, writing and image in the form of interviews to advertise the DVD set. Besides Elijah Wood and Howard Shore, the composer of *LotR*, Peter Jackson praises this product: "I'm a huge fan of special edition DVDs and I really think it's a great opportunity to be able to now restore material from the movie, about 30 minutes' worth of extra footage" (4-1, 0:45). John Gilbert, the editor, adds that "there's a lot of little things from the book" (4-1, 1:05), clearly addressing the readers who had been addressed directly from the beginning. Using speech when referring to the book context also functions as a personal promise for the quality of the product and as such entails a strong emotive function, even if spoken by a voice-over narrator: "Now, the power of Blu-ray lets you experience the wonder of *LotR* the way it was meant to be seen" (4-2, 1:27). Additionally, the emotive function is emphasized by the mode of writing, which underlines not only the quality of the films, e.g. by listing the Academy Awards won by the trilogy (4-3, 1:40), but also the quality of the individual products, e.g. as "THE MOST COMPLETE THE LORD OF THE RINGS TRILOGY" (4-3, 0:19) or stating "the brilliance of Blu-ray" (4-3, 1:23).

This comparison of trailers furthermore shows the close connection among the trailer functions that have been laid out in the beginning, as for example in the trailers that appeared after the cinema screenings, the emotive function refers to both the context of the film and the new context of the DVD and Blu-ray editions. In terms of (multi)modal patterns and their relation to Jakobson's functions, it is hard to present a clear-cut result, as the trailers use a variety of modes and multimodal combinations for the different trailer functions. However, this diversity of modes seems especially remarkable within the referential function, which is at the same time the most elaborate one, hinting at the special case of *LotR* as a filmic adaptation and film franchise.

4 Conclusion: The role of media convergence?

Since the first announcement of the film project was published in 2000 (www.theonering.net, Thompson 346), *LotR* has continued to be present on various levels, further enforced by the production of the prequel *The Hobbit*. The producers carefully embellished the franchise with not only the films, but also other media offering further contents such as the official website, books, board- and video-game adaptations and spin-offs,[27] as well as extended editions of the films, which all want to keep up the audience's interest. Certainly, the media conglomerate Time Warner Inc. as producer and distributor of the trilogy – and at the time "the world's largest media company" (Wasko and Shanadi 26) – is another piece of this franchise puzzle as it additionally opened further ways of addressing an audience via media coverage on television, in magazines etc. (ibid.).[28] Additionally, large numbers of merchandise articles (Wasko and Shanadi 28-32) from bags and books to jewellery, phone-cases and watches (WB Shop) were sold. While the latter will mostly serve to raise the revenue of the franchise, content relevant media products have wider implications considering the concept of transmedia storytelling, i.e. they contribute to and make up "stories that unfold across multiple media platforms, with each medium

---

27 For an overview of games see Young (346). Brookey and Booth examine the *RotK* video game adaptation.
28 Another example was the full trailer of *TTT* "exclusive" to AOL users according to the fan website www.theonering.net. Thinking of AOL as part of Time Warner Inc., this could count a strategic move.

making distinctive contributions to our understanding of the world" (Jenkins 334). The possibility and existence of these different stories can explain why the films reached such a broad audience (Barker and Mathijs).

As I have shown, the film trailers contributed to the advertising of the trilogy by orienting themselves towards the potential audience groups of fans, readers, and others, who were offered different stories respectively: An audience acquainted with the books could be presented with background information about the film production, while a mainstream audience was happy with the visual impressions of an adventure story that promised an entertaining film experience.

Moreover, this explorative study transfers Jakobson's claim that "a verbal message fulfils several functions, which are hierarchically ordered and whose predominant function is responsible for its verbal structure" (*On Language* 73; Waugh 58) to the realm of trailers: Regarding the complexity of trailers, there is no one-to-one relationship between a function and its modal structure, but the study indeed showed that there are reoccurring patterns and preferences within certain communicative functions. In the analysed *LotR* trailers, the conative function is almost exclusively executed by speech and writing. However, this explicit verbal address to the audience is backed multimodally by other functions. For example, the emotive function shows the positive stance towards the promoted films more diversely, via speech and writing, but also via images and orchestral music. The poetic function can be seen as the artistic focus on the trailer itself, for example in the use of graphical elements and music. Moreover, the trailer offers further contact to the audience by providing the website of the films in written form. Apart from that, the phatic function also tries to maintain the contact with the audience of the trailer by using sound in combination with other modes to attract and guide the audience's attention. The complementary combination of sound with other modes is typical of the intermodal function, too. This newly coined function proves to be the most complex one, as it per definition includes several combinations of modes. As could be suspected from the filmic scenes used in the trailers, there is a frequent combination of speech and images; however, also writing is used, often in the form of intertitles that are followed by film scenes. Given the diversity of multimodal patterns, the analysis resulted in the classification into five intermodal subfunctions that are aimed at a better comprehension, that is cognitive processing of the trailer:

identification, narration, emphasis, illustration and cohesion. The latter is mainly attained by the musical score. Finally, music, as well as images, writing, and speech are used for a referential function, which plays a central role for *LotR* trailers. In terms of multimodal patterns, it is especially interesting to notice the use of interviews in two trailers, with the combination of speech, writing, and image. It can be attributed to the special case of the trilogy being a film adaptation and the attempt of the producers to assure their target audience of the conscientious handling of the literary material, thus serving as a source for further word-of-mouth advertising within pre-existing fan structures.

The diachronic comparison of the trailers finally mirrors the long-term marketing strategy of the franchise and reveals a subdivision of the referential function in the three contexts of Tolkien's original work, the films of the trilogy, and the DVD/Blu-ray versions. As the trilogy was designed as a film franchise, it was necessary to not only appeal to a prospective audience as early as possible for having gained enough momentum at the launch of the trilogy. Also, the specific prospective audience consisting of readers and fans of Tolkien's works had to be convinced of the quality of the films, which was only possible by assuring them of the close connection between films and books (Shefrin 267), both orally and by showing them (visual) impressions of the films. During the trilogy, the producers had to keep the mainstream audience interested to be able to rely on them as future viewers and buyers of merchandise. This was done by referring to the other films within the trilogy, thus creating a new target audience of film fans (see also Mikos et al. 204-207). Finally, considering and addressing both film and book fans in the marketing of ancillary products like DVDs and Blu-rays, for example by using interviews again, can therefore be seen as a clever move to draw the connection back to Tolkien's underlying story of Middle-earth. Trailers, as I have shown, have been indeed an effective way to bind enthusiastic audiences in the darkness of the movie theatre, even though there could (luckily?) never be only one trailer to rule them all.

About the Author

HEIKE KREBS is a PhD candidate in the field of English Linguistics at the University of Augsburg. She graduated in 2010, majoring in English and Spanish. After her teacher's training she returned to academia. At the moment she is working for the Women's Representative and as a temporary lecturer for the Chair of English Linguistics.

In her research she focuses on media studies, multimodality, semiotics and film theory, combining these fields in her dissertation with the working title "The Multimodal Transcription Process between Film and Trailer." She has organized an interdisciplinary conference on gender and diversity ("Alles anders?") and several lecture series on gender, diversity and queer studies, as well as presented the results of her own research in various lecture formats, e.g. on Tolkien's *The Lord of the Rings*.

References

BARKER, Martin and Ernest MATHIJS, eds. *Watching the Lord of the Rings*. New York: Lang, 2008.

BATEMAN, John and Karl-Heinrich SCHMIDT. *Multimodal Film Analysis: How Films Mean*. New York: Routledge, 2012.

BORDWELL, David and Kristin THOMPSON. *Film Art: An Introduction*. New York: McGraw-Hill, 2008.

BROOKEY, Robert and Paul BOOTH. "Restricted Play: Synergy and the Limits of Interactivity in *The Lord of the Rings: The Return of the King* Video Game." *Games and Culture* 1.3 (2006): 214-230.

CONRICH, Ian. "A Land of Make Belief: Merchandising and Consumption of *The Lord of the Rings*." *From Hobbits to Hollywood: Essays on Peter Jackson's Lord of the Rings*. Eds. Ernest Matthijs and Murray Pomerance. Amsterdam: Rodopi, 2006. 119-136.

ENGADGET. Home Page. 14 Feb. 2017 <https://www.engadget.com/2011/03/21/the-lord-of-the-rings-extended-edition-blu-ray-set-officially-an/>.

GOLDEN TRAILER AWARDS. Home Page. 15 Feb. 2017. <http://www.goldentrailer.com/gta4-nominees/>.

Home Page. 15 Feb. 2017. <http://www.goldentrailer.com/gta5-nominees/>.

GRAINGE, Paul. *Brand Hollywood. Selling Entertainment in a Global Media Age*. New York and London: Routledge, 2008.

HEDIGER, Vinzenz. "Das vorläufige Gedächtnis des Films. Anmerkungen zur Morphologie und Wirkungsästhetik des Kinotrailers." *montage/av: Zeitschrift für Theorie und Geschichte audiovisueller Kommunikation* 2 (1999): 111-132.

Verführung zum Film: Der amerikanische Kinotrailer seit 1912. Marburg: Schüren, 2001.

HEDLING, Erik. "Framing Tolkien: Trailers, High Concept and the Ring." *The Lord of the Rings. Popular Culture in Global Context.* Ed. Ernest Mathijs. London: Wallflower, 2006. 225-237.

INTERNET MOVIE DATABASE. Home Page. 15 Feb. 2017. <http://www.imdb.com/company/co0046718/?ref_=ttco_co_1>.

IVERSEN, Fritz. "Man sieht nur, wovon man gehört hat. Mundpropaganda und die Kinoauswertung von Independents und anderen Non-Blockbuster-Filmen." *Demnächst in Ihrem Kino. Grundlagen der Filmwerbung und Filmvermarktung.* Eds. Vinzenz Hediger and Patrick Vonderau. Marburg: Schüren, 2005. 176-192.

JAKOBSON, Roman. *Selected Writings: Volume VII.* Ed. Stephen Rudy. The Hague: Mouton, 1985.

On Language. Eds. Linda R. Waugh and Monique Monville-Burston. Cambridge MA: Harvard University Press, 1990.

Language in Literature. Eds. Krystyna Pomorska and Stephen Rudy. Cambridge MA: Belknap, 1987.

JENKINS, Henry. *Convergence Culture.* New York: New York University Press, 2008.

JEWITT, Carey, Jeff BEZEMER, and Kay O'HALLORAN. *Introducing Multimodality.* Abingdon: Routledge, 2016.

JOHNSTON, Keith. *Coming Soon: Film Trailers and the Selling of Hollywood Technology.* Jefferson NC: McFarland, 2009.

KERNAN, Lisa. *Coming Attractions: Reading American Movie Trailers.* Austin TX: University of Texas Press, 2009.

KREBS, Heike. "Roman Jakobson Revisited. The Multimodal Trailer Event." *Image* 23 (2006): 17-29.

KRESS, Gunther. "What is mode?" *The Routledge Handbook of Multimodal Analysis.* Ed. Carey Jewitt. Abingdon: Routledge, 2014. 60-75.

KUIPERS, Giselinde and Jeroen DE KLOET. "Global Flows and Local Identifications? *The Lord of the Rings* and the Cross-National Reception of Characters and Genres." *Watching the Lord of the Rings.* Eds. Martin Barker and Ernest Mathijs. New York: Lang, 2008. 131-148.

LEWIS, Jon. "Following the money in America's sunniest company town: some notes on the political economy of the Hollywood blockbuster." *Movie Blockbusters.* Ed. Julian Stringer. London: Routledge, 2003.

Maier, Carmen D. "Visual Evaluation in Film Trailers." *Visual Communication* 8 (2009): 159-181.

Mathijs, Ernest, ed. *The Lord of the Rings: Popular Culture in a Global Context.* London: Wallflower, 2006.

Mathiot, Madeleine and Paul L. Garvin. "The Functions of Language: A Sociocultural View." *Anthropological Quarterly* 48.3 (1975): 148-156.

Mikos, Lothar, Susanne Eichner, Elizabeth Prommer, and Michael Wedel. *Die „Herr der Ringe"-Trilogie. Attraktion und Faszination eines populärkulturellen Phänomens.* Konstanz: UVK, 2007.

Movieweb. Home Page. 14 Feb. 2017. <http://movieweb.com/the-lord-of-the-rings-motion-picture-trilogy-extended-edition-blu-ray-hits-june-28th/>.

Pomorska, Krystyna and Stephen Rudy. "Semiotic Vistas." Roman Jakobson. *Language in Literature.* Eds. Krystyna Pomorska and Stephen Rudy. Cambridge MA: Belknap, 1987. 409-411.

Prommer, Elisabeth. "Filmauswahl unter crossmedialen Bedingungen." *Mediennutzung in konvergierenden Medienumgebungen.* Eds. Uwe Hasebrink, Lothar Mikos, and Elisabeth Prommer. Munich: Reinhard Fischer, 2004. 221-242.

Reddy, Michael J. "The conduit metaphor: A case of frame conflict in our language about language." *Metaphor and Thought.* Ed. Andrew Ortony. Cambridge: Cambridge University Press, 1979. 284-310.

Shefrin, Elana. "*Lord of the Rings, Star Wars*, and participatory fandom. Mapping new congruencies between the internet and media entertainment culture." *Critical Studies in Media Communication* 21.3 (2004): 261–281.

Shore, Howard. "The Ring goes south". *The Lord of the Rings: The Fellowship of the Ring.* (Original Motion Picture Soundtrack). 2001.

Stöckl, Hartmut. "In Between Modes. Language and Image in Printed Media." *Perspectives on Multimodality.* Eds. Eija Ventola, Cassily Charles, and Martin Kaltenbacher. Amsterdam: Benjamins, 2004. 9–30.

The Lord of the Rings Wiki. Homepage. 18 Feb. 2017. <http://lotr.wikia.com/wiki/Warg_riders?action=edit&section=6>.

Homepage. 18 Feb. 2017. <http://lotr.wikia.com/wiki/M%C3%BBmakil>.

Theonering. Homepage. 14 Feb. 2017. <http://www.theonering.net/torwp/2010/03/18/35663-theonering-net-exclusive-clip-lord-of-the-rings-on-blu-ray-in-stores-april-6th/>.

Homepage. 15 Nov. 2016. <http://www.theonering.net/torwp/2014/07/11/90933-the-ghosts-of-trailers-past-revisiting-the-lord-of-the-rings/>.

THOMPSON, Kristin. *The Frodo Franchise*. Berkeley: University of California Press, 2007.

TSENG, Chiaoi. *Cohesion in Film: Tracking Film Elements*. Basingstoke: Palgrave Macmillan, 2013.

TOLKIENGATEWAY. Homepage. 14 Feb. 2017. <http://tolkiengateway.net/w/ index.php?title=The_Lord_of_the_Rings:_The_Fellowship_of_the_Ring_(extended_edition)&oldid=259829>.

WASKO, Janet and Govind SHANADI. "More than just rings: Merchandise for them all." *The Lord of the Rings: Popular Culture in Global Context*. Ed. Ernest Mathijs. London: Wallflower, 2006. 23-42.

WAUGH, Linda. "The Poetic Function in the Theory of Roman Jakobson". *Poetics Today 2.1a (Roman Jakobson: Language and Poetry)* (1980): 57-82.

and Monique MONVILLE-BURSTON. "Introduction. The Life, Work, and Influence of Roman Jakobson." In Roman Jakobson. *On Language*. Eds. Linda Waugh and Monique Monville-Burston. Cambridge MA: Harvard University Press, 1990. 1-45.

WB SHOP. Homepage. 15 Nov. 2016. <http://www.wbshop.com/category/code/lotr.do>.

WILDFEUER, Janina. *Film Discourse Interpretation*. New York: Routledge, 2014.

YOUNG, Helen. "Racial Logics, Franchising, and Video Game Genres: *The Lord of the Rings*." *Games and Culture* 11.4 (2016): 343-364.

Filmography and trailers

	Name	Source / Channel	URL (last access 18 Feb. 2017)
0-1	Lord of the Rings (first trailer 2000)	Alex Nuñez	https://www.youtube.com/watch?v=2UDTbQrOGa0
0-2	Lord of the Rings: The Fellowship of the Ring – Trailer	Warner Movies On Demand	https://www.youtube.com/watch?v=z_WZxJpHzEE
1-1	The Lord of the Rings: The Fellowship Of The Ring (2001) Official Trailer #1 – Ian McKellen Movie HD	Movieclips Trailer Vault	https://www.youtube.com/watch?v=_e8QGuG50ro
1-2	The Lord of the Rings: The Fellowship Of The Ring (2001) Official Trailer #2 – Elijah Wood Movie HD	Movieclips Trailer Vault	https://www.youtube.com/watch?v=cKEGZ-CvWHk
The Fellowship of the Ring. Dir. by Peter Jackson. New Line Cinema, 2001.			
2-1	Lord of the Rings: The Two Towers – Trailer	Warner Movies On Demand	https://www.youtube.com/watch?v=cvCktPUwkW0
2-2	The Lord of the Rings: The Two Towers (2002) Official Trailer #2 – Orlando Bloom Movie HD	Movieclips Trailer Vault	https://www.youtube.com/watch?v=LbfMDwc4azU
The Two Towers. Dir. by Peter Jackson. New Line Cinema, 2002.			
3-1	The Lord of the Rings: The Return of the King (2003) Theatrical Trailer #2	Forever Cinematic Trailers	https://www.youtube.com/watch?v=5jWYWOFvO9o
3-2	The Lord of the Rings: The Return of the King (2003) Official Trailer – Sean Astin Movie HD	Movieclips Trailer Vault	https://www.youtube.com/watch?v=y2rYRu8UW8M

	Name	Source / Channel	URL (last access 18 Feb. 2017)
The Return of the King. Dir. by Peter Jackson. New Line Cinema, 2003.			
4-1	The Lord of the Rings: The Fellowship of the Ring – Special Extended DVD Edition Trailer [HD]	Movies Fan	https://www.youtube.com/watch?v=Bd5ZRJUhras
4-2	The Lord of the Rings Trilogy (2001-2003) Official Blu-ray Trailer LOTR Movie HD	Movieclips Trailer Vault	https://www.youtube.com/watch?v=xPblyMf2tOY
4-3	The Lord of the Rings Motion Picture Trilogy: Extended Edition – Trailer	Warner Bros. Home Entertainment	https://www.youtube.com/watch?v=bzfSb25Vtqs
4-4	The Lord of the Rings Motion Picture Trilogy: Extended Edition – Trailer 2	Warner Bros. Home Entertainment	https://www.youtube.com/watch?v=lkOSXG1JEx0

Birgit Schwan

Searching "For a Better Rhythm, or a Better Word or Phrase": J.R.R. Tolkien's Re-Telling of the Legend of King Arthur in Alliterative Metre

Abstract

The characters of Arthur King of Britain and his Knights of the Round Table had become a fixture in English culture by the end of the first millennium (A.D.) and, soon after, in the 11th and 12th centuries in European literature, too. Today, at the beginning of the 21st century, they are an important part of world literature, while indeed the stories around King Arthur have evolved from legend to myth over the centuries. It is no wonder, then, that a scholar like J.R.R. Tolkien, interested in all manners of medieval stories, decided to study them further. For J.R.R. Tolkien, studying medieval literature often meant translating it, sometimes while re-working and transforming it in order to transport it into another age. In his essay "The Poem in Arthurian Tradition", Christopher Tolkien has already placed the work of his father into the line of the Arthurian literature, starting with Geoffrey of Monmouth's work *Historia Regum Britanniae* and ending with Sir Thomas Malory's *Le Morte Darthur*, which is why I will not focus on the tradition of the story itself, but on the aspects in which Tolkien's story-telling differs from his sources, especially from Malory. By closely reading and comparing passages of Tolkien and Malory, Tolkien's work appears to be rather "un-medieval" despite the ancient metre. Today's reader of *The Fall of Arthur* may be especially struck by the alliterative metre, which nevertheless sounds quite dynamic to our modern ears and which helps rendering the old story in a cinematic way, while opening up new interpretatory avenues.

1 On J.R.R. Tolkien's *The Fall of Arthur* and translating medieval literature: some background information

When J.R.R. Tolkien decided to study the intricate tapestry of Arthurian legends, he did not only work on the various stories; for him, studying medieval literature often meant translating it, while sometimes re-working and transforming it in order to transport it into another age. He evidently started on his narrative poem The Fall of Arthur in the 1930s, worked on it for a few years, but later abandoned it for reasons unknown. In 2013, 40 years after the death of J.R.R. Tolkien, his son Christopher Tolkien published The Fall of Arthur (henceforth FOA). It is a re-telling of the end of King Arthur in alliterative verse,1 an originally Germanic poetic metre2 nowadays best known because of its use in the Old English epic poem Beowulf. To illustrate this metre, I quote the first three lines of Beowulf, marking the alliterating sounds in the lines:

(1) Hwæt, wē Gār-Dena   in geār-dagum
    þēod-cyninga   þrym gefrūnon,
    hū ða æþelingas   ellen fremedon.[3]

In Old English poetry, the poetic text is structured in lines (also called verses); each verse is made up by two half-lines containing two stressed syllables. The two half-lines then are linked by alliteration, i.e. the repetition of a consonant or any vowel.[4] This poetic metre has been used in various poems of subsequent centuries, such as *The Wanderer*, *Sir Gawain and the Green Knight* as well as the *Alliterative Mort Darthur*, which was one of the sources for J.R.R. Tolkien's work. Over the centuries, the rules for using alliterative metre had been relaxed slightly, i.e. the alliteration was not restricted to a maximum of three syllables in one verse anymore. To illustrate this, I quote the first three lines from the *Alliterative Mort Darthur*:

(2) Now grete glorious God   through grace of Himselven
    And the precious prayer   of his pris Moder
    Sheld us fro shamesdeede   and sinful workes

Translators need first to understand completely and then to interpret their source text in order to be able to transfer it into the target language, and thereby finding the equivalent text for the target language. However, this includes more than translating word for word or sentence for sentence. Umberto Eco,

---

1 Sudell's comprehensive study of the alliterative verse of the *FOA* was published only after my paper had been written and could not be taken into consideration. On Tolkien's use of alliterative verse in general, see Shippey "Tolkien's Development".
2 See Mitchell and Robinson 141: "The metrical unit is the half-line. Two half-lines alliterating together form the alliterative line which originated among the Germanic peoples in prehistoric times, was used for centuries by Old High German, Old Saxon, and other Germanic poets, as well as by the Anglo-Saxons, and which in England had a glorious flowering in the fourteenth century with such works as *Sir Gawain and the Green Knight* and *Piers Plowman*."
3 Trans. Heaney: "So. The Spear-Danes in days gone by / and the kings who ruled them had courage and greatness. / We have heard of those princes' heroic campaigns." Heaney also explains the Old English alliterative verse in his "Introduction" to his verse translation of *Beowulf* when he recalls the "requirements of Anglo-Saxon metrics" (XXVI): "These lines were made up of two balancing halves, each half containing two stressed syllables [...], there was alliteration linking [...] across the caesura" (XXVI).
4 See also the more detailed explanation of the Old English poetic line in Crystal 89-90.

who tried his hand successfully at translation and whose works were translated in many languages, wrote in his *Experiences in Translation* that "translations are not about linguistic *types* but rather about linguistic *tokens*. Translations do not concern a comparison between two languages but the interpretation of two texts in two different languages" (14).[5] This means that translators deal not only with words and their specific meaning, but also with the ideas and associations connected to them in certain contexts in each language, i.e. source as well as target language. One consequence of this understanding of the process of translation is that the idiosyncrasies and characteristics of a source language regarding grammar, syntax, and vocabulary as well as historical development and/or cultural use need to be taken into account when transferring a text. For those idiosyncrasies of the target language, this may even be called essential. This is also true for translations between the different diachronic stages of the same language, as Manfred Görlach stated: "The general problems of linguistic and cultural equivalence remain, and even formal imitation, if too close, can present a problem [...]" ("Translation" 92).

In the case of Tolkien's posthumously published work *The Fall of Arthur*, we are dealing not so much with a translation within the same language, taking up a medieval text and transferring it into Present-Day English. In my opinion, Tolkien's poem is a re-narration, a re-interpretation, and transformation of the final part of the legend of King Arthur. Although he spent a long time working on this poem, it remains unfinished.[6] Through Tolkien's narration of the end of King Arthur, even though it might be fragmentary, we see the legend of Arthur King of Britain through a differently coloured glass, partly

---

5 As I understand his text, Umberto Eco here takes up the difference between linguistic word types, i.e. every word counts for itself in a text or all words can be regarded as "particular words" (Bieswanger and Becker 77), and linguistic word tokens, i.e. the words used in a text are counted in accordance to their semantic content or the "occurrences of words" (Bieswanger and Becker 77). Yet, Umberto Eco develops this difference one step further and regards it as the important difference when translating: For him, one word needs not only be translated according to its inherent semantic meaning (denotation), but also according to its use within a certain context (connotation).
6 In his notes on the text as well as the essay "The Evolution of the Poem", Christopher Tolkien shows that his father must have spent an enormous amount of time working on this poem: "Very different indeed is the case of *The Fall of Arthur*, where there are some 120 pages of drafting [...] preceding the 'final' text given in this book. The movement from the earliest workings (often only partly legible) can be largely followed through succeeding manuscripts that underwent abundant emendation" (*FOA* 171).

transformed into a new poetic form, using the alliterative metre as it is used in Old Norse or Old English poetry.

2 The sources and antecedents of J.R.R. Tolkien's *The Fall of Arthur*

Concerning his essay "The Poem in Arthurian Tradition", which has been published together with the poem *The Fall of Arthur*, Christopher Tolkien states that it "is an account of the derivation of [his] father's poem from particular narrative traditions and its divergences from them" (*FOA* 13). Therefore, it can be supposed that J.R.R. Tolkien used many of the known sources of the legend for his work: Geoffrey of Monmouth's *Historia Regum Brittaniae* (ca. 1136) and Sir Thomas Malory's *Le Morte Darthur* (ca. 1470) as well as the anonymous *Stanzaic Morte Arthur* (ca. 1400) and the anonymous *Alliterative Mort Darthur* (ca. 1390). In order to begin to understand Tolkien's own poem, *The Fall of Arthur*, a very brief overview of the sources shall be given.

2.1 Sources of the legend of King Arthur

The English chronicler Geoffrey of Monmouth wrote his "History of the British Kings", the *Historia Regum Brittaniae*, in the first half of the 12th century (ca. 1136), probably using as his main sources the works of Gildas (from the 6th century), Bede (8th century), and Nennius (9th century) as well as the *Welsh Annals* (10th century). Geoffrey of Monmouth's pseudo-historical work was distributed and read widely; the Norman Robert Wace translated Monmouth's *Historia* into Anglo-Norman: "In all essentials of narrative, proportion, thematic content and historical colouring, Wace's *Brut* remains what the *Historia* is" (Barron and Weinberg XXVII). The Briton Layamon then used Wace's *Brut* as the basis for his translation, transferring the legend back to the British Isles in a slightly changed version. The stories spread and became more and more part of the British cultural heritage, being taken up time and again, as can be seen from two anonymous works: the *Stanzaic Morte Arthur* (ca. 1400) and the *Alliterative Mort Darthur* (ca. 1390).

At the end of the 15th century, Sir Thomas Malory decided to collect in one book all the stories about King Arthur and his Knights of the Round Table, *Le Morte Darthur*. It can be supposed that the stories were well-known legends at that time, as they were widely distributed in European literature and folklore and changed through transposition and transmutation.[7] Since Malory probably knew at least a version of Monmouth's chronicle,[8] it might be said then that Malory included at least some of the general aspects of the chronicle in his work, transformed others using his individual interpretation and style, and focused on some aspects of the stories more than others. This only means that Malory – just like Wace before him[9] – followed the respected manner of medieval *translatio*;[10] however, knowing that texts were not only translated into another language in medieval times, but into a different culture as well, explains the many changes that become obvious when following the development of one storyline or one character through time.[11]

Malory completed *Le Morte Darthur* (henceforth *MD*) around 1470. It is the single extant cycle of Arthurian legends in the English literature of the Middle

---

7 Cooper writes in her "Introduction" to Sir Thomas Malory's *Le Morte Darthur*: "The fashion started by Chrétien initiated an extraordinary literary flowering of Arthurian material across Europe. New romances were composed; French ones were translated and adapted into a multiplicity of languages, from Norse to Portuguese and Hebrew. Early in the thirteenth century in France, the stories contained in the verse romances of Arthur were given a new and extended form in prose. A connected series of these written by various authors, known as the Vulgate Cycle, covered the whole history of the Round Table [...]" (VIII).
8 Even if Malory had not read the *Historia Regum Brittaniae*, it is apparent that one of the versions of this chronicle must have been known to him; see also Kennedy 223-34, especially 225.
9 See Lacy, Ashe, and Mancoff 62. See also Weiss XVIII: "'Translate' in the Middle Ages did not have the narrow meaning it does today, and Wace, in bringing Geoffrey's 'history' to a yet larger audience unversed in Latin, felt free to amplify and embellish his chronicle."
10 *Translatio* signifies here the transferral of one text into another language as well as its probable interpretation and, if necessary, elaboration; it needs to be stressed, however, that at all times translators have been conscious of the implications of using various translation methods. In fact, the debate whether translation should be literal (*verbum pro verbo*) or free (*sensum de sensu*) goes back to antiquity; see the detailed study of Copeland on the development of rhetoric, hermeneutics and translation from Roman antiquity to the Middle Ages: "The familiar precepts about translation, which the Middle Ages borrowed from antiquity, center on the idea that translation may be literal (word for word) or loose (sense for sense);" (Copeland 9). The tradition of translating literary texts more loosely goes back to St Jerome, who translated the bible into Latin (end of 4th century) and "eschews literalism as clumsy and as an obstacle to the meaning" (Copeland 46) in the translation of non-scriptural texts. The development went so far that in the 14th century writers like Chaucer or Gower felt free to transfer their source texts in such a manner that their translations "tend to claim for themselves [...] a kind of originary discursive status, as if the translation, once achieved, displaces the source by assuming a certain canonical authority of its own" (Copeland 95). This phenomenon can be compared to the medieval concept of quoting; see Kirner-Ludwig and Zimmermann, especially 297-305.
11 Compare the development of a medieval literary character, for instance King Arthur, as described in Schuh 70-74.

Ages. Malory used the French Vulgate cycle as his main source, but tapped into other sources as well (Bethlehem 384). In the centuries thereafter, Malory's cycle has become one of the main sources for any kind of story-telling about King Arthur, his Knights of the Round Table, and his queen, Guinevere.

It is very telling, then, that J.R.R. Tolkien pointedly chose another path: "But from the first lines of *The Fall of Arthur* it is seen that my father was departing radically from the story of Arthur's last campaign overseas as told by Geoffrey of Monmouth and his successors" (*FOA* 75). This is one of the reasons why I regard Tolkien's work *The Fall of Arthur* not as a translation as such – at least not in the modern (but possibly in the medieval) sense of "translation" – but as an adaptation or even a transformation.

2.2 Differences and commonalities of Le Morte Darthur and The Fall of Arthur

Both works have been written at a time of historical change: Malory wrote *Le Morte Darthur* at the end of the 15th century, Tolkien worked on *The Fall of Arthur* during the 1930s and 1940s before abandoning it. Both points in time were marked by enormous change caused by political, social and cultural developments: During the 15th century, social and economic structures in England were changing due to an ever-increasing urban society. In addition, new technological developments, such as the printing press, the rise of a new social middle class as well as the end of the Hundred Years' War, and later with the establishment of the Tudor dynasty with a new policy (at home as well as abroad) – just to name a few important events for England – made for exciting times to live in. At the beginning of the 20th century, Tolkien experienced two world wars at close range as well as the intermittent period. The years between the world wars (1918-1939) were marked by political unrest throughout Europe and Russia, social instability, due, for instance, to the call for reforms, such as women's suffragette, or high unemployment rates, the rise of socialism and fascism, and economic catastrophes like hyperinflation. In Great Britain, change had become shockingly obvious with the abdication of King Edward VIII in 1936. New rules were applied to old systems, and like so many others both Sir Thomas Malory and J.R.R. Tolkien had to come to terms with the developments of their times. It is an axiomatic statement that creative work in all its regards can help to deal with life's unexpected challenges. For a later audience, however, it is important to remember that the creation of every text is influenced by its context.

In the case of Malory's *Le Morte Darthur* and Tolkien's *The Fall of Arthur*, both writers collected and combined their material as far as possible: Malory gathered all known stories of the Arthurian legend into one single cycle, combining, interpreting, and changing small aspects of the storyline, as well as modernizing some of the characters, especially the female ones. As a scholar, Tolkien used sources known to him and other material in his reach, which was connected to the Arthurian legend, re-working the final chapter of Arthur's life and exploits, and utilizing ancient metre to an astonishingly modern effect. Due to this, both works can be regarded as high points in the development of Arthurian lore.

The differences lie mainly in style. The term "style", however, needs to be clarified. In my essay, I follow the definition of Marie Borroff who writes: "Style may be generally described as the way language is used, the 'how' of expressing anything in words as opposed to the 'what'" (3). This means that one and the same content may be expressed in various, quite divergent styles, using different words, different structures, and different stylistic devices. In the case of the legend of King Arthur and our authors, the first thing one can observe is the choice of poetic metre or the lack thereof: Malory wrote prose, Tolkien used verse.

Such a decision has far-reaching consequences with regard to grammar, lexical choices, use of direct or indirect speech, and use of stylistic devices, such as alliteration, syntactical inversion, ellipsis etc. For instance, Malory's prose is a combination of sequential main clauses and complex constructions of main and subordinate clauses (see (3)). The long sequences of main clauses drive the plot onward; the constructions using subordinate clauses are mainly used to give background information to the audience, to give coherence to the text or to add causality. In addition, Malory employs dialogue very frequently (i.e. direct speech, see (3)), bringing the characters to life. Here is an example from the beginning of *Le Morte Darthur*:

(3) So there came into the thick of the press Arthur, Ban, and Bors [*main clause*], and slew downright on both hands [*main clause*], that their horses went in blood up to the fetlocks [*subordinate clause*]. But ever the eleven kings and the host was ever in the visage of Arthur [*main clause*]. Wherefore King Ban and Bors had great marvel [*main clause*], considering the great slaughter that there was [*subordinate clause*]; but at the last they were driven aback over a little river [*main clause*].

With that came Merlin on a great black horse [*main clause*], and said unto King Arthur [*main clause*], 'Thou hast never done, hast thou not done enough? Of three score thousand this day hast thou left alive but fifteen thousand, therefore it is time to say 'Whoa!' For God is wroth with thee, for thou wilt never have done. For yonder eleven kings at this time will not be overthrown; but and thou tarry on them any longer, thy fortune will turn and they shall increase. […]' [*direct speech*] (*MD* I.17, 18)

The first part of this short passage gives a vivid picture of the battle. The use of the imagery – "that their horses went in blood up to the fetlocks" – in combination with the choice of words – "the great slaughter" – causes the imagination of the reader to paint everything in even more detail. This supposition would, in all probability, hold true for anyone in the 15th century, because people then were only too well acquainted with battle scenes, if not directly and personally then at least indirectly and from hear-say;[12] today's (Western) audience may have a greater distance to war, but the imagery is pointed enough to trigger colourful images.

In the second part of this passage, Merlin admonishes Arthur. Through the dialogue, this character comes to life: Merlin starts with a rather forceful rhetorical question – "Thou hast never done, hast thou not done enough?" (see (3)) –, answers it himself by giving the results of the day's work ("Of three score thousand this day hast thou left alive but fifteen thousand", see (3)), and with the imperative onomatopoetic word *whoa* adds his admonishment to Arthur. He then goes on to give his reasons ("For God is wroth with thee, for thou wilt never have done", see (3)), employing common sense ("And therefore withdraw you unto your lodging and rest you as soon as ye may, and reward your good

---

12 Although most of the Hundred Years' War was fought on the continent, stories of the various battles were probably told in England. In addition, smaller skirmishes were not unusual, especially in the border regions to Scotland and Wales. In the second half of the 15th century, battles were fought in England between the Yorkists (supporters of the House of York, associated with a white rose) and the Lancastrians (supporters of the House of Lancaster, associated with a red rose), the so-called Wars of the Roses.

knights with gold and with silver, for they have well deserved it", *MD* I.17, 18) and even a hint of foreshadowing ("they shall increase", see (3)). Merlin's words are enough for Arthur to stop fighting; directly after this scene, the reader is informed that Arthur follows Merlin's advice: "'Ye say well,' said Arthur, 'and as thou hast devised, so shall it be done.'" (*MD* I.17, 19). Arthur may be young still, but he proves himself to be intelligent and ready to take counsel.

As Tolkien mostly used the final chapter of the Arthurian legends in *The Fall of Arthur*,[13] I cannot give the equivalent scene here. However, in order to get a feeling of Tolkien's completely different style, here are the first lines of the beginning of *The Fall of Arthur*:

> (4) Arthur eastward   in arms purposed
>   his war to wage   on the wild marches,
>   over seas sailing   to Saxon lands,
>   from the Roman realm   ruin defending.
>   Thus the tides of time   to turn backward
>   and the heathen to humble,   his hope urged him,
>   that with harrying ships   they should hunt no more
>   on the shining shores   and shallow waters
>   of South Britain,   booty seeking. (*FOA* I, 1-9)

The alliterative metre combined with the syntactic structure creates a driving rhythm. Tolkien employs a free word order as can be seen from the first line onwards: "Arthur eastward in arms purposed". Here, an adverbial of direction ("eastward)" and a modal adverbial phrase ("in arms") are set between the subject of the sentence ("Arthur") and the verb ("purposed"), breaking the usually employed rule of Present-Day English word order that the subject is directly followed by the verb. In combination with the rhythm created by alliteration and free word order, the chosen vocabulary blends into image after image that flash through the reader's mind: Arthur marches over marshland to the east; the sea and ships carrying invaders are visible in the background; raiders hopeful of grabbing rich treasure are making their way to the shore; and still one can imagine Arthur standing in front of his army, hopeful of victory in spite of the massive onslaught. When the poem is not read silently but aloud, the effect is multiplied. Then, the various sounds of the syllables emphasized through al-

---

13 For a detailed description of the sources used and their influence on Tolkien's work, see Christopher Tolkien, "The Poem in Arthurian Tradition."

literation (e.g. line 2 "his war to wage", line 3 "over seas sailing to Saxon lands", or line 5 "Thus the tides of time to turn backward") create a vivid picture. The alliterative metre often makes inverted word order necessary as the structure of this metre is rigid (e.g. in line 1 "Arthur eastward in arms purposed"): In the alliterative long line, the first half has at least one, quite often two stressed syllables, in the second half only one. For instance, in *FOA* I, 5-6: "Thus the *tides* of *time* | to *turn back*ward / and the *hea*then to *hum*ble, | his *hope* urged him" (for illustration, the alliterating sounds are marked in bold italics, while the stressed elements are marked in italics). Yet, the stress through alliteration is never on the last syllable; as can be seen in our example, the syllables "-ward" and "him" are unstressed. Naturally, this structure influences one's interpretation of a text. In the sentence quoted above "{Thus [*conjunction*] the tides of time [*object of infinitive clause 1*] to turn backward [*infinitive clause 1*] / and [*conjunction*] the heathen [*object of infinitive clause 2*] to humble [*infinitive clause 2*]} [*subordinate clause(s)*], his hope urged him [*main clause*]" (*FOA* I, 5-6), for instance, first main clause and subordinate clause in addition to the two objects of the infinitive clauses and the infinitive clauses themselves are inversed. These inversions emphasize the hope of Arthur to bring peace and prosperity back to his country and nation, because the main clause forms the second half-line of line 6, with the subordinate clauses filling the three half-lines before. Thus, the focus of the audience is skilfully guided to this important clause and its content. And since the alliterative stress falls on the noun "hope" in the second half-line of line 6, the reader concentrates then on this single word, making it the keyword of this passage.

3 A close reading of *Le Morte Darthur* and *The Fall of Arthur*: three instances of interpretation

I consider *translation* as well as *adaptation* as conceptual tools because they "facilitate a rich fusion of experiences through the simultaneous interpretation of multiple resources" (Tunç 96). In my opinion, Tolkien's re-working of the Arthurian legend is a superb example for such a simultaneous interpretation. In the following section, I am going to take a closer look at three instances; in all cases I will very briefly describe the story and context, and then concentrate on the way Malory as well as Tolkien use their respectively chosen style (free-flowing prose vs. alliterative metre). In my close reading, I am going to analyse the use of syntactic constructions, the phonological interpretation of some lexical choices as well as taking some morphological and/or semantic interpretations into account. I selected three passages that could be found both in *MD* and *FOA*. With this selection, I also want to give a closer look at three main characters of the legends around King Arthur: King Arthur himself, his queen Guinevere, and one of his most prominent knights, Lancelot.

3.1 The Judgement of Queen Guinevere

In the legend, Queen Guinevere undergoes three rescue situations. One of them is the rescue of Guinevere by Lancelot, when she is on trial for treason against the crown and is convicted to death by fire. Malory describes the actions leading to the Queen's judgement and the reasons for it minutely and in much detail, often employing dialogue in order to make it more life-like and to draw the reader more and more into the story.[14] The entire trial situation is caused by the suspicions voiced by Gawain and his brothers, their subsequent spying on the queen, and their actual discovery of the love affair between Guinevere and Lancelot. After the lovers were discovered together in the queen's chambers, Lancelot flees from the room fighting, thereby killing some and wounding others. After that fight, Mordred informs the King of this treasonous situation, starting the legal procedure of the trial process. Lancelot later returns in order to rescue the queen from certain death; in fact, Lancelot rushes his horse toward the Queen on the burning stake and spirits her away, while his friends and followers fight off the other knights. The following passage from *MD* starts with King Arthur's decision after he had been told of the events in the queen's quarters by Mordred:

(5) '[...] **And** now it is fallen so', said the King, 'that I may not with my worship but my Queen must suffer death' – **and** was sore moved.

So then there was made great ordinance in this ire, **and** the Queen must needs be judged to the death. **And** the law was such in those days, *that* whosoever they were, of what estate or degree, *if* they were found guilty of treason there should be none other remedy but death, **and** either

---

14 Malory uses these devices right from the start of this part of the legend, see also *MD* XX.1-2, 468-471.

> the mainour or the taking with the deed should be causer of their judgement. **And** right so was it ordained for Queen Guenivere: *because* Sir Mordred was escaped sore wounded, and the death of thirteen knights of the Round Table, these proofs and experiences caused King Arthur to command the Queen to the fire, and there to be burned.
> (*MD* XX.7, 478; emphasis added)

Here, the plot is driven by a combination of subsequent main clauses (as evidenced by the often used coordinating conjunction "and" as well as "so then", put in semibold in (5)) and a complex system of subordinate clauses (here, the subordinating conjunctions "that", "if", and "because", marked in italics in (5), are used). The conviction of Queen Guinevere to death by fire ("and there to be burned") is one of the turning points of the story to the worst. Since Lancelot saves her from death, both have to flee and seek exile in Lancelot's castle. Many knights of the Round Table are loyal to Lancelot and therefore leave with him, forsaking Camelot, Arthur's court, and the ideals and principles of the Round Table. Thus, the judgement of the Queen and all its consequences for the court, for the kingdom, and for Arthur himself, might be regarded as the obvious sign of an extensive decay that had been evolving for a long time. Arthur sees all that, and still "was sore moved". When Lancelot succumbed to his feelings for the queen and gave up his loyalty to his liege lord as well as the ideals of the Round Table, he hurt his king in his way of governing as well as in a very personal manner. Despite this (double) injury, the little sentence "was sore moved" shows that Arthur finds it in him to grieve for the loss not only of his beloved wife, but also of one of his most trusted knights and friends.

In comparison, Tolkien depicts the same situation in a condensed manner, using the alliterative metre. As a result, his choices in word order and vocabulary, applied to give his poem structure and rhythm, influence the story-telling, too, by imbuing the way in which the story is told with more force; here, the rhythm mirrors the urgency of the situation.

> (6) Swift swords were drawn   by sworn brethren
> and the Round Table   rent asunder
> in the Queen's quarrel.   Cold rang the blades.
> The Queen was taken.   With cruel justice
> ***fair as fay-woman***   they to fire doomed her,
> to death they condemned her.   But death waited. (*FOA* III, 71-76)

At this point in the narrative, the consequent use of consonants for the alliteration (marked in bold in (6)) ensures a driving rhythm, while the sequence of very short sentences enhances that the readers immediately picture scene after scene in their minds.

The phrase "fair as fay-woman" in (6), i.e. *FOA* III, 75, describing Queen Guinevere, is a repetition of an earlier description occurring 20 verses before:

(7)   Dear she loved him
    with love unyielding,   lady ruthless,
    fair as fay-woman   and fell-minded
    in the world walking   for the woe of men. (*FOA* III, 53-56)

Through the repetition of the half-line "fair as fay-woman" Guinevere is depicted as a beautiful woman who may be ruthless in getting her own wishes fulfilled. The description of Guinevere in (7) is written from the point of view of Lancelot, who thinks of her while he is in exile alone, remembering the course of their affair; that he still loves Guinevere dearly is made clear at the beginning of the third *canto*: "by leagues of sea from love sundered" (*FOA* III, 18). However, combining (7) and (8), the following interpretation may be reached: the rift between Lancelot and Arthur, his king, was not only caused by Guinevere's character, but even more so by Lancelot's actions (see (8) in the following section 3.2). It was Lancelot's betrayal of Arthur that led to his final exile, from which he does not return in Tolkien's version of the legend.

In comparing the styles of Tolkien and Malory, in which they tell this story, it can be said that both convey the urgency of the situation in different ways, but to an equal degree. Malory achieves an image of the rush and bustle through dialogue (see *MD* XX.1-2, 468-471) and long prose descriptions, in which he uses a complex pattern of main and subordinate clauses (see (5)). The use of rather formal vocabulary, such as "mainour", "ordained", "proofs and experiences", and phrases like "I may not with my worship" (meaning, "I cannot honourably do otherwise") or "whosoever they were, of what estate or degree" emphasizes on the one hand the seriousness of the situation, while on the other hand portraying the legal system. Tolkien, in comparison, focuses on the forceful energy in his portrayal of the scene. He uses consonants (/s/, /r/, /k/, /f/, /d/) to drive the rhythm onwards through alliteration, and a sequence of short sentences: "Cold rang the blades.", "The Queen was taken.", and finally "But death waited." This last sentence has nearly the ring of a knelling bell to it, due to the combination of sounds (/b/, /d/, /w/) resulting in an acoustic echo lingering in the mind of the reader.

3.2 Lancelot's exile

After Lancelot rescued Guinevere from burning at the stake, the legend tells that both went into exile together. However, in the hope of reconciling the estranged King and Queen, Lancelot persuades Guinevere to return to her husband. Although he may have hoped to be allowed to return to Camelot as well, Lancelot's wish was denied. He was told to stay in exile. Tolkien picks up the storyline at this point in the third *canto* of *The Fall of Arthur*. At the beginning of the *canto*, he portrays Lancelot at night, alone on the tower looking over the sea. Tolkien shows that in his interpretation Lancelot is grieving for everything he has lost:

> (8) Dark slowly fell.   Deep his anguish.
>   He his lord betrayed   to love yielding,
>   and love forsaking   lord regained not;
>   faith was refused him   who had faith broken,
>   by leagues of sea   from love sundered. (*FOA* III, 14-18)

In the second line of this passage, the nouns "lord" and "love" are juxtaposed, thereby designating opposing centres of Lancelot's loyalty, obviously referring to Arthur and Guinevere respectively. The third line takes up the juxtaposition in reversed order, giving thus a line of action: first, Lancelot left Arthur and the court for Guinevere's love, then, with Lancelot's agreement or maybe even encouragement, Guinevere returned to Arthur, but to no avail for Lancelot and his hopes for returning to Camelot. His banishment has not been revoked, leaving Lancelot separated from everyone and everything that he held dear. The noun "love" in the last line of this passage can refer to both "lord" and "love" of the second line, or even to much more. The passage is repeated twice, though slightly altered, later in the *canto* (III, 118-123; III, 139-142), signalling the importance of these emotions and concepts.

In *Le Morte Darthur*, Lancelot is allowed to state his grief at being exiled openly before the court:

(9) The Sir Lancelot sighed, and therewith the tears fell on his cheeks; and then he said thus: 'Most noblest Christian realm, whom I have loved above all other realms, and in thee have I got a great part of my worship! And now that I shall depart in this wise, truly me repents that ever I came in this realm, that I should be thus shamefully banished, undeserved and causeless. But fortune is so variant and the wheel so mutable that there is no constant abiding; [...]' (*MD* XX.17, 494f.)

Reading this speech of Lancelot, it is apparent that he sees himself as innocent of any crime but love. That loving the queen can also mean betraying one's king is implied in the use of the phrase "shamefully banished". Instead, the fickle Lady Fortune is seen as the cause for his misery and misfortune.

At the end of the third *canto* in *The Fall of Arthur*, it is stated clearly that Lancelot was taken up with his grief, his reflections, and emotions. Indeed, he was so taken up with his emotional turmoil that he was not able to alter this situation in any way:

(10) And Lancelot   over leagues of sea
    Looked and pondered   alone musing
    Doubtful-hearted.   Dark had fallen.
    No horn he blew,   no host gathered;
    He wavered and went not.   Wind was roaring
    The towers trembled   tempest-shaken. (*FOA* III, 187-192)

After this passage, Tolkien describes Lancelot's loneliness (*FOA* III, 200, "alone dreaming"), his life and death as a hermit (*FOA* III, 227f., "to return never / among waking men") in search of peace (*FOA* III, 204f., "but on lowly earth / peace had fallen") in stirring images of the rising sun (*FOA* III, 211, "with the flame of morn in his face burning"), shimmering light and waters (*FOA* III, 207, "washed with water the world shimmered") and the memory of music (*FOA* III, 212f., "the surge he felt of song forgotten / in his heart moving as a harp-music").

Malory sets Lancelot's choice to become a hermit right after a final dialogue between Lancelot and Guinevere, saying their last good-byes, thereby giving a very different reason:

(11) And at last he was ware of a hermitage and a chapel stood betwixt two cliffs; and then he heard a little bell ring to Mass, and thither he rode and alit and tied his horse to the gate, and heard Mass, and he that sang Mass was the Bishop of Canterbury. [...] And then he kneeled down on his knee, and prayed the bishop to shrive him and assoil him; and then he besought the bishop that he might be his brother. Then the bishop

said, 'I will gladly,' and there he put a habit upon Sir Lancelot. And there he served God day and night with prayers and fastings. (*MD* XXI.10, 521)

In Malory's description, Lancelot's decision to live as a hermit is the direct effect of having to say good-bye to Guinevere and of meeting the bishop, when he is in a state of absolute emotional turmoil. Another cause for Lancelot's decision to renounce his knighthood and the world of chivalry is a chance meeting with Sir Bedivere, who tells him about Arthur's death: "Sir Lancelot's heart almost brast for sorrow. And Sir Lancelot threw his arms abroad and said, 'Alas, who may trust this world?'" (*MD* XXI.10, 521).

In both works, Lancelot's decision to live the rest of his life as a hermit is motivated by the consequences of his earlier choices. However, Tolkien pictures Lancelot as a lonely figure, being frozen in hopes, wishes, and feelings of guilt; this state can only be unlocked by the search for peace in nature and faith. Malory, on the other hand, gives the meeting with several people and talking to beloved individuals as the cause as well as a sign for Lancelot to spend the rest of his days in penance, living the life of a hermit. Therefore, it can be argued that, for Malory, the reasons for any kind of decision may lie in internal (e-)motions, but any kind of decision-making process is started by social interaction, whereas Tolkien portrays individual (thinking and feeling) processes. These may be caused at least partly by social interaction, but other states – like a lonely night-watch, observing nature and pondering past, present, and future – play an important role, too.

3.3 Arthur's return to England

The last part of both works paints a harsh picture, full of battle scenes and depictions of death. Arthur returns to England from the continent, where he had been engaged in battle. In the beginning of Tolkien's poem, Arthur was fighting against the Saxons and for the freedom of his own people. Now Gawain and his host have to fight against the army of Mordred in order to win free passage into England – and the battle is brutal and gruesome:

```
(12) Boats were blazing,     burned and smoking;
     some on shore shivered    to shards broken.
     Red ran the tide     the rocks staining.
     Shields on the water    shorn and splintered
     as flotsam floated.    Few saved their lives
```

> broken and bleeding   from that battle flying.
> Thus came Arthur   to his own kingdom
> and the sea's passage   with the sword conquered,
> Gawain leading.   Now his glory shone
> as the star of noon   stern and cloudless
> o'er the heads of men   to its height climbing
> ere it fall and fail.   Fate yet waited.
> Tide was turning.   Timbers broken,
> dead men and drowned,   a dark jetsam,
> were left to lie   on the long beaches;
> rocks robed with red   rose from water. (*FOA* IV, 215-230)

The alliterating words mostly begin with stops (/b/, /t/, /g/, /k/) and fricatives (/f/, /s/, /ʃ/). The effect of these sounds is a sort of audio-image: In combination with the driving rhythm of short clauses, these consonants create a picture in the mind of breaking wood, mindless slashing and running blood and water.

Through an entirely different method, Malory achieved a similar effect. He used a sequence of main clauses, mostly beginning with "and so", "so" or a combination with "there". These small words begin with fricatives (/s/ and /ð/), too. However, Malory does not employ words with stops in initial position, thereby softening the harshness of the picture. But the initial effect reached by the use of fricatives is then intensified by the repetitive description:

> (13) And so as Sir Mordred was at Dover with his host, so came King Arthur with a great navy of ships and galleys and carracks. And **there was** Sir Mordred ready awaiting upon his landing, to let his own father to land upon the land that he was king over. Then **there was** launching of great boats and small, and full of noble men of arms; and **there was** much slaughter of gentle knights, and many a full bold baron **was laid** full low on both parties. […] So when this battle **was done**, King Arthur *let* search his **people that were hurt and dead**. And then was noble Sir Gawain found in a great boat, lying more than half dead. (*MD* XXI.2, 507f.)

Despite the rushing visuals created by the employment of fricatives, the overall effect is still more softened through the use of the passive voice in this passage (highlighted in (13)). The passive voice coupled with the prominent use of nouns creates a distance to the events depicted, since everything seems to have become abstract and remote. The images are transferred into the mind of the reader, but the events appear to be visible as if there were a mist hanging over them.

Interesting to note here is also the phrase "much slaughter of gentle knights". In fact, only one knight is mentioned by name, and that is Sir Gawain, "lying more than half dead". Directly after this passage, Malory describes the final meeting of Arthur and Gawain and the death of the latter in detail. However, in this instance, Sir Gawain – as nephew of King Arthur, loyal knight, and advisor of the king after Lancelot's exile – stands *pars pro toto* for all the other loyal knights and subjects to the king. The perspective of Arthur is pictured as well:

> (14) On the land he looked   lofty shining.
>   Treason trod there   trumpets sounding
>   in power and pride.   Princes faithless
>   on shore their shields   shameless marshalled,
>   their king betraying,   Christ forsaking,
>   to heathen might   their hope turning. (*FOA* V, 12-17)

Tolkien portrays Arthur shortly before the battle. In this depiction, Arthur is king in full measure. He might be grieving over the situation, but at the same time he is determined; the first line and here especially the use of the preposition "on" in initial position are hinting at this determination. The following lines give reasons for the battle (listed here in order of appearance): treason, lust for power, pride, persons in powerful positions lacking faith and having no shame or honour. In addition to all that, the people are not only betraying their king but also their religion, turning from Christianity back to the old belief system.

The first reasons are given by Malory as well. He adds to this list the evil of slander:

> (15) Thus was King Arthur depraved and evil said of. And many there were that King Arthur had brought up of nought, and given them lands, that might not then say him a good word. [...] For he that was the most king and noblest knight of the world, and most loved the fellowship of noble knights, and by him they all were upheld, and yet might not these Englishmen hold them content with him. Lo, thus was the old custom and usages of this land; and men say that we of this land have not yet lost that custom. (*MD*, XXI.1, 507)

In this passage, Malory might hint at a shift from Christianity to paganism, but it is not mentioned as such. Instead, he says that "thus was the old custom and usages of this land"; this might also refer to a general discontent with leadership as such, thereby having only political implications and showing no links to religion.

Close to the end of the poem, Tolkien describes Arthur's feeling for his people and his nation. Having achieved greatness, Arthur is portrayed as a leader who loves his land and each and every one of his people:

> (16) Now pity whelmed him
> and love of his land   and his loyal people,
> for the low misled   and the long-tempted,
> the weak that wavered,   for the wicked grieving.
> With woe and weariness   and war sated,
> kingship owning   crowned and righteous
> he would pass in peace   pardon granting,
> the hurt healing   and the whole guiding,
> to Britain the blessed   bliss recalling.
> Death lay between   dark before him
> ere the way were won   or the world conquered. (*FOA* V, 37-47)

Arthur might be tired of fighting constantly, but he is also gracious and has the best of interests for all in mind. However, he is not able to do everything as he may wish, as death and darkness lie before him.

Similarly in *MD*, where Malory states that "[n]ow more of the death of King Arthur could I never find, but that these ladies brought him to his grave" (*MD* XXI.6, 517). He goes on: "Yet some men say in many parts of England that King Arthur is not dead, but had by the will of Our Lord Jesu into another place; [...] but rather I would say, here in this world he changed his life" (*MD* XXI.7, 517). In short, no one knows what may have happened to King Arthur, although death is almost a certainty.

3.4 Summary

A close reading of three instances has shown that the focus of interpretation has shifted from social conventions and pressures to a more individualized point of view on relationships and resulting events. Malory portrays mostly external situations, for instance the discovery of the two lovers, their conviction and subsequent exile, giving only small clues and hinting at intellectual or emotional reasons (e.g. the added sentence "was sore moved"). Tolkien, on the other hand, states reflections and emotions clearly, while picturing the effect on actual events vividly. However, by repeating phrases as well as by emphasizing certain words through the structure of the poem (e.g. the repetition of "fair as fay-woman" or the emphasis on the word "hope"), it is obvious that Tolkien sees the emotional, moral, or even ethical pressures as much more important than the social one.

With regard to style, I am of the opinion that both authors used very different methods to achieve similar and, on the whole, equivalent effects (see Table 1):

	MD	*FOA*
Metre	Prose, free-flowing	Poetic: alliterative verse
Syntax	Pattern of main clauses interlaced with subordinate clauses	Pattern of longer sentences interrupted by sequences of short sentences
Word-order	Mostly SVO, but not as strict as in Present-Day English (usual for 15th-century English, as some inflections were not yet levelled)	Free word-order
Vocabulary	Combination of everyday words (mostly Germanic in origin) with frequently used French (or Romance) words, use of technical jargon when required	Combination of everyday words with archaic or rarely-used words to create alliteration as well as to convey a different connotation
Morphology	Use of 2nd person sg. personal pronoun *thou* in intimate situations	Use of archaic 3rd person sg. present tense indicative verbal suffix *-eth*
Phonology	Mostly unremarkable; instead, use of syntactic patterns and conjunctions for creating images	Conscious use of consonants (and sometimes vowels) to create audio-visual imagery

Table 1: Characteristics of Malory's *Le Morte Darthur* and Tolkien's *The Fall of Arthur*

Through various linguistic means, both Malory and Tolkien achieve the creation of vivid images. In fact, both create a different picture of the legend of King Arthur while keeping the story in its essence alive.

4 *The Fall of Arthur*

Turning now to Tolkien's unfinished poem, I am going to explore in more detail its probable effect on today's reader and possible causes for it. To do so, I am taking a closer look at the choice and use of poetic metre, use of vocabulary and morphological choices.

4.1 Poetic metre: choice and effect

As mentioned above, the structure of alliterative metre – as used in Old Norse or Old English poetry as well as by Tolkien – is rigid. It employs a so-called alliterative long line, consisting of two half-lines. In each half-line, some words were stressed through alliteration, resulting in respective patterns. J.R.R. Tolkien stated that "the patterns were made of *strong* and *weak* elements, which may be called 'lifts' and 'dips'. The standard lift was a *long stressed* syllable (usually with a relatively high tone). The standard dip was an *unstressed* syllable, long or short, with a low tone" ("On Translating" 61f.). By balancing unstressed syllables with stressed syllables and using the resulting patterns – six as defined by Tolkien in his essay "On Translating *Beowulf*" – it was possible to emphasize particular aspects of the story in more ways than only by lexical choices. Unsurprisingly, the forming of those patterns influences the choices of vocabulary as well as the use of syntax and word order. As Christopher Tolkien wrote in his "Foreword" to *The Fall of Arthur*: "The astonishing amount of surviving draft material for *The Fall of Arthur* reveals the difficulties inherent in such use of the metrical form that my father found so profoundly congenial, and his exacting and perfectionist concern to find, in an intricate and subtle narrative, fitting expression within the patterns of rhythm and alliteration of the Old English verse-form" (*FOA* 11f.).

Poems in alliterative metre have a very different structure to rhymed poetry, and their effect on the audience is also very different; this has partly been shown in section 3 and will be discussed in the following section 4.2. J.R.R. Tolkien was very aware of this: "he searched unceasingly for a better rhythm, or a better word or phrase within the alliterative constraints" (*FOA* 171f.).

4.2 The power of the suitably chosen word

In alliterative metre, the most important word comes – usually – at the beginning of a line, which is worded as follows by Tolkien: "The force was renewed and the tone raised at the beginning of the line (as a rule), and there the strongest and heaviest words were usually placed" ("On Translating" 70). Tolkien goes on to explain: "The more significant elements in the preceding final were frequently caught up and re-echoed or elaborated" ("On Translating" 70). This method can frequently be observed in his own work. Earlier I mentioned the repetition of the phrase "fair as fay-woman" in Guinevere's case, or the slightly altered, thereby "re-echoed" lines in the third *canto*.

With regard to the lexical choices, rarely used words are usually avoided in *The Fall of Arthur*, except when they fit seamlessly into the alliterative metre and the context. Here, I only give examples from the first *canto*: "**harrying** ships" (I, 7), "in the **van** of Arthur" (I, 58), "York is **leaguered**" (I, 160), "his heart **foreboded**" (I, 177), "legions **levy** through the lands" (I, 202), "knights more **puissant**" (I, 205). All these rather infrequently used words,[15] a handful in the entire first *canto*, have been not only chosen because of their (for alliteration) suitable initial sounds, but also because of their semantic contents: these words can be used as synonyms for more frequently used words or expressions (e.g. "raiding" for "harrying", "powerful" for "puissant"), but they convey other associations and connotations, too. These words either originated in Old English (e.g. "to harry" evolved from Old English *hergian* "to ravage") or were originally Romance loan-words (e.g. "puissant" evolved from the Anglo-Norman *pussant*

---

15 The *Oxford English Dictionary* (*OED*) states that these words are all used less frequently. The years of the last instances for each word are given by the *OED* as follows: "to harry" (1894); "van" (1879; however, the longer form 'vanguard' appears to be used even more infrequently than the abbreviation "van"); "to leaguer" (1860); "to forebode" (1895); "to levy" (1854; in the sense "to make war"); "puissant" (2005; used by Salman Rushdie).

"mighty"). Thus, they carry at least a feeling of archaic times, if not conjuring up pictures of dangerous medieval times and a knight in shining armour respectively. In his essay "On Translating *Beowulf*", J.R.R. Tolkien wrote on the use of archaic or dialectal forms:

> This sort of thing – the building up of a poetic language out of words and forms archaic and dialectal or used in special senses – may be regretted or disliked. There is nonetheless a case for it: the development of a form of language familiar in meaning and yet freed from trivial associations, and filled with the memory of good and evil, is an achievement, and its possessors are richer than those who have no such traditions. ("On Translating" 55)

As these words are "freed from trivial associations", their semantic content is often closer to the original. At the same time, these words were used frequently enough to remain part of the language, and because of their age, they carry a certain inherent tendency or "the memory of good and evil", as Tolkien calls it. Nevertheless, all of these words can be easily understood, especially when the context is taken into account, thus the use of them follows the maxim of Tolkien on the general use of words:

> Words should not be used merely because they are 'old' or obsolete. The words chosen, however remote they may be from colloquial speech or ephemeral suggestions, must be words that remain in literary use, especially in the use of verse, among educated people. ("On Translating" 55)

As a result, the chosen words often present a very suitable fit for a modern epic poem in an archaic style retelling a legendary tale.

Another instance of the use of archaic style can be found in the last lines of the fifth *canto*. Here, the archaic verbal suffix signifying the third person singular present tense indicative *-eth* is employed, when Arthur talks to Gawain and says: "My heart urgeth / that best it were that battle waited" (*FOA* V, 59f.). This suffix is employed in direct speech throughout this poem, starting with the message to Arthur that his country is in chaos: "unto Kent kindled the coast blazeth" (*FOA* I, 162). Thus, the archaic suffix is used consistently by Tolkien. Again, some lines later, there is a dialogue between Arthur and Gawain in the first *canto*: "Best meseemeth / swift word to send" (*FOA* I, 185f.), so says Arthur, and Gawain answers: "Best meseemeth that Ban's kindred / abide in Benwick" (*FOA* I, 191f.) In this last example, not only the older suffix is used, but also a syntactic construction using an impersonal verb and employing the personal pronoun of the first person singular in the dative case. This was usual for Middle English,[16] the language variant of English spoken during Chaucer's and Malory's time. Up until at least the 17th century, the inflectional morphemes *-s* and *-eth*, both indicating the third person singular present tense indicative, could have been used interchangeably.[17] Regarding the use of "meseemeth", the construction "it seems to me" is usually preferred today to "me seems" (as it would be in Present-Day English); in the *Oxford English Dictionary*, references from the literary works of William Morris (*Story of Sigurd*, III.307; published in 1874) and Ezra Pound (*Sonnets and Ballate of Guido Cavalcati*, 117; published in 1912) are given as the last two occurrences of "meseems".[18] It appears that Tolkien's maxim on the use of archaic words might be expanded to include phrases and/or inflectional morphemes, since the consistent use of the archaic suffix strengthens the medieval flair of the poem.

5 Conclusion

The term "style" as I use it here describes not what is told, but how the story is told. With regard to the legends of King Arthur, the story has been told in various ways over the centuries, most notably by Sir Thomas Malory at the end of the 15th century. J.R.R. Tolkien told the story in his own style, too. In his unfinished poem, he worked on the part of the legend describing the death of King Arthur and the events leading to it. Both authors used a very different style indeed: Malory chose to write in free-flowing prose, whereas Tolkien decided to create an epic poem using the archaic alliterative line. Nevertheless, the effect on the reader may be considered to be equivalent. In both works, the story unfolds in dramatic scenes, drawing the reader into the narration through the depicted imagery. And yet, the focus of both authors appears to rest on very different areas: Malory concentrates on situations and experiences that lead to certain results, i.e. on external events. In contrast, Tolkien portrays the events of the outside world, but at the same time con-

---

16 See, e.g., Burrow and Turville-Petre 50-51, Freeborn 332, and Brunner 107.
17 See Freeborn 332. The inflectional morpheme *-(e)th* appears to have been used more in formal texts, see Görlach, "Einführung" 72.
18 Cf. s.v. "meseems, v." *OED Online*, Oxford University Press, December 2016. A 19th-century dictionary of English pronunciation, published in 1834, has the entry "meseems" and gives as explanation: "I think, it appears to me" (Cobb 283).

centrates on reflections and emotional developments of the characters, thus depicting their inner world.

By taking a closer look at Tolkien's poem *The Fall of Arthur*, I have tried to show that his use of the archaic and – as some would consider it – old-fashioned alliterative metre proves to be effective in creating an astonishingly modern effect. Through the syntactic structures and inverted word order as well as by the words and sounds chosen, a vivid picture of everything and everyone is painted in the mind of the reader – flashes of images are supported by sound and together result in the creation of an imaginary film. The effect on the reader is dramatic and may even be called cinematic.

The use of the alliterative metre is also effective in creating a driving rhythm, often emphasizing a sense of urgency, very appropriate for the theme of the poem. Due to the alliteration and the necessary search for the perfect word, words have been chosen not only for their denotation, but also for their connotation: the chosen words fit perfectly into the rigid metre. Additionally, they convey different associations, and sometimes even a heavier touch than their modern equivalents, which is suitable for the age-old story and the archaic setting.

Taking all of this together, Tolkien has achieved a transformation of well-known stories of the Arthurian legend into something new, thereby modernizing the legend of Arthur, his knights and his queen. Tolkien focused on the interpretation of individualized facets of the characters, all the while staying true to the essence of his sources. In this way, just like Malory, he opens up new avenues for interpretation and ensures that the Arthurian legend will live on.

About the Author

BIRGIT SCHWAN works as a lecturer, teaching translation from English into German, at the Department of English and American studies at the Ludwig-Maximilians-University, Munich, Germany. She is currently working on her Ph.D. in the field of Historical English Linguistics and Medieval Literature. Her teaching and research interests cover a wide area in linguistic, literary, cultural and translation studies, but are always focused on the various relations and interconnections between these fields. Her interest in J.R.R. Tolkien's works stems from her youthful fascination with the world of Middle-earth, which led to a further exploration of all the aspects of Tolkien's career, concentrating on his lexicographical and academic work and its influence on his literary opus.

Bibliography

Primary sources

TOLKIEN, J.R.R. *The Fall of Arthur*. [= *FOA*] Edited by Christopher Tolkien. London: HarperCollins, 2013.

Sir Thomas MALORY. *Le Morte Darthur*. The Winchester Manuscript. [= MD] Edited and abridged with an introduction and notes by Helen Cooper. Oxford: Oxford University Press, 1998.

Beowulf. A new verse translation by Seamus Heaney. Bilingual edition. London: Faber and Faber, 2000.

King Arthur's Death. The Middle English Stanzaic Morte Arthur and Alliterative Morte Arthure. Edited by Larry D. Benson. Revised by Edward E. Foster. TEAMS Middle English Texts Series. Kalamazoo, Michigan: Medieval Institute Publications, 1994. Accessed online: http://d.lib.rochester.edu/teams/publication/benson-and-foster-king-arthurs-death (February 26, 2017)

Dictionaries

Oxford English Dictionary [= *OED*]: *OED Online*. Oxford University Press, December 2016. (Accessed February 26, 2017)

Cobb's Abridgment of J. Walker's Critical Pronouncing Dictionary, and Expositor of the English Language. Comp. & Eds. John Walker and Lyman Cobb. New York: Harper & Brothers, 1834.

Secondary Literature

BARRON, William R. J. and S. C. WEINBERG. "Preface." *Layamon's Arthur. The Arthurian Section of Layamon's Brut (Lines 9229 - 14297)*. Ed. & trans. W.R.J. Barron and S.C. Weinberg. Exeter: University of Exeter Press, 2001.

BETHLEHEM, Ulrike. *Guinevere – A Medieval Puzzle. Images of Arthur's Queen in the Medieval Literature of England and France*. Heidelberg: Winter, 2005.

BIESWANGER, Markus and Annette BECKER. *Introduction to English Linguistics*. Tübingen, Basel: A. Francke, 2010.

BORROFF, Marie. *Sir Gawain and the Green Knight. A Stylistic and Metrical Study*. Hamden, CT: Archon, 1973.

BRUNNER, Karl. *Die englische Sprache. Ihre geschichtliche Entwicklung*. Vol. 2. Halle (Saale): Max Niemeyer, 1951.

BURROW, J. A. and Thorlac TURVILLE-PETRE. *A Book of Middle English*. Oxford: Blackwell Publishing, 2005.

COOPER, Helen. "Introduction." *Le Morte Darthur. The Winchester Manuscript*. Ed. Helen Cooper. Oxford: Oxford University Press, 1998. VII-XXII.

COPELAND, Rita. *Rhetoric, Hermeneutics, and Translation in the Middle Ages. Academic Traditions and Vernacular Texts*. Cambridge and New York: Cambridge University Press, 1991.

CRYSTAL, David. *The Stories of English*. London and New York: Penguin Books, 2004.

ECO, Umberto. *Experiences in Translation*. Trans. Alastair McEwen. Toronto: University of Toronto Press, 2001.

FREEBORN, Dennis. *From Old English to Standard English. A Course Book in Language Variation across Time*. Basingstoke and New York: Palgrave Macmillan, 2006.

GÖRLACH, Manfred. *Einführung ins Frühneuenglische*. Heidelberg: Winter, 1994.

"The translation of Medieval and Renaissance texts." *Topics in English Historical Linguistics*. Heidelberg: Winter, 2003. 71-92.

HEANEY, Seamus. "Introduction." *Beowulf. A New Verse Translation*. London: Faber and Faber, 2000. IX-XXXIV.

KENNEDY, Edward Donald. "Sir Thomas Malory's (French) Romance and (English) Chronicle." *Arthurian Studies in Honour of P.J.C. Field*. Ed. Bonnie Wheeler. Woodbridge: D.S. Brewer, 2004. 223-34.

KIRNER-LUDWIG, Monika and Iris ZIMMERMANN. "Quoting and Plagiarising – Concepts of Both Now and Then?" *The Pragmatics of Quoting Now and Then*. Eds. Jenny Arendholz, Wolfram Bublitz, and Monika Kirner-Ludwig. Berlin and Boston: de Gruyter Mouton, 2015. 291-318.

LACY, Norris J. and Geoffrey ASHE, with Debra N. MANCOFF, eds. *The Arthurian Handbook*. 2nd ed. New York and London: Garland Publishing, 1997.

MITCHELL, Bruce and Fred C. ROBINSON. *A Guide to Old English*. Oxford: Blackwell Publishing, 2007.

SCHUH, Hans-Manfred. "Die Darstellung von König Artus bei Chrétien de Troyes." *König Artus lebt!* Ed. Stefan Zimmer. Heidelberg: Winter, 2005. 65-92.

SHIPPEY, Tom A. "Tolkien's Development as a Writer of Alliterative Poetry in Modern English." *Tolkien's Poetry*. Eds. Julian Eilmann and Allan Turner. Cormarë Series 28. Zurich and Jena: Walking Tree Publishers, 2013. 11-28.

SUDELL, T.S. "The Alliterative Verse of *The Fall of Arthur*." *Tolkien Studies* 13 (2016): 71-199.

TOLKIEN, Christopher. "The Evolution of the Poem." *The Fall of Arthur*. Ed. Christopher Tolkien. London: HarperCollins, 2006. 171-220.

"Foreword." *The Fall of Arthur*. Ed. Christopher Tolkien. London: HarperCollins, 2006. 9-14.

"The Poem in Arthurian Tradition." *The Fall of Arthur*. Ed. Christopher Tolkien. London: HarperCollins, 2006. 72-122.

"Introduction to the Translation." J.R.R. Tolkien, *Beowulf: A Translation and Commentary together with Sellic Spell*. Ed. Christopher Tolkien. London: HarperCollins, 2014. 1-11.

TOLKIEN, J.R.R. "On Translating Beowulf." *The Monsters and the Critics and Other Essays*. Ed. Christopher Tolkien. London: HarperCollins, 2006. 49-71.

TUNÇ, Tanfer Emin. "Adapting, Translating and Transforming: Cultural Mediation in Ping Chong's *Deshima* and *Pojagi*." *Translation, Adaptation and Transformation*. Ed. Laurence Raw. London and New York: Continuum, 2012. 81-98.

WEISS, Judith. "Introduction." *Robert Wace: Roman de Brut – A History of the British*. Ed. & trans. Judith Weiss. Exeter: University of Exeter Press, 1999. XI-XXIX.

Heike Schwarz

Wounds That Can(not) Be Wholly Cured: Ecopsychology, Solastalgia and Mental Substainability in J.R.R. Tolkien's *The Lord of the Rings*

Abstract

This essay employs an approach towards J.R.R. Tolkien's seminal epic *The Lord of the Rings* using an interdisciplinary angle of ecopsychological frameworks which understand the relevance of environmental well-being based on an embedment of individuals in undamaged ecological surroundings. Tolkien's *The Lord of the Rings* and its environment of the Middle-earth has attracted ecocritical scholars only recently yet quite distinctly. Obviously Tolkien can be categorized as ecocritical novelist whose concern of representing the opposition of a well-balanced environment of the Hobbit world and the Ent-society versus the machine-world of Sauron exemplifies how an interaction and interrelationship with an unspoiled environment seems necessary for physical as well as psychological balance. The very recent establishment of the discipline of ecopsychology, stressing the networked self being able to rely on an intact *umwelt* and thus establish mental stability, needs to be connected to not only nonfiction works, documentaries about natural catastrophes or decidedly realist fiction. Tolkien's high-fantasy work can very well be analyzed in an interdisciplinary way combining ecopsychological standpoints with a stress on how literature enforces empathy showing how especially the genre of fantasy helps establishing an interrelationship of "nature", environment and the human and non-human self. Ideas of nostalgia and ecology, reconceptualized by Australian philosopher Glenn Albrecht with the term of *solastalgia* shimmer through Tolkien's narration even though Albrecht's term was only established recently. Solastalgia as "nature distress syndrom" refers to the psychological impact of destruction of a formerly intact environment. This essay will explore the challenge and necessity of interdisciplinary approaches towards literature and psychopathology, carefully investigate (pop) psychological influences that shaped Tolkien's notion of psychopathological characters in *The Lord of the Rings* (such as Gollum/Sméagol), analyze misconceptions of psychological categories and diagnoses usually applied to some characters, explain how the concept of solastalgia applies, and how Tolkien negotiates trauma and post-trauma while at the same time allow for a development of environmental and thus ecopsychological healing in terms of a proposed concept of mental sustainability.

1 Introduction

This essay employs an approach towards J.R.R. Tolkien's seminal fantasy epic *The Lord of the Rings* using an interdisciplinary angle of an ecopsychological framework. I will apply an understanding of the relevance of *environmental* well-being based on an embedment of individuals in unspoiled, hence undamaged, ecological surroundings. Despite the fact that Tolkien studies in the fields of linguistic and historic or medieval approaches are dominant, Tolkien's *The Lord of the Rings* and the environment of Middle-earth by now has also attracted considerable academic analyses in terms of so-called "ecocriticism".[1] The interdisciplinary field of ecocriticism employs approaches of ethical, philosophical, various cultural or natural science theories when analyzing the representation of "nature" and the interrelationship of species and their environments predominantly in canonized and sophisticated, complex literary texts. Authors of fantasy and science fiction literature likewise offer ecocritical stances, hence they steadily become now the focus of ecocritical attention despite the dominance of attention given to non-fantasy literary texts.[2] However, Tolkien as writer of fantasy fiction can indeed be categorized as an ecocritical novelist, whose concern of representing the opposition of a well-balanced environment – the Hobbit world, the Ents' society or Elven woods versus the machine-world of Sauron and his quasi gene-modified organisms, the Orcs – exemplifies how an interaction and interrelationship with an unspoiled environment is essential for a physical as well as a psychological balance. Such a physically and also psychologically sustainable solidity is defined by the theory of ecopsychology that highlights the dependence on a balanced hence healthy environment. This paper draws attention to the relevance of fantasy literature within ecocritical

---

1 The journal *Tolkien Studies* now comprises 12 volumes. Out of the 83 essays published only three explicitly deal with ecological issues (Brisbois, Hirsch, Olson), while most of them refer to linguistics and medieval issues or myths and sagas. Yet several entries in Michael Drout's *J.R.R. Tolkien Encyclopedia* now refer to ecology, environmentalism and nature itself as an "integral dimension" (Curry, "Nature" 463). Interestingly, recent master theses by presumably young scholars connect Tolkien now to ecopsychology (Boulegroune) and concepts of place and solastalgia (Jones) yet do not classify Tolkien within a broader range of ecopsychological conceptions – an essential stance nowadays.
2 Usually ecocritical approaches to literary texts include their own canon of writers and novelists such as American nature writers and recently postcolonial works which all focus on actual or historical events damaging the natural surroundings. For further reading on such examples refer to Hubert Zapf. *Literature as Cultural Ecology: Sustainable Texts*. London: Bloomsbury, 2016. For further readings on ecocriticism and science fiction see Susan Bernardo. *Environments in Science Fiction: Essays on Alternative Spaces*. Jefferson, NC: McFarland, 2014.

studies and particularly understands Tolkien as an ecocritical writer whose works help emphasizing especially ecopsychological approaches.

In this essay the focus lies on harmful ecological transformations that influence environ*mental* health thus constituting an "eco-psychopathology" in Tolkien's *The Lord of the Rings*. Tolkien's mythopoeic quest fantasy demonstrates how ecological disasters affect the single characters physically and psychologically, hence marking an applicability of Albrecht's ecopsychological concept of "solastalgia". This concept of solastalgia stresses the psychological impacts of ecological destruction. Tolkien, however, also allows for a regeneration of nature and thus an ecopsychological healing of what could be termed as a concept of mental sustainability and ecological resilience. The emerging field of medical and environmental humanities explores the challenge and necessity of inter- and transdisciplinary approaches towards literature, medicine and treatment when gaining insight into causes of illnesses and also how reading, as an empathetic act, provides an understanding of those illnesses and how a possible treatment can be obtained or at least acknowledgment be reached. The natural science approach is certainly still necessary, but the combination of literature and the medical humanities is here defined as essential when it comes to fully comprehend underlying mechanisms or behaviors.[3]

2 What is ecopsychology?

Ecopsychology stresses the relationship between humans and non-humans, as well as the natural environment by interrelating ecological, ethical and psychological principles. Ecopsychology as an approach is not primarily connected to psychoanalysis or other distinct schools of psychological theory, although it focuses on social, hence environmental embedment. In the center of interest is the focus on interconnectedness, non-hierarchical thinking in terms of ecocentrism, which understands the equal existence of all life forms, and the importance of a well-functioning, non-toxic environment. A typical proponent of these issues is C.G. Jung who declares that "no man lives within his own

---

[3] This applies to psychological and more culture-bound syndromes as well as neurodegenerative illnesses such as Alzheimer's disease where exactly the comprehension derives not merely from natural science reports but from personal accounts and literary works.

psychic sphere like a snail in its shell, separated from everybody else, but is connected with his fellow-men by his unconscious humanity" (Jung cited in Sabini 14). Jung's collective unconscious, which understands shared values or standards of a society, however, employs an anthropocentric view condemning the machine world of modernism and its forces that separate men from nature and feelings of primordiality. Yet there is no existence without environmental embedment, no being without an ecosystem. Harm to the ecosystem means also harm to the being, hence causing what has been termed "ecosystem distress syndrome" (Rapport and Whitford) that exemplifies physical and psychological sickness connected to a polluted or toxic environment. The "multi-disciplinary appeal" of environmental psychology excludes artificial laboratory situations and focuses on real environments so that various occupational groups such as in the fields of urban sociology, urban or landscape architects, anthropologists and so on also benefit from it (Williams 23).

Within the natural sciences and the fields of psychology and psychiatry, ecological aspects now play a substantial role. In 2012, the National Forum and Research Report of the National Wildlife Federation published a study on "The Psychological Effects of Global Warming on the United States" where they argued mental health care needs to be significantly more supported as ecological disasters and climate change may cause not only physical but also mental and social disorders (ii). The classification of such an ecopsychological stance works usually in connection with real and often world-wide, transnational sets of problems such as global warming, natural disasters, floods, draughts and forced emigration which also cause drastic cultural changes within nations and societies. This report thus emphasizes that not only "traditional" causes of disorders such as trauma, depression, post-traumatic stress, alienation and others need to be in focus but that newer threats such as environmental questions in general must be added.[4] Another report given by the American Psychiatric Association called "Psychology and Global Climate Change" in 2011 already

---

4 "Traditional" causes here refer to personal experiences of loss, assaults, war trauma or recently the stress on terrorism – all aspects which vary in reference books such as the *DSM* (*Diagnostic and Statistical Manual of Mental Disorders*). Recently, ecological threats are considered suggesting that not only diagnoses are adapted and reshaped but that acknowledged causes reflect current trends and cultures in the psychological field.

researches the "psychological dimensions of climate change" (6), thus again adding and acknowledging the ecopsychological dimension.

Psychology as social science and especially its branch of social psychology always figured (human) beings as embedded in their environment intrinsically shaping them externally and internally. Concepts of "self" and "identity" are classified as formed essentially by such embedment, for example the concept of "reflected appraisal" that underlines how multiple factors constitute all social beings (Wallace and Tice). (Eco)psychology functions similarly to environmental social science as Susan M. Koger and Deborah Du Nann Winter exemplify in *The Psychology of Environmental Problems*. Ecological psychology in its inter- and transdisciplinary features includes biology, sociology, and neurosciences as well as individual impacts defining beings in their "biological nature" (Bell, Greene, Fisher and Baum) and stressing the social ecology framework (Ungar, Wheeler). Ecopsychology as "Umweltpsychologie" is now well established in terms of sustainable thinking, ecological consciousness and health or depression and post-trauma because of real experience of ecological disaster and/or the constant repetition of possible ecological threats and risks (Fliegenschnee and Schelekovsky, Hellbrück and Fischer, Hellbrück and Kals, Howard, Hunecke). Consequently, psychological factors are now acknowledged when ecological disasters or risks appear or are being discussed.[5]

The term of "ecopsychology", however, is similarly diverse as is the term of "ecocriticism", roughly referring to the accent of psychological and spiritual issues in relationship to our environment: "Ecopsychology integrates ecology and psychology in responding to both sets of questions" (Davis 50). In Douglas A. Vakoch and Fernango Castrillon's essay collection on relational phenomenology, ethics and psychology, the field of ecopsychology refers not only to the (non)human experience in nature, which might evoke transcendental notions, but also to the interconnection of nature and all life forms as relevant medium of producing a consciousness and a concern for a balanced interconnection. This seems to work in accordance to environmental ethics such as philosopher

---

5 The United Nations agreement of Paris on global warming mentions ecological threats to human societies constantly.

Hans Jonas' idea of stewardship and Tolkien's own ideas of a recovery in the re-balanced landscape world of the Hobbits' Shire.

Not only natural sustainability but also mental health is in the focus of numerous seminal ecocritical works of the twentieth century such as by Theodor Roszak in *The Voice of the Earth* about ecology and "mind and spirit" (202), the emotional philosophy and ecosophy by Deep Ecologist Arne Naess, and the transpersonal ecology by Warwick Fox, all relying on and deriving from classic ecological writers among which Tolkien can surely be placed now. Ecopsychology here is not meant to be exclusive to humans, thus evoking an anthropocentric stance, but its very core implies an ecocentric existence that embraces also mental balances. "Nature" here is equated with an ideal or myth referring to a positive and good (versus evil) existence, all the while causing definitional issues when it comes to explain what kind of "N/nature" seems to be applied. This definition discourse has been addressed by William Cronon in *The Trouble With Wilderness* or Timothy Morton in *Ecology Without Nature* where concepts or ideas of nature and wilderness might only be implicit in the imagination while real wilderness retreats may not exist any more. Philosopher Kate Soper's distinguishes three "nature" concepts: metaphysical (difference and specifity), realist (structures within the physical world), and surface/lay concept as all observable features (Soper 155-6; cited in Buell 143). Another level is necessary here, which is clearly depicted in Tolkien: the ecological unconscious (Roszack) and thus, next to the literary imagination (Buell), the environ*mental* imagination will prove essential. This imagination of a "good nature" is relevant for the success of "nature cure" theories and therapies[6] – however ineffective and even dangerous they can be when it comes to homeopathy, natural or holistic medicine theories and remedies. Nature as concept of the gentle healer may, if it does not cause danger and is used instead of more necessary treatments,

---

6 Relevant for ecopsychological views could be ideas of a physically and consequently mental healthy life within natural settings such as given by political or philosophical thinkers like Mahatma Ghandi in *Nature Cure* (1954) or movements within so-called romantic medicine as a literal antipode to drastic treatments provided by psychiatric or medical therapies. For such a philosophical critique of only seeing physical processes refer to Karl Jasper's *Allgemeine Psychopathologie*. Berlin: Springer, 1973.

work at least within the realm of placebo or transform into greenwashing or ecokitsch.[7] Yet with the implied author Tolkien (cf. Guanio-Uluru 8), the audience encounters nature as a necessary connection for mental healing as only a healed and positively coined nature signifies such new found balance. Tolkien's influence on environmental activity is well documented (Curry, "Environmentalism and Ecocriticism" 165), and his popularity may be especially helpful in promoting ecological issues.

The very recent establishment of the discipline of ecopsychology, stressing the networked self being able to rely on an intact *umwelt* and thus establish mental stability, needs to be connected to not only nonfiction works, documentaries about natural catastrophes or decidedly realist fiction. Tolkien's high-fantasy work can be analyzed in an interdisciplinary way combining ecopsychological standpoints with a stress on how literature enforces empathy. Especially the genre of fantasy, in which elements of the emotional, the supernatural and fantastic transgress bounderies, helps establishing an interrelationship of "nature", environment and the human and non-human self. Ideas of nostalgia and ecology, reconceptualized by Glenn Albrecht with the term of *solastalgia*, shimmer through Tolkien's narration even though Albrecht's term was only established recently. Solastalgia as "nature distress syndrom" refers to the psychological impact of destruction of a formerly intact environment. According to Australian sustainability scholar and environmental philosopher Glenn Albrecht the combination of homesickness and mourning of long lost cultures creates a psychological distress syndrome that needs to be seen as a reaction to environmental destruction. Nostalgia (Gk. *nostos* = "return to home or native land", Gk. *algia* = "pain or sickness", cf. Albrecht 42) pairs up with solace, thus "literally, solastalgia is the pain or sickness caused by the loss or lack of solace and the sense of isolation connected to the present state of one's home and territory" (Albrecht 45). Albrecht's term is suitable because it connects the idea and requirement of an intact environment with notions of nostalgia and psychological distress when an ecosystem is destroyed. Of interest in terms of

---

7 The marketing or "greenwashing" of naturopathy and holistic medicine is clearly constantly stressing the alternative and gentle form of such "natural" procedures even for severe conditions, denying some drastic side effects or sometimes ineffectiveness as placebos. The idea of nature as gentle cure remains strong also in quack medicine as a form of religion while the opportunity of living in a non-polluted environment has not met with that critique of charlatanry (for further information refer to Eric W. Boyle. *Quack Medicine*. Santa Barbara: Praeger, 2013).

solastalgia or eco-nostalgia is the former, more restricted meaning of "ecological", as Patrick Curry points out as "the word was coined in 1866 by the German natural philosopher Ernst Haeckel, who borrowed the Greed word *oikos*, meaning 'home' or 'household', to describe the scientific study of the relationships among organisms and between them and their environment" (Curry, *Ecological Ethics* 4). The environment, the surroundings, the *umwelt*, are the embedment of all organisms, human and non-human alike.

Ecopsychology thus emphasizes that an unhealthy environment can cause not only irritation but serious damage on a physical and mental scale. As Susan Jeffers points out in regard to Tolkien's narratives in *Arda Inhabited*, "the inhabitants of Middle-earth all relate to their places in terms of power relationship" where she distinguishes between "power with" (Ents, Hobbits, Elves), "power from" (Men, Dwarves), and "power over" (Orcs, Sauron, Saruman) (19). Any relationship, however, needs to be functional in the sense that the environment should be intact because a destruction of such functional and fruitful elements would immediately cause considerable impairment and could lead from a formerly singular defect to the defect of the whole ecosystem. American ecologist Aldo Leopold writes in his "Land Ethic" that "a thing is right when it tends to preserve the integrity, stability and beauty of the biotic community. It is wrong when it tends to do otherwise" (224). A possible or actual ecological damage is relevant for issues dealing with environmental activism and socioeconomic environmental justice for indigenous or minority communities as well as the general population (cf. Bullard). It also touches upon questions of globalism and wilderness preservation, destruction of landscapes via oil extraction, fracking and exploitation of resources. As Jung's and Leopold's statements accentuade, it is also the individual being, human or non-human, that will consequently be harmed – again not only physically but also mentally in terms of ecopsychology.

3 Ecopsychology, empathy and literature

Ecopsychological standpoints and the focus on physical and mental wellbeing within intact ecosystems can be understood particularly with the help of storytelling. Literary works are essentially approachable as the inner worlds of characters are presented often in interconnection with their natural surroundings, and these environmental interdependencies are closely networked to possible ecological threats. Long before ecopsychological theories emerged, similar angles can be traced back to romantic literature, dark romanticism and Gothic texts such as Edgar Allen Poe's "The Fall of the House of Usher" (1839) where the natural setting of a decaying house correlates with the inhabitants' loss of their physical health and mental stability. Modernist writers also work with ecopsychological patterns when describing the destruction and fragmentation of lost worlds in which its inhabitants merely experience alienation and deculturalization. Poems by T.S. Eliot or portraits of urban molochs as in Jon Dos Passos *Manhattan Transfer* (1925) enhance such emotions of dissociation and lack of coherence. A harming natural environment represented in naturalist fiction – for example Jack London – certainly causes mental degeneration but also calls for challenges within discourses of masculinity or oppositions between civilization and wilderness. Recent novels that predominantly discuss environmental issues such as climate change, natural catastrophes, toxicity or genetic engineering, also elaborate on the material/physical/psychological interdependence of all organisms within their *umwelt* and illustrate how a violation of an unspoiled environment causes illness and despair. This is also apparent in the *MaddAddam* trilogy (2003-13) by Canadian novelist Margaret Atwood about a postcatastrophic world in which traumatized characters need to survive in a hostile world. In *Lowboy* (2009) by American novelist John Wray the teen protagonist suffers from textbook schizophrenia and literally destabilizes when he experiences a temperature rise because of global warming. Lowboy believes that the ccodisastrous effect of global warming that he feels needs to be cured by lowering his own body temperature. Mental breakdowns because of climate change and the impact of the Anthropocene are evident in novels such as *EisTau* (2011) by German novelist Ilija Trojanow, in which the main character suffers from a mental breakdown, or postapocalyptic graphic novels such as *Sweet Tooth* (2009-13) by Canadian author Jeff Lemire, whose human-animal creatures dwell in a world without ecological balance. In all these examples one could detect exceptional emotional conditions such as depression or post-trauma and add the obligatory prefix "eco", because it is the destruction of the natural world that signifies the mental disintegration.[8]

4 Ecocritical trends: the material and the mental in Tolkien

Long before the establishment of ecocritical thinking (in academia that is) or the concinnity of ecology and health theory within standards of medicine, it was J.R.R. Tolkien whose narratives provided a connecting factor when it came to mediating ecopsychological principles. The approach applied in this paper, however, has rarely been mentioned in works of ecocritical analysis about Tolkien even though in ecocritical works about him the stress on interaction and interdependence of various characters and their belonging within one ecosystem is apparent. Yet such ecocritical approaches focus mainly on the various peoples and species in Middle-earth, such as the Ents, the Elves, the Hobbits, or the evil forces represented by Sauron, Saruman and his Orks. Trends within the field of ecocritical approaches stress the now prominent materialist turn within ecocriticism,[9] which has recently been well established by Serenella Iovino and Serpil Oppermann (cf. *Materialism* 2014) amongst others. This material turn underscores the relevance of matter and material such as "rain" or "water" or uses concepts like "porosity" (Iovino on Italian cities, cf. *Materialism*) and again highlights the smaller than atomic interconnection and transgressional material world of one environment. Yet even the material turn in ecocriticism as a study on matter and environmental issues does not deny the mental or psychological aspect needed to communicate how in the anthropocentric age ecological destruction or transformation impinges on mental systems. Affect theory and empathy within ecological film studies already emphasize mental conditions more clearly, as Alexa Weik von Mossner's studies prove.

---

8 Drastic actual examples of loss of solace and culture connected to a certain land are the physical and psychological effects on the displaced inhabitants of the Bikini Atoll in the Marshall Islands after the nuclear testing program by the United States from 1946. For further information see Jack Niedenthal. "A History of the People of Bikini Following Nuclear Weapons Testing in the Marshall Islands: With Recollections and Views of Elders of Bikini Atoll." *Health Physics* 73.1 (1998): 28-36. The topic of the impact of these tests was presented by Mita Banerjee at a conference at Augsburg University, showing how a destroyed environment influences the culture of a people.

9 For the various approaches the umbrella term of ecocriticism now offers see Axel Goodbody and Kate Rigby, eds. *Ecocritical Theory: New European Approaches*. London: University of Virginia Press, 2011.

The ecopsychological framework seeks to point out how environmental changes and ecological damage not only cause actual physical damage or material changes within a toxic world. It also underlines how especially a destruction of the environment evokes a psychological transformation that may transgress into an ecotrauma when real or imagined disasters reiterate a doom of a formerly functioning ecosystem. The imagination of a better, or ecologically balanced world – a Middle-earth recovery literally present in the final chapter in *The Lord of the Rings* – seems to be connected to a possible healing of the (Middle-)earth as well as the psyche of the protagonists, although some will not recover completely within their former environment.

What Tolkien's fantastic journey suggests in terms of empathetic ecological consciousness is a shift of perception evoking a "capacity for subverting human-centric perceptions of signs by substituting nature-centric perceptions" (Sacknoff 6) in order to make non-human agencies (landscapes, flora, fauna, species) and their suffering accessible. In alignment with Bentham's dictum that animals can suffer, Tolkien illustrates that every thing and being can suffer – by giving them a voice (Bentham 236). In *Becoming Animal*, American ecocritic David Abram generates an "earthly cosmology" of interconnection of the human/non-human that can be applied to Tolkien as well, revealing a Middle-earth cosmology, although not all species in *The Lord of the Rings* necessarily mingle but do exist separately and all within one networked world. It is the ability of fantasy literature with its transgression of real or realistic boundaries to form an acknowledgement of mechanisms beyond the material and hence create empathy for the seemingly Other.[10]

Within Tolkien's "nature" all beings differentiate, still closely connected to and dependent on their habitats; yet all share a larger ecosystem and consequently suffer when egoist greed brings about damage. As Michael Brisbois rightly points out, "the representation of nature in *The Lord of the Rings* is at once comforting in its familiarity and fantastic in its personifications" (197), showing that – apart from the reader's empathy towards the familiar – landscapes, mountains, lakes, and forests are likewise "persons" or emotional

---

10 On literature and empathy see Suzanne Keen's *Empathy and the Novel*. Oxford: Oxford University Press, 2010.

entities that may suffer and, with Tolkien's fairy tale closure, may also recover. This personification beyond Leopold's land ecosystem ethics highlights an ecocritical approach even more, adding a component of suffering, trauma, emotion, affect and (eco)psychopathology of all things/entities/organisms with the ability to access resilience.[11]

5 Ecopsychology and fantasy literature

Noteworthy is that ecopsychological or ecocritical approaches are not mainly tied to fictional works but prominently so to a wider range of non-fiction nature writers such as Henry David Thoreau or Ralph Waldo Emerson as well as travel scripts and natural history texts whose realist approach stresses their direct applicability, although traditional romantic literary texts have always functioned as counterworlds to ecological destruction or modernity and industrialization. This practicality is what makes the ecopsychological field so convincing and communicable, via personal experience, for example. What is more, its approach now seems to be established within psychological or psychiatric theories despite their partly contested grounds or some more controversial diagnoses (cf. McHugh, Szasz). Tolkien's novels and texts, however, belong to the manifold genre of fantasy literature, seemingly the opposite of realism or naturalism even in the literary sphere due to its allegedly superficial lack of mimetic principles and made-up universes. Tolkien famously explained that Middle-earth resembles spatial and actual reality even though its setting is represented within the mythopoeic fantasy literature genre:

> I am historically minded. Middle-earth is not an imaginary world. The name is the modern form (appearing in the 13th century and still in use) of *midden-erd* > *middel-erd*, an ancient name for the *oikoumenē*, the abiding place of Men, the objectively real world, in use specifically opposed to imaginary worlds (as Fairyland) or unseen worlds (as Heaven or Hell). (*L* 183)

In Tolkien's narratives, detectable characteristics of realism such as reflections on historical references, his condemnation of deforestation, a critique of modernity and industrial progress, are entangled with elements of quest fantasy

---

11 Leopold's land ethic already includes all bioforms. See Warwick Fox. *A Theory of General Ethics*. Cambridge, MA: MIT Press, 2006. 40.

mythology. It may not be crucial which approach – realism or fantasy – would fit ecocritical or ecopsychological issues best. Both aspects work well together when exemplifying the ecological distress of non-human and human agency. Chris Barratta's edited essay collection on *Environmentalism and the Realm of Science Fiction and Fantasy Literature* underlines how environmental thought and non-fiction genres even underline the ecological approach. Tolkien's *The Lord of the Rings* is defined as the prototypical example of fantasy literature in general due to its well-known pop-cultural influence (cf. Guanio-Uluru 12) yet it also makes use of real threats to natural worlds such as war, decay, destruction and exploitation. As such, Middle-earth is indeed "the canvas onto which Tolkien paints the ongoing issues and problems that the world continues to face" (Barratta, "No name" 32) and can be used as brilliant example of how to evoke empathy with the ecological Other.

This is also presented by Lykke Guanio-Uluru in her study on *Ethics and Form in Fantasy Literature* by combining an Aristotelian view on poetics and ethics with the moral philosophy of Martha Nussbaum, who equally stresses the ability of literary narrative to offer alternative views (10). Guiano-Uluru adds literary theories of the implied narrator (Wayne Booth) and classifies Tolkien's *The Lord of the Rings* as a quest fantasy which captures the reader's imagination and affect in order to impart ecological issues. Helpful is Guanio-Uluru's approach when she eludicates that "fantasy literature seems to tap into such 'obscure' psychological patterns and movements of will in ways that many readers find intuitively meaningful" (17). Additionally, "fantasy can reflect the numinous as well as aid in a revisioning of our normative perception of the natural world" (Brawley 95), and surely the painstakingly detailed descriptions in *The Lord of the Rings* provide a "startling sensation of primary reality" (cf. Jeffers 1, quoting Patrick Curry, *Defending Middle-earth* 49).

6 The ecological Tolkien

Until today the established mainstream ecocriticism in academia still tends to reject a thorough analysis of Tolkien's literary work (Siewer), despite the potential anti-modernism of his literary escapist writing style[12] and reflection of modernist upheaval. Alfred K. Siewer's detection of the academic lack of "a sustained and systematic way in mainstream discussion within the discipline of ecocriticism or environmental literary studies" concerning the acknowledgement of the ecocritical Tolkien still is true (166). This counteracts Tolkien's own stance and his influence on the fantasy genre in literature and film, for example *Avatar*, or even the Green movement (cf. Curry *Defending Middle-earth*). All mentioned studies on Tolkien as ecological writer also prove that the view on Tolkien as environmentalist is established. Although Tolkien's unique and unified ecosystem derives from a song that gave birth to the world (*Silmarillion*), the characters in *The Lord of the Rings* need their individual environments that may somehow coexist but also exist separately. The danger to all things, beings and coexisting elements is symbolized by the Ring and the egoistical greed it evokes: dominion and thus total destruction of this coexistence.

Ecocriticsm, when first applied in earlier Tolkien studies, mostly focused on the natural setting of the geography and geology of Middle-earth (Juhren) and compared Tolkien's occupation with and use of nature (Garcia de la Puerta), or analyzed single characters in terms of their relationship with nature, for example Tom Bombadil (Hargrove). The publications on the nature/character interrelationship, the personalized landscapes and trees, the elements and so on are numerous but have to my knowledge never been connected to ecopsychology. The popularity of Tolkien's *The Lord of the Rings* may have helped to create an awareness of ecological embedment and physiological and psychological health – at least its popcultural influences helped fostering ecological standpoints. Patrick Curry, whose seminal works on Tolkien's environmentalism demonstrated how relevant these issues are for Tolkien's narratives, can be included in more ecopsychological readings. Especially his essay "Less Noise and More Green" works within these terms when he mentions the "profound

---

[12] On the surface, Tolkien's narrative technique might seem to be devoid of modernist fragmentary experimental styles when compared to "proper" modernist writers like Čapek, Brecht, Eliot, Pound, Stein or Faulkner. But when various sections of *The Lord of the Rings* are compared the diversity of language and style becomes noticeable: dialogic segments are followed by songs, poems, and outstandingly detailed descriptions of traumatic war scenes before elevating nature settings are pictured. Those shifts in narrative styles would clearly mark Tolkien also as a modernist writer, which altogether cannot be described as a homogenous group anyway. Tolkien's success and popularity have added to his unintelligible exclusion from a more elitist writing canon (see Jeffers 123).

feeling" towards nature (21) that is frequently accentuated in *The Lord of the Rings*. Curry sees that "various races of people are rooted in, and unimaginable (both to themselves and us) without, their natural context" (Curry, "Less Noise" 21). Similarly, Brawley observes that the "deeply sensual appreciation of this world" (Brawley 204) seems essential for an understanding of the social network theory that constitutes ecopsychology and the acknowledgment of a biotic communitarianism meaning a coexistence of individuals in a shared ecosystem.

The complex structure of the novel *The Lord of the Rings* unravels a multifaceted network of various ecologies, not only of the natural environments but of mythologies, storytelling, literary genres, poetry, songs, insertions, foreshadowing and flashbacks, linguistic changes, shifts of perspective of non-human/human species, and elements of myth and legends. Hence, as an ecocritical approach would indicate, it is also the narratology of *The Lord of the Rings* that functions already within the ecocritical dictum of "everything is connected to everything else" (cf. Commoner), the first law of ecology as well as within the third law stating that "nature knows best" (cf. Commoner) as Tolkien shows the resurrection of a healed nature. Matter in *The Lord of the Rings* is inspirited through animism like the palantíri, the Seeing Stones. It has been widely illustrated by Curry, Campell, Simonson and others that Tolkien's appliance of a land ethics filters also through the treatment of landscapes as a character itself with feelings and reactions to destruction and changes (through humans and Sauron) thus applying Aldo Leopold's "land ethic" and an intrinsic value as well as agency and subjectivity to the different areas in Middle-earth such as the Shire, various woods, mountains, rivers and the sea (cf. Curry, "Nature" 453-54, Campbell 3, Simonson et al.). According to Liam Campbell, "[n]ature, the ennoblement of the non-human, and environmental concerns lie just below the surface of Tolkien's narratives", and she ascribes a visionary ecologist view to Tolkien (3). In Tolkien's seminal essay "On Fairy-Stories", he clearly marks the world of fantasy fiction – as he understands it – as ecologically intertwined and interconnected, thus stressing the network of beings, plants, and all things:

> Faerie contains many things besides elves and fays, and besides dwarfs, witches, trolls, giants, or dragons: it holds the seas, the sun, the moon, the sky; and the earth, and all things that are in it: tree and bird, water and stone, wine and bread, and ourselves, mortal men, when we are enchanted. (OFS 5)

Where such a coexistence of all organisms and matters is endangered by egoist tendencies (the poisoning Ring), Tolkien's seemingly pastoral world almost falls apart. "The heart of Faërie", as Tolkien mentions, is "the desire of men to hold communion with other living things" (OFS 15), and those living things may be, according to nature-myths, sagas, epics, legends, folk-tales, and *Märchen*, personified (OFS 23). His romantic nature balance is not absolute because it almost shatters, and through this process of endangerment the concept of nostalgia – longing for the ancient balance of a lost place and culture – and the ecopsychological solastalgia as "ecosystem distress syndrome" manifests. Literally, Frodo, when wearing the Ring, mentally enters another world where he is lost and isolated. The Ring itself is signifier of evil, greed, interruption and disturbance.[13] Sméagol/Gollum as the classic Jekyll/Hyde dual character demonstrates the condition of being torn between good/evil as he transforms both physically and psychologically. Sméagol/Gollum switches from one personality state to another and refers to himself/selves in the plural form (*LotR* 827), and the film adaptation by Peter Jackson provides a now classic visualization of the multiple personality or pop-culturalized dissociative identity/ies. The Ring as instrument to dominate Middle-earth is mere poison, a toxic element that eradicates the pastoral or the near wilderness spaces.

Albrecht's solastalgia and his reference to Casey's "place pathology" (Albrecht 43) connects to Fraser Harrison's "radical nostalgia" in Tolkien's *The Lord of the Rings*, where characters and landscapes alike literally fight the traumatic experience of war and machine-worlds. This radical nostalgia by Harrison as a concept of "homesickness" is later discussed by Curry (Curry, *Defending Middle-earth* 11). The connection to war and shell-shock experience in addition to longing for a lost home or "Heimat" is comprised within the notion of "nostalgia" as war-induced illness and its psychological consequences which Tolkien makes clearly apparent (cf. Lynch). Ecocritical approaches to Tolkien acknowledge the pastoral idyll in *The Lord of the Rings*, also noticeable in Peter Jackson's film adaptations; for one thing, they analyze Gandalfian stewardship, agriculture, horticulture and feraculture as well as Mordor's evil landscapes, environmentalism, transcendentalism and action (cf. Dickerson and Evans).

---

13 For a reference on the good/evil divide see W.H. Auden. "Good and Evil in The Lord of the Rings." *Tolkien Journal* 3.1 (#7) (1967): 5-8.

Other studies refer to the teaching environmentalism or concepts of the pastoral and ideas of sustainability by using Tolkien (Donovan 108, 157, 183). And further essays classify the communal nature of Ents, Elves, Hobbits, Men and Dwarves (Jeffers) or present Tolkien as tree lover and ecocentric thinker (Flieger). Recent publications concentrate fully on the representation of nature and ecology in Tolkien's work (Campbell, Curry *Deep Roots*, Simonson) with further elaboration on Sylvan biocentrism, the element of water, object-oriented ontology, cultural memory, postcolonialism (cf. Simonson) or environmental personae (Campbell). The well-known "eco-catastrophic magic" of Sauron opposes the quasi-utopia of Lothlórien (Ertsgaard 207), while the transcendental sublimity of Ents and Entwives is highlighted (Olson), as they are seen most prominently as symbols of ecological standards (Cohen). The Ents are classified as interacting and existing as a "community in their own right" (Denekamp 3).

7 Green "eucatastrophe" and mental recovery

Acknowledging environmental impacts on physical and psychological health does not necessarily mean only classifying negative environmental effects as individual mental disorders, but also showing how societal issues involve questions of ecologically protective measures. Tolkien's communitarian views on society with its individuals who share a community, its civil culture and citizens, are most evident in the representation of the Shire as he stresses this connection of individual and society. This still works despite clear stances of royal exceptionalism, fixed hierarchy and racial inclinations as "Tolkien's paternalism if not patriarchy is unmissable" (Curry, *Deep Roots* 14). The return to the first destroyed Shire exemplifies Tolkien's need for a clear recovery, and "its seeming finality is revitalized by the concluding chapters that turn away from the vast scope and the mythic dimension of the eucatastrophe towards more personal, domestic, and quotidian issues" (Hirsch 77). In accordance to Flieger's idea of nature/culture combination that sustains (Flieger "Matter"), in the end the audience encounters a culture landscape rather than unspoiled wilderness that the Ents already mourn. The cultivated re-established Shire, however, signifies a nature under control, although it resembles a connection to regenerated trees such as the White Tree of Gondor that can flourish again. This middle ground between wilderness and destruction has been read as Christian nature settings thus referring to Tolkien's subliminal Christian worldview in *The Lord of the Rings* and its roots in a "personalized and spiritually energized nature" (Siewers 167) that is still connected to ancient mythologies and story-telling. Relevant for an ecopsychological view is that the outside regenerative forces symbolize or correspond to the internal recovery. Frodo's deep traumatization, however, needs another level of nature balance, because he eventually needs to leave for the literally Undying lands and its mythological landscapes – again mental stability is connected to unspoiled surroundings.

Suffering and sadness overshadow both characters and landscapes – mountains, waters, and trees alike. Through this emotional reaction towards the evil destruction of greed and megalomania all entities do not only share a "transcorporeality" (Alaimo) but a condition that can be called a trans*psycho*reality. Tolkien, however, grants the world recovery and resilience, hence emphasizing prototypical ecological ethics. In the section "Recovery, Escape, Consolation", he writes

> And actually fairy-stories deal largely, or (the better ones) mainly, with simple or fundamental things, untouched by Fantasy, but these simplicities are made all the more luminous by their setting. For the story-maker who allows himself to be "free with" Nature can be her lover not her slave. It was in fairy-stories that I first divined the potency of the words, and the wonder of the things, such as stone, and wood, and iron; tree and grass; house and fire; bread and wine. (OFS 59)

Counteracting a hopeless, fatalist worldview, Tolkien's work within the genre of fairy-tales and fantasy does not merely provide a "fugitive spirit" (OFS 67) or escapist tendencies but contains references to the "real" world. In Tolkien's words, its "Morlockian horror of factories" (64) prevents any "oasis of sanity" (62). Tolkien's acknowledgement of all elements and species in Middle-earth,[14] a certain stance of deep ecology one could affirm, also forms a coalition against evil and thus offers the ability to self-regulating forces as the "desire to converse with other living things" to be powerful. The happy ending or "joy" of over-

---

14 To be precise, Tolkien does not acknowledge the darker forces Sauron is controlling. Those foreign species are also not really part of the ecosystem, they solemnly signify danger and pollution. This endangerment of a formerly functioning ecosystem is apparent in the chapters "The Road to Isengard" where Saruman creates and controls the Orcs and "The Scouring of the Shire" where Saruman attempts to exploit the land of the Hobbits.

coming traumatic adventures or various crises expresses the human desire for a positive closure within the fairy story as opposed to drama, something for which Tolkien coined the term "eucatastrophe". While he never denies the "existence of dyscatastrophe" (OFS 68) within the fairy tale, the ability of recovery and consolation – in *The Lord of the Rings* all working within ecopsychological frameworks and sustainable recovery of the environment – expresses Tolkien's trust in faith i.e. Christian belief in re-establishing harmony and balance as well as the intrinsic power of the natural world.

In the penultimate chapter of the *The Lord of the Rings*, "The Grey Havens", the intersubjective hence psychologically relational grief is perspicuous when both trees and Sam, whom the reader can identify with, are affected:

> The trees were the worst loss and damage, for at Sharkey's bidding they had been cut down recklessly far and wide over the Shire; and Sam grieved over this more than anything else. For one thing, this hurt would take long to heal, and only his great-grandchildren, he thought, would see the Shire as it ought to be. (*LotR* 1338)

Despite the destruction, resilience remains possible and relevant. A magic grey dust distributed by Galdadriel, plain but effective, will heal the places "where specially beautiful and beloved trees had been destroyed" reconnecting the post-war world to ancient strength (*LotR* 1338). The foreshadowing of the trees growing out of this earth illustrates a recovery in fast motion:

> Spring surpassed his wildest hopes. His trees began to sprout and grow, as if time was in a hurry and wished to make one year do for twenty...In after years, as it grew in grace and beauty, it was known far and wide and people would come long journeys to see it. (*LotR* 1339)

Eventually, Tolkien's optimism shines through the description of the healing landscape which eventually enjoys "wonderful sunshine and delicious rain" with "an air of richness and growth, and a gleam of beauty beyond all mortal summers that flicker and pass upon this Middle-earth" (*LotR* 1339). Tolkien's future Hobbits have "golden hair" and fair skin and are, again in accordance with the healed land, never ill – "everyone was pleased" (*LotR* 1339) – with a sustainable future for generations to come (*LotR* 1340). While Sam, Merry and Pippin are "full of merriment than ever before" (*LotR* 1341), Frodo's injury ("It is gone forever, and now all is dark and empty", *LotR* 1340) forces him to the Undying Lands. The mood of the world ("in the autumn there appeared a shadow of old troubles", *LotR* 1342) functions to enhance the inner landscapes of the characters. Almost similar to Sméagol/Gollum and his inner duality, Frodo tells Sam not to not be "torn in two" but to "be one and whole" in the new Shire (*LotR* 1347).

Again, memory, landscape and life are connected, in accordance with the Elves who remember as the trees remember (*LotR* 1347). The film audience of Jackson's adaptations will depart with the companions when the film provides the most ecopsychological pivotal pastoral: the sunset in the Grey Havens. Frodo's last peace is comprehensible, when in his dreams he pictures "white shores and beyond them a far green country under a swift sunrise" (*LotR* 1348), while comfort for the other companions is provided by their families.

The readers of Tolkien's novel, however, encounter another fight for regaining the destroyed Shire to transform this capitalist Saruman wasteland back into an idyllic landscape. Again, the interconnection of the devastated state of the personified landscapes and the mental state of the characters is implied, for example, when "in that lost land" also "their heart sank" (*LotR* 391) – this marks the suffering of all subjects, emphasizes their subjectivity, and accentuates the individual human or non-human agency within the concept of nature distress syndrome. Tolkien does not only refer to the individual distress of his characters but especially highlights the interrelationship and interdependencies.

The sickness that greed and egotism bring is closely related to destruction and ecocide. When Sam and Frodo enter Mordor, they experience a land devoid of vitality causing them to feel pain: "a land defiled, diseased beyond all healing – unless the Great Sea should enter in and wash it with oblivion. 'I feel sick,' said Sam. Frodo did not speak" (*LotR* 825). In the destroyed Shire, where Saruman attempts to install a monopolistic capitalism by exploiting both the Hobbits and the land, the characterization of the later emphasizes that "the land looked rather sad and forlorn" and therefore diseased (*LotR* 1309). Land and characters alike are "forlorn": "the voice of a forlorn and weary hobbit" (*LotR* 1188). The disease-related words Tolkien uses are striking when describing the Dead Marshes ("dreadful") and particularly Mordor: "dreadful", "loathsome", "gasping", "choked", "sickly", "fire-blasted", "poison-stained", "obscene", "desolated", "dark", "defiled" (cf. Dickerson and Evans 186). Because the reader identifies with the Hobbits the ecophobia or nature distress syndrome becomes explicit. To underline a depressive mood, Tolkien's environment is described as hostile – "before them the mountain frowned" (*LotR* 392), and "ominous water" (*LotR* 393).

Some of the most analyzed characters in the novel are the Ents (cf. Olsen). The loss of their culture and connectedness to unspoiled wilderness is linked to the Entwives and their cultivation of the landscape, but mainly due to severe damage of their old forest. I would argue that the Ents as solastalgian characters hence offer the deepest insight into a violated psyche due to the ecological disaster they have been experiencing. Especially Treebeard's songs about all "living creatures" (*LotR* 604) show the interconnection of words, meaning and the world as a balanced organism – and how destruction and deforestation affect everything: "Many of those trees were my friends, creatures I had known for nut and acorn; many had voices of their own that are lost forever now" (*LotR* 617). Tolkien's reference to destroyed landscapes under dark shadows and bad memories signify Treebeard's solastalgia (*LotR* 605). Treebeard's physical and psychological well-being is dependent on his relationship with the land ("roots are long", *LotR* 612) and endangered by Saruman's "mind of metal and wheels [while] he does not care for growing things" (*LotR* 616). The destruction of the forest, begun by evil spirits, even infects birds to become greedy and start their own destruction of the woods (*LotR* 630). The mention of birds – seemingly in accordance with a balanced forest – as threats to the trees ("unfriendly and greedy and tore at the trees", *LotR* 631) underlines the toxic forces of Saruman's destructive powers. In a world out of balance, no single species is immune.

As Jones describes, the various species in *The Lord of the Rings* are strongly linked to distinct places, and a loss of these places will cause solastalgia as solace and physical but also psychological well-being is lost. Tom Bombardil is "shepherding his own place" (Jones 14). The tree-like Ents and the conscious trees called Huorns belong to and literally are Fangorn Forest. Saruman's destruction of the forest will foster a solastalgian mourning as Isengard and Orthanc will destroy the balance Ents, Huorns and trees depend on. The passages in which Treebeard voices his realization of the future loss of intact forests suggests that a destruction of the land via deforestation will also eliminate his very identity.

This loss makes even him angry and puts him into a mood of war: "We go to war!/To land of gloom with tramp of doom" (*LotR* 632).

Eventually, Tolkien's tale allows for recovery. Isengard will be renamed into the Treegarth of Orthanc as a "garden filled with orchards and trees" with a lake of "clear water, and out of it the Tower of Orthanc rose still" (*LotR* 1281). Later, parts of the Shire will be restored and also renamed as if the memory of the landscape and its traumatization could thus be eliminated (*LotR* 1338). A return to stewardship and intact landscapes opposes Nordic myths of the apocalypse and the Ragnarök although Tolkien was influenced by Nordic sagas and the *Eddas* as well as Christian motives (cf. Chance 184). Tolkien's *Sillmarillion* has been compared to Nordic sagas while *The Hobbit* and *The Lord of the Rings* are connected to Christianity, yet Tolkien's concept of eucatastrophe succeeds (Vos 178).

Nature or the natural species display a quality of being acting entities, and as dynamic subjects they can actively seek revenge. Brisbois differentiates between a passive (essential, ambient) and an active (independent, wrathful) nature (203, quoted in Jones 18), thus signifying how Tolkien's depiction of nature not merely functions within romantic tropes or the sublime per se, but is given agency and, literally, a voice. Tolkien's "pastoral fantasy nostalgia" (Curry, "Less Noise" 20), in which Harrison's radical nostalgia functions as the prerequisite for a restoration of the Shire, is seen as "resacralisation of life" (Curry, "Less Noise" 40). With the means of the principles of subsidiarity and the Hobbit tradition of the "friendship with the earth" (*LotR* 2) a new order and idyll after the ecocide can be rebuilt. This renewal – symbolized by the new growing trees and the renaming of places – will foster life, new memories and attachment to the environment and create new myths: "The Third Age of the world is ended, and the new age is begun" (*LotR* 1272).

This interdependence of place and individuals in *The Lord of the Rings* is always firmly connected to intact memory power that all individuals share alike, for example Treebeard who is "filled up with ages of memory and long, slow, steady thinking" (*LotR* 603). Existence and identity are not possible without deep association to current or future places and their integrity and preservation. No individual – not even the evil forces of Saruman or Sauron – can exist without an "intact" environment that provides what they need. The evil power of the Ring and its radiating forces change an ecocentrically embedded self into an egocentric entity affecting characters such as Frodo, Sméagol/Gollum, Wormtongue, and others in various ways.

Eventually, Gandalf's story about Gollum, who has transformed into Sméagol, insinuates a minimal but relevant chance for recovery, which is again linked to the ecological. Gandalf's story is connected to Gollum as the most sorrowful figure, whose addiction to the Ring deprives him of any kind of autarkic subjectivity but still grants him a relationship with natural elements:

> Even Gollum was not wholly ruined. He had proved tougher than even one of the Wise would have guessed – as a hobbit might. There was a little corner of his mind that was still his own, and light came through it, as through a chink in the dark: light out of the past. It was actually pleasant, I think, to hear a kindly voice again, bringing up memories of wind, and trees, and sun on the grass, and such forgotten things. (*LotR* 72)

The healing or recovery of both characters in conjunction with nature and a restored environment is a refuge Tolkien in his fairy tale narrative grants, at least partially. Frodo's declaration that his wounds are of that kind "that cannot be wholly cured" makes clear that they are not only wounds of the inner but also of all natural landscapes (*LotR* 1295). Tolkien's constant emphasis of the interrelationship of physical and psychological states on the one hand and environmental states on the other hand offers insights into ecopsychological concepts: by showing how all characters can only obtain wholeness, intactness and integrity, when they are able to dwell in an intact ecosystem.

8 Conclusion

This essay has employed an ecocritical approach towards J.R.R. Tolkien's seminal epic *The Lord of the Rings* by applying an interdisciplinary angle of ecopsychology that understands the relevance of environ*mental* well-being based on an embedment of individuals in undamaged ecological surroundings. Tolkien's fantasy tale and the therein described environment of Middle-earth, as shown, has attracted ecocritical scholars' attention. Hence, Tolkien is clearly categorized as an ecocritical novelist whose concern of representing the opposition of a well-balanced environment of the Hobbit world and the Ent society versus the machine-world of Sauron exemplifies how an interaction and interrelationship with an unspoiled environment seems necessary for physical as well as psychological balance.

I have proposed that the very recent establishment of the discipline of ecopsychology, which particularly lays emphasis on the networked self as being able to rely on an intact *umwelt* and thus establish mental and also physical stability, needs to be connected not only to nonfiction works, documentaries about natural catastrophes or decidedly realist fiction. In addition to realist literary texts, it is the fantasy genre that can establish another innovative view on interrelationships of "nature", environment, the human and the non-human agencies due to the ability of the fantasy genre to transgress boundaries and offer creative story worlds. Particularly Tolkien's high-fantasy work enhances interdisciplinary approaches that combine ecopsychological standpoints and ecocriticism with literary texts as storytelling enforces empathy with the (ecological) Other. Aspects of nostalgia, ecotrauma and solastalgia shimmer through Tolkien,'s narratives, and such aspects employ recent concepts of ecology, ecocriticism and environmental standpoints. The necessity of interdisciplinary approaches towards literature, psychology, psychopathology and studies on empathy is relevant within the newly established fields of medical and environmental humanities. Nonfiction studies may undoubtedly employ relevant data. Yet literary works as well as highly popularized narratives such as Tolkien's tales function as transmitters for understanding the complex interrelationship between ecological wholeness and physical and psychological well-being.

Nature destruction and recovery is an ever-recurring phenomenon of our day. The PBS documentary film *Radioactive Wolves* (2011) highlighted how the natural world around the Chernobyl nuclear power plant has recovered in an unbelievably sustainable and resilient way. The area, however, remains toxic for humans – Chernobyl as functioning community for humans will remain only a solastalgian memory. Nature recovery is also present on the Marshall Islands where the nuclear tests have polluted the landscape for humans but not for flora and fauna.[15] Fictional texts and particular the fantasy genre may reestablish seemingly lost unspoiled ecosystems. In Tolkien's world, the physical as well as the mental recovery within his concept of eucatastrophe is relevant. In Tolkien's narratives a resacralisation of the environment remains an option for all beings. Despite fairy tale enchantments, the recovery of the shared ecosystem is gained through constructive stewardship. Such a commitment to regain a balanced environment marks the quest fantasy also as ecological warning that all beings need a non-toxic unspoiled environment in order obtain physical and also mental health, sustainability and resilience.

About the Author

HEIKE SCHWARZ is a postdoctoral researcher in the Department for American Studies (Amerikanistik) and an adjunct professor at the Department of Comparative Studies at Augsburg University, Germany. She earned her Ph.D. in American Studies in 2013 with her monograph *Beware of the Other Side(s): Multiple Personality Disorder and Dissociative Identity Disorder in American Fiction* (2013 transcript, American Culture Studies Series). She has published on psychopathology and psychological proto- and stereotypes in literature and film. Her research interests focus on issues of mental health and mental illness represented in literature and film. Her studies analyze interdisciplinary fields of literature, psychiatry and medical humanities, cultural psychiatry, history of madness and psychiatry, trauma studies, ecocriticism and ecopsychology. She is currently editing a collection of essays on states of mental transgression in international fiction and film with the volume *Madness in the Woods* (forthcoming; Lexington, Ecopsychological Research) and is also working on her new research project on neuro-degenerative diseases such as Alzheimer's disease and its depiction in literature and film.

Homepage: https://www.philhist.uni-augsburg.de/lehrstuehle/anglistik/amerikanistik/mitarbeiter/schwarz/

---

15 For further information see Zoe T. Richards. "Bikini Atoll coral biodiversity resilience five decades after nuclear testing." *Marine Pollution Bulletin* 55.3 (2008): 503-15.

List of Abbreviations

L   CARPENTER, Humphrey, ed. with the assistance of Christopher Tolkien. *The Letters of J.R.R. Tolkien.* London: George Allen & Unwin, 1981. Reprinted Boston: Houghton Mifflin, 2000.

LotR   TOLKIEN, John Ronald Reuel. *The Lord of the Rings.* London: HarperCollins, 2007.

OFS   TOLKIEN, J.R.R. "On Fairy-Stories." *The Tolkien Reader.* New York: Ballantine Books, 1966. 3-84.

Bibliography

ABRAM, David. *Becoming Animal.* New York: Vintage, 2011.

ALBRECHT, Glenn. "Solastalgia: A New Concept in Health and Identity." *PAN* 3 (2005): 41-55.

ALAIMO, Stacy. *Bodily Nature: Science, Environment, and the Material Self.* Bloomington IN: Indiana University Press, 2011.

BARRATTA, Chris, ed. *Environmentalism in the Realm of Science Fiction and Fantasy Literature.* Newcastle: Cambridge Scholars Publishing, 2012.

———. "'No name, no business, no Precious, nothing. Only empty, only hungry': Gollum as Industrial Casualty." *Environmentalism in the Realm of Science Fiction and Fantasy Literature.* Ed. Chris Barratta. Newcastle: Cambridge Scholars Publishing, 2012. 32-46.

BELL, Paul A., Thomas C. GREENE, Jeffrey D. FISHER, and Andrew BAUM, eds. *Environmental Psychology.* Fort Worth: Harcourt College Publishers, 2005.

BENTHAM, Jeremy. *An Introduction to the Principles or Morals and Legislation.* Oxford: Clarendon Press, 1789.

BOULEGROUNE, Adel. *An Ecocritical Perspective of Medieval Myth and Fantasy in J.R.R. Tolkien The Lord of the Rings.* MA Thesis. Mohamed Kheider University-Biskra. 2015. Web. 3 Sep. 2016.

BRAWLEY, Chris. *Nature and the Numinous in Mythopoetic Fantasy Literature.* Jefferson, NC: McFarland, 2014.

BRISBOIS, M. J. "Tolkien's Imaginary Nature: An Analysis of the Structure of Middle-earth." *Tolkien Studies* 2 (2005): 197-216.

BUELL, Lawrence. *The Future of Environmental Criticism: Environmental Crisis and Literary Imagination.* Malden, MA: Blackwell, 2005.

BULLARD, Robert D. "Environmental Justice For All." *Environmental Ethics: The Big Questions*. Malden, MA: Blackwell, 2010. 491-501.

CAMPBELL, Liam. *The Ecological Augury in the Works of JRR Tolkien*. Zurich and Jena: Walking Tree Publishers, 2011.

CARPENTER, Humphrey, ed. with the assistance of Christopher TOLKIEN. *The Letters of J.R.R. Tolkien*. London: George Allen & Unwin, 1981. Reprinted Boston: Houghton Mifflin, 2000.

CHANCE, Jane, ed. *Tolkien and the Invention of Myth*. Lexington KT: Kentucky University Press, 2004.

COHEN, Cynthia. "The Unique Representation of Trees in *The Lord of the Rings*." *Tolkien Studies* 6 (2009): 91-125.

COMMONER, Barry. *The Closing Circle: Nature, Man, and Technology*. New York: Random House, 1971.

CURRY, Patrick. *Defending Middle-earth: Tolkien Myth and Modernity*. London: HarperCollins, 1998.

Ecological Ethics. Cambridge: Polity, 2006.

"Environmentalism and Ecocriticism." *The J.R.R. Tolkien Encyclopedia*. Ed. Michael D.C. Drout. New York: Routledge, 2006. 165.

"Nature." *The J.R.R. Tolkien Encyclopedia*. Ed. Michael D.C. Drout. New York: Routledge, 2006. 453-4.

Deep Roots in a Time of Frost. Cormarë Series 33. Zurich and Jena: Walking Tree Publishers, 2014.

"'Less Noise and More Green': Tolkien's Ideology for England." *Deep Roots in a Time of Frost*. Cormarë Series 33. Zurich and Jena: Walking Tree Publishers, 2014. 11-42.

DAVIS, John. "Diamond in the Rough: An Exploration of Aliveness and Transformation in Wilderness." *Ecopsychology, Phenomenology, and the Environment*. Eds. Douglas A. Vakoch and Fernando Catrillón. New York: Springer, 2014. 47-64.

DENEKAMP, Andrea. "Sylvian Biocentrism in *The Lord of the Rings*." *Representations of Nature in Middle-earth*. Ed. Martin Simonson. Cormarë Series 34. Zurich and Jena: Walking Tree Publishers, 2015. 1-28.

DICKERSON, Matthew and Jonathan EVANS. *Ents, Elves, and Eriador: The Environmental Vision of J.R.R. Tolkien*. Lexington, KT: Kentucky University Press, 2006.

DONOVAN, Leslie A., ed. *Approaches to Teaching Tolkien's The Lord of the Rings and Other Works*. New York: Modern Language Association, 2015.

ERSTGAARD, Gabriel. "'Leaves of Gold There Grew': Lothlórien, Postcolonialism, and Ecology." *Representations of Nature in Middle-earth*. Ed. Martin Simonson. Cormarë Series 34. Zurich and Jena: Walking Tree Publishers, 2015. 207-230.

FLIEGENSCHNEE, Martin and Anreas SCHELAKOVSKY. *Umweltpsychologie und Umweltbildung*. Wien: Facultas University Press, 1999.

FLIEGER, Verlyn. "Taking Part of the Trees: Eco-Conflict in Middle-earth." *J.R.R. Tolkien and His Literary Resonances*. Eds. George Clark and Daniel Timmons. Westport, CT: Greenwood Press, 2000. 147-158.

"J.R.R. Tolkien and the Matter of Britain." *Mythlore* 23.1 (#87) (2000): 47-59.

GARCIA DE LA PUERTA, Maria. "J.R.R. Tolkien's Use of Nature: Correlation with Galicians' Sense of Nature." *Mythlore* 22.1 (#83) (1997): 22-25.

GUANIO-ULURU, Lykke. *Ethics and Form in Fantasy Literature: Tolkien, Rowling and Meyer*. New York: Palgrave, 2015.

HARGROVE, Gene. "Who is Tom Bombadil?" *Mythlore* 13.1 (#47) (1986): 20-24.

HELLBRÜCK, Jürgen and Manfred FISCHER, eds. *Umweltpsychologie*. Göttingen: Hogrefe, 1999.

HELLBRÜCK, Jürgen and Elisabeth KALS. *Umweltpsychologie*. Wiesbaden: Springer, 2012.

HIRSCH, B. "After the "end of all things": The Long Return Home to the Shire." *Tolkien Studies* 11 (2014): 77-107.

HOWARD, George S. *Ecological Psychology*. Notre Dame, IN: Notre Dame University Press, 1997.

HUNECKE, Marcel. *Psychologie der Nachhaltigkeit: Psychische Ressourcen für Postwachstumsgesellschaften*. München: oekom, 2013.

JEFFERS, Susan. *Arda Inhabited: Environmental Relationships in The Lord of the Rings*. Kent, OH: The Kent State University Press, 2014.

JONAS, Hans. *Das Prinzip Verantwortung*. Frankfurt: Suhrkamp, 1979.

JONES, Renae. 'A Close Friendship With the Earth': Place in The Hobbit and Lord of the Rings. Master Thesis. Radford University. 2014. Web. 3 Sep. 2016.

JUHREN, Marcella. "The Ecology of Middle Earth." *Mythlore* 2.1 (#5) (1970)/ *Tolkien Journal* 4.2 (#12) (1970): 4-6, 9. Reprinted 20.2 (#76) (1994): 5-9.

KOGER, Susan M. and Deborah DU NANN WINTER. *The Psychology of Environmental Problems: Psychology for Sustainability.* New York: Psychology Press, 2010.

LEOPOLD, Aldo. *Sand County Almanac, and Sketches Here and There.* Oxford: Oxford University Press, 1949.

LYNCH, Andrew. "Archaism, Nostalgia, and Tennysonian War." *Tolkiens Modern Middle Ages.* Eds. Jane Chance and Alfred K. Siewers. New York: Palgrave, 2005. 77-92.

MCHUGH, Paul R. *Try to Remember: Psychiatry's Clash over Meaning, Memory, and Mind.* Chicago: Chicago University Press, 2008.

OLSEN, C. "The Myth of the Ent and the Entwife." *Tolkien Studies* 5 (2008): 39-53.

RAPPORT, D. and W.G. WHITFORD. "How Ecosystems Respond to Stress." *Bioscience* 49 (1999): 193-203.

ROSZAK, Theodore. *The Voice of the Earth.* New York: Schuster, 1992.

SABINI, Meredith, ed. *The Earth Has a Soul: C.G. Jung On Nature, Technology and Modern Life.* Berkeley, CA: North Atlantic Books, 2008.

SACKNOFF, Lance Michael. *Fantastic Eco-semiosis: An Analysis of Fantasy as Nature-text in The Lord of the Rings.* Master Thesis. Iowa State University. 2014. Web. 6 Sep 2016.

SASZ, Thomas. *Psychiatry: The Science of Lies.* Syracuse, NY: Syracuse University Press, 2008.

SIEWERS, Alfred K. "Environmentalist Readings of Tolkien." *The J.R.R. Tolkien Encyclopedia.* Ed. Michael D.C. Drout. New York: Routledge, 2007. 166-167.

SIMONSON, Martin, ed. *Representations of Nature in Middle-earth.* Cormarë Series 34. Zurich and Jena: Walking Tree Publishers, 2015.

TOLKIEN, John Ronald Reuel. *The Lord of the Rings.* London: HarperCollins, 2007.

"On Fairy-Stories." *The Tolkien Reader.* New York: Ballantine Books, 1966. 3-84.

UNGAR, Michael, ed. *The Social Ecology of Resilience.* New York: Springer, 2012.

VAKOCH, Douglas A. and Fernando CATRILLÓN, eds. *Ecopsychology, Phenomenology, and the Environment.* New York: Springer, 2014.

Vos, Holger. *Die Weltdeutung im Silmarillion von J.R.R. Tolkien.* Berlin: epubli, 2014.

WALLACE, H.M. and D.M. TICE. "Reflected appraisal through a 21st-century looking glass." *Handbook of Self and Identity.* Eds. M.R. Leary and J.P. Tangney. New York, NY: Guildford. 2012. 124-140.

WHEELER, Stephen M. *Climate Change and Social Ecology.* London: Routledge, 2012.

WILLIAMS, Stephen M. *Environment and Mental Health.* Chichester: John Wiley & Sons, 1994.

Magdalena Spachmann

Ethereal Elvish and Horrid Orkish: An Attempt to Capture J.R.R. Tolkien's Controversial Theory of Linguistic Aesthetics and Phonetic Fitness

Abstract

J.R.R. Tolkien was a genuine word-lover who invented a considerable number of languages with the utmost meticulousness. In need of a world in which some of his invented languages could become alive, he created the famous mythology of Middle-earth, which is therefore largely a product of his philological convictions. Close inspection reveals that the linguistic universe unfolded in *The Lord of the Rings* implicitly, and yet decidedly, contradicts established linguistic theory, i.e. de Saussure's arbitrariness of the linguistic sign. For instance, the principle of arbitrariness is challenged by Tolkien's decision to equip the heroes of his novel with pleasantly sounding languages and, in turn, the villains with abominably sounding ones. His language making depends on the concepts of phonetic fitness and linguistic aesthetics and represents a plea in their favour. In this essay, several of Tolkien's invented languages are examined with a special focus on tracing their underlying linguistic aesthetics and phonetic fitness. Due to the lack of a single coherent account of his convictions, this essay aims at compiling a Tolkienian linguistic theory by drawing on some of his literary and scholarly works as well as his rich written correspondence.

1 Objectives of this paper

When reading *LotR* with the eyes of a linguist, one gets the impression that its author incorporated innumerable linguistic considerations and convictions into the novel. Significantly, Tolkien himself once affirmed this impression explicitly by stating: "*The Lord of the Rings* is to me largely an essay in 'linguistic aesthetic'" (*L* 205). Closely linked to his "linguistic aesthetic" is the notion of *phonetic fitness*, i.e. the aptness and direct linkage between a sound and its meaning. While linguistic aesthetics and phonetic fitness were the foundation for his literary and scholarly works, there is surprisingly little[1] published on this thought-provoking topic, which may be due to the fact that mainstream linguistics usually does not take it into consideration.

---

[1] For instance Ross Smith, *Inside Language: Linguistic and Aesthetic Theory in Tolkien* (2007), and Part II (63-115) in Dimitra Fimi, *Tolkien, Race and Cultural History* (2009).

In fact, there is hardly any topic in linguistics that could be more controversial than phonetic fitness as it goes hand in hand with questioning the principle of arbitrariness, which excludes a natural relationship between the sound sequence and the concept of an entity (Kortmann 16). To put it more succinctly, proposing a direct linkage between sound and meaning stands in contradiction to an arbitrary relation between signifier and signified.[2] Oddly, since Ferdinand de Saussure established the notion of the arbitrary linguistic sign at the beginning of the 20th century, modern linguistic theory has not seriously challenged this "law". Although opposing interpretations of de Saussure's *Cours de linguistique générale* (1916) do exist (cf. e.g. Jules Levin's "Saussure and the *arbre* 'tree': A Fundamental Misunderstanding."), such diverging views are usually not taken into account in today's mainstream linguistic discourse.[3] Thus, most linguists may dodge the issue of phonetic fitness a priori or dismiss it as untrue and marginal, e.g. Kortmann's introduction to English linguistics, which regards structuralist thinking as "largely undisputed in present-day linguistics" and does not mention differing views (17). Other linguists defend phonetic fitness and similar concepts as the only truth.[4] However, an analysis of Tolkien's philosophy of language requires the permission to call into question the well-established linguistic credo of an arbitrary linguistic sign.

In this paper, a small selection of Tolkien's scholarly works, some of his private and professional written correspondence, and his fantasy narrative *LotR* including the appendices E and F shall be scrutinised for relevant passages on phonetic fitness and linguistic aesthetics. The main idea is to capture Tolkien's controversial yet deeply revealing views on language and to compile a coherent theory on linguistic aesthetics and phonetic fitness subsequently. For this purpose, it is necessary to extract relevant statements from the texts under investigation. Bearing in mind both the challenges and the chances of touching upon a true "Cinderella field" in linguistics, this paper seeks to reveal the relationship between sound and meaning from a new perspective, the Tolkienian one.

---

2 *Signifier* denotes the sound-image, e.g. tree /triː/, and *signified* the concept, e.g. a tree is a tall, woody plant having a trunk, branches, and leaves.
3 For further reading on nonconformists, see Jules Levin.
4 Margaret Magnus, *Gods of the Word: Archetypes in the Consonants* (1999); Dwight L. Bolinger, "The Sign Is Not Arbitrary" (1949); Genette, Gérard Genette, *Mimologics: A Voyage into Cratylusland* (1995).

2 Tolkien on phonetic fitness

2.1 Tolkien's "Secret Vice", an open secret

Tolkien described his passion for the creation of artificial languages as his "secret vice", referred to as "'home-made or invented languages'" (*MC* 3-4) – even today there is no consensus among critics in regard to the exact number of languages he did invent.[5] Estimates range from five (Segura and Peris 32) to thirteen (Noel 102), depending on varying defining criteria: for instance, some would not consider the language of the Riders of Rohan to be an invented one, since it is merely synthesised out of Old English elements. In "A Secret Vice", Tolkien elaborates on children's linguistic faculty and the pleasure that children take in a playful use of language and in inventing secret languages (*MC* 201). The quintessence of "A Secret Vice"[6] is summed up particularly well by Tolkien's statement in the following paragraph. It contains many of the issues elaborated in the essay.

> This idea of using the linguistic faculty for amusement is however deeply interesting to me. I may be like an opium-smoker seeking a moral or medical or artistic defence for his habit. I don't think so. The instinct for 'linguistic invention' – the fitting of notion to oral symbol, and pleasure in contemplating the new relation established, is rational, and not perverted. (*MC* 206)

The metaphor of the opium-smoker mirrors Tolkien's major passion, the creation of languages, all too well. The habit of inventing languages had accompanied him from childhood up to a high age, continually polishing, first and foremost, his Elvish languages without ever (wanting) to reach a definite version. The quote furthermore hints at his inner strife between embarrassment and pleasure regarding his invented languages and their disclosure to the public. His final remark seems like a defence for his invented languages having a sound, rational basis and for being neither perverted nor unsubstantiated. The quote also reflects his strong conviction of the existence of phonetic fitness, the relation between a word's sound and its meaning on the one hand, and between a word's form and its meaning on the other hand. Tolkien gives priority to phonetic fitness,

---

5 Regarding real languages, Tolkien knew around seventeen, speaking several of them fluently (Segura and Peris 31-32).
6 The text has been recently re-edited in a critical edition by Dimitra Fimi and Andrew Higgins (see Tolkien *Secret Vice*, 2016).

being his "main source of pleasure" (*MC* 206) and what he was "personally most interested" in (*MC* 211).

While "A Secret Vice" contains a fair amount of information on Tolkien's predilections and a strong defence of his views, he does not call a spade a spade. It becomes clear from the statements commented on above that he is convinced of phonetic fitness and the *non*-arbitrariness of the linguistic sign. However, the lecture lacks further concretisations of his theory on phonetic fitness, a gap that will hopefully be closed after having scrutinised his much later lecture "English and Welsh".

2.2 "English and Welsh" and a "pleasurable" cellar door

The lecture "English and Welsh" was delivered in Oxford in 1954, more than two decades after "A Secret Vice" and in the same year the first and second volume of Tolkien's monumental opus *The Lord of the Rings* were published. After so many years, the element of pleasure and Tolkien's conception of phonetic fitness were still on his mind.

"English and Welsh" covers, amongst other aspects, the historical-linguistic features of the English and the Welsh languages in different stages of their development. Once again, Tolkien's broad knowledge in historical linguistics is displayed, even though he is repeatedly pointing out that his contribution is nothing more than "a curtain-raiser to […] a long series of lectures by eminent scholars" (*MC* 162). Towards the end of the lecture, Tolkien begins talking about the beauty of the Welsh language and elaborates on the aesthetic pleasure that certain sounds of beautiful languages can evoke in people. A central point he makes pertains to the differentiation between a basic and a higher dimension of aesthetic pleasure. While basic pleasure is caused by the style and the phonetic elements of a language, a higher dimension is reached only when associating these word-forms with meanings (*MC* 190). By calling attention to examples of what is not meant by aesthetic pleasure, he defines and refines the notion. In his opinion, the aesthetic pleasure is neither comparable to the pleasure of reading poetry, nor to the feeling of mastering a foreign language and having practical knowledge of it (*MC* 190). Much more so, he argues that every person has his or her own so-called "native language", which does not at all refer to the mother tongue in the understanding of modern linguists such as Crystal (3), but to a sort of individually different linguistic potential and personal preferences (*MC* 190).

What follows these thought-provoking remarks is a frequently cited and quite controversial passage, in which Tolkien makes a daring proposition:

> Most English-speaking people [...] will admit that *cellar door* is 'beautiful,' especially when dissociated from its sense (and from spelling). More beautiful than, say, *sky*, and far more beautiful than *beautiful*. Well then, in Welsh for me *cellar doors* are extraordinarily frequent, and moving to the higher dimension, the words in which there is pleasure in the contemplation of the association of form and sense are abundant. (*MC* 190-91)

Tolkien was very conscious of the problematic nature of such a proposition and of aesthetic pleasure in general, as he knew that there were no empirical studies to back his statements. Yet, Tolkien sought to illustrate that there was an abundance of Welsh words that caused in his linguist's mind auditory pleasure: in order to draw people's awareness to beautifully sounding words, he chose a commonly known word. Yet, it is impossible to tell if, by "most English-speaking people", Tolkien was really referring to all the possible pronunciations in the very dissimilar dialects and varieties of English or to his southern UK English only – an issue also discussed by Smith (64). What is more, "most" is very vague and generalising and thus wholly inconsistent with his idea of individually different linguistic predilections. On top of that, he used an English example, although he emphasised a few sentences later that aesthetic pleasure was perceived mostly with second-learned languages for those were not used as inattentively as one's first language. The cellar door incident therefore seems very much like an effort made to put into words the pleasure he derives from the Welsh language.[7]

The quintessence of Tolkien's theory of linguistic aesthetics and phonetic fitness is that he believed that certain sounds or combinations thereof could offer

---

7 Besides his love for the Welsh language, Tolkien revealed his sentiments for other languages during the lecture. While Latin and Greek had more of a historical appeal to him, French did not give him much pleasure (*MC* 191). He was very fond of Spanish, deeply moved by Gothic, and overwhelmed with emotion when it came to Finnish (*MC* 192). Tolkien stressed that neither a list of isolated pleasurable words, nor the translation of a favourite passage could convey the aesthetic pleasure he found in reading or hearing Welsh because the phonetic fitness of a linguistic style makes a language aesthetically pleasing (*MC* 192-93).

clues about their meaning and evoke divergent reactions in people. One of these reactions is certainly the pleasure Tolkien so frequently alluded to, or else the opposite reaction, i.e. distaste. He argued that people can tell by intuition what a certain unit of speech may mean, just by the mere sound of a word and without knowing the language itself.

To sum up, "English and Welsh" represents a further, more developed stage of the views expressed in "A Secret Vice". Although the number of commentaries on linguistic aesthetics, phonetic fitness, and pleasure in "English and Welsh" is per se limited, Tolkien's claims and arguments are well-wrought and structured. Shippey classifies the Tolkienian theory displayed in "English and Welsh" as "a considered though not scientific attempt to say what makes a language beautiful" (129). As mentioned before, Tolkien himself seems to have been highly conscious of the fact that his remarks were not backed by scientific findings. Shippey suggests that, when delivering the lecture at the age of 62, Tolkien possibly may not have been craving for the foundation of a new branch of learning any more (129), which could indeed be an explanation for the lack of a coherently compiled theory on linguistic aesthetics on his part.

2.3 Written correspondence

The *Letters of J.R.R. Tolkien,* edited by Humphrey Carpenter and Christopher Tolkien, is a significant collection of Tolkien's private and professional correspondence ranging from 1914 to 1973. The biographical focus inherent in this compilation presents itself as very fruitful for the purpose of synthesising a Tolkienian philosophy of linguistic aesthetics. After all, in contrast to essays and fiction, letters have the advantage that they contain plain, (supposedly) sincere statements, especially when written in a private, sheltered context such as Tolkien's lively correspondence with his son Christopher.

The use of the catchphrase "aesthetic pleasure", and parts and variations of it, such as "aesthetic linguistics" and "linguistic aesthetic", is noticeably frequent in Tolkien's letters (*L* 172; 175; 176; 213; 216; 231; 264; 265 etc.). This fact alone shows that the aspect of aesthetic pleasure was a topic of primal concern to Tolkien, especially in the 1950s apparently, according to the dating of the letters. To a close friend of his family, Tolkien for instance described the pleasure he perceived from the mere form of words, particularly in foreign or distant languages such as Old English (*L* 172). On a different occasion, Tolkien wrote that, while he gained pleasure from literature or history, none of these could ever outweigh "the acute aesthetic pleasure derived from a language for its own sake, not only free from being useful but free from being the 'vehicle of a literature'" (*L* 213; 264). These remarks define the pleasure Tolkien meant and show that he regarded language as an end in itself. In his view, his invented languages did not have to be useful or serve any purpose, simply because they had a value in themselves and, what is more, they were pleasurable. Had Tolkien not experienced immense pleasure constructing languages, surely he would not have bothered investing a lifetime to come up with "two organized philologies and grammars and a large number of words" (*L* 216).

Tolkien enjoyed describing his love for language(s) to others, while emphasising the fact that he was "primarily interested in the aesthetic rather than the functional aspects of language" (*L* 231). From these and other similar remarks, one can conclude that his love for certain languages was not utilitarian at all but very much nurtured by their nature and sound. At the same time, it needs to be noted that this is a rather unusual love, as it arguably differs widely both from the linguist's and from the literary scholar's pleasure gained from language. Nevertheless, Tolkien seemed convinced that the pleasure he derived from the phonetic structure of languages was also felt by others who either shared his favoured sound patterns or had other preferences (*L* 175-76). He referred to this as an individual's "native tongue", probably denoting the same concept he called "native language" in "A Secret Vice" and "English and Welsh" (*MC* 190; 211). If Tolkien had had his way, he would have included many more Elvish passages in *The Lord of the Rings* (*L* 216). By composing the Elvish tongues, he forged his personal taste into phonetic structures. Assuming that it was impossible to please all members of the heterogeneous group of readers, he flamboyantly concluded: "I have therefore pleased myself" (*L* 176).

Despite numerous attempts to find the right words to express his theory, Tolkien knew about the elusiveness of the concept of aesthetic linguistics. A very revealing letter for that matter and other issues is the following, addressed to his son Christopher in 1958:

I do not know what I mean, because 'aesthetic' is always impossible to catch in a net of words. Nobody believes me when I say that my long book is an attempt to create a world in which a form of language agreeable to my personal aesthetic might seem real. But it is true. An enquirer (among many) asked what the L.R. [*LotR*] was all about, and whether it was an 'allegory'. And I said it was an effort to create a situation in which a common greeting would be *elen síla lúmenn' omentielmo* [a star shines upon the hour of our meeting], and that the phrase long antedated the book. (*L* 264-65)

The quoted passage addresses several important points and one of them is that he must have felt misunderstood regarding *The Lord of the Rings* and the statement he had intended to make by it. It also shows that Tolkien himself regarded the concept of linguistic aesthetics as very complex and hard to grasp or put into words. This intricacy is the reason why he created Middle-earth, a world in which he could overcome such mundane difficulties and in which an Elvish greeting, so pleasantly sounding to him, would be part of everyday life. Apart from that, this is the letter in which Tolkien expresses his dislike for reading *The Lord of the Rings* allegorically in any way, an interpretation that many (literary) critics tried. Also, he emphasised again that the invented languages were his number-one priority and preceded the fiction by far.

3 Looking for Tolkien's applications of phonetic fitness and linguistic aesthetics in his literary works

3.1 A linguistic universe, or speech matching character in *The Lord of the Rings*

Needless to say that the frame narrative in *The Lord of the Rings* is written in English, simply because otherwise nobody except Tolkien himself would have been able to read it. Tolkien, always striving for philological preciseness, equated what he called the *Common Speech*, or *Westron*, with Modern English; only the other languages in the book remained untranslated.[8] As we infer from appendix F in *The Lord of the Rings*, the Common Speech came to be the lingua franca in entire Middle-earth over the years, and some peoples, the hobbits for example, even adopted it as their first language (1127). Tolkien sought to pay tribute

---

8 See Honegger "Westron turned into Modern English".

to the differences in usage by writing in several varieties and styles of English and by having the people of Gondor speak a rather formal and archaic English in contrast to the rustic hobbits (*LotR* 1133; app. F). The varying styles are exemplified in the following dialogue between a hobbit and an elf. While the former uses contracted forms of auxiliaries, the latter avoids using them. Also, their choice of words differs widely, e.g. *folks* belongs to an informal register while *alas!* is rather archaic.

(1) 'No, Lady,' he [Frodo] answered. 'To tell you the truth, I wondered what you were talking about. […] But if you'll pardon my speaking out, I think my master was right. I wish you'd take this Ring. You'd put things to rights. […] You'd make some folks pay for their dirty work.' 'I would,' she [Galadriel] said. 'That is how it would begin. But it would not stop with that, alas! We will not speak more of it. Let us go!' (*LotR* 366; book II, ch. 7)

3.1.1 Gollum's Westron

Gollum (formerly Sméagol and a hobbit) speaks an unpleasantly sounding variety of Westron that represents his wicked character adequately. Many regional variations and different sociolects among the speech communities in *The Lord of the Rings* are identifiable,[9] but few show Tolkien's deliberate use of phonetic fitness for characterisation as perfectly as Gollum's idiolect. In Gollum's speech, the predominant phoneme is the voiceless alveolar fricative /s/, which is mainly responsible for the unpleasant impression given to the reader, and surely even more so to the listener, if the novel were read out loud. The following passage demonstrates this neatly:

(2) 'Ach, sss! Cautious, my precious! More haste less speed. We musstn't rissk our neck, musst we, precious? No, precious – *gollum*! […] We hate it,' he hissed. 'Nassty, nassty shivery light it is – sss – it spies on us, precious – it hurts our eyes. […] Where iss it, where iss it: my Precious, my Precious? It's ours, it is, and we wants it. The thieves, the filthy little thieves. Where are they with my Precious? Curse them! We hates them.' (*LotR* 613; book IV, ch. 1)

Evidently, the high number of grammatical and orthographical "mistakes" serves a purpose. The deliberate word choice, the incorrect doubling of <s> and the

---

9 See Johannesson "Speech of the Individual".

overuse of the inflectional morpheme {-s}, marking the third person singular present tense indicative, lead to an extremely high occurrence of the voiceless sibilants /s/ and /ʃ/. The effect of these phonetical features in Gollum's speech is in fact explicitly stated in the passage above: he does not speak, he "hisses". According to Gymnich's interpretation, Gollum's hissing perfectly mirrors his wickedness and alludes to a snake, the universal symbol of evil (21).

What is more, Gollum's speech is reminiscent of early-child speech owing to the grammatical mistakes in subject-verb agreement, e.g. "'they jumps on us'" (*LotR* 614; book IV, ch. 1) and the flawed use of the personal pronouns, e.g. "'We promises, yes I promise!' said Gollum" (*LotR* 618; book IV, ch. 1). Adding the plural morpheme {-(e)s} to word forms already marked as plurals is another type of overgeneralization found in child speech (Gymnich 21-22): plural formation of this sort as in "hobbitses" or "mices" thus increases the number of sibilants even further (*LotR* 614; book IV, ch. 1). Based on the phonetical displeasure that Gollum's use of Westron causes, his language is meant to characterise him as sinister and evil. At the same time, however, the childlike aspect of his idiolect allows for the understanding that he is not fully villainous, but merely corrupted by the power of the ring. Gollum is an excellent example for Tolkien's making use of phonetic fitness for the creation of certain atmospheres and characters.

3.1.2 The Orcs' Black Speech

It is only consistent that an aesthete like Tolkien divides the world into word-lovers and word-abusers and thus raises the dichotomy of good and evil in correspondence with these categories. The Elves, whose languages I will specifically focus on in 3.2 below, are described throughout all meta-linguistic comments as aesthetically superior and more skilled in words and culture than any other peoples of Middle-earth (*LotR* 1134; app. F). Their incompatible counterpart is the enemy Sauron and his slaves, the Nazgûl, Orcs, and Trolls, whose language, the Black Speech, is downright harsh and guttural (Hostetter 343). Among the dominating sounds are sh and gh, phonetically realised as the sibilant [ʃ] and the "back spirant" [gʰ] (*LotR* 1117; app. E), as in *ghâsh* 'fire' (*LotR* 327; book II, ch. 5).

The Orcs speak "without love of words or things" in an utterly "degraded and filthy" manner (*LotR* 1134; app. F); their talk was "dreary and repetitive with hatred and contempt, too long removed from good to retain even verbal vigour, save in the ears of those to whom only the squalid sounds strong" (*LotR* 1134; app. F). In other words, being the wretched creatures they are, they have lost the capacity to feel the vitality and pleasure that beautiful language can convey, and as a consequence of their hatred, they are unable to form any fine language.

Such statements and such a world view vest language with a major power. When captured by the Orcs, hobbit Pippin observes that they are filled with so much malice that any word out of their mouths – regardless of whether it is uttered in their own "abominable tongue" (*LotR* 445; book III, ch. 3) or in their harsh variety of Common Speech – sounds cursing, aggressive, and brutal. Within the same scene, one sentence of the overall sparingly used Black Speech is uttered by an Orc of Mordor, most likely Grishnákh:

(3) *Uglúk u bagronk sha pushdug Saruman-glob búbhosh skai.*
(*LotR* 445; book III, ch. 3)

According to Tolkien's draft of appendix F, which was posthumously published by his son Christopher in *The Peoples of Middle-earth*, the translation is as follows: "*Uglúk to the cesspool, sha! the dungfilth; the great Saruman-fool, skai!*" (*PME* 83). While "Úgluk" is the name of another Orc-leader, "sha" and "skai" could be interpreted as Orcish interjections of rage. At any rate, Tolkien did not provide a translation for the reader, presumably believing that the speaker's attitude and the meaning of the utterance was conveyed by the "harsh and hideous sounds and vile words", how he expressed it (*PME* 35), which makes the Orcs' Black Speech another powerful example of phonetic fitness in *The Lord of the Rings*.

3.1.3 The Dwarves' Khuzdul

A people who seem to be an exception to the rule in regard to the connection of beautiful language and non-evil character are the Dwarves. Although their tongue Khuzdul is described as "strange", "guttural", and "a fair jaw-cracker" (*LotR* 285; book II, ch. 3; 1132-34; app. F), Dwarves are not evil characters in the story. Tolkien is consistent with the fact that they like to keep their language secret, tending it as precious heritage, which is why the instances of Khuzdul are highly rare: in *The Lord of the Rings*, Khuzdul only appears in few place names like *Khazad-dûm*, whose equivalent in Common Speech is "Dwarrowdelf" and refers to *Moria*, which in turn is an Elvish name meaning "black chasm" (*LotR* 1137; app. F). Gimli's battle-cry is the only full sentence in Khuzdul in *The Lord of the Rings*:

> (4) "*Baruk Khazâd! Khazâd ai-mênu!* 'Axes of the Dwarves! The Dwarves are upon you!'" (*LotR* 1132; app. F)

Unlike the Orcs, the Dwarves seem to love (their) language and speak it with skill, adapting themselves easily to their company. Galadriel, one of the oldest and most powerful Elves, even ascertains that Gimli is most skilled in using words and that Dwarves are not at all as ungracious and greedy as their reputation would suggest (*LotR* 376, book II, ch. 8). Perhaps the special position of these mysterious craftsmen can be explained by them being "a race apart" (*LotR* 1132; app. F), hard to classify and oscillating between the two poles of aestheticism and ugliness. Nevertheless, certain consonant clusters contribute to an unpleasant impression the recipient gets from the language.[10]

3.1.4 Entish – "long-winded" and "sonorous"

The most ancient people in Middle-earth are the living trees, the Ents, who do not need to keep their language secret for nobody else would be able to even learn it (*LotR* 1131; app. F). Treebeard is the archetype of the Ents being the oldest one in Middle-earth; his name is as long as his life story and thus is continually growing as he lives on (*LotR* 464-65; book III, ch. 4).

The reader learns most about Entish from the dialogue Treebeard and the hobbits Merry and Pippin have. For one thing, although it was the Elves who woke up the trees and taught them how to speak, Entish does not have much in common with Elvish at all. Both peoples are very skilled in languages but in very idiosyncratic ways. Since Tolkien created his fictional characters based

---

10 It is relevant to note that this might be due to the structure and phonetics of Khuzdul being based on Semitic languages, which entails that roots are formed by three consonants in a row (Hostetter 341). See also Vink on the links between the Dwarves and the Semitic people.

on the aesthetics and nature of his invented languages, the Ents' speech (just as much as all others') is clearly reminiscent of their character and outer appearance: their "slow, sonorous, agglomerated, repetitive, indeed long-winded" tongue is very distinct and different from the quick-worded and agile Elves (*LotR* 1130; app. F; cf. 3.2 below).

In his dialogue with the two hobbits, Treebeard wonders about the short lexeme "hill" denoting an entity that has stood there forever and finds it too "hasty" a word (*LotR* 466; book III, ch. 4). In Treebeard's view, the monosyllabic hill with its short front-vowel /ɪ/ is not an adequate representation of "a thing that has stood here ever since this part of the world was shaped" (*LotR* 466; book III, ch. 4). In accordance with the Ents' logic, such an old entity would deserve a long name, reflecting the hill's everlasting permanence.

Also, when telling the hobbits that the Elves shortened *Laurelindórenan* to *Lothlórien* in the course of time, he remarks that "perhaps they are right: maybe it is fading, not growing" (*LotR* 467; book III, ch. 4). According to Treebeard, the golden woods of Lothlórien were formerly called "'Land of the Valley of Singing Gold'" but are now referred to as the "'Dreamflower'" (*LotR* 467; book III, ch. 4). By shortening the name, he enigmatically hints at evil forces threatening the golden wood (*LotR* 1131; app. F).

These two observations are representative of the Entish philosophy of language and show that the length of their words results from their belief of a direct connection between a word's sound and its concept, closely resembling each other. Gymnich provides a concise analysis of what the Ents' language means in terms of linguistic thinking.

> According to the Ents, the words of a language ought to reflect the nature of the entities they denote. Thus, Ents apparently do not conceive of words as linguistic signs in the Saussurean sense, namely as *arbitrary* connections of a signifier and a signified. Instead, the Ents assume that the relationship between signifier and signified should be motivated. Since Entish words even reflect the *history* of the entities they denote, linguistic signs in Entish have to be inherently instable, perpetually growing longer as the entities they refer to become older. (23)

One could argue that, by creating Entish, Tolkien (deliberately?) went against the Geneva school and its founding father de Saussure: instead of declaring the relationship between signifier and signified as arbitrary, the Ents actually regard this relationship as motivated and thus create words in a length adequate to their individual history. This is why Treebeard's real name grows all the time, "etymologically" telling his story.

Another example of *Entish* – in fact only a small part of the word Treebeard is referring to – is given as sample (5),

(5) '*a-lalla-lalla-rumba-kamanda-lind-or-burúmë.*' (*LotR* 465; book III, ch. 4)

This agglutinative string of morphemes, which, according to Tolkien's information given in appendix F is a representation of "a fragment of actual Entish" (*LotR* 1131; app. F), sounds rather childlike, yet pleasant, and is reminiscent of the playful way Tom Bombadil speaks: "Ring a ding dillo del! derry del, my hearties! (*LotR* 128; book I, ch. 7). Since the latter is also among the oldest still dwelling in Middle-earth, this "coincidence" might in fact not be as coincidental as it may seem.

What is definitely intentional on Tolkien's part is that he does not uncover the secret of Tom Bombadil's existence and language (*L* 174). What Shippey terms "Bombadil-style" refers to Tolkien's firm belief in a genuine language beneath it all, one "'isomorphic with reality'" with "a close connection between thing-signified, person-signifying, and language-signified-in" (130). Thus, by reference to Treebeard and Bombadil, both Gymnich and Shippey support the thesis that Tolkien did regard the connection between signifier and signified as motivated. Therefore, he conspicuously shaped the languages of these characters in a way that made concept and sound-image resemble and complement each other, inherently negating the core of structuralist thinking.

To sum up, the isomorphic Entish reveals that Tolkien was convinced of the *non*-arbitrariness of the linguistic sign. Moreover, Tolkien made use of phonetic fitness when constructing the phonetically unpleasant languages, among them the Black Speech, Khuzdul, and Gollum's variety of Common Speech. Without explicitly formulating a theory, Tolkien put his linguistic convictions into practice and proved them right by provoking the very same positive and negative emotions in the readers when coming across these languages in *The*

Lord of the Rings. The icing on the linguistic cake, however, were the Elvish languages, which he perfected through to the last detail.

3.2 Tolkien's strongest examples of language making: Quenya and Sindarin

The two Elvish tongues Quenya and Sindarin form the core of Tolkien's mythology and offer a considerable size of material, also due to their advanced stage of development. It is arguable whether the youngest stages of Quenya and Sindarin are the ultimate and the only valid ones, thus the following description of Quenya and Sindarin refers only to their stages in *The Lord of the Rings*, without intending to say that these were more valid than earlier and later stages.

Tolkien forged Quenya on a Latin base and enriched it with Finnish and Greek features, since he perceived a particular phono-aesthetic pleasure in the two latter languages (*L* 176). Despite many similarities to those three underlying languages,[11] Tolkien made Quenya less consonantal than these, supposedly for phono-aesthetic reasons. Overall, Quenya, or High-Elven or Elvish (*L* 176), is a sort of "Elven-Latin", a register for ceremony, song, and lore. Suitably, it is exclusively spoken, in fact mostly sung, by the wisest in Middle-earth, among them Galadriel, e.g. when she bids the fellowship of the Ring farewell (*LotR* 377; book II, ch. 8).

Speaking of Galadriel in the context of Quenya, one should rather call her *Altariel*, since tracing back the Sindarin form of her name *Galadriel* would unveil the following processes. The unrecorded form **galata-rīg-elle* is assumed to mean "lady {elle} with a garland {rīg} of sunlight {galata}" resulting *Altariel* in Quenya due to loss of <g>, syncope of the second <a>, loss of the final <e>, and reduction of <ll> to <l> (Hostetter 337). The fact that earlier, unrecorded forms can be deduced systematically says a lot about the complexity of Tolkien's Elvish tongues. By adding the diachronic dimension, Tolkien bestows depth upon them and they nearly reach the rank of real languages.

---

11 For further reading on the agglutinating and inflecting nature of Quenya see Hostetter 337; Noel 68; Smith 90-91.

The living Elvish tongue and hence the one usually present in *The Lord of the Rings* is Sindarin or Grey-Elven. Despite having evolved from a shared prototype language, Sindarin has a very different linguistic character from Quenya (Noel 54). Certainly Tolkien's intention, Sindarin bears resemblance to Welsh so to mirror the Celtic echo of the legends told in Middle-earth (*L* 176). According to Hostetter, Sindarin resembles Welsh primarily in terms of phonology and grammar (333), which can be seen in the occurrence of the characteristic Welsh voiceless lateral fricative [ɬ], spelt <ll> in Welsh and <lh> in Sindarin (340).

In "English and Welsh", Tolkien discloses his personally preferred sounds and sound patterns by adhering to Welsh, which he finds "very attractive" (*L* 176). He is particularly fond of the nasal sound [n], but also of the semivowel [w], and the voiced fricatives [v] and [ð] (*MC* 193-94). These preferences are easily recognisable in Sindarin lexemes, names, and passages, as Gandalf's spell demonstrates:

> (6) *Annon edhellen, edro hi ammen! Fennas nogothrim, lasto beth lammen!*
> (*LotR* 307; book II, ch. 4)

Tolkien's intention when creating the Elvish tongues was to make them European in style and structure on the one hand and to be particularly pleasant on the other hand (*L* 175). While definitely having succeeded in bestowing a European layer upon Quenya and Sindarin, the second resolution was far more difficult to achieve. Tolkien was conscious of this challenge, knowing that "individuals' personal predilections, especially in the phonetic structure of languages, varies widely" (*L* 175).

What is of special interest in this paper's context is the Elven tongues' effect on the unlearned reader, as here the impact of phonetic fitness can be observed best. Several critics' voices confirm the impression that the invented languages must have a significant effect on the linguistically illiterate reader (Gymnich 10). Shippey goes as far as to claim that Tolkien "clearly believed that *untranslated* elvish [sic] would do a job that English could not" (130). I will again claim that the only possible explanation for such an impact can be found in phonetic fitness, the direct link between sound and meaning. It is beyond doubt that Tolkien himself was convinced of this genuine connection and consequently based his invented languages on this belief (Smith 56-57). He dissolved the boundaries between sound and sense and proved the arbitrariness principle wrong by doing so. The systematic usage of Elvish and other non-English elements and the uniform reactions Tolkien evoked among a multitude of readers are genuinely convincing.

3.3 A nomenclature for *The Lord of the Rings*

As Tolkien constructed the names of individuals, entire peoples, and creatures, but also of places and objects in *The Lord of the Rings* with so much passion for details, he felt quite offended by poor quality translations ("Nomenclature" 750). Concerning names, Tolkien left nothing to chance, not even their translation into other languages. He therefore composed a nomenclature explaining on approximately thirty pages the origin of the majority of names in *LotR* in order to provide a guide for their successful translation. Naturally, a complete nomenclature for Middle-earth cannot and should not be given in the context of this paper.[12] Yet, some entries will be mentioned here because many names in *The Lord of the Rings* provide evidence for the existence of phonetic fitness.

Similar to the fact that Tolkien invented a language first and created a story world later, his love for words went so far as to inventing the name of a character before forming the actual character. He did so by drawing on his knowledge of Old English, Old Norse, and other languages on the one hand, and by making use of phonetic fitness on the other. The Ents, for instance, "grew rather out of their name, than the other way about" simply because he liked the peculiar Old English word *ent*, meaning "giant" or "mighty person of long ago" (*L* 208).

Smith seeks to demonstrate the phonetic fitness of Tolkienian names by interchanging them, which results in a "severe phonetic unfitness" in his view (57). In his line of reasoning, calling the valiant, noble Lord Denethor Lord Bombadil instead does not sound quite right, since it is phonetically unfit. The name Bombadil arguably suits the good-hearted Tom Bombadil, because it consists mainly of the pleasant, soft sounding voiced phonemes /m/, /b/, and /l/. It is equally possible, however, that the learned reader regards the name as phonetically suitable only because he already knows the character. Smith's

---

12 For suchlike purposes, *A Reader's Companion* (2005) by Wayne G. Hammond and Christina Scull is the perfect work of reference. See also Nagel, *Hobbit Place-names* (2012).

interchanging of names is a promising approach, but it would be best to conduct a survey asking people who are not familiar with *LotR*. Another example mentioned in this context are the two rivers Anduin and Withywindle, the former being great, long, and majestic and the latter playful, winding, and bordered by many withies ("Nomenclature" 779).

Also, the names of the wizards Gandalf and Saruman deserve a closer look. One of the major sources for Gandalf's nature is the Norse God Óðinn, as both are wanderers and associated with sun or fire (Tolley 53). The origin of Gandalf's name *Gandálfr* is to be found in an Icelandic poem, *gandr* being a sort of "spirit" or "seer" and *álfr* meaning "elf" (Tolley 54).[13] Appropriately enough, there is a certain uncertainty concerning the Old Norse origin of Gandalf's name, like his character in *The Lord of the Rings*, who always remains somewhat enigmatic. Pleasant phonemes like the smooth alveolar lateral approximant /l/ and the equally voiced alveolar and velar stops /d/ and /g/ in the name "Gandalf" reflect the nature of his character. Exchanging the name of the benevolent Gandalf for Saruman, the perfidious wizard, seems unreasonable. Saruman was given a name of Old English origin which already hints at his dishonest, deceitful disposition: *searu* essentially means "cunning" or "treacherous" (Tolley 55). Furthermore, it contains the rather unpleasant voiceless alveolar fricative /s/ and close back rounded vowel /u/. Anticipating the legitimate question of why his name is "Saruman" instead of "Searuman", this decision can be put down to Tolkien's personal preference for the Mercian rather than the West Saxon dialect, which is also revealed in his composition of the Rohirrim, who call their land "the Mark", an English form of *Mercia*, which is again a Latinised form of Old English *merce* for "people of the frontier" living in a borderland (Tolley 56-57).

The examples given above show the immeasurable depth of Tolkien's nomenclature as they comment on nothing more than a fraction of all the names in Middle-earth. Of course, the reader could certainly not be expected to have a knowledge even close to Tolkien's, which is why Tolkien most certainly relied on the mechanisms of phonetic fitness just the more. A respective example would

---

13 Shippey translates *gandr* as "staff" => Gandalf = staff-elf. Geir T. Zoëga's *A Concise Dictionary of Old Icelandic* gives for *gandr* "magic staff", Walter Baetke's *Altnordisches Wörterbuch* translates it as "Zaubertier".

be his commentary on "Mount Doom" claiming that "doom" has in English "partly owing to its sound [...] become a word loaded with senses of death; finality; fate" ("Nomenclature" 768). Several times he affirms that "doom" together with the associated "boom" is "descriptive of sound" by generating the sense of disaster ("Nomenclature" 768-69).

In *The Lord of the Rings*, Tolkien relies on this effect of sound when the Fellowship of the Ring travels through the Mines of Moria:

(7) *Doom, boom, doom* went the drums in the deep. (*LotR* 324, book II, ch. 5)

Repeatedly, this sentence is inserted into the text in variations throughout the chapter. Thereby, Tolkien succeeds in creating a growing sense of disaster, danger, and death that culminates in Gandalf's fall into the abyss with the monstrous Balrog at the end of the chapter. This is an excellent example of phonetic fitness in Tolkien's choice of names and words. He explicitly stated "doom" to work via sound, mostly because of the longed close back rounded vowel [u:]. For the same reason, Tolkien decided to name the Orcs "Orcs". According to his own explanation in a letter to his proof-reader Naomi Mitchison, he derived *orc* from an Old English noun "only because of its phonetic suitability" (*L* 177-78). Tolkien's wording seems to suggest that the meaning 'demon' was of less importance to him than the phonetic fitness of orcs for the horrible creatures he created afterwards.

The items listed in this chapter show how Tolkien proceeded when he created names and the characters and creatures fitting these names. Apart from that, the numerous statements provide useful insights into Tolkien's mind, for instance how phonetic suitability took top priority for him.

4 Conclusion

Tolkien's statements in his letters and the two essays "A Secret Vice" and "English and Welsh" discussed in Chapter 2 were revealing with regard to his theory on linguistic aesthetics, and the analysis of the invented languages in Tolkien's literary work *The Lord of the Rings* in Chapters 3.1 and 3.2 turned out to be complementary to what Tolkien had defined as phonetic fitness. Yet, the statements I gathered from his essays did not disclose more than first beginnings of a "Tolkienian theory about linguistic aesthetics and phonetic fitness", as they are neither complete nor concrete enough.

What the analysis has enhanced, though, is a deeper understanding of Tolkien's philosophy of language. He was fully aware of how elusive and problematic the concept of linguistic aesthetics was. His fictional worlds, however, were suitable spaces for him to overcome the theoretical difficulties and incongruities without having to defend his thinking. He could satisfy his personal aesthetic predilections and tell his tales in what he deemed phonetically fit wording.

For the most part, Tolkien divided Middle-earth into philologists and misologists who were associated with good and evil respectively. In line with this worldview, he created the characters and languages of Middle-earth with Khuzdul, the language of the Dwarves, adopting a special position in-between the aesthetically superior Elves and the word-abusing, inferior Orcs. Since linguistic aesthetics works both ways, Gollum's idiolect, for example, will be perceived as phonetically unpleasant. Entish, too, is a highly revealing language in regard to Tolkien's philosophy. The Ents' continually growing words tell stories and are, therefore, inherently motivated. Tolkien thus negates and rejects the arbitrariness of the linguistic sign.

Finally, Tolkien's most developed languages Quenya and Sindarin have a great appeal to (historical) linguists and non-specialist readers alike. The fact that Tolkien included numerous instances of these varieties without translating them shows how convinced he was of the principles of phonetic fitness and of the fact that untranslated Elvish influenced the reader in a way that English could not have achieved. By including the Elvish tongues to such an extent, Tolkien effectively contradicted the principle of arbitrariness as he proclaimed a connection between certain combinations of phonemes and meaning. Finally, the nomenclature of *The Lord of the Rings* presents even more notions of phonetic fitness. On many occasions, Tolkien chose names that fitted the character of places and persons in Middle-earth, not only in meaning, but primarily in sound. Tolkien's notion of phonetic fitness had great potential to become a serious alternative concept to the arbitrariness principle, but his fear of being ridiculed as eccentric presumably prevented him from becoming more explicit in formulating his theories. Despite the lack of a coherent theory, linguistic aesthetics and phonetic fitness remain the founding principles of Sindarin and all the other invented languages. Thus, linguistic signs that are non-arbitrary and phonetically fit are omnipresent in Tolkien's fiction. His works ultimately speak for themselves, particularly to the readers who are aware of Tolkien's convictions.

About the Author

MAGDALENA SPACHMANN is a graduate in English and Spanish linguistics and literature at the University of Augsburg, Germany. She has worked as a language teacher in secondary educational and university contexts in Spain, Ireland and Germany. Her special interest in historical English linguistics led to an intense involvement with J.R.R. Tolkien, the medieval linguist. Among renowned experts on Tolkien like Prof. Dr. Thomas Honegger she contributed to a successful interdisciplinary public lecture series on J.R.R. Tolkien at the University of Augsburg in summer 2015. Last year, she completed her dissertation on Tolkien's linguistic aesthetics and phonetic fitness, two rather neglected research topics.

List of Abbreviations

L	CARPENTER, Humphrey, ed. with the assistance of Christopher TOLKIEN. *The Letters of J.R.R. Tolkien*. London: George Allen & Unwin, 1981.
LotR	TOLKIEN, John Ronald Reuel. *The Lord of the Rings*. 50th anniversary edition. London: HarperCollins, 2007.
MC	TOLKIEN, John Ronald Reuel. *The Monsters and the Critics and Other Essays*. Ed. Christopher Tolkien. London: George Allen & Unwin, 1983.
PME	TOLKIEN, John Ronald Reuel. *The Peoples of Middle-earth*. Ed. Christopher Tolkien. Boston: Houghton Mifflin, 1996.

Bibliography

BOLINGER, Dwight L. "The Sign Is Not Arbitrary." *Thesaurus Boletín del Instituto Caro y Cuervo* 5 (1949): 52-62.

CARPENTER, Humphrey, ed. with the assistance of Christopher TOLKIEN. *The Letters of J.R.R. Tolkien*. London: George Allen & Unwin, 1981.

CRYSTAL, David. *English as a Global Language*. Cambridge: Cambridge University Press, 2003.

FIMI, Dimitra. *Tolkien, Race and Cultural History. From Fairies to Hobbits*. London and New York: Palgrave Macmillan, 2009.

GENETTE, Gérard. *Mimologics: A Voyage into Cratylusland*. Trans. Thaïs E. Morgan. Lincoln: University of Nebraska Press, 1995.

GYMNICH, Marion. "Reconsidering the Linguistics of Middle-earth: Invented Languages and Other Linguistic Features in J.R.R. Tolkien's *The Lord of the Rings*." *Reconsidering Tolkien*. Ed. Thomas Honegger. Cormarë Series 8. Zurich and Berne: Walking Tree, 2005. 7-30.

HONEGGER, Thomas. "The Westron Turned into Modern English: The Translator and Tolkien's Web of Languages." *Translating Tolkien*. Ed. Thomas Honegger. Cormarë Series 6. Zurich and Berne: Walking Tree Publishers, 2004. 1-20.

HOSTETTER, Carl F. "Languages Invented by Tolkien." *J.R.R. Tolkien Encyclopedia: Scholarship and Critical Assessment*. Ed. Michael D. C. Drout. New York: Routledge, 2007. 332-344.

JOHANNESSON, Nils-Lennart. "The Speech of the Individual and of the Community in *The Lord of the Rings*.' *News from the Shire and Beyond – Studies on Tolkien*. Eds. Peter Buchs and Thomas Honegger. Second edition. First edition 1997. Cormarë Series 1. Zurich and Berne: Walking Tree Publishers, 2004. 13-57.

KLOCZKO, Edouard. *Dictionnaire des langues elfiques*. Toulon: Tamise Production, 1995.

Dictionnaire des langues des hobbits, des nains, des orques. Argenteuil: ARDA, 2002.

KORTMANN, Bernd. *English Linguistics: Essentials*. Berlin: Cornelsen, 2005.

LEVIN, Jules F. "Saussure and the arbre 'tree': A Fundamental Misunderstanding." *The Semiotic Bridge. Trends from California*. Eds. Irmengard Rauch and Gerald F. Carr. Berlin et al.: Mouton de Gruyter, 1989. 355-362.

"The Sign Is Still not Arbitrary: Some Semiotic Principles of Language Origin." *Interdigitations. Essays for Irmengard Rauch.* Eds. Gerald F. Carr, Wayne Harbert and Lihua Zhang New York et al.: Peter Lang, 1999. 519-528.

MAGNUS, Margaret. *Gods of the Word: Archetypes in the Consonants.* Kirksville, MO: Thomas Jefferson University Press, 1999.

NAGEL, Rainer. *Hobbit Place-Names. A Linguistic Excursion through the Shire.* Cormarë Series 23. Zurich and Jena: Walking Tree Publishers, 2012.

NOEL, Ruth S. *The Languages of Tolkien's Middle-earth.* Boston: Houghton Mifflin, 1980.

SEGURA, Eduardo, and Guillermo PERIS. "Tolkien as Philo-Logist." *Reconsidering Tolkien.* Ed. Thomas Honegger. Cormarë Series 8. Zurich and Berne: Walking Tree Publishers, 2005. 31-44.

SHIPPEY, Tom. *The Road to Middle-Earth.* London: HarperCollins, 2005.

SMITH, Ross. *Inside Language: Linguistic and Aesthetic Theory in Tolkien.* Cormarë Series 12. Zurich: Walking Tree Publishers, 2007.

TOLKIEN, John Ronald Reuel. *The Lord of the Rings.* 2nd ed. of 50th anniversary edition. London: HarperCollins, 2007.

The Monsters and the Critics and Other Essays. Ed. Christopher Tolkien. London: George Allen & Unwin, 1983.

"Nomenclature of *The Lord of the Rings.*" Wayne G. Hammond and Christina Scull. *The Lord of the Rings. A Reader's Companion.* London: HarperCollins, 2005. 750-782.

The Peoples of Middle-earth. Ed. Christopher Tolkien. Boston: Houghton Mifflin, 1996.

A Secret Vice. Eds. Dimitra Fimi and Andrew Higgins. London: HarperCollins, 2016.

TOLLEY, Clive. "Old English Influence on *The Lord of the Rings.*" *Beowulf and Other Stories: A New Introduction to Old English, Old Icelandic and Anglo-Norman Literatures.* Eds. Richard North and Joe Allard. Edinburgh: Pearson Education, 2007. 38-62.

VINK, Renée. "'Jewish Dwarves'. Tolkien and Anti-semitic Stereotyping." *Tolkien Studies* 10 (2013): 123-145.

Sebastian Streitberger

Concepts of Space in Middle-earth's Landscapes or the Potential of Fantasy and Film for School Geography

Abstract

Peter Jackson's Oscar-winning *The Lord of the Rings* trilogy followed in the footsteps of J.R.R. Tolkien and the defining importance of his novel for fantasy literature. Film and literature have certainly both been imported into everyday educational life all around the world. Fantasy arguably has not. Thus, this paper argues that supposedly non-educational (fantasy) films can in fact be used effectively for educational purposes if educators view them through their individual scientific – in the case of this essay geographical – glasses. I seek to demonstrate my point by taking Peter Jackson's filmic interpretation of J.R.R. Tolkien's *The Lord of the Rings* as a starting point and by bringing it together with the fundamental geographical concept of space.

After establishing a theoretical basis for using film (as a medium) and fantasy (as a genre) in the classroom, the second part of this paper will focus on a discussion of strategies to adapt Tolkien's Middle-earth for geography education. To embed these discussions within a geography teaching frame, I will introduce various perceptions of geographical space: from the early – yet not outdated – concept of "material space" (e.g. through the concept of "ecozones") and "systematically ordered space" (e.g. through the "Central Place Theory") to a more constructivist perspective on spaces (e.g. through concepts of "individually perceived space" or "socially constructed space"). In doing so, various geographical and non-geographical educational media such as maps, graphs, text information and drawings from and of Tolkien's oeuvre will be used to enhance Jackson's *The Lord of the Rings* for the classroom and steer students through Middle-earth's landscapes, while changing their spatial perception on the way. Likewise, teachers and educators are provided with an example so to unlock the educational potential of film and fantasy for their classrooms.

1 Introduction: Objectives of this paper

"Why don't we watch a film, Mr Keating?" – this question seems to re-echo every time during the school year when holidays are drawing closer. While both teachers and pupils will tend to be willing to grasp the opportunity of responding to such a request in light of the nearing break, they will most likely disagree on the genre let alone the actual film. Teachers, on the one hand, may favour documentaries on recently discussed topics; pupils, on the other hand, may unanimously agree on the latest Hollywood smash hit picture. Being a geography educator and film lover myself, I would argue that there is a wealth of films and series for a teacher to choose from while still ensuring a balance of information and entertainment appropriate for the classroom.

Hence, this paper argues that supposedly non-educational films can in fact be used effectively for educational purposes, if teachers view them through their scientific – in this case geographical – glasses. I seek to demonstrate my point by taking Peter Jackson's filmic interpretation of J.R.R. Tolkien's *The Lord of the Rings* as a starting point and by bringing it together with the fundamental geographical concept of "space".

After establishing a theoretical basis for using film (as a medium) and fantasy (as a genre) in the geography classroom, the second part of this paper will focus on a discussion of strategies to adapt Tolkien's Middle-earth for geography education. To embed these discussions within a geography teaching frame, I will introduce various perceptions of geographical space: from the early – yet not outdated – concept of "material space" (e.g. through the concept of "ecozones") and "systematically ordered space" (e.g. through the "Central Place Theory") to a more constructivist perspective on spaces (e.g. through concepts of "individually perceived space" or "socially constructed space"). In doing so, various geographical and non-geographical educational media such as maps, graphs, text information and drawings from and of Tolkien's oeuvre will be used to enhance Jackson's *The Lord of the Rings* for the classroom and steer students through Middle-earth's landscapes, while changing their spatial perception on the way. Likewise, teachers and educators are provided with an example of how to unlock the educational potential of film and fantasy for their classrooms.

2 Film as an educational medium! Fantasy as catalyst for learning?

While the value and potentials of the mass medium film for educational purposes has been acknowledged since the very beginnings of this medium (when the brothers Lumière created an international stir with their moving pictures in the late 19th century), the first purely educational films began to emerge some years later in 1910 with *The Minute Men* or *Life History of the Silk Worm* (Saettler 96-99). In 1913, renowned inventor and progressive Thomas Edison confidently uttered his belief that "[it] is possible to teach every branch of human knowledge with motion picture [and that our] school system will be completely changed in ten years" (Saettler 98). And yet, contrary to Edison's predictions, modern-day education does not orbit around film: When different journals for geography education are tested for specific keywords in a purely quantitative approach, German journals show only ten,[1] the English-language *Journal of Geography* 27 entries for "film" in issues published since 1980.[2]

In order to be able to talk about modern film further on, the terminology should be established. Film – both with respect to its origins and a contemporary understanding of this mainstream medium – is constituted of three overlapping spheres, which had been developed by the late 19th century: For one thing, it deals with authentic reality. This also includes any form of a vaguely plausible reality: a secondary world like Middle-earth, for example, is not real per se; however, it is realistic and therefore authentic in its own ontology. Otherwise, fictional films could not be considered part of the definition. Second, films use a narrative structure; movies tell stories. Even documentaries use literary devices in order to establish some form of narration. Narrators guide the recipient through the mass of information. Third, films use scenes, i.e. sequences of continuous action, which convey a sense of live broadcast (Faulstich 17-18). Each of these three characteristics on its own is not radically new for a medium. Yet together, they create the pillars of this undisputedly popular mass medium. Moreover, from an educator's perspective, each of them can easily be linked to classroom teaching situations: Teachers always try to "bring reality" into the classroom by using real problems, real situations and real topics. They also try to weave a continuous thread that runs through their lessons, thereby establishing a narrative structure that highlights information relevant for their students' learning processes and which omits anything not relevant

---

1 The journals under scrutiny are *Praxis Geographie, Geographie heute, Geographie aktuell & Schule* (and its predecessor), *Zeitschrift für Geographiedidaktik and Geographie und ihre Didaktik* (since its first issue).
2 The following keywords were used: "film", "movie", "video", "DVD", "television (TV)", and their German equivalents. The entries were not tested for appropriateness with regard to non-educational films, however.

(Schekatz-Schopmeier 21-26).³ And finally, teachers can only focus on a very specific and often limited fragment of information, which might be shown in just a few scenes. Due to these similarities, films as a medium can be assumed to be appropriate for the classroom.

In a didactic sense, films are first and foremost, what has already been established, a medium. Media, in turn, can be described as carriers of information and are usually used "where genuine encounters are not possible"⁴ (Brucker, "Womit unterrichten" 64). Since genuine encounters between students and an educationally relevant subject matter are indeed rarely possible – one cannot simply bring, for example, a volcano to the classroom – media play a major role inside of classrooms, potentially creating communication opportunities for teachers and students. However, educators often struggle with other problems. For one thing, viewers must overcome their expectations to be solely entertained when watching a movie. Moreover, teachers must settle technical and organisational issues: how to play the film, where to borrow the equipment (e.g. players, speakers) from, etc. Only some schools offer broadband wifi connections in their classrooms, while others do not, which may complicate matters. What is more, films require at least a modest degree of media literacy: students must be aware of a film's bias and their awareness needs to be raised in regard to the fast-paced succession of images and sounds therein. The former is particularly true for the teacher who seeks to include telecinematic materials in their lessons. In addition, a teacher will have to work with what they are provided with: a film cannot be changed or adjusted by the teacher according to their didactic wishes. On the contrary, teachers must either aimfully choose a film that can be smoothly and efficiently integrated in their lesson plan or change their own plans in accordance with a certain film's content, message, structure or potential interactivity (Wüthrich 153).

When it comes to school audiences, moving images show their potential in other aspects, nonetheless. First of all, motivation plays a major role in the process of learning (Krapp, Geyer, and Lewalter 209). As teachers we may encourage our

---

3 This is also known as "Didaktische Strukturierung" and forms a crucial part in developing or improving lessons according to the idea of "Didaktische Rekonstruktion" which again tries to consider both the perspectives of the individual learner and each discipline's requirements. For more information see Kattmann.
4 The original German reads: "wo die originale Begegnung nicht möglich ist".

students to watch films for their explicit visualisations on the one hand; on the other hand, films depict a certain degree of the real world and allow for this reality to enter the classroom. Furthermore, films can usually show dynamic processes much better than other – more static – media may be able to. While their high pace might make it more difficult for some viewers to process the information presented, films also offer the chance to rewind and pause but also interlace sound and imagery (Brucker, "Klassische Medien kreativ nutzen" 180).

It is this interlacing Allen Paivio underlines in his "Dual-Coding Theory". According to him, there are two different codes for representing information: the verbal and the imaginal. While verbal code (e.g. language) can stand by itself, imaginal code always includes verbal code. When an image comes to one's mind, most recipients will process and potentially remember it both visually and verbally. They will verbalise the visual representation to a certain degree. Therefore, imaginal types of media can enhance memorising information and retrieving this memory at a later point in time (Clark and Paivio 151-156, 165-166; Paivio). Research by Beentjes and van der Voort from 1993 supports Clark and Paivio's theoretical assumptions: students would remember information better when they had extracted it from films rather than print media (Nieding and Ohler 389-390). Much of the potential of films is lost, however, when they are only used passively. The whole process of watching must be enriched by a process of working with the information given (Biddulph, Lambert, and Balderstone 195). This holds particularly true for landscapes in films which will be our main object of discussion later on. Carl argues that

> [w]hen reading landscapes in film, it is important to distinguish between the landscape prior to filming and the 'product' that we view in the film. Therefore, different layers of meanings, texts and symbols have to be acknowledged as well as the intention of the filmmaker to translate landscape into film; all of which can alter the pre-filmed landscape. In detail, we need to consider how and why the landscape was transformed. This leads to the mise-en-scène (in which way the image was shot and what was chosen to be the image in film), montage, sound and the narrative structure in which the landscape is portrayed. (33)

Non-educational feature films equally call for a much more active form of watching: "Seeing does not mean perceiving" (di Palma 48); only active engagement on the part of students might develop a deepened understanding of geographical contents and enhance geographical knowledge. Here, media literacy also includes that students understand the use of camera angles, lighting, colour, exposition and its sequence of images; they learn to interpret cinematographic language. Likewise, they will gain insights into cultural parameters which constitute film, and learn to see its complexities as well as its (over-)simplifications (di Palma 48-49). Since films tend to exaggerate, they might also amplify geographical topics (Wilhelmi 57). In addition, narrative cinema allows for viewers to see the world from the very beginning of the film unlike literature, which must establish the frame step by step, word by word, over dozens of pages (Aitken 105). Thus, non-educational films can offer both a variety of opportunities for educational purposes when their challenges are addressed, and a unique way to gather information, especially for geographers, as Lukinbeal remarks:

> Film offers geographers a realm of information which combines multiple perspective[s], imagination, art, objective and subjective qualities, geographical information and geographical imagination. Films may also provide one way to explore personal and cultural perceptions and attitudes towards landscapes. (5)

Furthermore, non-educational films are part of popular culture; nowadays, they often constitute only one small cog in the huge marketing machinery, which may involve books, video and board games, toys and other consumables but also landscapes and with them touristic destinations (Carl 42-43):

> Our modern civilisation, like all civilisations before it, has settled around a set of myths and legends as the basis of its culture. They are more complex, more interesting, more sophisticated, and with a much richer interaction between creators and fans than you might think. Far from being mere films or comic books, they are whole extended fictional universes, entirely self-consistent, with deep histories, hundreds of characters, and even a form of theological scholarship. (BBC)

When di Palma argues fictional films to be easier deconstructed as they lack the pseudo-objectivity of documentaries (48) or for them being distinct by their "ontological rupture" (Fowkes 5), fantasy films should be even more deconstructible. Not only do they lack objectivity, but they openly enunciate their own fabricated reality. Cinematic images and their semiotic landscapes are reconstructed by their viewers; they assign meaning to the images (Aitken and Zonn 7-8). This "reminds us why fantasy films may be particularly rich: they excel in employing multi-faceted symbols that engage viewers on many levels" (Fowkes 173).

Whereas film and literature have both been imported and woven into everyday educational life all around the world, fantasy, arguably, has not. Using the same approach as before with the keyword "film", the results for "fantasy"[5] indicate only two (German journals) and six (English-language *Journal of Geography*) instances, respectively. Altogether, both film and fantasy – and especially the latter – can be considered a niche at best in our educational world. This is startling, as fantastical narratives have in fact been a well-established genre since the beginnings of film-production in the early 20th century. George Méliès' *Le Voyage dans la Lune* can be regarded as not only the first feature-length film with its barely double-digit running time but also the forerunner of modern film in general and modern fantasy films like *The Lord of the Rings* in particular (Faulstich 19-21). From a psychological standpoint, this also seems to be peculiar since it is especially genres with an arc of suspense (e.g. action, adventure or horror films) which activate their viewers on a cognitive level (Schweizer and Klein 160-161). The crux for educational use, however, lies in an emphasis on entertainment regarding these genres: "Fantasy films (like all mainstream movies) are first and foremost designed to entertain" (Fowkes 172). Thus, it is more challenging to use films in a learning environment than a cinema hall. Students must acquire the competence to draw information from these films first – as already pointed out before. Certainly, fantasy's inherent charm makes it all the more obvious for modern geographical education: "looking at the familiar from an unfamiliar perspective" (Worley 270). It is the unfamiliar perspective on Middle-earth which we shall zoom in on in the following.

3 *The Lord of the Rings* in geography education

A milestone for the fantasy film genre, Peter Jackson's *The Lord of the Rings* trilogy followed in the footsteps of J.R.R. Tolkien and his defining importance for fantasy literature (Fowkes 134). The vast scope of Tolkien's closed world with its own immanent history, languages and geography can be studied almost as thoroughly and coherently as the physically existing earth in which we live. Since fantasy does not entail unrealistic but rather unreal pieces of information and, hence, follows the rules which apply for reality as well, Middle-earth

---

[5] The following keywords were used: "fantasy", "narrative (text)", "fairytale", "fiction", "fictional (text)".

might be exactly the right choice when one seeks to integrate a fantastical basis into real-life geography education: It was Tolkien's "wonder and delight in the Earth as it is, particularly the natural earth" (Resnick 41) as well as his belief that a secondary world must not differ all too much from its primary source world which led to an "inner consistency of reality" (*TL* 48). This consistency is visible throughout *The Lord of the Rings* (Fonstad ix):

> Northward the dale ran up into a glen of shadows between two great arms of the mountains, above which three white peaks were shining: Celebdil, Fanuidhol, Caradhras, the Mountains of Moria. At the head of the glen a torrent flowed like a white lace over an endless ladder of short falls, and a mist of foam hung in the air about the mountains' feet. (*FR* 347)

While Tolkien applies many descriptions of his world, only Jackson's visualisation can instantly offer access to it and prompt a complex network of individual images (Pinkas 145). Jackson brilliantly succeeds in rebuilding Tolkien's detailed world and in populating it; his world appears consistent and understandable (Butler 80-84). Landscape plays a major and active role within this world and the narrative of the films – not only as a background behind the story but also as meaningful environment that influences the characters (Carl 150). Nonetheless, Middle-earth's geography is fictitious and potential geographical topics within it are detached from reality. This, however, does not have to be a disadvantage for pupils might be able to think outside the box more easily when focusing on Middle-earth: "It feels familiar and nonetheless not quite the same" (John Howe on Jackson, *FR* disc 1). This also comes in handy when the teacher introduces rather abstract ideas like the inherently geographical concept of spatial perception, which I will present in the upcoming section; I will do so by choosing Tolkien's world and the images evoked through Jackson's films as my setting.

4 Spatial perception: everywhere and nowhere

Spatial perception or the perception of space is a key concept of geography and can be described as part of each geographer's conceptual content knowledge (Biddulph, Lambert, and Balderstone 143; Mittelstädt 140; L. Taylor,

9).[6] The German Geographical Society emphasises its pivotal position in geographical curricula as follows:

> Space, as well as time, is an existential aspect of our lives and it is therefore urgently necessary to consider it in detail. The ability to orient oneself spatially in different ways is therefore an important geographical competence, going well beyond the possession of basic topographic knowledge and serving as the foundation for the development of further geographical competences. However, students do not only acquire spatial orientation competence, but also analyse regions of the Earth at different scales, [...] from different perspectives and with regard to various problems. In this way, they acquire fundamental regional geographical knowledge about regions, nations and groups of nations as well as the potential to develop a considered awareness of their home country, awareness as Europeans and cosmopolitan attitudes between the global and the local. (Deutsche Gesellschaft für Geographie 6)

Yet, each definition of the concept is very limited due to the wide array of geographical fields which all choose alternative approaches (Jackson 199). Accordingly, "space can be conceptualised radically different and applied in totally different ways depending on the scientific focus" (Seebacher 65).[7] Thus, these differing concepts are rarely amalgamated. Merging them nonetheless, might lead to epistemological or methodological problems (Seebacher 66). Hence, I will introduce only two variants of the concept and will do so sequentially: "space" versus "place" and Wardenga's four concepts of space.

4.1 Spatial perception: space versus place

This chapter will focus on the distinction between "space" and "place" as they – according to Tuan – "together define the nature of geography" ("Humanistic Perspective" 133; *Experience*). I would argue that they cannot even be defined satisfyingly without involving the other (Cresswell, "Space and Place" 55). Space, to begin with, has constituted a central aspect of geographical science for a long time. Yet, it cannot be reduced to its connotation of emptiness, which it shows

---

6 Geographers do not necessarily agree on the terminology. In German-language geography "space" and "place" are often translated as one: "Raum". Furthermore, geographical concepts of space do not necessarily align with non-geographical ones, see Christine Vogt-William's essay in this volume, in particular chapter 5 "Liminal green "Othered" spaces". For more information on different approaches and the general geographical discussion about space and place see Seebacher (and here in particular pages 67-68) and Köck.
7 The original quote reads "[...] dass 'Raum' als Konzept höchst unterschiedlich gedacht wird und je nach Forschungsperspektive in völlig unterschiedlicher Weise [...] eingesetzt werden kann."

in everyday speech and has been in existence since Plato. According to Newton and Leibniz space does not necessarily relate to emptiness but rather to a form of reality that is objectively measurable (Jonietz 20-21). Space in films can be visible through the landscape, for example. However, landscape in this sense is limited to a minor role as a mere setting that is somehow interchangeable (Carl 32).

> At one level, the space created by film is simply the frame within which a subject is located, and twenty-four of these frames pass before our eyes every second. This space enables the subject of the film to unfold in a variety of ways that may be controlled by the filmmaker. More than neutral space, however, these shots demand to be read as real places with their own sense of geography and history. (Aitken and Zonn 15-16)

The Shire, for instance, is described in many a material detail – verbally in Tolkien's books, visually in Jackson's films. Its perception transcends the physical description: it rather conveys a "sense" of the Shire: Its landscape seems inviting, harmonic and reassuring. It feels like home (Carl 62-63). Here, landscape has a more integral part in the narrative of the film and transforms the formerly known space into a place (Lukinbeal 68). Place, in short, "is a space with attitude" (P. Taylor 10). *The Lord of the Rings* uses landscapes much more actively and attributes certain features to these places (Carl 32). Landscape is thereby endowed with a certain purpose: "Place is a meaningful site that combines location, locale and sense of place" (Cresswell, "Place" 169).[8] While "location" can be defined by the measurable coordinates of a place, "locale" includes its surroundings, e.g. buildings, trees or specific areas. "A sense of place", however, adds emotional impressions to an otherwise objectively perceivable space. These emotions do not necessarily have to be distinct amongst individuals but can in fact be shared. It is especially this sense of place which is widely used in fantasy films and novels (Carl 33; Cresswell, "Place" 169-170) and may open a discussion of diegesis in *The Lord of the Rings* – and films in general. For instance, to what extent does Jackson's score change the visuals on an extradiegetic level? When do you see the subjectivity of the *The Lord of the Rings* otherwise stable and homogenous yet impossible world? Does this subjectivity lead to an instability

---

8 For more information on how Tolkien has imbued his locations with locale and a sense of place see authors Wayne G. Hammond and Christina Scull in their art collections (*Hobbit; Lord of the Rings*). I find the development of Rivendell or Hobbiton especially noteworthy.

of the world (Pinkas 148-151)? Furthermore, places cannot exist without people (or hobbits, elves, dwarves etc.). Since places carry meaning for the creatures that inhabit them, they have been named: their names imply subjective, personal or collective pictures and connotations (Uhlenwinkel 182-187; on place names also cf. Tober and Traxel in this volume).

Categorisations of space and place are not cast in stone as already mentioned. Spaces, for instance, can turn into places when people begin to integrate them into their everyday lives. Individuals connect spaces with their experiences so that they eventually develop associations (Cresswell, "Place" 169-170). *The Lord of the Rings* and *The Hobbit* may have transformed many of their viewers' perspectives on New Zealand from being a mere space (with landscape) into being an actual place (of meaningful landscape). Experience may add another crucial factor in changing space into place: through kinaesthetic familiarity. There are specific environments through which individuals can move without thinking about where to put their feet; they are familiar with the place around them. Thus, place can be both constructed actively when attributing meaning to a space and experienced in unconscious ways as well (Cresswell, "Space and Place" 56).

Both space and place are visible in *The Lord of the Rings* in many different scenes and with regard to many different perspectives. When Frodo first learns about his quest and its purpose, i.e. to throw the One Ring into the fires of Mount Doom, he only begins to give meaning to the route to and into Mordor. Up until that moment, it had been but a distant location irrelevant for his life. But now, the space between his home and his goal becomes a burden, and hence a place (*FR*). Likewise, Gandalf hesitates to enter the Mines of Moria. He knows of its meaning which becomes visible in the many names given to this place: Halls of Durin, Khazad-dûm, Dwarrowdelf, Hadhodrond or Phurunargian (*FR*).

Not only the characters of *The Lord of the Rings* distinguish between space and place, also the viewers (or readers) do. Landscapes in *The Lord of the Rings* are usually used as places rather than spaces when they are described or visualised: dark landscapes, e.g. Mordor or Isengard (at least after Saruman's defection), imply lifelessness, destruction and – more generally – evil, whereas bright landscapes are full of sound, lush nature and good forces (Carl 61-70). Peter Jackson used meaningful places even when the spaces did not carry this meaning themselves: he changed, pre- or post-edited and ultimately distorted certain filming sites, e.g. the Shire – as I will discuss later on in more detail – in order to transport the intended associations (Carl 62-64). Probably even more meaning is infused into Mordor in its video game adaptation in *Middle-earth: Shadow of Mordor*. There, Mordor is incorporated much more focally and from a different perspective, featuring the more fertile Núrn and the bleak Udûn as in-game locations, while the Plateau of Gorgoroth is merely visible in the background. Native New Zealander and Weta Workshop Creative Supervisor Richard Taylor sums up different viewpoints on one and the same landscape when he says: "The sad thing about a lot of the sceneries in these movies is a lot of the world's population will think there's some clever piece of digital effect when actually they're just real locations around the country" (Jackson, *TT* disc 1 around 01:20 with creation design commentary on).

4.2 Spatial perception: four concepts of space

Sometimes overlapping, sometimes different from the aforementioned discussion between space and place, there is another element of geographical conceptual content knowledge that deals with different approaches to spatiality: Wardenga's four concepts of space.[9] They are regarded central in German geography education, e.g. by the Arbeitsgruppe Curriculum 2000+, and relate to changing core views on space in the history of this discipline. Here, Wardenga distinguishes between four concepts of space: material space, systematically ordered space, individually perceived space and, finally, socially constructed space (Deutsche Gesellschaft für Geographie 6; Wardenga, "Räume"; Wardenga, "Raumkonzepte" 8-11). While the former two concepts see space as a real, material geographical space, the latter two follow a perception-based stance. Nonetheless, all four concepts are accepted in geographical discussions but may lead to a different range of topics (Kaminske 21-25). Accordingly, they are illustrated in the following with regard to specific geographical contents within and surrounding Middle-earth.

---

9 For purposes of misleading translations, only the term "space" will be used when referring to Wardenga's list of concepts. See also the Deutsche Gesellschaft für Geographie (6).

4.2.1 Material space

Geography has seen itself as a scientific discipline that defines its raison d'être by space itself. Alfred Hettner had introduced this idea well before it began to gain popularity in the late 19th century, when an increasingly complex and extensive world made it necessary to present information in more concise ways. Regional geography has ever since approached spaces by defining and specifying them and then to describe their geographical contents. The concept of space used to be understood and applied as if it were a very restricted container for holding information, which again would be constituted of the material, i.e. a measurable and openly perceivable world. Space would include natural (e.g. rock formations, climate, biota), anthropogenic (e.g. people, cities, infrastructure) and every other physically present detail without further reflection (Wardenga, "Räume" 47-49; Wardenga, "Raumkonzepte" 8-9). The focus was on location and locale without attaching sense.

When regional geographers described the uniqueness of certain landscapes as a specific container, they applied the concept of material space which can be described as a rather static piece of landscape. Likewise, Peter Jackson – as much as many other directors – regularly uses shots of static landscapes as openers for entire scenes as is visible in the collage of stills (see Figure 2). It is such shots that show a particular potential for the classroom (Wardenga, "Raumkonzepte" 9) and their abundance bears upon Tolkien's storytelling, in which a plethora of sceneries unfolds over the course of events, e.g. Hobbiton's green hilly countryside, the snow-capped Misty Mountains or the swampy Dead Marshes (Carl 59). Tolkien seems to have been very keen on delivering primary world geography to his Middle-earth by not only introducing landforms, vegetation etc., but also by creating entire ecosystems that show the dynamic interaction of these elements (Fonstad 179).

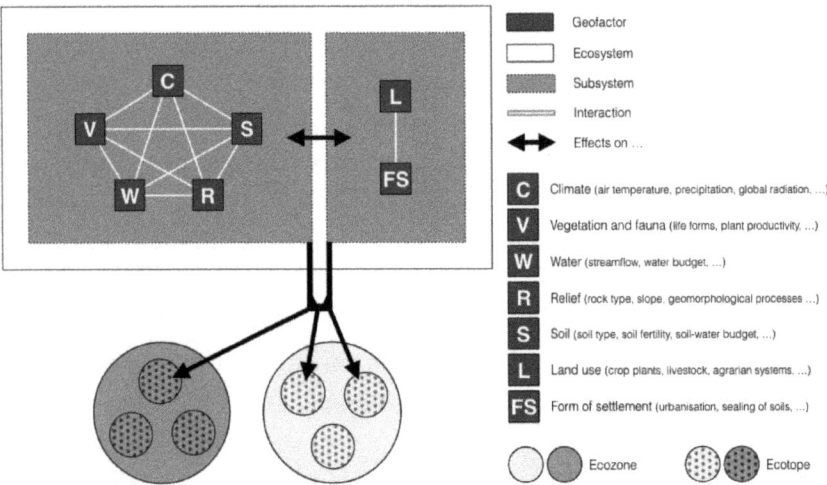

Figure 1: Relation between geofactors, ecosystems, ecotopes and ecozones (Bailey, *Ecosystem* 41-50; Engelmann and Scholz 9-10; Schultz 23-24)

In the classroom, the footage of such extraordinarily marked landscapes – interwoven with descriptions voiced by the narrator or the characters – can be analysed by adhering to the so-called concept of "ecozones".[10] By ecozones geographers generally refer to large-scale areal representations of ecosystems that are subject to geofactors such as climate, soils, water, vegetation and anthropogenic influences (see Figure 1). Their smallest sub-category is usually called "ecotope" or "microecosystem" (Bailey, *Ecosystem* 3-20; Engelmann and Scholz 8-10; Schultz 18-25). One may find clues about geofactors making up ecozones/ecotopes by exploring and examining specific landscapes in detail. Examples I will discuss are Jackson's Shire, Rohan and Mordor.[11] Independent from the landscape(s) chosen by a geography teacher, the task for the classroom might be something along the following lines: "Look at the landscape. Where could you film these scenes? Choose a single country which features all the geographical characteristics for you to shoot each one of these three scenes."

---

10 There are differences in the terminology within this idea. While some use the term "ecoregion" (Bailey, *Ecosystem*; *Ecoregion*), others use "geo-ecozones" (Engelmann and Scholz) or simply "ecozones" (Schultz). The scientific understanding does not vary considerably between these terms. For Schultz (18) it is merely a differentiation with regard to scale. For more information please see the aforementioned authors.

11 Obviously, there are many more examples for Middle-earthian landscapes to be scrutinised under the concept of ecozones, e.g. Rivendell, Isengard or the hills of Emyn Muil (Carl 62-76).

Sebastian Streitberger: Concepts of Space in Middle-earth's Landscapes

Figure 2: Stills from *The Lord of the Rings* by Peter Jackson
(A = Shire; B = Rohan; C = Mordor)

The Shire[12] (as in Figure 2, A) could be described with regard to its anthropogenic (or "hobbitogenic") overprint: Hobbiton is characterised by various species of livestock, e.g. cattle, pig, goat and sheep, and its visible agriculture; fields are ploughed and hoed; flowers, vegetables and other crops are cultivated. This already indicates highly fertile land. Lush and full vegetation – grass, bushes, hedges and trees – reinforce this impression, as well as streams, ponds and lakes suggest an adequate amount of precipitation and a humid climate. Deciduous forests alternate with fields; blooming flowers are omnipresent. The air temperature seems to be quite warm and stable when you compare nighttime to day-time since the hobbits celebrate Bilbo's birthday in short sleeves. All this portends to the humid temperate domain with a maritime component and, thus, to merely 0.92 % of the global land area, e.g. in West Europe, British

---

12 The information given here is mainly drawn from scenes in *FR* (Jackson, disc 1 08:52-16:30 and 20:00-25:49).

Columbia's coastal region, west Chile and New Zealand's southernmost part of the South Island (Bailey, *Ecosystem* 86-89 and the enclosed map). Since soft hills dominate Hobbiton's relief, the list of potential filming locations can be reduced further: British Columbia's coastal region, for example, is primarily composed of mountainous terrain, which contradicts the lack of mountains in Hobbiton's scenery – unless digitally removed.

The factual landscape in the films is located around New Zealand's North Island's Matamata in the Hinuera Valley. It, too, is characterised by agriculture, more specifically by sheep farming. This form of agriculture has led to a mosaic of smaller parcels of pine forests and larger pastures for the livestock. While settlers have deforested the area in order to create the pastures, it was their sheep which grazed the under-storey vegetation almost entirely bare. For the films, Jackson post-edited the pine trees in a way that they resembled oak trees, thus alluding to Tolkien's idea of the Shire as home, i.e. England and Wales. This allusion was further established by using European field crops and flowers on set; the non-native plants had to be injected with hormones that protected them against predators and kept them in a presentable state. In order to enhance this false authenticity of England/Wales, European clothing from centuries ago and a black-headed breed of sheep, which were primarily common in England, were used (Carl 62-64).[13] This fake material space thus blends authentic New Zealand ecozones with such elements meant to lead the audience to believe that it actually resembles a genuine English/Welsh ecozone. On the one hand, this might be quite difficult for students to grasp; on the other hand, it could help bridging to the concept of constructed space – which I will discuss later on – especially when the students learn to use cinematographic terms in order to describe alterations for the sake of the narrative or the director's intentions. For example, both colour and shading can be discussed when the mis-en-scène is brought into prominence (Aitken and Zonn 16-17).

By contrast, B (Rohan[14]) shows extensive plains of treeless grassland in shades of dominantly brown and green. Similar to Hobbiton and the Shire, there are also

---

13 Mind you, there were up to 12,000 sheep on site. Jackson imported them although the Shire scenes were filmed on a working sheep farm.
14 The information given here is mainly drawn from scenes in *The Two Towers* (Jackson, disc 1 18:40-19:15, 22:00-23:03, 24:05-24:18; disc 2 00:00-01:45) and *The Return of the King* (Jackson, disc 2 29:07-29:32).

indications of anthropogenic influences: huts, livestock and settlements such as Edoras. Moreover, Rohan is surrounded by snow-capped mountains (Carl 73-74). Aragorn comments on its climate when he says that the Riddermark "'is cold until the sudden spring, and [they] may yet have snow again'" (*FR* 397). This indicates a rather continental climate (Fonstad 182). Its low temperatures are also implied in a scene in *The Return of the King* in which Aragorn meets Legolas on the terrace of Edoras' palace at night-time: Legolas wears the hood of his cloak – possibly against the cold. Furthermore, the film scenes point towards a geographical mosaic within Rohan's landscapes. While the steppe-like appearance is consistent, there is also a varying ratio of grass to shrubs and boulders to be seen now and then. In addition, Edoras sits at a height lower than other parts of Rohan, which is implied by the mountains surrounding the capital being only covered with snow at their very tops. Earlier shots of Rohan in the films show mountains being covered with snow almost down to their feet, too. Snow coverage and lakes here and there also indicate a relatively high amount of precipitation.

According to Bailey all these observations are typical descriptions of a temperate, semi-arid climate in the mid-latitudes, i.e. to only 1.22 % of the global land area, or the humid temperate domain with its semi-humid prairies – 3.02 % of the global land area (*Ecosystem* 86-89). However, since prairies are characterised by taller species of grass than their semi-arid counterparts, Jackson's Rohan suggests the latter. Its cooler air temperatures, especially in winter, might lead to a relatively low level of evapotranspiration. Hence, the vegetation is of small growth and mainly comprised of different species of shortgrass which have adapted to seasonal levels of precipitation (Bailey, *Ecoregions* 63 and 75-76). Yet, Rohan's treelessness might be caused by azonal influences as well: local lee-side aridity or its location in the precipitation shadow of the Misty Mountains (Fonstad 182-184). With these findings, students are able to narrow filming sites down to prairie and steppe ecozones in central North America, East Europe, central East Asia and Central Asia, South-East Australia and New Zealand's South Island east of its Alps (Bailey, *Ecosystem* and the enclosed map).

According to Tolkien himself, C (Mordor[15]) draws inspiration from the Mediterranean volcanic basin and Stromboli being Mount Doom (Fonstad 90). It is visualised as a dark, volcanic landscape without water or vegetation. It is enclosed by mountains on three sides and shows man-made (or rather Orc-made), primarily military structures. The North Island's central Tongariro National Park was chosen for Mordor's shooting location. The setting was digitally enhanced in post-production so to highlight Mordor's bleakness and its – for both story and landscape – pivotal volcano Mount Doom (Carl 70). The near-to-complete lack of vegetation hints at a semi-arid to arid climate. Its black rocks could be composed of intrusive igneous gabbro or the extrusive igneous basalt (Fonstad 90).[16] According to Fonstad (90) basalt's columnar weathering may cause the described "tall piers and jagged pinnacles of stone on either side, between which were great crevices and fissures blacker than the night" (*TT* 319).

Another aspect is that there is no mention of snow or ice in Mordor (Fonstad 90); this suggests either that the air temperatures there must be above zero or that the ground must be heated by volcanic activity. Since Mount Doom towers at ca. 4,500 feet (Fonstadt 91), the overall temperature must be above zero atop the mountains and in the valley for there is no visible deposition of snow or ice in either of these areas. Yet, Sam shudders when he and Frodo take a rest after having rid themselves of the Orc armour; from the context, this seems to be caused by the clouded skies.

Light deprivation due to airborne volcanic aerosols might also be a major factor for the limited plant growth in the Plateau of Gorgoroth. Since it is an active volcanic region, stress from toxic gases, lava streams or eruptions might also shorten the vegetation period to the extent that the plateau remains largely barren. Hence, Sauron's troops must draw their supplies from other regions of his

---

15 The information given here is drawn from scenes in *The Fellowship of th Ring* (Jackson, disc 1 02:25-04:40 and 32:40-32:45) and *The Return of the King* (Jackson, disc 2 55:48-56:14, 01:00:50-01:02:29 and 01:04:17-01:06:37).
16 While intrusive igneous rock (e.g. gabbro) consists of crystallised magma that had intruded into otherwise unrelated wall rock, extrusive igneous rock (e.g. basalt) is a result of cooling down lava, i.e. magma which has reached the earth's surface (Vinx 130). Mordor's black landscape suggests the dark grey to black basaltic rocks, basanite or gabbro (Vinx 195 and 228).

kingdom. Volcanic areas often co-occur with fertile soils fertilised by volcanic ashes; thus, the ash plain Lithlad might serve this purpose (Fonstad 91).

Focusing on Mount Doom, its composition of relatively great height and steep slopes indicates a stratovolcano. Its shape is a result of highly viscous lava that is rich in silicon dioxide; this type of lava can usually be found in volcanic effusions at continental edges (Götze et al. 373). Recent volcanic activities like lave flows and the aforementioned igneous aerosols suggest that this volcano is highly active (Fonstad 146). Analogous to mountain ecozones, volcanic areas are azonal with regard to latitude, i.e. they can theoretically occur all around the globe (Bailey, *Ecosystem* 70). However, there are regions of lower and higher volcanic activity; high volcanic activity frequently occurs with close proximity to tectonic plate boundaries (Michael 242-243). Referring back to the task for the students – "Choose a single country which features all the geographical characteristics for you to shoot each of these three scenes." – the selection is already rather limited as the Shire and Rohan require temperate regions as a backdrop for filming. Taking into account that stratovolcanoes are more likely to occur at continental edges (Götze et al. 373), the Pacific Ring of Fire is the most likely for visualising Mordor and thus Middle-earth.[17]

All three examples as well as other regions of Jackson's Middle-earth share some common denominators which might lead a school class to locate a single country that comprises these ecozones and ecotopes. It must be a country featuring flatlands, hills, mountains, coastal areas and volcanic activity. Moreover, it must show a dominance of broadleaf vegetation and very few coniferous forests as visible in Jackson's films. Tolkien's descriptions also suggest prevailing westerly winds and an overall mild climate (Fonstad 180-184). Thus, not only winterless climates of low latitudes and summerless climates of high latitudes can be excluded (Bailey, *Ecosystem* 54-55), but the country must also be located both in temperate and dry mid-latitudes due to its west wind drift (Bailey, *Ecosystem* 204; Schultz 168). Since there are only two areas in the world which lack high summer temperatures within the dry mid-latitudes – these being Eastern Patagonia and New Zealand (Schultz 169) – potential filming locations were

---

17 "The Ring of Fire" is a circum-Pacific highly active volcanic belt that stretches from New Zealand in the south west to the Malay Archipelago, Japan, the Kamchatka Peninsula, the Aleutian Islands, West Canada, West USA, Mexiko and southwards along the west coast of South America.

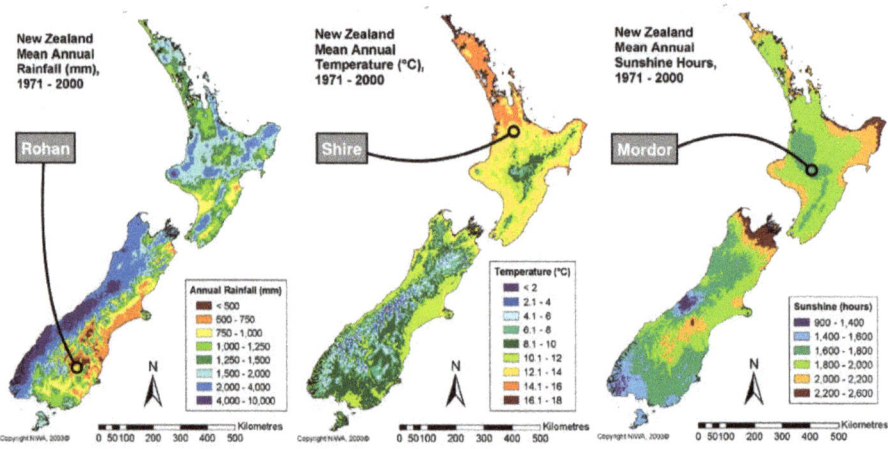

Figure 3: New Zealand climate (annual rainfall, temperature and sunshine hours) and the filming locations of Peter Jackson's Shire, Rohan and Mordor (New Zealand Institute of Water and Atmospheric Research, *Climate; New Zealand as Middle-earth* on the extended editions of Jackson's trilogy)

already reduced to a manageable number that can be thoroughly checked. Rainfall, temperature and sunshine (as illustrated in Figure 3) and climate data from the New Zealand Institute of Water and Atmospheric Research (*Overview; Summaries*) all substantiate the selection of the filming location in the South West Pacific country: New Zealand.

4.2.2 Systematically ordered space

Systematically ordered spaces, different from material ones, cannot be shown in a single screenshot. As the notion already indicates, a systematically ordered space refers to a system of locations; the confinements of the aforementioned container are blurred or have vanished entirely. This category of space now focuses on distances in between two or more spaces as well as their relationship to one another. In doing so, space is captured in its holistic entirety. Still very materialistic, systematically ordered spaces shape societal reality and highlight the dispersion and the integration of these spaces under the influence of the Anglo-American spatial approach of the 1970s (Wardenga, "Räume" 49;

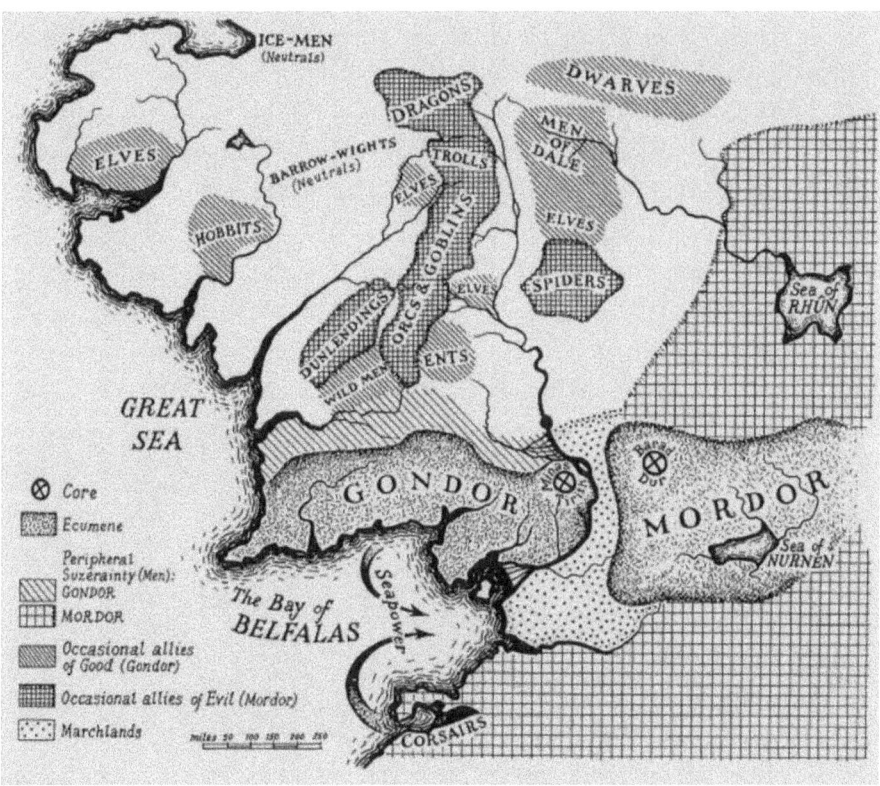

Figure 4: Political geography in Middle-earth (Porteous 35)

Wardenga, "Raumkonzepte" 9-10). *The Lord of the Rings* reveals the connections which are necessary for this spatial concept, for example, through war, history and trade; the focus is on relations between different areas and their people. This is visible in the Porteous map showing the political spaces (see Figure 4). Here, not only the great East-West divide is visualised, but also the interdependencies between the different peoples are charted.

An interesting theory which follows the concept of systematically ordered space is the "Central Place Theory" by German geographer Walter Christaller (1933). His deductive approach endeavours to explain hierarchies within settlement structures on the basis of economic interaction. In his theory Christaller argues that a greater distance between consumer and seller, or product respectively, equally raises transport charges, increases its price and lowers the level of demand for said product. Hence, every product has a maximum threshold with regard to its range, i.e. the threshold beyond which haulage is too high to find buyers for it. From the point of view of the seller there is another threshold: a product must find enough buyers so that the production is profitable – the minimum threshold. If the maximum threshold exceeds the minimum threshold, the area in-between contains the profitable market for both consumer and producer. Different product types require different thresholds. A loaf of bread, for example, usually is of a very low order or so-called "centrality"; its maximum and minimum threshold is close to the site of production: The number of bakeries is generally high, which makes it highly unlikely that consumers travel great distances for bread. Yet, bakeries can survive with a relatively small consumer market due to their low production and transportation costs. Places of high centrality offer not only products of high order but also products of every lower order (Schätzl 72-79).[18] London, for instance, might offer highly specialised financial services as well as top-brand clothes and the regular loaf of bread, whereas Reading might only offer a simple piece of garment and bread, and Silchester only a stale piece of bread.

Like Silchester, Hobbiton does not resemble a central place of a high order. It plays a rather marginal, more isolated role with regard to other regions and settlements in Middle-earth (Carl 62). There is no indication of any outsiders in Hobbiton except for Gandalf, who does in fact not immerse in its atmosphere or make use of its almost non-existent service sector but is visiting Bilbo and Frodo. "The village was so small that it had no inn or public house, and its residents were forced to walk 'a mile or more' to Bywater to visit *The Ivy Bush* and *The Green Dragon*" (Fonstadt 118). Bree, on the other hand, is of a higher order regarding centrality. Its service sector, especially and perceptibly its pub *The Prancing Pony Inn*, draws people in from farther afield. Its role for hobbits is visible in the hobbit-peephole at the town gate or the hobbit-sized beds at the inn (Carl 65). Bree lies at the intersection of two roads which follow in a North-South and West-East direction through Middle-earth, which is indexical for its centrality regarding traffic and trade (Fonstad 124).

---

18 See Schätzl (63-96) for a more detailed overview of Christaller's Central Place Theory and also its advancement through Albert Lösch.

When Théoden and his people retreat to Helm's Deep, the fortified stronghold fulfils a higher order with regard to defence and for the provision of the Rohirrim people in case of emergency in comparison to Edoras, despite its lower order regarding administration and infrastructure (Carl 74). Minas Tirith is probably the one city which possesses an even higher centrality with regard to defence: its setup of seven concentric city walls out of "more than two million tons of stone" (Fonstad 138) surpass even Helm's Deep's fortifications. Gandalf agrees when he tells Pippin that "'there [Minas Tirith] you will be as safe as you can be anywhere in these days'" (*RK* 20). Moreover, Minas Tirith is the king's residence and hence possesses administrative centrality (Fonstad 138). Its high density of products is also acknowledged indirectly by the fact that horses are rarely used within the walls, making it accessible on foot so to reach any products needed (*RK* 23). The films also include respective hints to established shops within Gondor's capital: goods are sold on tables in front of certain houses (Jackson, *RK* disc 1 42:30-43:58). In Helm's Deep, there is no evidence of shops, but only of provisions distributed in the streets (Jackson, *TT* disc 2 16:10-17:50). Another example of the White City's high centrality is visible in the Houses of Healing since they not only provide medical care but offer "the leechcraft of Gondor [which] was still wise, and skilled in the healing of wound and hurt, and all such sickness as east of the Sea mortal men were subject to" (*RK* 136). Pursuant to these examples, I argue that Minas Tirith is Middle-earth's city with the highest centrality – at least for humankind and respective human norms.

In accordance with Christaller's theory, New Zealand's centrality has increased as well since Peter Jackson started filming the *The Lord of the Rings* trilogy there: on the one hand, more potential tourists consider New Zealand an intriguing destination and hence place – to which I will come back later in section 4.2.4; on the other hand, the country has become more visible and attractive for foreign film productions – not least because of the expanded infrastructure for filming (Carl 51). Among the films which were (partly) shot in New Zealand or in cooperation with Kiwi production infrastructure after *The Lord of the Rings* had "pioneered" are *The Last Samurai* (2003), *King Kong* (2005), *Bridge to Terabithia* (2007), *Underworld: Rise of Lycans* (2009), *X-Men Origins: Wolverine* (2009), *Avatar* (2009), and *Dawn of the Planet of the Apes*

(2014) as well as television series like *Power Rangers* (2003-), the *Legend of the Seeker* (2008-2010) or *The Shannara Chronicles* (2016-) (Film New Zealand).

4.2.3 Individually perceived space

When Christaller's theory was published, apparently "[s]patial scientists were not very interested in how people related to the world through experience. Theirs was a world of simple people" (Cresswell, "Space and Place" 54-55), who did not change spaces into places by endowing their environments with individual meaning. This started to change in the 1970s and early 1980s when constructivism had reached spatial science and the notion of "subjectivity" had gradually spread to various disciplines. Space becomes dependent on individual perception. As a consequence, there is no clear-cut, objectively measurable space that could be agreed upon anymore. Instead, it is very much dependent on each person's individual experience with and within it (Wardenga, "Räume" 49-50; Wardenga, "Raumkonzepte" 9-10). It is this experience and knowledge with which Tolkien and Jackson play when they use symbolic, non-real landscapes to provoke specific emotions: Hobbiton's rurality symbolises a harmonic style of life – both amongst its inhabitants and between the latter and nature surrounding them. Although, as shown before, its filming site ironically is deforested farmland. In turn, caves like Moria evoke fear and discomfort. Rivers are associated with life or change. They fight for the good forces and their waters often prevent the progress of evil forces or even lead to their demise, as is shown e.g. at the battle of Isengard, Arwen's invocation of the river Bruinen (in Jackson's adaptation), or the hobbits' escape on a raft (Carl 76-78).

It is also notable that Tolkien implicitly describes the landscapes from the point of view of hobbits; most of them have not had any first-hand knowledge of these landscapes, but experience them for the first time during their quest. Hence, the hobbits arguably perceive them in a more fearful and uncomfortable state than natives of said landscapes who have grown accustomed to their – for hobbits – strange lands (Carl 76). Likewise, different characters in *The Lord of the Rings* react to locations in a different manner. This becomes apparent when the fellowship realises that the mountain pass is blocked and Gandalf proposes the Mines of Moria: "Only Gimli lifted up his head; a smouldering fire was in his eyes. On all the others, a dread fell at the mention of that name. Even to the hobbits it was a legend of vague fear" (*FR* 308-309). While Gimli eagerly follows Gandalf into "the halls of Durin" (*FR* 310) as the dwarves call them, Aragorn shows much more reluctance to enter them (*FR* 310). Boromir even considers it a "'trap, hardly better than knocking at the gates of the Dark Tower itself'" (*FR* 309). Gandalf, however, disagrees vehemently and maintains Sauron's stronghold to be a far greater peril, based on his past experience with the Dark Lord, which Boromir does not share (*FR* 309). The wizard also sums up the different perceptions of this one space when he says: "'In the ruins of the Dwarves, a dwarf's head will be less easy to bewilder than Elves or Men or Hobbits'" (*FR* 310). Similarly, Lothlórien evokes divergent connotations: Boromir voices his opinion "of that perilous land" (*FR* 352); Aragorn understands that it is perilous, but claims that "only evil need fear it" (*FR* 352) and Legolas attributes only pleasant memories to it (*FR* 349).

The idea of individually perceived spaces also becomes visible when Tolkien's books and Jackson's films are juxtaposed with the imagination of the respective reader or viewer. So to "pre-investigate" into this, I presented two friends with the following description of Mordor (taken from snippets of *RK* in their native language) and it was their task to make a pencil drawing from it. The two participants had not read Tolkien's novels, but one of them had seen Jackson's filmic adaptation.

> (1) 'Bless me, Mr. Frodo, but I didn't know as anything grew in Mordor! But if I had a'known, this is just what I'd have looked for. These thorns must be a foot long by the feel of them; they've stuck through everything I've got on. Wish I'd a'put that mail-shirt on!' (*RK* 194)

> (2) Away to their left, southward, against a sky that was turning grey, the peaks and high ridges of the great range began to appear dark and black, visible shapes. (*RK* 196)

> (3) They had trudged for more than an hour when they heard a sound that brought them to a halt. Unbelievable, but unmistakable. Water trickling. Out of a gully on the left so sharp and narrow that it looked as if the black cliff had been cloven by some huge axe, water came dripping down: the last remains, maybe, of some sweet rain gathered from sunlit seas, but ill-fated to fall at last upon the walls of the Black Land and wander fruitless down into the dust. Here it came out of the rock in a little falling streamlet, and flowed

across the path, and turning south ran away swiftly to be lost among the dead stones. (*RK* 197-198)

(4) In the morning a grey light came again, for in the high regions the West Wind still blew, but down on the stones behind the fences of the Black Land the air seemed almost dead, chill and yet stifling. Sam looked up out of the hollow. The land all about was dreary, flat and drab-hued. On the roads nearby nothing was moving now; but Sam feared the watchful eyes on the wall of Isenmouthe, no more than a furlong away northward. South-eastward, far off like a dark standing shadow, loomed the Mountain. Smokes were pouring from it, and while those that rose into the upper air trailed away eastward, great rolling clouds floated down its sides and spread over the land. (*RK* 210)

As expected the depiction of Mordor based on the text excerpts (1) to (4) varied (see Figure 5, A and B). Although they were both presented with the identical text excerpts, were so for the first time and were given the same amount of time, each drew his or her own version of Mordor.[19] While A depicted a rugged landscape with a tangle of thorn bushes, on the one hand, and beautiful elements like a meandering stream and a grove of trees, B, on the other, highlighted the bleakness of Mordor, with the mountain range being steep and jagged; the sun hidden behind a grey curtain of clouds; the thicket of thorns ubiquitous; no gently-flowing rivulet or riverside copse. Yet, the protruding feature probably is Mount Doom, which is much more dominant here than in A's interpretation.

This little experiment illustrates the idea behind the concept of individually perceived and constructed space: Even though there is exactly the same material description of a very specific space, in this case Mordor, it is still very unlikely that individuals will construct this space in exactly the same manner. For one thing, this may be due to different interpretations of the source text. It can also be argued that B, who had seen Jackson's Mordor (C) and with it the focus on Mount Doom and Sauron's tower, may have used her different set of experiences unconsciously when putting the Land of Shadow to paper. Just as much as the two participants, Peter Jackson is but an interpreter of Tolkien's descriptions himself. He not only construed Mordor from the original texts

---

19 The participants had to describe their intentions after they had drawn Mordor. Accordingly, the interpretation of each version is based on those verbal descriptions as well as the drawings themselves.

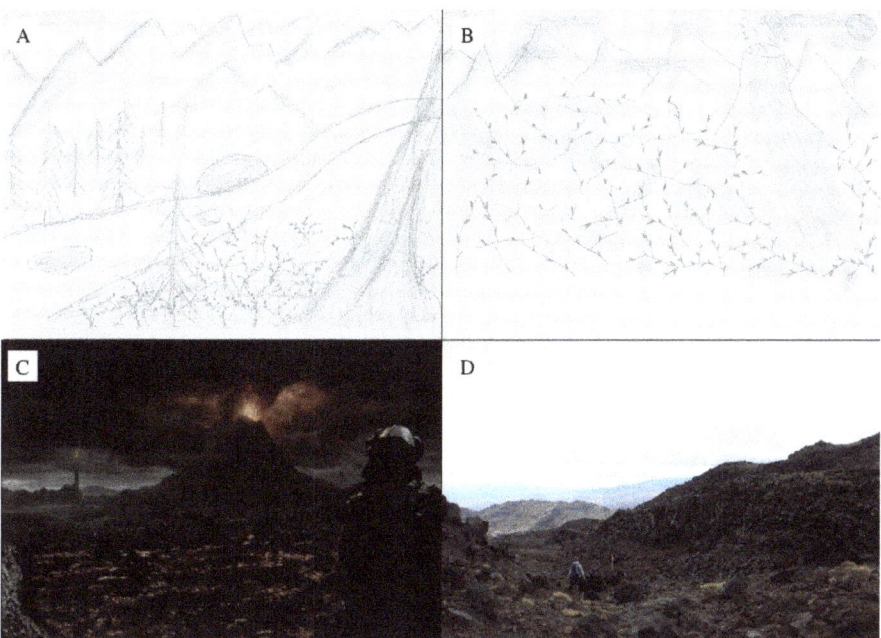

Figure 5: Mordor (A: based on Tolkien's description without knowledge of Jackson's adaptation; B: based on Tolkien's description with knowledge of Jackson's adaptation; C: Peter Jackson's Mordor; D: unedited landscape which Jackson used for his version of Mordor)

and the script but rather used his personal experiences to shape it by changing certain features of an already existing material space: Tongariro National Park (D) on New Zealand's North Island.

4.2.4 Socially constructed space

Lastly, socially constructed space replaces the individuality of the experience within the individually perceived space with a much more collaborative approach. As the name implies spaces are rather constructed by society and not merely perceived and constructed by an individual. According to this concept, spaces are built by communication between and the actions of people. This idea was already established in 1986 by Helmut Klüter,[20] but I will focus on Benno

---

20 For more information on socially constructed space see Klüter.

Werlen and his refined proposal of 2000 that individuals not only relate the world to themselves but also shape it by their actions (Wardenga, "Räume" 50-51; Wardenga, "Raumkonzepte" 10-11). Werlen's idea also agrees with Christina Kennedy's and Chris Lukinbeal's recommendation to use a transactionalistic approach, when working with geography in films, i.e. "a holistic approach to human-environment transactions" (36) that takes both the portrayed space, the creator of the image, the medium (i.e. film), and the audience into consideration (36-37). It is particularly the creator's and the audience's capacity to construct spaces and give them meaning "through a series of perceptual filters based on their life experiences and goals" (Kennedy and Lukinbeal 37) that may shape socially constructed spaces.

One of the more prominent examples of socially constructed spaces in the Tolkienian fan world certainly is New Zealand with regard to its touristic impact. Upon accessing the official travel website for New Zealand (see Figure 6) when researching for this essay, I was greeted by a picture of Milford Sound on the South Island. Directly below it, it is Middle-earth that is introduced as a valid association for New Zealand as well. This association is cemented further through expressions like "HOME OF MIDDLE-EARTH", so-called "Middle-earth itineraries" and "Middle-earth experiences" including e.g. a "16 Days Lord of the Rings Self Drive Vacation", the "Elven Magic" tour or "A Halfling's Ramble", which are all advertised on different subsites (Tourism New Zealand). Tour companies have jumped on the bandwagon in offering "the real Middle-earth" (Hobbiton Tours) or "a pilgrimage through Middle-earth" (Red Carpet Tours).[21] The campaign also included – among other things – interviews with high-profile fans like Chinese actress Yao Chen, several actors from the cast of *The Lord of the Rings* and *The Hobbit*, DVD featurettes of New Zealand, branded postage stamps and gold coins, a "Welcome to Middle-earth" stamp in each visitor's passport when you enter the country, an Elvish weather forecast and the marketing of Air New Zealand as the official airline of Middle-earth, together with a highly "Middle-earthian" on-board safety video (Carl 51, 125 and 130; Tudor 49-50). Ultimately, there are the films themselves which act like hours-long infomercials about the landscape of New Zealand (Carl 42 and 50-53).

---

21 For more information on film tourism with regard to *The Lord of the Rings* see Carl (80-120).

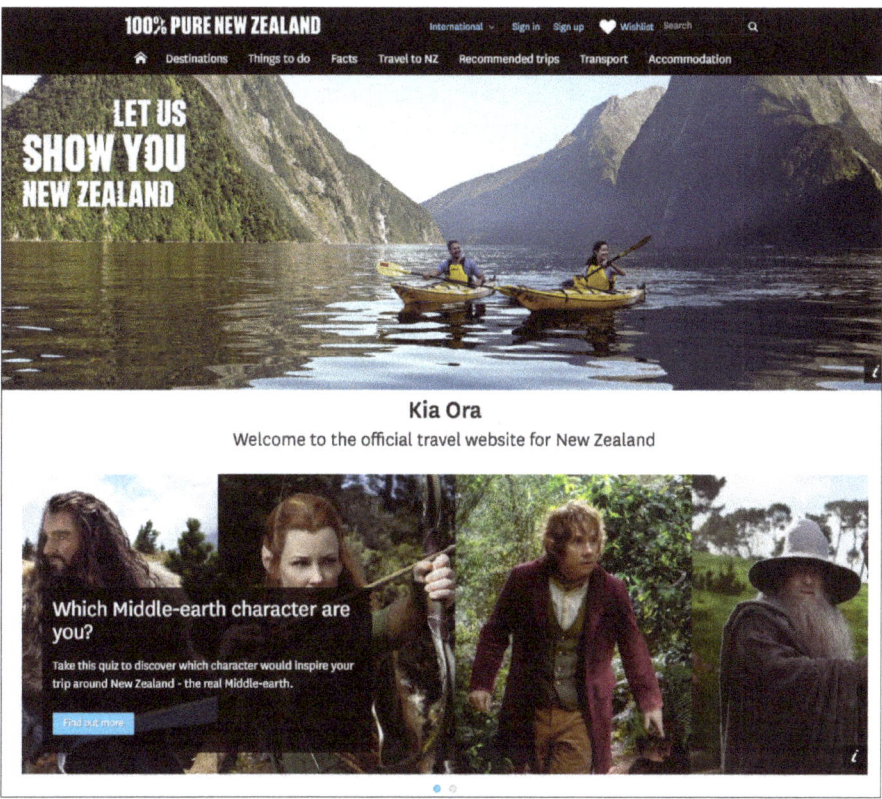

Figure 6: Website of the official travel website of *100 % Pure New Zealand* from 22 Jan. 2017 (see Tourism New Zealand)

Even though Tourism New Zealand, Air New Zealand, Peter Jackson, and Sir Ian McKellen (aka Gandalf in the *The Lord of the Rings* films), who comments on New Zealand as "the Middle-earth [he] had always pictured" (Tourism New Zealand) agree, it is evident that Tolkien could not have had this southern-hemisphere country in mind when he developed his Middle-earth. Still, the *The Lord of the Rings* franchise has had a major impact "on both New Zealand's economy and national self-perception. […] LOTR invited New Zealanders to see their country as one that could 'punch above weight'" (Dunleavy and Joyce 258). After all, New Zealand was ranked first in a study carried out by HBO Entertainment in 2015, in which 2,000 interviewees named their top 30 TV and film destinations. One in every four participants also chose their holiday destination with specific regard to filming locations. *The Hobbit* trilogy and the simultaneously running tourism campaign may have influenced up to 21 % of New Zealand travellers in doing so (Tudor 47-48).[22] A survey by Carl (130-148) showed that 49.2 % of the respondents in fact consider New Zealand to be Middle-earth. According to Barker and Mathijs this is no mere coincidence but a very successful transfer of meaning from film to location and eventually contingent upon "New Zealand's landscapes and views" (110).[23]

These examples also concur with one fundamental idea of socially constructed spaces: such spaces cease to exist when they are not reproduced time and time again (Wardenga, "Räume" 50). New Zealand will probably notice this development when Peter Jackson's films fade from the memory of their audiences' or when they are replaced by one of Hollywood's constant reboots, reshoots or remakes. However, as long as there are people reiterating the concept of New Zealand as Middle-earth, it will be constructed as such.

In addition to extradiegetic spaces, Tolkien's stories also show spaces which have been constructed socially on a diegetic level. The example of Lothlórien, which I have already discussed with regard to individually perceived spaces, is a fitting one here as well. Lore, according to Aragorn and Boromir's dialogue shortly before they enter the Elven forest, shapes the acceptance and perception of Lothlórien. While the Golden Wood is considered perilous by Gondor's people at this stage – although there seems to be no witnesses who attest to any danger or frightening events from personal experience – it had been positively connotated before (*FR* 352-353). Gondorians forgot about Lothlórien and thus lack awareness of its sense. Instead, they have formulated their own version of reality and imposed it on the forest, just as Middle-earth has been imposed on New Zealand.

---

22 The New Zealand Institute of Economic Research showed in its report covering the year 2013 *Western market visitor growth* (2014) that 21 % of German, 19 % of US, 12 % of UK, 7 % of Australian, 6 % of Japanese and 4 % of Canadian holidaymakers regard *The Hobbit* as a factor for visiting New Zealand (7).

23 For more insight into how, whether and to what extent New Zealand has become Middle-earth see Anne Buchmann, who interviewed people whose work related to the *The Lord of the Rings* films, in *How We Became Middle-earth. A Collection of Essays on The Lord of the Rings*. Eds. Adam Lam and Nataliya Oryshchuk.

5. Conclusion

As I have sought to demonstrate in this paper, *The Lord of the Rings* facilitates a particularly geographical perspective, which can be efficiently used within a teaching frame. In Tolkien's novel, the world is not only a stage but arguably much more than a mere backdrop for the story: "The greatest entity in the story of Middle-earth was Middle-earth itself. The world, the land is a character that delivered the Ring and accepts the Ring back" (Richard Taylor in Jackson, *FR* disc 1 around 06:25). Geographers (since I am one myself, I dare to claim this) are usually not very talented at analysing characters, but when the character is a landscape, they will know how to approach it. In this paper, I have discussed various spatial geographical concepts by presenting adequate examples from Middle-earth. I have provided evidence for using *The Lord of the Rings* and all that surrounds Tolkien's fiction: Students can learn about modern pop culture, cinematographic techniques, language, literature and film history as well as material space, systematically ordered space, individually perceived space and socially constructed space. Learning about and applying these concepts will, as I have claimed, not only increase the students' consciousness about space and place but also facilitate their understanding and adaptation of, e.g., the Central Place Theory or the concept of ecozones and constructivist perceptions to a topical frame that is likely to be both entertaining and informative for them. By showing the connections between an entertaining fictional film and different pieces of implicit geographical information, I have been given chapter and verse for my central thesis: it is not only possible but in fact can be beneficial to use non-educational films for educational purposes and – as shown in this case study – providing geographical education on the basis of fantastical worlds as the ones created by e.g. J.R.R. Tolkien. This may not only motivate students to engage with the topic, but in fact facilitate the holistic understanding of space and its relevance.

About the Author

SEBASTIAN STREITBERGER is a lecturer for the Chair of Geography Education at the University of Augsburg, Germany. He earned his B.Ed. with his monograph titled *The Potential of Internet-based Digital Atlases for Geography Education at School With the Example of the Energy-Atlas of Bavaria* (2014; original title: *Potentiale der Arbeit mit internetbasierten digitalen Atlanten im Geographieunterricht am Beispiel des Energie-Atlas Bayerns*). His teaching and research interests focus on educational media in geography education, e-learning and heterogeneity in the classroom as well as visualising knowledge. Both this and his study and teacher training in English have led to a great interest in using J.R.R. Tolkien's works in an educational environment. Consequently, he has contributed to interdisciplinary projects regarding this topic.

List of Abbreviations

FR TOLKIEN, John Ronald Reuel. *The Fellowship of the Ring*. London: George Allen & Unwin, 1966; respectively Peter JACKSON, dir. *The Lord of the Rings: The Fellowship of the Ring*. Extended-Edition Blu-Ray. 228 Min. New Line Cinema, 2001.

TT TOLKIEN, John Ronald Reuel. *The Two Towers*. London: George Allen & Unwin, 1966; respectively Peter JACKSON, dir. *The Lord of the Rings: The Two Towers*. Extended-Edition Blu-Ray. 235 Min. New Line Cinema, 2002.

RK TOLKIEN, John Ronald Reuel. *The Return of the King*. London: George Allen & Unwin, 1966; respectively Peter JACKSON, dir. *The Lord of the Rings: The Return of the King*. Extended-Edition Blu-Ray. 263 Min. New Line Cinema, 2003.

TL TOLKIEN, John Ronald Reuel. *Tree and Leaf*. Boston: Houghton Mifflin, 1965.

Bibliography

AITKEN, Stuart C. "A Transactional Geography of Image-event: The Films of Scottish Director, Bill Forsyth." *Transactions – The Institute of British Geographers* 16 (1991): 105–118.

— and Leo E. ZONN. "Re-Presenting the Place Pastiche." *Place, Power, Situation and Spectacle. A Geography of Film*. Eds. Stuart C. Aitken and Leo E. Zonn. Lanham: Rowman & Littlefield, 1994. 3-25.

ARBEITSGRUPPE CURRICULUM 2000+ DER DGFG. "Grundsätze und Empfehlungen für die Lehrplanarbeit im Schulfach Geographie." *Geographie heute* 200 (2002): 4-7.

BAILEY, Robert G. *Ecosystem Geography. From Ecoregions to Site*. 2nd ed. New York: Springer, 2009.

— *Ecoregions. The Ecosystem Geography of the Oceans and Continents*. 2nd ed. New York: Springer, 2014.

BARKER, Martin, and Ernest MATHIJS. "Seeing the Promised Land from Afar: The Perception of New Zealand by Overseas *The Lord of the Rings* Audiences." *How We Became Middle-earth. A Collection of Essays on The Lord of the Rings*. Eds. Adam Lam and Nataliya Oryshchuk. Zurich and Berne: Walking Tree, 2007. 107-128.

BBC. "Viewpoint: Why do Fictional Universes Matter?" *BBC Magazine* 17 October 2015. 26 January 2017 <http://www.bbc.com/news/magazine-34552953>.

BIDDULPH, Mary, David LAMBERT, and David BALDERSTONE. *Learning to Teach Geography in the Secondary School. A Companion to School Experience*. 3rd ed. London: Routledge, 2015.

BRUCKER, Ambros. "Klassische Medien kreativ nutzen." *Geographie unterrichten lernen. Die neue Didaktik der Geographie konkret*. Ed. Hartwig Haubrich. 2nd ed. Munich: Oldenbourg, 2006. 173-206.

— "Womit unterrichten wir? Medien." *Geographiedidaktik in Übersichten*. Ed. Ambros Brucker. 2nd ed. Hallbergmoos: Aulis, 2012. 64-65.

BUCHMANN, Anne. "Creating Middle-earth: The Insiders' Views." *How We Became Middle-earth. A Collection of Essays on The Lord of the Rings*. Eds. Adam Lam and Nataliya Oryshchuk. Zurich and Berne: Walking Tree, 2007. 33-61.

BUTLER, David. *Fantasy Cinema. Impossible Worlds on Screen*. London: Wallflower, 2009.

CARL, Daniela Susann. *Cultural Representation of New Zealand's Landscapes in the Films of The Lord Of The Rings and its Implications for Tourism*. Wellington: N.N., 2004.

CLARK, James M., and Allan PAIVIO. "Dual Coding Theory and Education." *Educational Psychology Review* 3 (1991): 149-210.

CRESSWELL, Tim. "Space and Place (1977). Yi-Fu Tuan." *Key Texts in Human Geography*. Eds. Phil Hubbard, Rob Kitchin, and Gill Valentine. London: SAGE, 2008. 53-59.

—. "Place." *International Encyclopedia of Human Geography*. Eds. Rob Kitchin, and Nigel Thrift. Amsterdam: Elsevier, 2009. 169-177.

DEUTSCHE GESELLSCHAFT FÜR GEOGRAPHIE. *Educational Standards in Geography for the Intermediate School Certificate. With Sample Assignments*. 2nd ed. Bonn: DGfG, 2012.

DI PALMA, Maria. "Teaching Geography Using Films. A Proposal." *Journal of Geography* 108 (2009): 47-56.

DUNLEAVY, Trisha, and Hester JOYCE. *New Zealand Film & Television. Institution, Industry and Cultural Change*. Bristol: Intellect, 2011.

ENGELMANN, Dieter, and Fred SCHOLZ. *Geoökozonen. Großräumliches Differenzierungsmodell der Erde*. Braunschweig: Westermann, 2009.

FAULSTICH, Werner. *Filmgeschichte*. Paderborn: Wilhelm Fink, 2005.

FILM NEW ZEALAND. Home Page. 22nd Jan. 2017. <http://www.filmnz.com/made-in-new-zealand>.

FONSTAD, Karen Wynn. *The Atlas of Middle-earth*. Boston: Houghton Mifflin, 1991.

FOWKES, Katherine A. *The Fantasy Film*. Chichester: Wiley-Blackwell, 2010.

GÖTZE, Hans-Jürgen, Dorothee MERTMANN, Ulrich RILLER, and Jörg ARNDT. *Einführung in die Geowissenschaften*. 2nd ed. Stuttgart: Eugen Ulmer, 2015.

HAMMOND, Wayne G., and Christina SCULL. *The Art of The Hobbit by J.R.R. Tolkien*. London: HarperCollins, 2011.

—. *The Art of The Lord of the Rings by J.R.R. Tolkien*. London: HarperCollins, 2015.

HOBBITON TOURS. Home Page. 22 Jan. 2017. <http://www.hobbitontours.com>.

JACKSON, Peter. "Thinking Geographically." *Geography* 91 (2006): 199-204.

JACKSON, Peter, dir. *The Lord of the Rings: The Fellowship of the Ring*. Extended-Edition Blu-Ray. 228 Min. New Line Cinema, 2001.

The Lord of the Rings: The Two Towers. Extended-Edition Blu-Ray. 235 Min. New Line Cinema, 2002.

The Lord of the Rings: The Return of the King. Extended-Edition Blu-Ray. 263 Min. New Line Cinema, 2003.

JONIETZ, David. *From Space to Place – A Computational Model of Functional Place.* Augsburg: N.N., 2016.

KAMINSKE, Volker. *Die räumliche Wahrnehmung. Grundlage für Geographie und Kartographie.* Darmstadt: WBG, 2012.

KATTMANN, Ulrich. "Didaktische Rekonstruktion – eine praktische Theorie." *Theorien in der biologiedidaktischen Theorie. Ein Handbuch für Lehramtsstudenten und Doktoranden.* Eds. Dirk Krüger and Helmut Vogt. Berlin: Springer, 2007. 93-104.

KENNEDY, Christina, and Chris LUKINBEAL. "Towards a Holistic Approach to Geographic Research on Film." *Progress in Human Geography* 21 (1997): 33-50.

KLÜTER, Helmut. *Raum als Element sozialer Kommunikation.* Gießen: Geographisches Institut der Justus-Liebig-Universität Gießen, 1986.

KÖCK, Helmuth. "Raumkonzepte in der Geographie – methodologisch analysiert." *Geographie aktuell & Schule* 209 (2014): 3-14.

KRAPP, Andreas, Claudia GEYER, and Doris LEWALTER. "Motivation und Emotion." *Pädagogische Psychologie.* Eds. Tina Seidel and Andreas Krapp. 6th ed. Weinheim: Beltz, 2014. 193-222.

LUKINBEAL, Chris. *A Geography in Film, a Geography of Film.* Hayward: N.N., 1995.

MICHAEL, Thomas, ed. *Diercke-Weltatlas.* Braunschweig: Westermann, 2015.

MITTELSTÄDT, Fritz-Gerd. "Der Raum als geographiedidaktisches Polylemma." *Geographie und ihre Didaktik* 3 (2011): 140-143.

NEW ZEALAND INSTITUTE OF ECONOMIC RESEARCH. *2013 Western Market Visitor Growth. What Explains the Increase in Advanced-Economy Visitors?* <http://nzier.org.nz/static/media/filer_public/8b/f7/8bf74d73-e8a6-436d-bda6-206b4132c0e2/understanding_western_market_growth.pdf>.

NEW ZEALAND INSTITUTE OF WATER AND ATMOSPHERIC RESEARCH. *Overview of New Zealand's climate.* Home Page. 28 Jan. 2017. <https://www.niwa.co.nz/education-and-training/schools/resources/climate/overview>.

Climate summaries. Home Page. 28 Jan. 2017. <https://www.niwa.co.nz/education-and-training/schools/resources/climate/summary>.

NIEDING, Gerhild, and Peter OHLER. "Mediennutzung und Medienwirkung bei Kindern und Jugendlichen." *Medienpsychologie*. Eds. Bernad Batinic and Markus Appel. Heidelberg: Springer, 2008. 379-400.

PAIVIO, Allan. *Mental Representations. A Dual Coding Approach*. New York: Oxford University Press, 1986.

PINKAS, Claudia. *Der phantastische Film. Instabile Narrationen und die Narration der Instabilität*. Berlin: de Gruyter, 2010.

PORTEOUS, John Douglas. "A Preliminary Landscape Analysis of Middle-Earth during its Third Age." *Landscape* 19 (1975): 33-38.

RED CARPET TOURS. Home Page. 22 Jan. 2017. <http://www.redcarpet-tours.com>.

RESNICK, Henry. "Interview with Tolkien." *Niekas* 18 (1967): 37-43.

SAETTLER, Paul. *The Evolution of American Educational Technology*. Englewood: Libraries Unlimited, 1990.

SCHÄTZL, Ludwig. *Wirtschaftsgeographie 1. Theorie*. 9th ed. Paderborn: Ferdinand Schöningh, 2003.

SCHEKATZ-SCHOPMEIER, Sonja. *Storytelling – eine narrative Methode zur Vermittlung naturwissenschaftlicher Inhalte im Sachunterricht der Grundschule*. Göttingen: Cuvillier, 2010.

SCHWEIZER, Karin, and Klaus-Martin KLEIN. "Medien und Emotionen." *Medienpsychologie*. Eds. Bernad Batinic and Markus Appel. Heidelberg: Springer, 2008. 149-175.

SCHULTZ, Jürgen. *Die Ökozonen der Erde*. 5th ed. Stuttgart: Eugen Ulmer, 2016.

SEEBACHER, Marc Michael. *Raumkonstruktionen in der Geographie. Eine paradigmenspezifische Darstellung gesellschaftlicher und fachspezifischer Konstruktions-, Rekonstruktions- und Dekonstruktionsprozesse von "Räumlichkeit"*. Wien: Universität Wien, 2012.

TAYLOR, Liz. "Basiskonzepte im Geographieunterricht. Schlüssel, um die Welt besser zu verstehen und den Unterricht besser zu planen." *Praxis Geographie* 7-8 (2011): 8-11.

TAYLOR, Peter J. "Places, Spaces and Macy's: Place-Space Tensions in the Political Geography of Modernities." *Progress in Human Geography* 23 (1999): 7-26.

TOLKIEN, John Ronald Reuel. *Tree and Leaf*. Boston: Houghton Mifflin, 1965.

The Fellowship of the Ring. London: George Allen & Unwin, 1966.

The Two Towers. London: George Allen & Unwin, 1966.

The Return of the King. London: George Allen & Unwin, 1966.

TOURISM NEW ZEALAND. *Home Page.* 22 Jan. 2017. <http://www.newzealand.com/int/>.

TUAN, Yi-Fu. *Space and Place. The Perspective of Experience.* Minneapolis: University of Minnesota Press, 1977.

"Space and Place. Humanistic Perspective." *Raum und Ort.* Eds. Anton Escher and Sandra Petermann. Stuttgart: Franz Steiner, 2016. 133-166.

TUDOR, Gabriela-Cosmina. "Film Tourism. A Successful Journey for New Zealand. The Way towards Being the World's Top Film Tourism Destination." *Cactus Tourism* 12 (2015): 45-53.

UHLENWINKEL, Anke. "Geographical Concept: Place." *Metzler Handbuch 2.0 Geographieunterricht. Ein Leitfaden für Praxis und Ausbildung.* Eds. Manfred Rolfes and Anke Uhlenwinkel. Braunschweig: Westermann, 2013. 182-188.

VINX, Roland. *Gesteinsbestimmungen im Gelände.* 4th ed. Berlin: Springer, 2015.

WARDENGA, Ute. "Alte und neue Raumkonzepte für den Geographieunterricht." *Geographie heute* 200 (2002): 8-11.

"Räume der Geographie. Zu Raumbegriffen im Geographieunterricht." *Wissenschaftliche Nachrichten* 120 (2002): 47-52.

WILHELMI, Volker. "Umweltbildung und Film. Von der virtuellen Filmwelt in die Schülerwelt am Beispiel des Spielfilms 'Avatar'." *Praxis Geographie* 7-8 (2015): 56-59.

WORLEY, Alec. *Empires of the Imagination. A Critical Survey of Fantasy Cinema from George Méliès to The Lord of the Rings.* Jefferson NC: McFarland, 2005.

WÜTHRICH, Christoph. *Methodik des Geographieunterrichts.* Braunschweig: Westermann, 2013.

Sabine Timpf

Insights into Mapping the Imagined World of J.R.R. Tolkien

Abstract

In April 1953 in a letter to his publisher (*L* 168) J.R.R. Tolkien writes: "Maps are worrying me. One at least (which would then have to be rather large) is absolutely essential." Why were maps so important to Tolkien? How were the maps produced that graced the first publication of *The Lord of the Rings*? And how do these maps differ from Tolkien's imagined worlds? Every map tells a story and different maps fulfil varying functions. How are these functions linked to the acts of creating a world, exploring its geographical extent and content, getting an overview or presenting the world to a group of readers? While examining the relationship between Tolkien's sketches, maps and his writing it becomes clear that J.R.R. Tolkien was too deeply immersed in his world to produce an overview map. The act of exploring and collating material for a story produces a cognitive collage. By contrast, the act of presenting the geography of the final story demands a map. Mapping imagined worlds requires detachment from the richness of the described geography.

1 Every map tells a story

Maps in literature add to the sense of immersion. They invite the reader to let their own imagination roam within and outside of the map. In that sense every map tells at least one story, often several. This seems to be Tolkien's opinion as well judging from what he writes in his letter to his publisher: "The maps. [...] They are essential [...] there should be picturesque maps, providing more than a mere index to what is said in the text" (*L* 171).

Maps in a narrow cartographic sense are scaled-down, two-dimensional representations of an actual geographical area (MacEachren). However, in discussions about maps, cartographers also include maps of imaginary places or those based on literary texts. Thus, the relevant property of maps does not seem to be the relation to real-world geography, but rather the relation to a perceived space (also cf. Streitberger in this volume). In Tolkien's case this perceived space was being invented or (as he insisted) re-discovered in the process of writing his (hi)stories. Tolkien was not only interested in producing an overview map, i.e. a mere index; he was interested in conveying a rich geography as a result of history including cultural references such as meaningful place names. Tolkien believed that a secondary world must not differ all too much from its primary source world.

Not only was Tolkien aiming at descriptions of geographical spaces, but at creating evocative settings (Schoggen) containing enough recognizable features for the reader that additional information would be unnecessary, thus building an expectation of how the world would most likely function. Ekman defines "settings" as an important constituent of fantasy worlds, although his definition, in contrast to Schoggen's, is more focused on the spatial/geographical and less on the psychological interpretation of a place. Settings seem to be the best way to present something new (a plot) that might not exist in our world today (such as magic), while at the same time playing on the familiar associations elicited from the readers' minds; they provide structure and coherence and allow for inferences of additional knowledge from similar experiences, i.e. a jungle is hot, even if the map will not show this "hot-ness". In my opinion this is what Tolkien implied by the term "picturesque maps", i.e. not only maps that show geography, but also maps that evoke feelings and familiarity, the taste and smell of a place.

1.1 Functions of maps

Maps have different functions: Maps show the known and hint at the unknown, i.e. they allow for exploration in imagined and in real or literary spaces. They often take the perspective of a bird, i.e. showing the world from above as if the observer was hovering in the atmosphere. Maps are objects of power: having a map allows for different decisions to be made than being immersed in the real world without knowledge about what lies behind the next turn of the road or a nearby hill. We can distinguish between overview maps showing spatial and thematic relations between objects in the world (e.g. a topographic map – see Fig. 1a) and route maps or travel maps that focus on the pathways and the connectivity of places (e.g., the famous Gough map of Britain – see Fig. 1b).

Maps also have the feel of veracity – we tend to believe what a map tells us, primarily because it is printed (Wood and Fels).

Fig. 1:   a) part of a topographic map (© OpenStreetMap[1] contributors) and
b) excerpt of Gough route map of Britain (www.goughmap.org)

In history, maps have been used to impart information about the believed structure of the world. For example, TO-maps dating from around the 7th century (see Fig. 2) show the known-inhabited world (at that time Asia, Europe and Africa) with the dividing main water bodies (The Mediterranean Sea, the Nile and the Don) forming the "T" and a surrounding world ocean forming the "O". These *mappaemundi* (world maps) were embellished in medieval times showing the Heavens outside of the world ocean, adding a specific philosophical interpretation to the geographical information.

---

1   www.openstreetmap.org/copyright.html

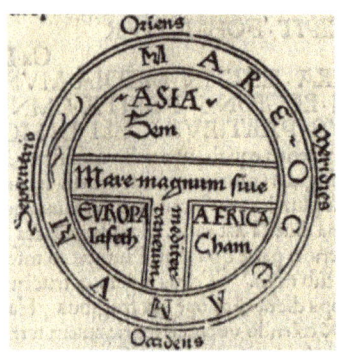 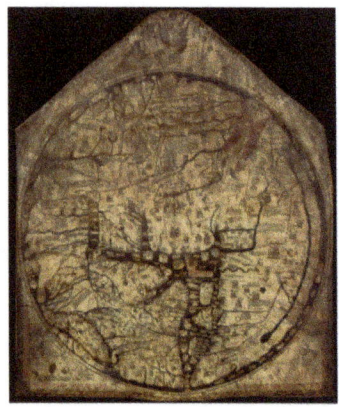

Fig. 2: A schematic TO map (from Isidore's *Etymologiae*, ca. AD 600, left)[2] and a classic TO map (*Hereford Mappa Mundi*, ca. AD 1300) on the right[3]

Maps may structure the imagination by providing boundaries on the imagined spaces; they construct spatial categories (water, buildings, streets…), thus determining how to talk and think about the world and, by extension, how to understand the world (MacEachren). "World" in this context means as much a realistic geographic world as an imaginary, literary world. Looking at historical maps through time, we can infer the story of how the world was seen and interpreted and how the interpretation changed with time.

Ekman, taking a topofocal stance, discusses characteristics of "fantasy maps" from a reader's perspective: most of these maps have a scale, which means that objects may be measured, making the recipient's experience more real. Roads on these maps allow for exploration – they lead us to unknown and known places and produce relations between places by connecting them. Barriers, such as shores or mountain ranges, produce a feeling of safety or of containment. Adding labels, i.e. names of peoples who live in these places, adds to the experienced mystery of these places. Fantasy maps may tell stories about the fantasy world in a fashion similar to real worlds. The more features occur in the map (not being part of the fantasy world), the more they suggest a rich background world and hint at other stories.

---

2 en.wikipedia.org/wiki/T_and_O_map
3 www.unesco.org.uk/wp-content/uploads/2015/03/Mappa-flat-copy.jpg

1.2 Functions of maps in literature

In literature, maps may illustrate the world described in the text – their main reason for inclusion is to provide an overview. See for example the maps used in the *Shadowrunner* books by Lynn Flewelling or the *Dragonrider* books by Anne McCaffrey. This type of map does not provide a lot of detail, but they are necessary for relating different locations mentioned in the text within one geographic framework. These worlds supposedly exist as a "coherent whole" in the minds of the authors often before the narrative is even begun.

Maps may visually bring together different narratives throughout the course of the work of an author, as is the case with the *Discworld* novels by Terry Pratchett or the adventures of *Flinx* by Alan Dean Foster. Here, the world or universe did not exist as a completely thought-out world or universe at the beginning of the first narrative, but evolved over the course of different novels over years. In fact, it often turns out not even to be necessary to consult the map unless one is interested in relating the different parts of an author's oeuvre.

Maps may also be used as guides – not only for the reader but also for the protagonists themselves. This is the case with Thror's map in *The Hobbit* or the Marauder's Map in *Harry Potter*. Stories of long, detailed journeys need maps to guide the reader, to show progress and to help the characters orientate themselves in their world.

Finally, maps may be used as a means to produce a coherent world in which distance, angles and views remain "correct" or in keeping with the story. One example for this category is Louis Stevenson's *Treasure Island* map: the map was drawn first and the story unfolds on the basis of this map.

1.3 Literary cartography

Literary cartography deals with the analysis of the relationship between places and narratives using maps as a means to make these relationships and patterns visible (Moretti). Most researchers on maps in literature focus on "maps as communicative devices" (e.g. Rosetto; Diane Duane or Frank W. Day and Clare Ranson [as cited in Ekman]; Bushell; Padron; Peraldo; Turchi; Wyatt).

The main research question in literary cartographies is how the spatial or geographical information within the narrative augmented by one or several maps is transmitted to the reader. Most research in literary cartographies is concerned with the mapping process depicted in Fig. 3.

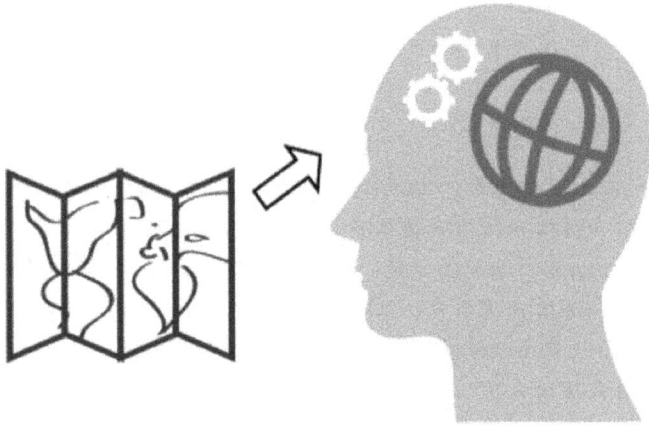

Fig. 3: The mapping process by the reader

In this mapping process, a reader visually perceives features and their relationships on the map, interprets these in combination with the literary text(s) and actively builds a mental representation of the features and their relationships in his/her memory.

My focus in this paper is on examining the role of maps and mapping during the creative process of writing a large oeuvre of fiction. As Ekman (5) states, "[f]antasy writers are free to make up whatever they like for their worlds, and change the laws by which these worlds work; but once the laws are in place, even the author is bound by them." This is certainly one of the reasons why Tolkien himself stated in a letter to Rayner Unwin: "[…] in such a story one cannot make a map for the narrative, but must first make a map and make the narrative agree" (*L* 168).

Although this approach seemed to be clear to Tolkien, he did not in fact follow his own advice. Indeed, as I will argue in this paper, he would not have been able to follow it as he was engaged in a process of world building at the same time as he was writing his narrative.

These two different but parallel activities, although clearly related, require distinct types of mapping processes and they will in turn produce different types of maps. In the following sections, I will first discuss different mapping processes and present the theory of cognitive mapping, contrasting it with the cartographer's task. I will examine Tolkien's exposure to mapping and discuss the relationship between his sketches and maps as they are known or published. Next, I will differentiate maps types during the acts of exploring and presenting a writer is engaged in. Finally, I will argue that Tolkien was caught in the quandary of needing an overview, while being immersed in his fantastic world, and I will give and discuss some insights into the mapping processes required for a writer and creator.

2 Mapping a world – cognitive mapping

Maps do not necessarily reproduce or represent a world – especially in literature – they (re)construct an aspect of a real or literary world. As Monmonnier (25) states: "a good map tells a multitude of little white lies – it suppresses truth in order to help the user see what needs to be seen." A specific aspect of the real world will be put on the map while other aspects will be neglected. An ethical cartographer will always make sure that the choice is made transparent to prospective readers of the map. However, the fact remains that a selection or reduction process needs to take place and that this process might produce different outcomes depending on the cartographer, the map's purpose, the intended audience and the technology used.

Christopher Tolkien put most of his father's map-sketch into a publishable form. He remarks:

> The large-scale map of Gondor and Mordor was closely based on a map of my father's. [...] My father's map is in some respects hard to interpret, for it was made roughly and hastily in point of its actual execution, the 'contour-lines' being very impressionistic, while the Nindalf and the Dead Marshes are shown merely by rough pencil hatching, for which I have substituted conventional reed tufts; but I have attempted to redraw it as precisely as I can. (*WR* 118, note 12)

This quote shows the processes of selecting aspects and emphasizing specific important features in action. These are only two of a multitude of tasks a cartographer faces when producing a map.

2.1 The cartographer's task

The difficulties a cartographer has to overcome when drawing a map are numerous and multifaceted. The main problem is that the world to be mapped is always larger than the resulting map, thus the knotty problem of cartographic generalization comes into play, requiring a reduction in detail. Luis Borges (Borges) played on this problem in his essay on "exactitude in science". His protagonist boasted of having the most accurate map possible covering the entire country at a scale of 1:1, although this map had to be abandoned because the farmers kept complaining and the map was too unwieldy. Cartographers

Fig. 4: The cartographer's mapping process

have developed rules and principles for this reduction process; however, they are given some leeway so to implement these guidelines according to their own understanding of what the purpose of the final version of that map is going to be. This might mean, for instance, that on a map of bicycle paths, highways that do not allow bicycles are de-emphasized in favour of bike-able routes, and vice-versa.

The reduction processes include abstraction from patterns, simplification of shapes, selection and aggregation of features and their shapes, scaling (i.e.

making smaller) and typification of the features (i.e. depicting types of features instead of individuals), displacing them from their original location, and finally symbolization of features in order to make a specific argument, to show a spatial pattern, to emphasize spatial relations, or for other purposes such as clarifying the overview or enhancing a route to be followed. These different shape-and-location-changing processes are not independent from each other: e.g. enhancing aspects of a feature will usually require that any surrounding features be displaced or further simplified. Among these processes, selection requires the highest effort of interpretation by the cartographer, who should, at that point, have the purpose of the final product in mind.

Considering the complexity of these processes, it is no wonder that J.R.R. Tolkien felt unequal to the task. Even more than being detracted by the complexity of the task, Tolkien was engaged in a different creative process: cartographers deal with the mapping process as depicted in Fig. 4, whereas Tolkien as writer and creator of a world was engaged in a cognitive mapping process as shown in Fig. 5.

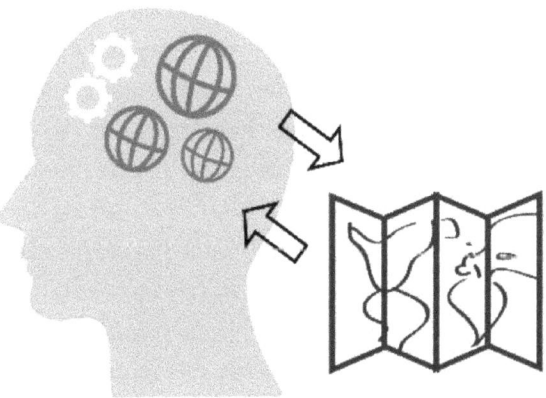

Fig. 5: The creative writer's mapping process

2.2 Cognitive mapping

The maps sketched by J.R.R. Tolkien are the results of mapping the internally constructed world of Middle-earth (a purely mental representation called cognitive map) at a specific time in the creative process into a visual form constrained by the space and margins of a (large) sheet of paper; from mental to material map, so to speak (see Fig. 5). This process produces a cognitive sketch map.

The process of cognitive mapping "may be defined as a process composed of a series of *psychological transformations* by which an individual acquires, codes, stores, recalls, and decodes information about the relative locations and attributes of phenomena in the spatial environment" (Downs and Stea 9). The result of such a process may be externalized through sketching and the final result may be called a cognitive (sketch) map or cognitive collage. Cognitive mapping research "seeks to comprehend how we come to understand spatial relations gained through both primary experience and secondary media (e.g. maps)" (Kitchin and Freundschuh 1) or texts.

E. C. Tolman first used the term "cognitive map" in 1948 to describe a hypothesized representation that allows rats to orient themselves spatially as an explanation for spatial behaviour. By his definition, the cognitive map comprises a flexible, schematized structure, which allows individuals to insert and revise knowledge about the real world. In other words, information fragments are collected such that they produce an ever changing whole. Tolman understood a cognitive map to be the result of an on-going mental construction process. Tversky suggested using the term "cognitive collage" instead of cognitive map, because "collage" suggests a relatively loose collection of spatial knowledge that does not necessarily have to be integrated, whereas the term "map" suggests a finished integrated product without contradictions. Hirtle proposed the alternative concept of "cognitive atlas" as another metaphor for the collection and organization of spatial knowledge.

In most cartographic discussions, the relationship to the "real world" is emphasized. However, the maps of Tolkien cannot have a relationship with a "real world" in the strict sense of the word, because they originate in the imagination of a writer of tales – i.e. features on the map could not be observed and measured by someone other than Tolkien himself. We can, however, gain a glimpse of the richness of the world through his literary endeavours by reading carefully and trying to re-construct in our minds the world as he imagined it – which is what K. Fonstad and B. Strachey did for their atlases.

3 Tolkien's sketches and maps

Tolkien learned map reading while in the army training camp in 1915 (Garth 164). He decided to specialize in signalling, which comprised training in map reading and presumably also mapping. This task appealed to him, being profoundly interested in languages, codes, words and messages. During his military service he put his learned knowledge to good use by devising a point-code with which his wife Edith was able to trace his movements on a map she had put on the wall at home (Garth 174).

This (supposedly first) exposure to mapping procedures might have influenced Tolkien in regard to his later endeavours to produce overview maps for *The Lord of the Rings*. One argument for this suggestion is that the makeup and map keys of the Map of Rohan, Gondor and Mordor (see Table 1) are similar to the colour coding and map key of British Army maps of the area where Tolkien was stationed[4] in France in 1916. However, the Map of Rohan, Gondor and Mordor is different in style from other published maps, such as the Map of Wilderland or Thror's map. These maps look more like sketches or charts and are much more reminiscent of Tolkien's drawings.

Wyatt (184) notes that Tolkien, throughout his life, ceaselessly produced sketches and drawings of places, characters, and of geographic places. These were the "devices" for controlling his emerging narratives and for establishing the history he was interested in (re-)creating. In his creative process, Tolkien seems to have started from scenes that he wrote and views that he sketched – see for example the sketches and watercolours of Orthanc, Rivendell and Nargothrond to be found on the Website of the Tolkien Estate.[5] In their book, Hammond and Scull write about various instances in which Tolkien first

---

4 www.lib.cam.ac.uk/deptserv/maps/tolkien.html?
5 http://www.tolkienestate.com/en/painting/landscapes/landscapes.html

visualized and then wrote about a specific scene, i.e. apparently visualisation preceded language. I will come back to the relationship between visualisation and language in section 4.

I would like to point out that having a three-dimensional perspective (as evident in Tolkien's written text and in his sketches) is a sign of being immersed in the narrative as well as in the geography, i.e. the world. This is very different from having an overview in which one seemingly flies above the world, and the higher one flies the more the world seemingly turns flat and two-dimensional (i.e. resembling a map).

It is hard to retrace the genesis of the published maps in Tolkien's oeuvre. I have made an attempt in Table 1 to distinguish between initial sketches of a geographic area on the one hand and the maps as they were first redrawn or published on the other hand. I did not take into account later publications such as Pauline Baynes' map of Middle-earth or Sibley and Howe's booklet with maps.

The maps in table 1 are ordered according to when they were first sketched. As far as I could trace their genesis, J.R.R. Tolkien himself did all sketches. By contrast, all maps were redrawn and published by his son Christopher Tolkien, with the exception of Thror's map published in *The Hobbit*.

map name	sketch	remarks	map type	re-drawn	by
Silmarillion	1926	2 major versions, continuous revisions	overview	1977	CT
Beleriand	ca. 1930	on the basis of 2nd Silmarillion map	overview, travel map	1977	CT
Thror's map	1930-1932	depends on its text, drawing lacks scale and detail, no road guide, vertical line, called "chart", *Hobbit*	treasure map	1937	JRRT

map name	sketch	remarks	map type	re-drawn	by
Wilderland	1936	sketch, color, showed topographic contours, vertical line, called "map", *Hobbit*	overview, travel map	1936	CT
Map of the Shire	1939	simple overview to give an orientation	overview	1953	CT
Middle-earth (West) "The first map"	1942	more detailed geography and more cultural details, does not fit the details of the *Hobbit*, 1943 map by C. Tolkien (*TI* 295ff)	overview, travel map	1954	CT
Rohan, Gondor and Mordor	1940-1953	many revisions, working map during writing of Book 5 of *LotR*	detailed, travel map	1955	CT
Númenor	1960	lacks detail, few features and names, colour	overview	1980	CT

Table 1: Tolkien's map sketches and their first publications

Thror's map stands out as the only treasure map in this collection: it shows where the treasure is (in a mountain), the dangers (Smaug) and it also shows the key for entering the place under certain conditions (moonlight at a specific day in the year). However, the map does not give instructions as to how to best get to the mountain – in that respect it is relatively sparse – thus, it is not a travel or road map. The map is part of the story, not separate from it. By contrast, all other published maps are additional materials produced especially for the readers in order to facilitate their understanding of the relationships and distances featured as well as for illustration purposes. In contrast to the books, the map of Middle-earth was included in the movie of *The Lord of the Rings: The Return of the King*.

As C. Tolkien notes (*TI* 300), redrawing a map (by hand) from a sketch involves not only meticulous copying skills, but also accurate re-scaling, employing different symbolisations and simplifications, and deciding which truth to copy and depict, if several exist. For publication, maps must be even more simplified, reduced in colour and made more legible. I argue that this onerous task was left to Christopher Tolkien not only due to time pressure, but mainly because the process of zooming out and imposing coherence on a map was a task almost impossible for J.R.R. Tolkien himself. He was too immersed in his created fantastic world to be able to allow himself to produce a version of this world that would be less detailed and thus inaccurate compared to the design he was imagining. A cartographer needs a special eye (and training) for producing a

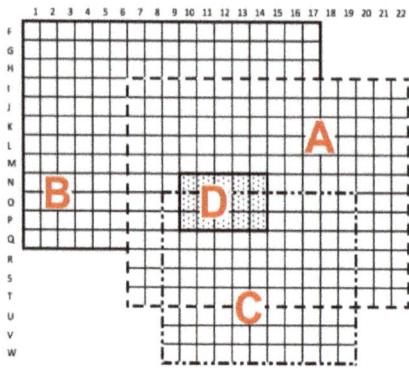

Fig. 6: Schema of construction of the working map after *TI* 297

final product that is both faithful to the original, less detailed but only as such fit for reproduction.

J.R.R. Tolkien himself used a working map as a reference map, which was changed when needed. C. Tolkien called it "a strange, battered, fascinating, extremely complicated and highly characteristic document" (*TI* 295).

Contemplating Tolkien's working map as explained in (*TI* 295-323), we can easily recognize its collage character (see Fig. 6), mirroring the process of creation with revisions and re-inventions: first sketch map A was drawn, then extended towards the West (sketch map B), redrawn with more detail and extended towards the south (sketch map C), and more detail added in sketch map D due to exigencies of the narrative. Parts of the maps were revised over time and glued to each other such that a reconstruction of this document's genesis has become impossible. Evidence for the transient character may be found in (*TI* 300) "[…] this map was a continuous development, evolving in terms of, and reacting upon, the narrative it accompanied." Tolkien's working map carries the characteristics of a cognitive sketch map.

4 Writing the map or mapping the story

We know that the brain treats pictorial and textual information differently – the right hemisphere is mostly in charge of language (among other things) and the left hemisphere mostly in charge of holistic (visual) thinking ("Cerebrale Dominanz"). Thus, a combination of words and maps caters to all parts of the brain, which allows for a deeper immersion into the narrative. Turchi (12) states that writing can be divided into two separate acts that overlap and mutually affect each other: the act of exploring and the act of presenting or communicating. The writer as an explorer will thus need to morph into the writer as a guide during the gestation process of a narrative.

4.1 Act of exploring

The first act in writing leads into the unknown, off or beyond the map, so to speak. From accounts of writers we know that they, by writing or sketching, explore specific scenes or settings, develop characters, write part of a story, only to drop or rewrite them completely. Tolkien, throughout his life, produced sketches and drawings of places, characters, and maps (Wyatt 184) in addition to actual text fragments, snippets and dialogues, which were also subject to numerous revisions. Various sections in the History of Middle-Earth point towards Tolkien first trying to visualize and sketch his impressions or specific scenes before integrating them into the narrative (MacLeod and Smol 117). It seems that text and image were intricately linked and interwoven during Tolkien's explorative act.

In the case of map-making the "act of exploring" corresponds to inventing places, sketching settings, or determining measures (distances, angles) of a world.

Among Tolkien's sketches we can find alternative ways of arranging topographical features, for example the winding (or not so winding) path to The Hill in relation to The Mill (Hammond and Scull 100-106). In a similar manner the entrance to the Elvenking's Hall is depicted in several sketches varying the surrounding topography and the path towards the bridge in front of the hall (Hammond and Scull 124-125). Tolkien himself did not like to publish his artistic sketches, claiming that they were not up to a good standard. He also once stated, that "fantasy is a thing best left to words, to true literature" ("On Fairy-Stories" as cited in MacLeod and Smol 117). He wanted the readers to produce their own pictures in their minds. One could say that all the materials combined would create a cognitive collage – forming a whole in Tolkien's mind. As we know from cognitive collages, they often do not mesh well, since each part of a collage is a fragment by and consistent in itself, whilst not necessarily consistent with the other fragments.

I suggest using the term "cognitive collage" for the collection of material used in imagining the spaces, places and spatial relationships for a narrative. This better differentiates the collection of materials used for creating a geography from the final product meant for reading, which may appropriately be called 'map'.

4.2 Act of presenting

The second act in writing, that is, the act of presenting (Turchi 12), is the way of the author to organise material, to arrange it into a sequence, to follow a red line or logical thread in order to arrive at the final stage of a finished text. As there is always more material in existence than will be published in the final version, this second stage is akin to selecting the best pieces for the flow of the narrative. Tolkien himself was known to continuously edit his creations and he often inserted major corrections into the final proofs (Wyatt 184). This is an extreme form of intermingling of the two acts and in my opinion proof of Tolkien's perfectionism.

The "act of presenting" a map corresponds to drawing the final map, observing all cartographic necessities (such as title, North arrow, scale, author, year, etc.). Organizing knowledge on a map at a reduced scale, showing only the important pieces (because there is not enough space to put in more) may lead to the discovery of patterns. Seeing the whole might lead us to identify new relationships, which in turn might incite new discoveries and unsuspected or unintended associations. This is certainly one of the goals of including a map as part of a work of fiction. However, for the writer, who is still in the act of exploring, these new discoveries and associations will either show up inconsistencies, blanks on the map or engender new and additional scenes to include in the narrative. Fonstad notes that the more of a map you draw, the more you realize what you do not know until you decide which are the things that need to be included and which are not (paraphrased from Fonstad ix).

One cause for Tolkien's difficulty in producing the final maps was his perfectionism and attention to detail. Tolkien "felt he [had to] ensure that every single detail fitted satisfactorily into the total pattern. Geography, chronology, and nomenclature all had to be entirely consistent" (*Bio* 198). Tolkien complained in 1955 in a letter to Rayner Unwin: "The map is hell! I have not been as careful as I should in keeping track of distances" (*L* 210). Campbell (405) states, that "Tolkien's geography was imagined and developed for his stories. He combined places where he had travelled, in England and Europe, with places from literature history, and his imagination. [...] The maps were an integral part of Tolkien's writing process, and were intended to be spatially accurate."

Literary texts are the result of plans that the writer formulates in terms of his or her general knowledge of the object world (Bjornson 57). Especially when the creative phase lasts a long time (as in *The Lord of the Rings*) or covers a large area (also true for *The Lord of the Rings*), the externalization of the plan (be it in form of outlines, text passages, sketches or maps) seems advisable. It was important to Tolkien to construct a consistent world and history – since the underlying endeavour of his literary work was the wish to produce a mythology he could dedicate to England, as he wrote to Milton Waldmann (*L* 144).

While reading, humans try to synthesize a composite image of the imaginary territory mapped in the text (Bjornson 58). They tend to begin with a general idea of what they are reading and then construct the whole image piece-by-piece. Textual images are flexible cognitive constructs, which employ the same cognitive mapping techniques people use for orientation in the world.

Tolkien gave the impression that he thought reading *The Lord of the Rings* without maps would be much harder than with maps. I do not entirely agree with his assessment – he was a gifted writer, capable of recreating a world in the minds of his readers of such a detailed nature that the recreation would be possible with or without map. I wonder if Naomi Mitchison agreed or how she responded to his assertion that it must have been hard to read *The Lord of the Rings* without access to the geography (*L* 177). Fonstad mentioned that the richness of descriptive detail in *The Lord of the Rings* was such that she felt compelled to produce maps from the description alone (Fonstad ix).

5 Some concluding insights

Maps were important to Tolkien for several reasons at different stages in his world building and creative writing process that he was engaged in throughout his life. Distinguishing between the act of exploring and the act of presenting allows for a coarse differentiation into map sketches and published maps.

Maps as sketches of places and settings play an important role in the act of exploring the topic. Each spatial sketch or map draft may be considered an information fragment of a vaguely perceived or imagined whole. At this stage of the process we cannot call this collection of fragments a map in the conventional sense; instead I propose the notion "cognitive collage". Cognitive collages do not require consistency in every relationship between the different fragments. There may even exist contradictory and alternative information fragments at the same time. Cognitive collages are the product of cognitive mapping. After some time of collecting information fragments, structures may emerge from and within the collage.

The "act of presenting" requires the writer to select a spatial structure and to integrate existing spatial information fragments into a coherent whole. This process forces the writer to detect blank spaces in the imagined geographic space and contradictions within the written text (mostly pertaining to distances and angles), but the writer may also find new associations and inspiring ideas. The final product of this process may then be called a map in the conventional sense.

Tolkien was not just writing a story – he was at the same time re-creating a geography, a history and different cultures. His *The Lord of the Rings* working map (this strange, battered document mentioned in *TI* 295) was his way of trying to keep everything consistent. Making a finer distinction between the different types of maps used in the creative process, this map could be called an overview map with a given structure in which spatial information fragments were inserted in a non-contradictory fashion. The map had a small scale, i.e. it showed a large area, but not much detail, although more detail was added later in a central portion of the map.

Although the working map was not very detailed, the descriptions in the text are so vivid and contain so much details that a re-creation of the world in the reader's mind is relatively simple and straightforward – which inspires so many people to try their hand at mapping parts of the journey or even additional information (see the *Atlas of Middle-earth* for example). The world of Middle-earth as described in *The Lord of the Rings* is much richer (both in language and history) than the world in *The Hobbit*. This is also reflected in the maps that were published together with the corresponding books: Thror's Map is a treasure map but shows only a little of the surrounding culture and topography, e.g. topographic names are simple – tailored to the way children see the world. By contrast, the map of Middle-earth is full of topographic place names that do not occur in Tolkien's stories, insinuating a rich history exactly as Tolkien had intended.

Maps have power – once they are printed, they suggest a truth about the world. The richer the map, the more it is perceived to reflect history and culture. At the same time a map provides settings for other (hi)stories to happen. Tolkien's maps of Middle-earth in the *The Lord of the Rings* exhibit this richness of settings enticing readers to continue adding to the (hi)story.

About the Author

Prof. Dr. SABINE TIMPF is a researcher in Geographic Information Science interested in how humans perceive, reason about, and visualize geographic information, and act on this information in geographic space. She has contributed to research in wayfinding and navigation by applying and extending theories from cognitive science, especially ecological psychology, and by implementing models of human spatial knowledge representation, reasoning and decision making in geographic contexts such as intelligent navigation assistance in smart cities and landscape appraisal for quality-of-life in urban environments.

List of Abbreviations

Bio CARPENTER, Humphrey. *J.R.R. Tolkien. A Biography.* First published 1977. Paperback edition. London: HarperCollins, 1995.

L CARPENTER, Humphrey, ed. with the assistance of Christopher Tolkien. *The Letters of J.R.R. Tolkien.* London: George Allen & Unwin, 1981. Reprinted Boston: Houghton Mifflin, 2000.

LotR TOLKIEN, John Ronald Reuel. *The Lord of the Rings.* 50th Anniversary One-Volume Edition. Boston and New York: Houghton Mifflin, 2004.

TI TOLKIEN, John Ronald Reuel. *The Treason of Isengard.* The History of Middle-earth 7. Ed. Christoph Tolkien. First published 1989. London: Grafton, 1993.

WR TOLKIEN, John Ronald Reuel. *The War of the Ring.* The History of Middle-earth 8. Ed. Christoph Tolkien. First published 1990. London: Grafton, 1992.

Bibliography

BJORNSON, R. "Cognitive Mapping and the Understanding of Literature." *SubStance* 10.1 (1981): 51-62.

BORGES, J. L. "On Exactitude in Science." *Collected Ficciones*. London: Penguin, 1998. 704-705.

CAMPBELL, A. "Maps." *J.R.R. Tolkien Encyclopedia: Scholarship and Critical Assessment*. Ed. M. D. C. Drout. New York: Routledge, 2007. 405-408.

CARPENTER, Humphrey. *J.R.R. Tolkien. A Biography*. First published 1977. Paperback edition. London: HarperCollins, 1995.

ed. with the assistance of Christopher Tolkien. *The Letters of J.R.R. Tolkien*. London: George Allen & Unwin, 1981. Reprinted Boston: Houghton Mifflin, 2000.

"Cerebrale Dominanz." (20 April 2017). *Lexikon der Neurowissenschaften* (http://www.spektrum.de/lexikon/neurowissenschaft/cerebrale-dominanz/1972).

DOWNS, R. M., and D. STEA, eds. *Image and Environment – Cognitive Mapping and Spatial Behaviour*. Chicago: Aldine, 1973.

EKMAN, S. *Here be Dragons – Exploring Fantasy Maps and Settings*. Middletown CT: Wesleyan University Press, 2013.

FONSTAD, K. W. *The Atlas of Middle-earth*. Harcourt: Houghton Mifflin, 2014.

GARTH, J. *Tolkien and the Great War. The Threshold of Middle-earth*. London: HarperCollins, 2003.

HAMMOND, W. G., and SCULL, C. *J.R.R. Tolkien – Artist & Illustrator*. Boston and New York: Houghton Mifflin, 1995.

HIRTLE, S. "The Cognitive Atlas: Using GIS as a Metaphor for Memory." *Spatial and Temporal Reasoning in Geographic Information Systems*. Eds. M. J. Egenhofer and R. G. Golledge. New York: Oxford University Press, 1998. 263-271.

KITCHIN, R., and S. FREUNDSCHUH. *Cognitive Mapping Past, Present and Future*. London: Routledge, 2000.

MACEACHREN, A. M. *How Maps Work – Representation, Visualization, and Design*. New York: Guilford, 1995.

MACLEOD, J. J., and A. SMOL. "A Single Leaf: Tolkien's Visual Art and Fantasy." *Mythlore* 27.1-2 (2008): 105-126.

MONMONNIER, M. *How to Lie with Maps*. Chicago: University of Chicago Press, 2014.

MORETTI, F. *Atlas of the European Novel*. London and New York: Verso, 1998.

Schoggen, P. *Behavior Settings*. Stanford CA: Stanford University Press, 1989.

Sibley, B., and J. Howe. *The Maps of Tolkien's Middle-earth*. Boston: Houghton Mifflin, 2003.

Strachey, B. *Journeys of Frodo: An Atlas of J.R.R. Tolkien's The Lord of the Rings* New York: Ballantine Books, 1981.

Tolkien, John Ronald Reuel. *The Lord of the Rings*. 50th Anniversary One-Volume Edition. Boston and New York: Houghton Mifflin, 2004.

The Treason of Isengard. The History of Middle-earth 7. Ed. Christoph Tolkien. First published 1989. London: Grafton, 1993.

The War of the Ring. The History of Middle-earth 8. Ed. Christoph Tolkien. First published 1990. London: Grafton, 1992.

Tolman, E. C. "Cognitive Maps in Rats and Men." *The Psychological Review* 55.4 (1948): 189-208.

Turchi, P. *Maps of the Imagination: The Writer as Cartographer*. San Antonio TX: Trinity University Press, 2007.

Tversky, B. "Cognitive Maps, Cognitive Collages, and Spatial Mental Models." *Spatial Information Theory: A Theoretical Basis for GIS*. Eds. A. U. Frank and I. Campari. Vol. 716. Heidelberg and Berlin: Springer, 1993. 14-24.

Wood, D., and J. Fels. *The Power of Maps*. New York: Guilford Press, 1992.

Wyatt, J. *Use of Imaginary, Historical, and Actual Maps in Literature: How British and Irish Authors Created Imaginary Worlds to Tell their Stories (Defoe, Swift, Wordsworth, Kipling, Joyce, Tolkien, etc.)*. Lewiston: Edwin Mellen, 2013.

Carolin Tober

How J.R.R. Tolkien Used Kennings to Make *The Lord of the Rings* into a Medieval Epic for the 20th Century

Abstract

My paper examines the stylistic device of the kenning and analyses why and how Tolkien used it in his novel *The Lord of the Rings*. I argue that the strict rules and premises that the elaborate form of the kenning achieved in the Old Norse poetry cannot and should not be regarded as binding for the Old Celtic and Old English kennings that can also be considered as models for Tolkien – nor are they direct models for the Tolkienian kennings themselves. There are many Tolkienian kennings that fully comply to even the strictest requirements of the Old Norse kennings, but just as many deviate from the Old Norse tradition and show greater affinity to Old English kennigs, and should therefore be examined with regard to their kenning-character.

1 Introduction

The Lord of the Rings does not only tell a story of a quest in a medieval world of a mythical past, full of monsters, heroes and great deeds of valour, but also utilizes particularly archaic language. There are numerous expressions, poems and songs as well as whole passages that distinctly recall the choice of words and tone of the Old English poem *Beowulf*. Professor Tolkien spent a lot of time working on *Beowulf* and even wrote an eloquent prose translation, which was published posthumously by his son Christopher in 2014. The influence of his work with Old English (OE) poetry on his fictional writing cannot be overestimated. By recycling distinctly medieval stylistic elements in his *The Lord of the Rings*, Professor Tolkien used his own craft, i.e. historical linguistics, to create a medieval epic for the 20th century. One of the stylistic devices he employed very artfully and effectively to achieve this pseudo-medieval style is the kenning, on which I want to shed some light in this paper.

To understand how Tolkien used the device of the kenning, I will first try to establish a definition of the kenning based on the works of scholars who analysed Old Norse (ON) and Old English (OE) kennings. Then, I will consider how far Tolkien's own stance on the kenning complies with the newly established definition and thereafter focus on the analysis of different kennings found in *The Lord of the Rings*. The aim of this paper is to reveal how Tolkien succeeded in creating a medieval style for his epic by crafting more or less prototypical kennings in several languages of his Middle-earth.

2 Understanding kennings

2.1 The kenning's historio-linguistic background and earlier research

Kennings (ON *kenningar*) are stylistic devices especially typical for and characteristic of Old Germanic poetry. They reached their most elaborate forms in the alliterative Eddic and skaldic poetry of medieval Norway and Iceland (Mohr 1), but also shaped, to a lesser, yet still considerable amount, the style of Anglo-Saxon (OE) poetry (Marquardt 103). While the term "kenning" itself is Icelandic and means "description" (Tolkien, "On Translating" 59), which could be argued does not seem too complex, the contrary is the case with regard to its definition by (historical) linguists. There exists so far no unanimous definition of this quite elaborate medieval stylistic device. The common denominator amongst scholars, however, is in alignment with the following elaboration of mine: Kennings are metaphorical compound-like structures used in poetry, serving the purposes of variation in ON and OE alliterative verse. They are used to substitute prosaic terms, mostly nouns. An example would be the OE kenning *yð-hengest*, which literally translates as "sea-stallion". It is, however, not to be taken literally, but metaphorically: A "stallion of the sea" is a pictorial expression for "ship". The second element of a kenning generally suggests an element of comparison based on similarity to the noun it substitutes, while the first element specifies the comparison and adds pictorial quality. In the case of "sea-stallion", the noun that the kenning substitutes in the poem is compared to a stallion, more specifically a stallion of the sea. The image that was supposed to come to mind is the one of a ship (Lee and Solopova 43).

It is agreed upon that a medieval poet would use kennings for stylistic reasons mainly, i.e. so to avoid repeating key notions contained in common Northern heroic verse, such as king, warrior, the sea, ship and battle (Marquardt 115). The kenning is, however, not only useful to provide synonyms and avoid repetition within a text, but also used to be cherished for its poetic, pictorial quality, as Tolkien himself notes:

> The compound offers a partial and often imaginative or fanciful description of a thing, and the poets may use it instead of the normal 'name'. [...] For the kenning flashes a picture before us, often the more clear and bright for its brevity, instead of unrolling it in a simile. ("On Translating" 59)

Research regarding the kenning is quite sparse, and mostly dates back to the 1920s and 1930s with scholars such as Rudolf Meissner and Hendrik van der Merwe Scholtz, Wolfgang Mohr, Wolfgang Krause, and Hertha Marquardt. Their understanding of kennings is mainly based upon the skaldic and Eddic kenning, as it occurs in Snorri Sturluson's compilation of ON poems including explanations of skaldic poetic style, variably called *Snorra Edda*, *Younger Edda* or *Prose Edda* (compiled about AD 1220). Since, however, Snorri himself did not provide a clear definition of the term and gave very little explanation of the exact concept of the kenning or how it is constructed (Krause 4), the aforementioned scholars still could not agree on a unanimous definition of kenning.

With regard to OE kennings, there is no medieval document known that would share meta-information about any principles of use and composition. In general, one may argue that they are similar enough to ON kennings and thus have largely been described by means of the latter's criteria (Mohr 30). While it needs to be noted that OE kennings differ from ON ones in a few crucial aspects after all, they tend to be overshadowed by the much more prominent ON kenning in the literature – undeservedly, particularly as Marquardt (1938) and Krause (1930) have demonstrated, and as shall be argued in this paper.

2.2 A working definition of kenning

I have established the three most consistent characteristics for the kenning, drawing from the existing research. On this basis, I will seek to compose a suitable working definition of the kenning for the purposes of this paper as well as for any potential future research on this versatile phenomenon.

1) The kenning is a poetic paraphrase consisting of two nouns (cf. 2.2.1)
2) There has to be a transfer of meaning to an exocentric head (cf. 2.2.2)
3) In its poetic applicability it has to be variable and should not rely on its context to unfold its meaning. Instead, the metaphor employed should ideally clash with the context to create a more powerful and abstract image (cf. 2.2.3).

2.2.1 A poetic paraphrase consisting of two nouns

This first criterion raises largely questions of function and form. According to Meissner, kennings have their origin in the poet's desire "to replace a worn out or rather inexpressive, ordinary term with a more colourful, vivid and imaginative one" (25).[1] The term replace is of special importance here since a kenning is defined first and foremost by its quality of providing a poetic, creative and vivid substitute or paraphrase for an ordinary prosaic word.

In order to be perceived as a poetic paraphrase, the free lexical morphemes[2] a kenning consists of have to belong to a typical poetic sphere (Krause 5). For example, OE *guð* and *hild* are the most frequently used words for "fight, battle" in OE poetry – but they do not appear in a single work of prose (Marquardt 119). So, it is fair to argue that they belong to the poetic sphere or a poetic class of lexemes[3] and are highly eligible to form kennings. Two examples from *Beowulf* are *hildeleoma* (1143), "battle-light", a kenning for "sword", and *gúð-beorn* (314), "battle-bear", a kenning for "warrior". *Beorn* is the poetic form of *bera*, "bear". It was used to refer to man in heroic poetry (Tolkien, "On Translating" 54). The implied comparison to bear would intensify the image of the referent by adding its associations with "strong" and "bold".

---

[1] In the original: "einen blasseren, abgenutzten, gewöhnlichen Ausdruck durch einen lebhafteren, farbigeren zu ersetzen."
[2] This is a term of morphology, the study of word formation. The basic units of meaning of a language are called "morphemes". E.g. the word *singers* can be divided into three morphemes, each carrying meaning: *sing*, *-er*, and *-s*. A free lexical morpheme or content word is a morpheme that can stand alone and unbound and signfies an extralinguistic concept. Therefore, of the examples cited before, only *sing* is a free lexical morpheme (Kortmann 49-52).
[3] *Lexemes* are also units of meaning in a language. They are content words that are headwords in the dictionary. To resume the example of *singer*: *sing* as well as *singer* are lexemes, whereas *singers* is a word form of *singer* (Kortmann 50).

What is so special about poetical paraphrase like *hildeleoma*, "battle-light", and *gúð-beorn*, "battle-bear", is that

> the literal meaning of the expression is inseparably linked to the pictorial imagination it evokes. The listener or reader is intended to perceive both, the literal meaning of the combination of the two lexemes [...] as well as the picture their combination elicits. (Mohr 22)[4]

The combination of lexemes evokes not only the replaced term they refer to but also a new image created from their combined meanings: A "battle-bear" is a warrior that fights as fiercely and ferociously as a bear, "battle-light" stresses the radiance of the naked steel. They also carry different connotations and emotions, which is one of the reasons why the poets have brought forth many synonymous kennings for one prosaic word (v. d. Merwe Scholtz 8).

Since a paraphrase must, by definition, consist of at least two elements (Marquardt 111), the kenning must be composed of two or more lexemes (c.f. also Krause 4, Meissner 2). It seems like the poets felt that a term made up of a combination of two or more lexemes would fit their purpose better than one single lexeme: "It seems that a single lexeme does usually not suffice the poet and that he strives for combinations and compounds to give his words more colour and substance" (Mohr 33).[5]

To substitute a noun, the kenning has to function as a noun within the grammatical dimensions of the syntax. Meissner (2-3) thus divided the constituents of the kenning into a base (G *Grundwort*) and one or more modifiers (G *Bestimmungen*). The base takes over the syntactic function of the replaced noun and therefore has to be a noun or nominalized word. It is usually preceded by one or more modifiers. The base serves as the characterizing or sensualizing element of the kenning (Meissner 25), which means that the base contains the element of comparison or similarity to the substituted term. Meissner also notes that a great number of kennings contain a *nomen agentis*[6] in the base because the

---

4 In the original: "das Tatsächliche ist unlöslich mit dem Bildhaften verbunden, wir sollen zweierlei erleben, das Bild und den wirklichen Inhalt."
5 In the original: "es sieht so aus, als ob dem Dichter der einteilige Ausdruck in der Regel nicht genüge, und daß er zweiteilige Ausdrücke suche, um seinen Worten mehr Fülle und Gewicht zu verleihen."
6 In linguistics, a *nomen agentis* is a lexeme that is derived from a verb or noun denoting an action. The new lexeme designates a person that performs that action. E.g. the nomen agentis *cleaner* is created by adding the suffix -*er* to the verb *clean*. This process is called "agentive nominalization" (Dixon 306).

personification contained in the word-formation inspires imagination (6). ON examples are *hræsvelgr* "corpse-swallower", a kenning for "eagle", or *húsbrjótr* "house-breaker", a kenning for "wind" (Meissner 9).

The word class of the modifier poses more problems and the scholars differ in their opinions. According to Meissner, the proper ON kenning contains not only a noun as base but also a noun as modifier and thus recommends restricting the term of "kenning" to those that are made up of two or more nouns (3). He states that "it is distinctive for a definition of the kenning in a stricter sense that it expresses relations between two nouns" (Meissner 6),[7] thus indicating that there is a narrower and a wider definition. Mohr on the other hand defines the kenning as "a poetic denomination consisting of a noun and one or more elements that modify the noun" (15), not making any restrictions regarding the word class to which the modifying elements have to belong.

So, I would like to stress that while it is a characteristic of the kenning in the stricter sense to express a relationship between two (or more) nouns, there are kennings in a wider sense that do not necessarily follow this rule and can thus contain a modifier belonging to a different word class. Also, as will be shown in the following chapter (2.2.2), it is the transfer of meaning that makes the ultimate quality of a kenning.

Since kennings are composed of two or more lexemes, the question arises whether to call them compounds, since that is what they look like at first sight. However, it is important to note that if kennings become "well-established compounds, their poetic character fades and they may enter the ordinary, prosaic sphere" (Meissner 18).[8] Hence, I would like to argue that kennings are characterized by being rather loosely tied combinations or just word-forms joined together without being compounded. I will therefore call them combinations rather than compounds. Another point in favour of this terminological choice is that numerous kennings contain inflected forms of their constituents, which is very atypical of compounds as well, as Bauer states: "The prototypical compound is simply the collocation of two unmarked lexemes" (346).

---

7 In the original: "für die Kenning im engeren Sinne ist […] charakteristisch, daß Beziehungen zwischen zwei Substantiven ausgedrückt werden."
8 In the original: "zu einer sich im Gebrauch festsetzenden Komposition, so verblaßt eine solche Bildung leicht und kann in den allgemeinen Sprachgebrauch übergehen."

2.2.2 Transfer of meaning to an exocentric head

As already mentioned in 2.1, the kenning is a metaphorical expression that substitutes a plain, prosaic term. The quality that makes it especially elaborate and challenging is that some kind of transfer of meaning must result from the combination of the base and the modifier. Meissner stresses that we can only speak of a kenning if the base of the combination cannot in its literal sense be connected to the modifier, and if a comparison, a transfer of meaning or a pictorial imagination is necessary to make sense of the combination (Meissner 27). To put it in a nutshell: When the combination of the two lexemes is to be taken in its literal sense and can be explained from the context, it is no kenning.

In this respect, the kenning works like an exocentric compound, where the semantic head is external to the compound itself. Headedness is shown most clearly by hyponymy: An endocentric compound as a whole is a hyponym of its head as can be seen in the example of *traffic-light*. The semantic head is *light*, and *traffic-light* is a subordinate term of *light*. An exocentric compound, by contrast, is not a hyponym of one of its elements, and thus appears to have a head external to the compound itself (Bauer 349). This is the case for the kenning. For example, OE *hēafodgim*, a kenning for "eye", is composed of the nouns *hēafod* "head" and *gim* "jewel", thus literally translates as "head-jewel". The meaning of the combination is the semantical head "eye", but a "head-jewel" is not a hyponym or subordinate term of "eye". The kenning is exocentric and we need to comprehend the transfer of meaning, i.e. the metaphor, to understand what it refers to.

Mohr (33) remarks that a strikingly high number of what he calls "Scheinkenningar" – expressions that look very similar to kennings – can be found in *Beowulf*. He quotes explanatory metaphors like *heofenes hwealf*, "heaven's vault" (*Beowulf* v. 2015), or combinations where the modifiers are just specifying or emphasizing the head noun like in *ellengæst* "powerful spirits" (*Beowulf* v. 86), a kenning for Grendel. They are not like the proper, metaphorical ON kennings, as they are to be taken rather literally lacking the crucial transfer of meaning. In Marquardt's opinion, however, these examples just illustrate that many OE kennings cannot necessarily be taken metaphorically but are often merely descriptive or sensualizing (116). For example, *guðwine* "battle-friend", a kenning for "sword"

(*Beowulf* v. 1810), is not specifically pictorial. Even though the head is still exocentric ("sword"), the metaphor it employs is quite easily deductible from the context. By the standards set beforehand, it would thus be a kenning in the wider sense. Marquardt states that OE sword kennings like *guðwine* typically rarely display a transfer of meaning but render actual relations between the lexemes, without lacking poetic quality (117). Van der Merwe Scholtz comes to the same conclusion and remarks that OE kennings are not always used in a figurative sense, but often in a rather specifying way (47). I would agree with Marquardt and van der Merwe Scholtz and argue that OE kennings just have different standards, the metaphorical kenning being very rare, while the specifying or descriptive kenning prevails.

2.2.3 Poetic application: Variability and independence from the context

After having described the form of the kenning and its metaphorical or descriptive character, the next step is to look at how it is employed in the text and why ancient poets bothered making up these artful exocentric combinations. Meissner (12) already declared that it is essential for the kenning to be perceived as a suitable substitute for another lexeme and as such must fulfil the demands of variability and independence from the context.

Variability means that the lexemes that form a kenning also have to be eligible to form other kennings. For example, the ON sword kennings (taken from Meissner 158) *hjaldrblik, hjaldrs eldr, hjaldrs bál, hjaldrs hyrr, hjaldrkyndill, hjaldríss, hjaldrliðr, hjaldrseiðr* illustrate that *hjaldr*, "battle, fight", can combine with many other lexemes to form variable kennings. If there is no such internal variability the combination cannot be considered a kenning, which is true for the OE *hláf-weard*, "bread-warden". It could be classified as a kenning for "lord" were it not a conventionalized compound whose constituents do not combine with other lexemes (112). Variability is one of the most prominent stylistic features of Old Germanic poetry, which explains why especially the ON poets came up with so many different kennings (Krause 4).

However, the criterion of variability does not apply to OE kennings in the same way as for ON kennings, since they were simply not used as frequently as stylistic devices (Marquardt 115). The surviving texts suggest that the OE poets did not have a nearly as big a set of interchangeable kennings at their disposal as their ON colleagues, and neither as many possibilities of variation in regard to the kennings' lexical constituents.

The other important feature of the poetic application of kennings seems to be independence from the context, since ON kennings are mostly found to be independent from a specific contextual situation (Krause 6, Meissner 12). That means that the further away from the context the lexemes and the metaphor employed in the kenning are, the higher the quality of the kenning. The reason for that seems to be quite simply that otherwise, it would be too easy to invent kennings. Meissner as a scholar of the ON kenning explains that the ON poets seemed to regard the invention of kennings as an appealing game, since they liked to use clashing images that did not connect to the context at all and were therefore not bound to any contextual situation (12). The kenning *hjaldrs orri* (Meissner 2) may serve as an example: It translates as "battle-partridge", which conjures up bizarre images because the ideas and connotations of "battle" and "partridge" clash. Put into a poem without explanation, there could hardly be a context that helps to make sense of this expression. Therefore, this kenning for "raven" (Meissner 2) is independent from the context and illustrates the poet's metaphorical inventiveness.

The independence from the context is further strengthened since the kenning relies on its tradition and the shared cultural knowledge (thus salience[9]) of the listeners or readers. Thus, a poet may have mostly used such kennings that he expected to be known and recognized by his audience – at least he would have believed that his audience would have a good shot at being able to guess what the expression refers to. Therefore, kennings tend to be highly opaque to an audience from a different cultural or temporal background like modern-day readers. Especially kennings referring to mythological contents could hardly be understood unless the listener knew the respective sagas and stories. Mohr gives

---

9 This is a pragmatic notion used in cognitive linguistics to describe the fact that some information is "foremost on one's mind" (Giora 15) because of its conventionality, familiarity, frequency and prototypicality for members of a certain culture or community. It thus refers to the phenomenon that members of all kinds of communities will perceive certain notions or concepts as particularly common or natural, or even self-explanatory. The ancient poets relied on a kenning's high degree of salience within their audience. See Giora (15-17) for a detailed explanation of the term.

the example of *otrgjöld* (17), which literally translates as "otter-recompense". This kenning for "gold" is impossible to deduce unless one knows that in ON mythology there was a shape-shifter called Otr, who was killed accidentally by Loki whilst in his otter-shape. Hence Loki offered Otr's father recompensation by covering the dead otter body in gold (Hampton Belton 277). This anecdote makes apparent the transfer of meaning and the semantic exocentricity of the kenning *otrgjöld* – and only those who are acquainted with it would be able to make the necessary connection.

Thus, it is evident that the kenning is culture-dependent, which renders a kenning an actual culture-specific kind of code. Mohr remarks that ON and OE kennings often look very much alike and use lexemes that would be understood in the other language respectively – but that their meaning or the referents they point to in some cases differ considerably: OE *hildelēoma* for example may well have been decoded as a sword kenning by an Old Norse recipient, since the meaning of the base, *lēoma* "light, radiance" was a component typically employed for ON sword kennings; in OE however it meant "dragonfire" (Mohr 31).

Yet again, the OE kennings are different from the ON regarding the feature of independence from the context. In contrast to ON kennings that prefer to stand alone as free lexical elements they often appear in form of a context-embedded apposition,[10] which means they rather accompany than substitute the noun they refer to. In the following example from *Beowulf* I have highlighted the appositional kenning: *Álédon þá léofne þéoden* **béaga bryttan** *on bearm scipes* (v. 34-35; emphasis mine); "then they laid down the beloved prince, ring-bestower, in the bosom of the ship." *Béaga bryttan* is a kenning for *þéoden*, but instead of using the kenning to substitute the noun, the poet placed both terms in apposition.

On this basis, Krause makes an interesting observation: Using the kenning in form of a context-embedded apposition seems to be one of the formal roots of this device (Krause 9-10). The art of the kenning seems to have originated in such context-bound appositional paraphrases and then gained increasing independence the more established the device became with the poets and

---

10 An apposition links noun phrases of equivalent grammatical status and identical reference (Greenbaum 87).

audiences. This can be illustrated with the already mentioned OE example of *béaga bryttan* and the very similar ON *baugbroti* "ring-breaker" (Mohr 17). First, expressions like that were probably used appositionally as an additional description for a person that actually bestows or breaks rings, the prince or king. Since the bestowing or breaking of rings was a common act for a king, the kennings were comprehensible without the explicit contextual reference to "king", and thus the poets could play with the transfer of meaning, using the kenning as a free lexical element independently from the context (Mohr 17). At least that is what the ON poets did, the OE ones rarely achieved this development. According to Krause, the Catholic Christian culture is to blame for that: The classical style seems to not have agreed with the barbaric stylistic device of the kenning, which is why the Christian influence in Britain put an end to the OE development of the kenning, while the ON kenning could thrive (10).

Marquardt supports Krause's claim by stating that "the older age of the OE poetic manuscripts gives reason to expect greater originality or a more pristine character, which leads us closer to the roots of the kenning" (103).[11] What one infers from these statements is that the OE kenning may represent an earlier stage of development than the ON one. That would then count as one of the reasons why the OE kenning does not seem as typical, as special, or as artful as the ON one. In many instances, it could be argued that even though the form is not yet a fully developed kenning in the ON sense, the idea, the image, and the metaphor behind it already is.

2.2.4 A new definition for kenning

The preceding chapters have illustrated the claim that the ON kenning was much more elaborate and abstract than the OE kenning came to be. In many cases, OE kennings can hardly be called "proper" kennings, and yet they are more than just pictorial compounds. My most important point has been to show that the strict rules and premises that the elaborate form of the kenning had assigned to itself in ON poetry cannot and should not be

---

11 In the original: "wegen des höheren Alters der poetischen Denkmäler eine größere Ursprünglichkeit erwarten läßt und uns näher an die Wurzeln der Kenning heranführt."

regarded as equally binding for OE kennings – after all, the latter have been shown to be more archaic than the ON ones and thus need to be measured by different standards.

I would thus like to propose a revised and more comprehensive definition of kennings that also take into consideration the variations of OE kennings and is able to do them justice all the same: A kenning is a formation made up of two or more lexemes occurring in the poetic genre. It serves as replacement for a noun of prosaic character in verse. The kenning is no conventionalized compound, but rather a more or less loose, often spontaneous combination, which does not preclude that these combinations enter the thesaurus or corpus of the poets and can be used in the same form repeatedly in different poems and by different authors, hence establishing a poetic tradition. A kenning should ideally be independent from the context to support the stylistic device of variation, and show traces of an experienced transfer of meaning to an exocentric semantic head, making it rather metaphorical or pictorial, at the very least sensualizing, emphasizing or characterizing.

Working with this definition, we can now approach the Tolkienian kennings as used in *The Lord of the Rings*.

3 Tolkien's stance on the kenning

Tolkien as a major scholar and Professor of Anglo-Saxon (OE) of course was familiar with the stylistic device of the kenning. In fact, he worked out his own working definition of kennings as presented in the commentary on his prose translation of *Beowulf*. In his understanding, a kenning is "a technical term for those *pictorial descriptive compounds or brief expressions which can be used in place of the normal plain word*" (Tolkien, *Beowulf* 141, emphasis in the original). So, how does this definition, which has certainly laid the ground for the Tolkienian kennings in *The Lord of the Rings*, comply with the other researchers' point of view and the newly established definition of the kenning in the previous chapter, and what the implied differences are?

In general, Tolkien also defines the kenning as a paraphrase and as pictorial, thus agreeing to the transfer of meaning to an exocentric head. However, there are a few notable differences that are entailed in his definition and his use of kennings. Most interestingly, he turns away from the exclusively compound-like character of the kenning and includes what he calls "brief expressions". Unfortunately, he does not specify what expressions he means by that. There is only a hint in his notes, where he comments on his efforts at translating OE kennings from *Beowulf* into Modern English. He laments that a literal translation will "certainly not [be] modern English, even if it is intelligible" ("On Translating" 58). In regard to the dilemma of rendering the compounded character of a kenning into modern English, he explains that there are two possibilities to do so, namely either name the denoted item with its modern English equivalent (mostly a single-word term of prosaic character), or render the combination into a phrase:

> The former method retains the compactness of the original but loses its colour; the latter retains the colour, but even if it does not falsify or exaggerate it, it loosens and weakens the texture. Choice between the evils will vary with occasions. One may differ in detail from the present translation, but hardly (if one respects modern as well as ancient English) in general principle: a preference for resolution. ("On Translating" 58)

What we infer from his words is that Tolkien expresses his preference of content over form. He would rather "retain the colour" of a kenning and render it into a phrase than to give it a monolexemic form. We can therefore deduce that Tolkien, noting the difficulty to form Modern English kennings after medieval patterns regards a "brief expression", a phrase-structure, as a kenning-equivalent as long as it retains the colour and the character of a kenning. He is therefore ready to neglect the premise of combinations made up of nouns.

4 Kennings in *The Lord of the Rings*

When taking a closer look at *The Lord of the Rings*, it becomes obvious that Tolkien's work and world are interspersed with expressions that very much look like kennings. They appear in all languages and cultures of his Middle-earth: In names like *Wormtongue* and *Treebeard* the exocentric, compound-like combination is conspicuous, and also most of the Elvish names like *Aragorn* "king-courage", *Lothlórien* "flower-dreamer" and *Glamdring* "foe-hammer" are modelled on the principle of kennings. A considerable number of them also appears with the Riders of Rohan, which does not come unexpectedly, since their language is actually rendered by OE (also cf. Spachmann, this volume) and thus innately prone to feature kennings. We find kennings used as personal names like *Éomer* "great war horse", *Éowyn* "horse-joy" or *Éomund* "horse-protector", place kennings like *Meduseld* "mead-seat/hall", *Dwimordene* "delusion-valley", *Sunlending* "sun-landing" and *Riddermark* and the Beowulfian sword kenning *Gúthwine* "battle-friend".

We have to keep in mind that the kenning was a stylistic device of alliterative poetry in Germanic cultures in medieval times. Tolkien, however, was not writing epic poetry but epic prose. This is a significant difference, since either style is based on a very different set and range of lexemes and expressions. For obvious reasons, the kenning being a stylistic device of poetry only, would hardly be borrowed into prose, simply because it would not be suitable and cohesive with the genre (Meissner 15). As a result, one will hardly find many genuine kennings in the sense of poetical paraphrases for prosaic expressions in *The Lord of the Rings*. Yet it is obvious that many names for persons, places and weapons are modelled on the concept of the kenning to support the pseudo-medieval character of Tolkien's writing and his fictional world. This is what I want to illustrate by analyzing a few examples of Tolkienian kennings.

4.1 Sword kennings

Kennings for weapons, especially swords, were typical in Old Germanic heroic poetry, as they referred to the salient concept of heroes, adventures and battles. As Meissner states about the numerous ON sword kennings in general, "it is especially the brilliance of the naked steel that the poets like to emphasize in the base: fire, flame, ray, light, glow, torch, candle, as well as lightning and further the lights of the sky distinguish the sword" (150).[12]

One example where Tolkien followed this concept would be Aragorn's sword *Andúril*, which is a Quenyan compound composed of *andúne* "sunset, west" (*S* 430) and *ril* "brilliance" (*S* 439), thus translating as "Flame of the West"

---

12 In the original: "[d]er Glanz der blanken Waffe ist es vor allem, den die Dichter durch das Grundwort hervorheben: Feuer, Flamme, Strahl, Licht, Glut, Fackel, Kerze, dann der Blitz, seltener die Leuchten des Himmels kennzeichnen das Schwert."

(*LotR* 277). Pesch remarks that *númen* is the usual Quenyan word for "West" (249), thus suggesting that *andúne* might be a more poetical term and therefore especially prone to be used as part of kennings.

Andúril was reforged from the shards of Elendil's sword, *Narsil*, which is also a Quenya kenning. It contains the elements *nár* "fire", which derives from the ancient root *(a)nar* (also cf. *Anar* "the sun"; *S* 437), and *-sil*, contained in *Isil* "the Moon" (*S* 441). These two examples are unmistakably created upon the example of ON sword kennings. Both contain a base that is related to the fire or flame of the blade and *Narsil* furthermore is made up of a determiner that refers to one of the "lights of the sky".

ON sword kennings also often contain a hitting-tool as their base, for example the hammer: *morðhammarr* (Meissner 156). This seems to have been the model for naming Gandalf's sword *Glamdring*, "foe-hammer", formed of Sindarin *glam* "shouting, wild noise, figuratively: an orc" (Pesch 426) and *dring*, "hammer" (Pesch 408). In Old Icelandic *glamm* also means noise (Meissner 16) – so it seems conspicuous where Tolkien got the inspiration for this one.

Sword kennings with a lexical component for "battle" in the modifier are rather frequent in OE verse (Meissner 159) and seem to have also inspired Éomer's sword *Guthwine*, containing OE *guð* "battle, fight" (cf. 2.2.1) and *wine* "friend". This kenning appears to be borrowed directly from *Beowulf* (v. 1810). Mohr states that it is quite unusual for a kenning referring to an inanimate object such as the sword to be formed by an agent noun in the base and quotes *guðwine* as one of the rare examples (31). See 2.2.2 for a discussion of this kenning.

The name of Théoden's sword is *Herugrim*, composed of OE *heoru* "sword" and *grim* "fierce". The name "fierce sword" does not make up a kenning, it is however an interesting combination, since *heoru* is a poetical lexeme and is found in kennings like *heorudrync*, "sword-drink", a kenning for "blood" (Mohr 31). It could be argued that Tolkien intended to make this sword name look like a kenning.

4.2 Name kennings

The Anglo-Saxon poets did not only paraphrase those concepts that were typical for heroic poetry (like "king", "warrior", "ship", "sea" etc.), but also demonstrated quite an inclination towards forming kennings for terms that played an important role only in one particular poem. Especially personal names were often paraphrased by a kenning because the kenning is not just another word or name for something, but aims to express the essence of the denoted referent (Marquardt 115-116). The pictorial, metaphorical or specialising effect of the kenning serves that aim very well, which has very clearly inspired Tolkien's "name-making". Many of his characters' names reflect their personalities or fates in one way or another, such as the Elvish kenning and personal name *Aragorn*, Sindarin for "king-courage" (Pesch 386).

A very good example of a Rohirric kenning is Gandalf's byname *Stormcrow*, which is bestowed upon him by the Rohirrim because he would typically show up bringing bad news in difficult times. *Stormcrow* thus contains a strong and vivid metaphor comparing him to a crow that brings on a storm or stormy times. The transfer of meaning is thorough, with the kenning deviating far from its literal sense and evoking a clear picture of Gandalf's personality in the eyes of the Rohirrim. Gandalf's other byname in Rohan, *Greyhame*, also carries a pictorial quality, but does not show the same elaborate transfer of meaning. It is a modernized form of OE *græg* and *hama* "grey-covering", referring to his outward appearance as he is always cloaked in grey. Another example for the description of the outer appearance is the name of the leader of the Ents, *Treebeard*.

The horse name *Firefoot* as well as the byname Aragorn receives from Éomer, *Wingfoot*, are modern English kennings modelled on the kennings of the OE type with their characterising, specifying and descriptive functions. The metaphor they contain is quite easy to understand, namely the speed of their name bearers, but they still transfer meaning to an exocentric semantical head, the horse and Aragorn respectively. The same holds true for Gríma's byname *Wormtongue*.

Also the OE hero's name *Beowulf* itself is a kenning for "a man as strong as a bear", but there is no full consent as to how exactly it has been contrived: Shippey explains it as a compound of *beo* "bee" and *wulf* "wolf" and thus a kenning for *bera* "bear" (lit. "the wolf of bees"), which in turn was a poetic word for "a strong, bold man" (301). Also note the quasi-homophony between *bera* "bear" and *beorn* "warrior", which may have even enhanced the salient association between animal and man. Bosworth and Toller however explain it as derived from the compound *beado-wulf*, a "war-wulf", as such likely a kenning for "warrior".

Tolkien constructed similar kennings in *The Lord of the Rings*: One of Elrond's sons is named *Elrohir*, which consists of *êl* "star" (*S* 433) and *rohir* "horse-lord, rider" (Pesch 477). Since the elves associate themselves closely with stars, calling themselves *Eldar* "people of the stars" (*S* 393), *êl* according to Pesch even seems to have become a poetic word for "Elf", which leads him to render *Elrohir* as "elf-rider" (413) and, analogously, *Aranel* as "king-star/king-elf" (386). The kenning "star/elf-rider" could also be taken as a poetic expression or kenning for "a noble knight".

Éomer is a similar formation, consisting of *eoh* "war-horse" and probably *mære* "great, excellent, splendid". For the Rohirrim, who are so much defined by their horsemanship, this kenning may just mean "great warrior" since a great warrior is only great because his horse is. A striking number of Rohirin names contain *eoh*, like *Éowyn*, *Éomund*, *Éothain*, *Éored* or *Éotheod*, which, in their word formational productivity and variability seems to be a linguistic reflection of the cultural importance of horses: *Éowyn* "horse-joy", *Éomund* "horse-protector" but also *Théodwyn* "people-joy", *Théodred* (*þeod* + *ræd* "people-counsel") illustrate the interchangeability of the lexemes *eoh*, *þeod*, *wyn* within the kennings, therefore satisfying the premise of variability. *Mund* also appears in the Rohirrims' name for Minas Tirith, *Mundburg*, while *ræd* was already productive in OE proper names, as in *Æðelræd* "noble advice".

Also, the lexeme *helm* is prone to form name kennings in Rohirric. There is *Elfhelm* as well as *Dernhelm*, the latter a word-formation of *derne* and *helm* "secret/hidden-helmet", or possibly, as in the specific scenario of Éowyn choosing this alias for herself when riding into battle disguised as a man, "[the hair/the woman] hidden beneath the helmet."

Having mentioned the culture-related importance and appreciation of horses in Rohan, this is additionally underlined by the kenning-like names they give their horses. These are mostly pictorial names like *Shadowfax* "shadow-hair", *Snowmane, Hasufel* "ash-coloured skin" or *Firefoot*. This is in alignment with ON poetry, where horse names like *gullinfaxi* "golden-hair" and *gollfaxi* "gold-hair" appear, which Meissner, however, does not classify as kennings due to their strong adjectival function (4). While the same holds true for *Snowmane* and *Hasufel*, I think *Shadowfax* is a kenning. It is a modernised form of the non-existent, but fairly transparent (at least for Anglo-Saxonists) OE compound *sceadu-feax* "shadow-hair" ("Guide" 172). I would argue that Tolkien did not just mean to say that the horse is "shadow-coloured"; in fact, it is described as "shining like silver" and "glistening" (*LotR* 504). To me, another interpretation is salient upon the collocation of *shadow* and *hair*, namely Lúthien Tinúviel, the fairest elf-maiden that ever lived in Middle-earth. She is also associated with shadows and twilight since "her hair was as dark as the shadows of twilight" (*S* 194). The notion of *shadow* in connection to "good" creatures carries a mythical, beautiful, noble connotation for Tolkien. Thus, I am convinced of the kenning-character of *Shadowfax* in the Tolkienian universe. Moreover, I think he kept the archaic *-fax* in order to demonstrate Shadowfax's noble and ancient lineage (being one of the Mearas, the finest horses of Rohan), as opposed to *Snowmane*. Here, instead of using the same name-pattern *snáw-feax* or *snowfax*, *feax* was translated into its modern English equivalent *mane*.

4.3 Place kennings

The same premises as discussed for the name kennings also hold true for the place kennings, which the ON skalds were also fond of (Meissner 85). Shippey alleges that all geographical names originally used to carry meaning and that Tolkien, "with his tendency to stress relationships between lands and languages and peoples" (305), evidently liked to have place names that meant something, too. This goes hand in glove with the claim that kennings express the essence of a denoted concept. For example, the Riders of Rohan call their country *Riddermark*,[13] hinting at their history of being Gondor's mark-wardens.

There is one particularly interesting kenning to be found in one of the Rohirric alliterative poems (*LotR* 803): *Sunlending* (l. 15) is explained by Tolkien ("Nomenclature" 776) to be the name in the language of Rohan for *Anórien*, Sindarin for "sun-land" (Pesch 385), the northernmost region of Gondor that is just on the border to Rohan. *Anórien* is a heraldic name related to the ancient King *Anárion* and the city he founded, *Minas Anor*. However, I'm of the opinion that the second lexical item of the compound could be interpreted differently. While the first lexeme of *Sun-lending* is certainly derived from *sunne*, "sun", I don't see why the second lexeme *lending* should be translated as "land" since there are two other OE lexemes with that meaning: *land* and *lond*. In my opinion, it should be translated literally as "landing-place". Thus *Sunlending* translates as "the sun's landing place". This, at first for anyone not closely familiar with Tolkien's fictional world, hardly makes any sense. The meaning behind it is indeed much more complex: The emblem of the founder of Gondor, Anárion, was the sun, also incorporated in his name, which is Quenya for "sun-son" (Pesch 248), and in the city he founded, Minas Anor ("Tower of the sun") (Pesch 454). After the downfall of Númenor, Anárion landed in the Bay of Belfalas where he founded the realm of Gondor. Therefore Gondor is indeed the landing place of the "sun", here to be understood as a poetic name for Anárion. Therefore I argue that *Sunlending* is a poetic synonym for Gondor. Its special metaphorical character, its culture-specificity, the fact that it could not be understood at all if one was unaware of Gondor's Númenórean history, and the fact that it is an exocentric compound all strongly suggest that we have a kenning on our hands.

Also some of the Elvish place names refer to historical or mythological contexts of their culture like *Lothlórien*, the name of the Elven realm that Galadriel rules. It is a kenning contrived of Sindarin *loth*, "flower, blossom" (Pesch 449) and Quenya *lóriën*, "dreamer" (Pesch 300). *Lóriën* is also the byname of the Vala Irmo, one of the "gods" of the Elves, who is one of the *Feanturi* or masters of spirits and watches over the gardens where tired souls can rest and find solace.

---

13 *Mark* is the Mercian dialect version of the standard West-Saxon *mearc*, meaning "limit, boundary".

The name of his realm is *Lórien*, from which he derives his byname. Naming the Golden Wood after this Vala adds another layer of culture-specific meaning. The Riders of Rohan however refer to this Elven kingdom as *Dwimordene*, a descriptive kenning composed of OE *dwimor*, "illusion, delusion" and *dene*, "valley", displaying their fearful and sceptical attitude towards the Elves.

There is one place kenning directly borrowed from *Beowulf* (v. 3065): *Meduseld*, the name of the Golden Hall of the Kings of Rohan in Edoras. The kenning is composed of *medu* "mead" and *seld*, "seat" – in the literal as well as in the figurative sense as in "mansion, hall, residence". The kenning translates as "mead-seat" or "the residence of mead" or "mead hall". It therefore denotes a happy place for laughter, drinking and feasting. In *Beowulf*, the kenning *meduseld* is used to refer to the golden hall Heorot, which seems to have inspired Tolkien since the Rohirric Meduseld is also described as a great hall of men, thatched with gold (*LotR* 507).

4.4 Particularly unconventional kennings

It is very notable that *The Lord of the Rings* abounds in expressions that certainly show a "kenning-ish" character in their pictorial, characterizing or descriptive functions but it is often debatable whether they are "real" kennings as they are frequently to be taken in a literal sense or may contain phrasal structures; to give only a few examples: *the Black Pit, Durin's Bane* and *Isildur's Bane, the Firstborn, the Ring-bearer, Elvenhome, the Hither shores, the Great Eye* or even expressions like *the Flame of the West* and *the sword-that-was-broken* – could these still be regarded as kennings in Tolkien's world and work?

It is striking that, in many cases, Tolkien provided an array of kennings or kenning-like synonyms to refer to a person or a place. *Moria* is variably called the *Mines of Moria, Khazad-dûm, the Black Pit, Dwarf-kingdom, halls of Durin,* and *Dwarrowdelf*.[14] All of these expressions are too literal and endocentric to be considered kennings. The same holds for *the Firstborn* (the Elves), *Elvenhome* (Valinor), *the Hither shores* (Middle-earth) and *the Great Eye* (Sauron); only the latter example might qualify as an exocentric combination since *Eye* here is not

---

14 In *Dwarrowdelf* Tolkien has used the archaic plural of *dwarf*.

to be taken literally (or meronymically) as one of Sauron's body parts but rather as a symbol and representation of his person and power – it is also strongly opaque for this reason. Yet, the fact that they are all made up of combinations of two or more lexemes is reminiscent of Mohr's observation regarding the medieval kenning mentioned above, namely that a single lexeme would usually not seem to suffice the medieval poet, which is why he would strive for combinations and compounds to give his words more colour and substance (33). The same holds true for Tolkien. Since he frequently uses these combinations of two or more lexemes as synonyms for a more simple or plain word he basically imitates the medieval poets. Just like them he tries to make up colourful, metaphorical, poetical paraphrases to substitute the plainer term. I think that these expressions were intended by Tolkien as devices reminiscent of kennings, even though they do not fulfil the formal requirements. The fact that they are all listed in the index of *The Lord of the Rings* (for e.g. *Moria*, see *LotR* 1165) supports this claim.

Kennings proper are surely *Isildur's Bane* and *Durin's Bane*, even though they at first do not look like it. But parallel constructions exist in ON poetry: Meissner quotes expressions like *Hjalmars bani* and *Fáfnis bani* as sword kennings – it would not be uncommon to personify the sword as the "killer" of a person (163). Tolkien uses *Isildur's Bane* (*LotR* 243) as a kenning for the One Ring, which, after all, was responsible for the death of Isildur, while *Durin's Bane* (*LotR* 317) serves as a poetical paraphrase for the Balrog that killed Durin VI and drove the dwarves out of Moria. I would consider them kennings, since they have been constructed on a medieval model and are exocentric. The fact that both expressions are also used when the original context, i.e. the deaths of Isildur and Durin, are of no importance in the respective context, supports my claim (cf. Meissner 13-14). This is the case with *Isildur's Bane* when it stands alone as a free lexical element like the ON kennings in a song in Boromir's dream (*LotR* 246), and shifts the expression into a clearly poetic sphere. However, it also appears in the form of an apposition like the OE ones: "the Ring, Isildur's Bane" (*LotR* 247), which hints at where the kenning originated from.

Another interesting expression is *Ring-bearer*. I cannot help but draw a parallel to the ON *baugbroti*, "ring-breaker" and the OE *béaga bryttan*, "ring-bestower", both kennings for "king" (both cf. 2.2.3). I think *Ring-bearer* is definitely meant to recall these kennings and additionally might be a kenning in the making. It satisfies the formal requirements, being made up of two nouns and the base being an agent noun. *Bearer*, moreover, is a rather poetical word as opposed to the rather prosaic equivalent *carrier* as in *water carrier*. In its use in *The Lord of the Rings*, *Ring-bearer* is still endocentric and thus to be taken literally since Frodo and Bilbo, who it refers to, still literally carried the One Ring. But one could imagine that in the fictional world of Middle-earth the expression might live on to be used for heroic people who have to carry heavy burdens in the literal or metaphorical sense. Thus, the direct link, the literal meaning, would be worn down in the process and the expression would become opaque.

There are also a few curious phrasal expressions in *The Lord of the Rings* that I would like to label as kennings. My favourite one is *the Sword that was Broken*. At first glance, it does not look like a kenning at all, but it is repeated several times throughout the text and is usually (but inconsistently) capitalized like a proper name and at least in one instance hyphenated: *the-Sword-that-was-Broken* (*LotR* 268). I assume that this is one of the "brief expressions" that Tolkien had in mind when producing his definition of the kenning. Since the expression sounds quite poetic and is a paraphrase for the sword *Narsil* or its reforged form *Andúril*, both kennings in their own right as shown above (cf. 4.1), I would regard it as a proper Tolkienian kenning. The same goes for *The Flame of the West*, which is another synonym for *Andúril*. I get the impression that Tolkien may first have intended to call it *West-Flame*, which would have been a proper kenning, but then may have changed the name to a phrasal construction for the sake of acknowledging Modern English language use. After all, he clearly stated (cf. 3.) that he would rather give up the compound-structure of a kenning in favour of a phrasal structure, if that meant he could still render the colour, i.e. the character of the kenning. Since Tolkien was no writer of the Middle Ages, of course, but of the 20th century, the linguistic building blocks he had at his disposal and the principles of using them had much changed since the heyday of the kenning. The Romance influence and the ever-increasing analytic character of the English language had estranged it more and more from its Germanic roots. I therefore believe that Tolkien's *Flame of the West* can be regarded as a modern kenning, adapted to and acknowledging the synchronic principles of Modern English word- and phrase-architecture.

5 Conclusion

The ON kenning is defined by its independence from a specific context on the one hand and by its lexical variability on the other hand. Since this paper has been focussing on Tolkienian kennings in *The Lord of the Rings* only, it is rather difficult to discuss them within the limited framework of strict rules established for ON kennings. Had I taken into account these criteria only, I would have to say that most of Tolkien's kennings lack the independence and variability that the ON kennings used to share. In ON poetry the same kennings would appear in different texts and be employed by different authors. However, the Tolkienian kennings discussed in this paper are (meant to be) perfectly understandable within his fictional world. If any other writer would sit down to work out stories set in Middle-earth, he could re-use Tolkien's kennings in a different context and they would still be understood by readers who are familiar with the Middle-earth canon.

As I have shown, the kenning is a very complex and rather complicated stylistic device linked to several fields of linguistics like word-formation, morphology, syntax and semantics. Its "ancientness", the fact that research has been so sparse, and that the kenning seems to have almost passed into oblivion for several centuries, does not make it easier to grasp the concept. Yet, I hope to have given a comprehensive account of this piece of poetic art as well as a new definition that helps bringing the different aspects of kennings together.

Some of the kennings in *The Lord of the Rings* are perfectly wrought, proper kennings, while others convey the idea of a kenning without complying to the standards worked out in my working definition. And yet, they all support that medieval style that contributes so much to the complexity and authenticity of Tolkien's world. Employing the kenning in names for persons, places, horses, and weapons of Middle-earth, in prose as well as in alliterative poetry, again contributes to the distinct pseudo-medieval character of Tolkien's world and work. Since the usage of the kenning faded with the eras of ON and OE poetry, it has retained a strong and distinctly archaizing effect, which Tolkien employed very skillfully in combination with other linguistic and literary devices so to create a medieval epic for the 20th century – and presumably future centuries to come.

About the Author

CAROLIN TOBER studied for a teaching degree in the subjects English, French and Philosophy at the University of Augsburg, Germany, where she obtained her degree in 2016. During her studies on English historical linguistics, she started to engage with Tolkien's work as medievalist and scholar of Old English, and her dissertation dealt with Tolkien's presentation of the Riders of Rohan as a pseudo-medieval people by linguistic means.

List of Abbreviations

LotR   TOLKIEN, John Ronald Reuel. *The Lord of the Rings*. 50th Anniversary One-Volume Edition. Boston and New York: Houghton Mifflin, 2004.

S   TOLKIEN, John Ronald Reuel. *The Silmarillion*. Ed. Christoph Tolkien. New York: Del Rey, 2002.

Bibliography

Dictionaries of Old English and Old Norse

BOSWORTH, Joseph. *An Anglo-Saxon Dictionary Online*. Ed. Thomas Northcote Toller and Others. Comp. Sean Christ and Ondřej Tichý. Faculty of Arts, Charles University in Prague, 21 Mar. 2010. Web. 5 Nov. 2013. <http://www.bosworthtoller.com/>.

ZOËGA, Geir Tómasson. *A Concise Dictionary of Old Icelandic*. Oxford: Clarendon Press, 1910. Web. Ed. Tim Stridmann. <http://norse.ulver.com/dct/zoega/i.html>.

References

BAUER, Laurie. "Typology of Compounds." *The Oxford Handbook of Compounding*. Eds. Rochelle Lieber and Pavol Štekauer. Oxford: Oxford University Press, 2009. 343-357.

DIXON, Robert M. W. *Making New Words: Morphological Derivation in English*. Oxford: Oxford University Press, 2014.

GIORA, Rachel. *On Our Minds: Salience, Context and Figurative Language*. Oxford: Oxford University Press, 2003.

GREENBAUM, Sidney. *The Oxford English Grammar*. Oxford: Oxford University Press, 1996.

HAMPTON Belton, James. *An Encyclopedia of Norse Mythology*. 2009. <http://uploads.worldlibrary.net/uploads/pdf/20120922030454encyclopedia_of_norse_mythology___first_edition_pdf.pdf>

KORTMANN, Bernd. *Linguistik: Essentials: Anglistik, Amerikanistik*. Berlin: Cornelsen, 1999.

KRAUSE, Wolfgang. "Die Kenning als typische Stilfigur der germanischen und keltischen Dichtersprache." *Schriften der Königsberger Gelehrten Gesellschaft, Geisteswissenschaftliche Klasse* 7.1. Halle: Niemeyer, 1930. 1-26.

LEE, Stuart D. & Elizabeth SOLOPOVA. *The Keys of Middle-earth: Discovering Medieval Literature through the Fiction of J.R.R. Tolkien*. Basingstoke: Palgrave Macmillan, 2005.

MARQUARDT, Hertha. *Die Altenglischen Kenningar. Ein Beitrag zur Stilkunde Altgermanischer Dichtung*. Halle: Niemeyer, 1938.

MEISSNER, Rudolf. *Die Kenningar der Skalden. Ein Beitrag zur Skaldischen Poetik*. Bonn and Leipzig: Schröder, 1921.

Mohr, Wolfgang. *Kenningstudien. Beiträge zur Stilgeschichte der Altgermanischen Dichtung.* Stuttgart: Kohlhammer, 1933.

Pesch, Helmut. *Elbisch. Grammatik, Schrift und Wörterbuch der Elben-Sprache von J.R.R. Tolkien.* Bergisch Gladbach: Bastei Lübbe, 2003.

Shippey, Tom A. "Creation from Philology in *The Lord of the Rings*." *J.R.R. Tolkien, Scholar and Storyteller. Essays in Memoriam.* Eds. Mary Salu and Robert T. Farrell. Ithaca and London: Cornell University Press, 1979.

Tolkien, John Ronald Reuel. *Beowulf: A Translation and Commentary together with Sellic Spell.* Ed. Christopher Tolkien. London: HarperCollins, 2014.

"Guide to the Names in *The Lord of the Rings*." *A Tolkien Compass.* Ed. Jared Lobdell. La Salle: Open Court, 1975. 153-201.

The Lord of the Rings. First published 1954/55. 50th Anniversary One-Volume Edition. London: HarperCollins, 2004.

"The Nomenclature of *The Lord of the Rings*". *The Lord of the Rings: A Reader's Companion.* Eds. Wayne G. Hammond and Christina Scull. London: HarperCollins, 2005. 750-782.

The Silmarillion. Ed. Christopher Tolkien. First published 1977. New York: Del Rey, 2002.

"On Translating *Beowulf.*" *Beowulf: The Monsters and the Critics and Other Essays.* Ed. Christopher Tolkien. London: Allen & Unwin, 1983. 49-71.

Van der Merwe Scholtz, Hendrik. *The Kenning in Anglo-Saxon and Old Norse Poetry.* Utrecht: Dekker, Vegt & Leeuwen, 1927.

Oliver M. Traxel

Exploring the Linguistic Past through the Work(s) of J.R.R. Tolkien: Some Points of Orientation from English Language History

Abstract

On a number of occasions, Tolkien's literary works contain words or even small passages that may sound alien to the modern reader. However, these are not always mere inventions. In fact, many expressions used to be part of the English language, even if they have become extinct or have changed to such an extent that they are no longer recognisable to speakers of Present-Day English. But there are also other languages or language stages that served as an inspiration for particular forms, such as Welsh or Old Norse. For example, some striking evidence is found in the names of certain characters in Middle-earth, which often reflect inherent traits if translated from their source language, such as *Théoden*, the Old English word for "ruler". Éomer even addresses him with the Old English greeting "Westu hál!". Such occurrences are therefore an ideal resource to create an interest in language history among those who are not yet familiar with it. This article shows how both Tolkien's fiction and scholarly work can serve to introduce both students and general readers to some key aspects of historical linguistics, in particular with regard to English.

1 Introduction

On a number of occasions, Tolkien's literary works contain words or even small passages that may sound alien to the modern reader. However, these are not always mere inventions. In fact, many expressions used to be part of the English language, though they may have become extinct in Modern English or changed to such an extent that they are no longer recognisable today. But there are also other languages or language stages that served Tolkien as an inspiration for particular forms, such as Welsh or Old Norse. For example, some striking evidence is found in the names of certain characters in Middle-earth, which often reflect inherent traits if translated from their source language, such as *Théoden*, the Old English word for "ruler". Éomer even addresses him with the Old English greeting "Westu [...] hál!" ("be thou well!"; *LotR* 518; Bk 3, ch. 6). Such occurrences are therefore an ideal resource to create an interest in language history among those who are not yet familiar with it.

There is already some literature available on how Tolkien's works can be used didactically.[1] Particularly noteworthy is Lee and Solopova on the medieval texts that exhibit parallels and served as inspirations for Tolkien's fiction. Similarly, Solopova (*Languages*) provides some basic background information on several linguistic, literary and historical influences on his works. These two publications can certainly be recommended as resources to be used in university courses dealing with Tolkien in one way or another.[2] This article seeks to expand on such approaches and focuses specifically on language issues. It shows how both Tolkien's fiction and scholarly works can serve to introduce both students and general readers to some important aspects of historical linguistics, in particular with regard to English.[3] The initial focus is on two eras that are particularly relevant within the field of Tolkien Studies, namely the Anglo-Saxon and the Middle English period. Subsequently, some linguistic concepts are explained and illustrated with examples from Tolkien's fiction, namely etymology, lexicology, and onomastics.[4] The points addressed in this article are intended to motivate Tolkien's audience to find out more about some of his inspirations.[5]

---

1 See, for example, Donovan, Kotlarczyk or the final chapter in Risden (181-199).
2 Some more valuable material including a number of "education packs" has been provided by the Tolkien Society, but is currently no longer accessible online. An archived page including working links is found at <https://web.archive.org/web/20161104105758/http://www.tolkiensociety.org/education/teaching-tolkien/>.
3 A more elaborate overview is provided by Insley, which may be recommended to advanced students and academics. A brief popular academic article in German dealing exclusively with the Old English lexicon is Traxel, "Wörter". Cf. also ScienceNordic's interview with Traxel in *The Names of Tolkien's Universe Explained* at <http://sciencenordic.com/names-tolkiens-universe-explained>.
4 Words which are attested also/only after the Old English period are referred to by their exact *Oxford English Dictionary* (henceforth *OED*) entry; words which are attested only in Old English may be found in *Bosworth-Toller Anglo-Saxon Dictionary* (henceforth *BT*), *A Concise Anglo-Saxon Dictionary* (henceforth *CASD*) and/or *Dictionary of Old English* (henceforth *DOE*). *CASD* and *DOE* as well as most modern editions of Old English texts employ a macron to indicate vowel length, whereas Tolkien preferred an acute accent, as is used in *BT* as well as in editions of Old Norse texts. If the source for words or quotations does not indicate vowel length, it has been added by me.
5 I would like to thank Thomas Honegger (University of Jena) for his helpful suggestions regarding this article.

2 The significance of Old English for Tolkien

The origin of Old English is traditionally dated to the middle of the fifth century when the continental Germanic tribes of the Angles, Saxons, Jutes and Frisians started to settle in Britain and drove away the Celtic population (Baugh and Cable 39-103). However, the first extant written records are not found until ca. AD 700. In fact, the largest amount of Old English texts date from as late as the end of the ninth century onwards, starting with the West Saxon king Alfred the Great and his literary circle. However, it is very likely that initially many texts, in particular poems, circulated orally and were not written down until much later. Moreover, many manuscripts have been lost, for which reason the surviving corpus does not provide a full picture. The language of that time is generally referred to as *Old English* whereas the term *Anglo-Saxon* is used in historical and cultural contexts. Old English was by no means homogenous, but can be divided into various dialects of which West Saxon is the most significant. Historically, the Anglo-Saxon period ended with the conquest of England by the Norman Duke William, who was crowned in AD 1066 after defeating the last Anglo-Saxon king Harold Godwinson. However, it took several decades until the language had changed to such an extent that one can label it Middle English.

As the Rawlinson and Bosworth Professor of Anglo-Saxon at Oxford from 1925-1945, Tolkien had a special relationship to that time period, and some of his literary works were overtly inspired by it (Atherton, "Old English"; Bolintineanu; Tolley). *The Homecoming of Beorhtnoth Beorhthelm's Son*, for instance, is a dialogue between two fictional characters taking place in the aftermath of the historical Battle of Maldon in AD 991. This fight is also the subject of an Old English poem on which Tolkien drew for his composition. For this purpose he even applied the alliterative rhyme scheme prevalent in Old English poetry to a Modern English text. In fact, alliteration in conjunction with poetic metre is found several times in *The Lord of the Rings*, for example in Treebeard's "Long List of the Ents" (*LotR* 464; Bk 3, ch. 4) and Théoden's "Call to Arms" (*LotR* 517; Bk 3, ch. 6).

There are further Old English stylistic devices which are mirrored in Tolkien's fiction. One prominent example is Aragorn's passage in *The Lord of the Rings* which begins with "Where now the horse and the rider" (*LotR* 508; Bk 3, ch. 6).⁶ Not only does it feature alliteration, but it also contains the *ubi sunt*-motif found, for example, in an Old English poem known as *The Wanderer*. Significantly, the text identifies this passage as a translation from the language of the Rohirrim, and Old English is often used in connection with Rohan (Tinkler), as is reflected, for example, in many of its names (see ch. 7 below; cf. Spachmann, Tober, this volume).

There are also many cultural similarities between the Rohirrim and the Anglo-Saxons (Honegger), although Rohirric is not based on the West Saxon but on the Mercian dialect. In fact, the term *Mark* for Rohan developed from Old English *mearc* ("boundary, frontier") and is etymologically related to the name of the Anglo-Saxon kingdom of *Mercia*. (Gilliver, Marshall and Weiner 158-160). Tolkien even composed texts in what may be called "neo-Old English" in order to distinguish it from authentic material (cf. Traxel, "Old English"). Examples are the "Annals of Valinor" (*SME* 334-350), which are written in the style of the *Anglo-Saxon Chronicle* (Artamanova), and "Sellic Spell" (Tolkien, *Beowulf* 407-414), a prose version of a possible folktale underlying the first part of the Old English epic poem *Beowulf*.

In fact, it is *Beowulf* itself that Tolkien was particularly fascinated by. In the seminal 1936 Gollancz lecture *'Beowulf': The Monsters and the Critics* he praised the literary value of the poem (cf. Kirner-Ludwig, this volume), and he also produced a translation which was published posthumously (Tolkien, *Beowulf*). Moreover, there are several motifs that inspired Tolkien, such as the dragon that is awoken by the theft of a cup from his treasure hoard and seeks revenge on a nearby town (Klaeber 76-79, ll. 2231-2311), as featuring in *The Hobbit*. Such parallels were also incorporated by "Tolkien linguist" David Salo into Peter Jackson's movie version of *The Lord of the Rings*, most notably in Éowyn's "Lament for Théodred" at his funeral.⁷ For this purpose the *Beowulf* passage "Bealocwealm hafað fela feorhcynna forð onsended" (Klaeber 78, ll. 2265b-2266)⁸ is adapted to "Bealocwealm hafað frēone frecan forð onsended"; the

---

6 In Peter Jackson's film adaptation a condensed version is recited by Théoden.
7 It does not feature in the theatrical release but appears only in the Extended Version of *The Two Towers*.
8 Tolkien translates it as "Ruinous death hath banished hence many a one of living men" (Tolkien, *Beowulf* 79, ll. 1904-1905).

plural noun phrase "fela feorhcynna" ("many a one of living men") is thereby altered into a singular one, i.e. "frēone frecan" ("the noble warrior"), so to describe an individual burial. In fact, the passage is even expanded into more than four lines of neo-Old English poetry including alliteration (Boyens and Salo):[9]

> [...] Bealocwealm hafað
> frēone frecan   forð onsended.
> Giedd sculon singan   glēomenn sorgiende
> on Meduselde   ðæt he manna wǣre
> his dryhtne dīerest   and maga dēoreost.
> [Bealo ...][10]

Apart from providing even more instances of Old English for the movies (not all of which have actually made it onto the screen), Salo also composed passages in some of Tolkien's invented languages, such as Elvish, Dwarvish and Black Speech (Smith, *Inside* 117-124; Velten; cf. Spachmann, this volume). However, Salo has been criticised for including instances of a "standardised" neo-Elvish which Tolkien had supposedly never intended in this form (Hostetter, "Elvish"). A similar problem concerns Old English, for which there was not one standard but a great deal of dialectal as well as diachronic variation. Nevertheless, as we have seen, composing in neo-Old English was dear to Tolkien's heart and this practice may also be employed in modern university courses due to its didactic value (Traxel, "Old English"). Tolkien even produced a Modern English to Old English dictionary which contains more than 400 entries and could be consulted for this purpose, though it remains unpublished (Gilson 41).

3 Adapting a script: runes in Anglo-Saxon England and Middle-earth

Originally, the Anglo-Saxons wrote in runes (Findell; Page). The alphabet, generally referred to as *Futhorc*, consisted of up to 31 characters and was an

---

9 A longer, untransmitted version is preceded by another 5 ½ lines of neo-Old English (Boyens and Salo). All instances of <th> in that transcription are here replaced by more authentic <ð>; appropriate lengthmarks have also been added.
10 The last word does not appear in Boyens and Salo, but is clearly heard in the movie; "An evil death has sent forth the noble warrior. A song shall sing sorrowing minstrels in Meduseld, that he was of men dearest to his lord and bravest of kinsmen. Pain." (translation by Philippa Boyens in Boyens and Salo; translation of the last word supplied by me). The word "Meduselde" is an inflected form of Old English *meduseld* ("mead-hall"), but is here used as a place name and therefore not translated. The passage is also transcribed and translated in Velten, though she interprets "manna" as "mā nō" ("no more"; 225), which, in addition to some other changes, is in contrast to the official version.

augmented version of the *Elder Futhark*, an earlier Germanic writing system. Texts written entirely in runes are relatively brief and are usually carved into Anglo-Saxon artefacts, such as the whalebone box known as *Franks Casket* and the large stone *Ruthwell Cross*, both of which have been dated to the early eight century (Findell 41-54). When Christianisation came, the *Futhorc* was gradually discarded and the Latin script was adopted instead, though short runic inscriptions can still be found until the ninth century. Two runes were retained and incorporated into the Old English alphabet as there were no equivalent letters to represent the respective sounds: these are ᚦ (<þ>; "thorn") for /θ/ (realised as either [θ] or [ð]), and ᚹ (<p>; "wynn") for /w/. In addition, some Latin graphemes were modified to produce new Old English letters: these are <ð> ("eth"), the shape of which is based on <d> and representing an alternative to <þ> and its respective sounds, as well as <æ> ("ash"), which is a ligature of <a> and <e> and was used for /æ/ and /æ:/. Occasionally, runes would reappear in Anglo-Saxon manuscripts in order to serve a specific purpose. The most prominent examples are the *Rune Poem*, which explains the literal meaning of runes in stanzas consisting of 3-5 lines each, as well as four poems attributed to Cynewulf, about whom not much is known, but whose name is found scattered in runic form throughout his compositions.

Tolkien provides two major types of runic script in his works (Gilliver, Marshall and Weiner 182-184; Smith, "Certhas"; Smith, "Runes"). The Anglo-Saxon *Futhorc* is used in *The Hobbit* to represent Dwarven writing, as found, most prominently, on Thror's Map. The foreword to *The Hobbit* explains that "runes are in this book represented by English runes" (*H* 10).[11] Tolkien thereby makes a clear reference to the *Furthorc*, which is not only credited as his source but is also supposed to facilitate the readers' understanding of the respective passages with the help of the equivalent modern letters (*H* 9). The foreword is also headed in runes, namely ᚦᛖ ᚻᚪᛒᛒᛁᛏ ᚩᚱ ᚦᛖᚱᛖ ᚪᚾᛞ ᛒᚪᚳᚴ ᚪᚷᚪᛁᚾ, which spell out the full title "THE HOBBIT OR THERE AND BACK AGAIN" (*H* 9).[12] Tolkien mostly chose a one-to-one correspondence between these runes and the Latin-based letters of Modern English. However, there are some exceptions where a

---

11 The foreword first appeared in the third edition, published in 1966.
12 Remarkably, some translations into other languages follow this practice. For example, the runes heading the foreword in the latest Norwegian edition spell "HOBITTEN ELLER FRAM OG TILBAKE IGJEN" (Agøy 7).

particular rune is transcribed by two letters, such as <þ> and its transcription <th>, as seen, for example, in "the", which is depicted as ᚦᛖ (<þe>) rather than ᛏᚻᛖ (<the>). Furthermore, since no runes existed for letters which were not used in Old English, Tolkien represented these by alternative means, such as the combination ᚳᚹ (<cw>) for <q>, and the "dwarf-rune" ᛣ for <z> (*H* 9).[13]

In *The Lord of the Rings*, on the other hand, we find a completely reshaped system of runes. These are called *Cirth* and also include several specifically devised forms not paralleled in the *Futhorc* (*LotR* 1117-1126; App. E). There are 58 main and two additional *Cirth*, which incorporate many runes of the *Futhorc*, though these are often assigned different sound representations. Examples include *Cirth* ᚹ for /p/ rather than Old English /w/, and *Cirth* ᚱ for /b/ rather than Old English /r/ (*LotR* 1124-1125; App. E). As with the runes in *The Hobbit*, the *Cirth* runes are also associated with Dwarves. There are two similar, related *Cirth* alphabets, which Tolkien refers to as *Angerthas Moria* and *Angerthas Erebor* respectively and which are modifications of an earlier Elvish version called *Angerthas Daeron* (*LotR* 1123-1126; App. E). This elaboration of an originally Germanic model shows how well Tolkien could adapt authentic material for his own creative output.

4 Tolkien and the Middle English period

The twelfth century is generally regarded as a transitional period between Old English and Middle English, which is why it is impossible to draw a clear line between these two language stages (Baugh and Cable 104-194). However, there is one instance which reflects the transition from Old English to Middle English rather clearly: a scribe responsible for the Peterborough version of the *Anglo-Saxon Chronicle* copied the annals up to 1121 from an Old English text, whereas his own entries from 1122-1131 as well as those by a later scribe have been regarded as early Middle English (Irvine ciii-clxvi). Similarly, the end of the Middle English and the beginning of the Early Modern English period cannot be defined either. There are some factors which date this line

---

13 In the *Furthorc*, the rune ᛣ ("calc") is only found in some Northumbrian inscriptions, where it represented the sound /k/ (Findell 36). In order to represent the grapheme <k>, Tolkien used ᚻ, an alternative shape of the rune ᚳ ("cen") for <c> (cf. ᛒᚫᚳᚻ for <back> above).

to the later fifteenth century, amongst others the discovery of the New World, the beginning of several sound changes concerning long vowels known as the *Great Vowel Shift*, and the introduction of the printing press, which paved the way for the gradual standardisation of English (Baugh and Cable 195-246).

Just as for Old English, Middle English shows many dialectal variations (Baugh and Cable 408-420). Tolkien was particularly interested in the West Midland dialect, which had evolved from a western variety of Old English Mercian, another dialect that he loved (cf. ch. 2 above). This fondness can certainly be explained by his close connection to the West Midlands, the region in which he spent his youth. Several of his academic publications deal with texts written in the respective dialect (Solopova, "Middle English"). One of his greatest achievements was the discovery of a literary standard in the late twelfth/early thirteenth century which may even represent a derivation from an Old English tradition. It appears in some religious prose pieces known as *Ancrene Wisse* and the *Katherine Group*, a collection of five texts. Tolkien named it "AB-Language" after the sigla of two significant manuscripts. A northern West Midland variety was used by an unknown author known as the "Gawain-Poet", who lived in the fourteenth century. The four texts of the only extant manuscript containing his work are written in alliterative poetry and are therefore reminiscent of Old English metre, possibly hinting at an unattested or oral continuation from that period. The best-known text, *Sir Gawain and the Green Knight*, was edited by Tolkien together with E. V. Gordon. In addition, Tolkien wrote part of the introduction to Gordon's edition of the poem *Pearl*, another text composed by the "Gawain-Poet" (xi-xix). Tolkien also produced translations of *Sir Gawain and the Green Knight* and *Pearl*, which were issued posthumously (Tolkien, *Gawain, Pearl and Orfeo*). Another Middle English alliterative poem, the anonymous *Morte Arthure*, served as one of Tolkien's inspirations for an unfinished Modern English version of the Arthurian story in alliterative verse, namely *The Fall of Arthur* (cf. Schwan, this volume).

Tolkien's translation of *Sir Gawain and the Green Knight* and *Pearl* is accompanied by his translation of a verse romance with end rhyme known as *Sir Orfeo* (*GPO*). In 1944, he had already edited this text anonymously in the form of a small booklet to be used in one of his courses (Tolkien, *Sir*

Orfeo; Hostetter, "Sir Orfeo").[14] This Middle English retelling of the classical story of *Orpheus and Eurydice* played a significant part in the depiction of Tolkien's Elves, which echoes many elements associated with the creatures of the Otherworld,[15] where Orfeo's wife had been abducted to (Lee and Solopova 199-208). This source may also account for the discernible evil traits found in the Wood-elves of Mirkwood, the capturers of the Dwarves in *The Hobbit*.

A dark characterisation of elves did in fact already feature in Old English literature, where they are usually described as supernatural beings who could be either good or evil (Hall). The modern view of elves as small fairy-like creatures is post-medieval and became popularised, for example, by the works of William Shakespeare. The difference between these two rather opposing views of *elf* is evident in the German translations of Tolkien's fiction, where the older idea is evident in the spelling *Elb* with <b>, which represents the correct etymological development of an earlier Germanic form (see ch. 5 below). Tolkien wrote that the more commonly used German form *Elf* were to be avoided in translations of his works into German, as these are post-medieval English loanwords generally used for the later depiction ("Nomenclature" 756).

5 Where do words come from? The role of etymology

As the example of *elf* demonstrates, Tolkien's works can serve as an excellent introduction to the concept of word history, commonly called *etymology* (Durkin). He even used this term for one of his writings, namely "The Etymologies" (*LR* 341-400).[16] Two words that can be traced back to a common origin are known as cognates, the original form itself is called *etymon*. English *elf* and German *Elb* as well as the Middle High German female form *Elbe* are therefore cognates which derived from the reconstructed Proto-Germanic etymon *albo-z* (*Oxford English Dictionary* (henceforth *OED*) *elf*, n.1; *Deutsches Wörterbuch* (henceforth *DWB*) *elb*, m.; *elbe*, f.).[17] Many similarities between the Germanic languages can be explained by their common origin, such as English *dwarf*, German *Zwerg*,

---

14 *Sir Orfeo* as well as excerpts from *Sir Gawain and the Green Knight* and *Pearl* are also edited in Sisam, for which Tolkien provided a glossary, his first published book (*Middle English Vocabulary*).
15 This Otherworld corresponds to the Underworld of Hades in Greek mythology.
16 It is a lexicon of linguistic roots on which words in the Elvish languages are based.
17 Cf. also related German *Albtraum* ("nightmare").

Low German *Dwarg*, Dutch *dwerg*, Swedish *dwärg* and Norwegian *dverg*, all of which ultimately go back to **dwergo-z* (*OED dwarf*, n. and adj.).[18] With regard to Tolkien, this noun is of particular interest, not only because he includes it (and thus the concept it refers to) frequently in his works, but also because he had a certain issue with its conventional English plural form *dwarfs* (*LotR* 1136; App. F). Tolkien preferred the spelling *dwarves*, which he called "just a piece of private bad grammar" (*L* 23; no. 17), though it had been in occasional use before, probably created in analogy with forms such as *loaf* – *loaves* and *elf* – *elves* (Gilliver, Marshall and Weiner 104-108).

The case of *dwarves* was not Tolkien's only idiosyncratic preference: as he lets his readers know, he regretted not having used either *dwarrows*, as it would have been the correct further development of the Old English plural form *dweorgas*, or the corresponding singular *dwarrow*, which would have been inspired by the plural (*L* 23-24; no. 17; *LotR* 1137; App. F). In this case, the Germanic cognates have comparable senses, but there are many instances where the meanings of related words have drifted apart. One prominent example is Modern English *knight*, which in Old English denoted a "boy" or a "boy or lad employed as an attendant or servant" (*OED knight*, n., I.1, I.2). It has since changed its meaning, a process called *semantic change*, as a result of which it now bears the sense "military servant or follower (of a king or some other specified superior)" (*OED knight*, n., I.3). In Modern German *Knecht* ("servant"), however, the older meaning has been retained.

Apart from these many individual instances Tolkien found worthwhile to look at, his interest in etymology is also reflected in his contributions to the *Oxford English Dictionary* (*OED*), where he was employed from 1919-1920 (Gilliver, Marshall and Weiner). As its original name *A New English Dictionary on Historical Principles* suggests, it differs from most modern dictionaries in that it pays particular attention to the origin and development of the English lexicon. In fact, it covers all words attested since 1150, even extinct ones, but not those that are found only before this cut-off date. Tolkien was mainly responsible for early entries of the letter *W*, several of which had difficult etymologies. These

---

18 In the *OED* entry, which has not been thoroughly revised since 1897, not all modern spellings are correct.

provided a challenging but ideal opportunity for him to get acquainted with various key issues in historical linguistics.

His entry on *walnut* is one that deserves some discussion, as it has been pointed out that, besides the well-done listing of cognates in this entry, it holds some more details in store for the attentive reader (Gilliver, Marshall and Weiner 49-51). As one issue, Tolkien addressed the first element of this compound as being etymologically related to *Wales* and *Welsh*, which can both be traced back to West Germanic *walhaz, which in Old English developed into *wealh* ("foreigner"; Schrijver 20). Tolkien was particularly interested in this complex etymology and explained it further in his 1955 inaugural O'Donnell Memorial Lecture "English and Welsh" (*MC* 162-197).

Another important term in historical linguistics which may also be of interest to the general reader is *loanword*, which refers to a word that is taken from another language and integrated into the native lexicon. One relevant *OED* entry that Tolkien was working on is *wallop*, n., which, alongside the slightly later attested *wallop*, v., was adopted from Old Northern French during the Middle English period. Etymologically related *OED gallop*, n.1, and *OED gallop*, v., were not adopted until the sixteenth century and their different spelling with initial <g> illustrates that they were borrowed from a different dialect, namely Central Old French.

A final example for an *OED* entry that Tolkien was concerned with is *wan*, adj.1. Here one can observe a semantic change: it meant "dark" in Old English, but is nowadays generally used in the sense of "pale". Tolkien occasionally employed the older meaning in his works, for example in "There was a black look in the sky, and the sun was wan" (*LotR* 286; Bk 2, ch. 3).

6 The importance of words: lexicology

Etymology as well as lexical semantics are regarded as subdisciplines of a larger linguistic field called *lexicology* (Jackson and Amvela), which is concerned with all aspects of vocabulary, including word formation. Tolkien's fiction contains a large number of words that are of linguistic and specifically lexicological interest, illustrating various features the general reader would most certainly not be acquainted with.[19] Even the title *The Lord of the Rings* itself includes some fascinating historical linguistic facts.

At first sight, *lord* looks like a straightforward one-syllable word, but it used to be a compound consisting of two lexical parts (*OED lord*, n. and int.): the modern form is a contraction of *loaf* and extinct *ward* (*OED ward*, n.1 ("keeper")),[20] an element which is still found in some German compounds, such as *Torwart* ("goalkeeper"). The blending process had already begun during the Old English period, where the most frequent spelling used to be *hlāford*. Such cases are called *obscured compounds* and the English language has a few more of these, for instance *daisy*, which is a contraction of the phrase *day's eye*, in Old English *dæges ēage* (*OED daisy*, n.).[21] Similarly, the term *ring* shows an interesting development. In Old English, it still had initial *h* in both spelling and pronunciation. The consonant clusters *hr-*, *hl-* and *hn-* (cf. *OED ring*, n.1, *OED loud*, adj., and *OED nut*, n.1 and adj.2) were all simplified during the Middle English period. Other initial consonant clusters, such as *gn-*, *kn-* and *wr-*, have kept their respective spellings but have lost their first sound, which implies that these combinations were pronounced for a longer time than those clusters beginning with *h*.

When looking at the title of Tolkien's other very popular work, *The Hobbit*, we are faced with a much greater lexicological problem, as the origin of this word is not entirely clear (Gilliver, Marshall and Weiner 142-152; Nagel, *Hobbit* 16-23). It might represent another obscured compound, in this case consisting of the Old English words *hol* ("hole") and *bytla* ("builder"), but this combination is not attested. However, a properly inflected possible Old English plural form is mentioned by Théoden: "Are not these the Halflings, that some among us call the Holbytlan?" (*LotR* 557; Bk 3, ch. 8). The matter is further complicated by the appearance of *hobbit* in a nineteenth-century list of supernatural beings within a text known as *Denham Tracts*, which might have influenced Tolkien on a subconscious level, though there is no evidence that he had actually read it

---

19 A particularly rich resource is provided in the chapter on "Word Studies" in Gilliver, Marshall and Weiner (87-224), where no less than ninety-eight entries are discussed in alphabetical order.
20 Semantically similar Modern English *warden* is a Middle English adoption from Old Northern French (*OED warden*, n.1).
21 Cf., for example, Bilbo's riddle in *The Hobbit* which Gollum correctly answers with "Sun on the daisies" (*H* 98; ch. 5). Other obscured compounds in Modern English are *lady*, *window* and *woman*.

(Gilliver, Marshall and Weiner 146-149; Nagel, *Hobbit* 16-17; Shippey, *Author* 3). Whatever its exact origin, it is striking evidence of Tolkien's fondness for linguistic wordplay.

One of Tolkien's most frequently employed strategies in his fictional works is the inclusion of words which used to be part of the English language but have become extinct (Atherton, *There* 194-200). A prominent example is *orc*, a Latin loanword meaning "demon", which is attested in Old English (Gilliver, Marshall and Weiner 174-176; *OED orc*, n.2). Tolkien himself stated that he revived it (*L* 177-178; no. 144; "Nomenclature" 761-762), though *OED* lists it under the same entry as a, probably etymologically related, Italian loanword which was adopted during the seventeenth century. In Old English, this word also appears in compounds, for example in *orcnēas*, as used in *Beowulf*: "eotenas ond ylfe ond orcnēas" (Klaeber 6, l. 112).[22] This line is particularly interesting as it also contains a plural variant of *elf* as well as the plural of *eoten* ("giant"; *OED eten, ettin*, n.), which Tolkien used in a modernised form in *Ettenmoors*, a part of the region of Eriador, west of the Misty Mountains.

Another Old English word for "giant" is *ent*, an obvious inspiration for the race of the same name (Gilliver, Marshall and Weiner 119-121). This word is also attested in conjunction with one of Tolkien's "revived" lexemes, i.e. *orthanc*, which occurs in a text known as *Maxims II:* "orðanc enta geweorc" ("the skilful work of giants"; Lee and Solopova 266, l. 2). He even explains one of its meanings: "*orthanc* signifies [...] in the language of the Mark of old the Cunning Mind" (*LotR* 555; Bk 3, ch. 8).[23] This language is based on Old English, as has already been pointed out (see ch. 2 above). The second element of this word has survived into Modern English but has undergone a semantic change (*OED thank*, n.), whereas *or-* is an Old English prefix that besides "cunning" could also mean "original" or even "without" (*OED or-*, prefix).[24]

---

22 Tolkien translates it as "ogres and goblins and haunting shapes of hell" (Tolkien, *Beowulf* 16, ll. 90-91).
23 Tolkien points out that *orthanc* "had (by design or chance) a twofold meaning" and that the second one denotes "Mount Fang" in Elvish (*LotR* 555; Bk 3, ch. 8). In fact, it literally means "forked height" in Sindarin and its coincidence with the Rohirric word may be seen as an "accident" (*UT* 518).
24 Cf. also the cognate German prefix *ur-* as well as *Orald*, the name for Tom Bombadil used by the Northern Men (*LotR* 265; Bk 2, ch. 2), which denotes "very ancient" ("Nomenclature" 761).

Tolkien's fiction also contains Old English words which have survived but are now restricted to dialectal usage, such as *attercop* ("spider"; *OED attercop*, n.; Gilliver, Marshall and Weiner 91-92). As the example of *Ettenmoors* has shown, extinct words could also be revived in a modernised form. The word *mathom* represents Old English *maðm* ("treasure"), and it is nowadays even found in non-Tolkienian contexts, where it refers to a "trinket, a piece of bric-a-brac" (*OED mathom*, n.; Gilliver, Marshall and Weiner 161-162). Another example is *smial*, a word for a Hobbit tunnel based on Old English *smygel* ("burrow"; Gilliver, Marshall and Weiner 190-191; cf. ch. 7 below).

Words which have survived in a different spelling could appear in an archaic form to make them sound more "legendary" and to avoid any unwanted modern connotations. One such example is *oliphaunt*, a thirteenth-century Anglo-Norman loanword which is cognate to *elephant* ("Nomenclature" 761; *OED oliphant*, n.; Gilliver, Marshall and Weiner 172-173). In fact, Tolkien himself adopted words from other languages and incorporated them into his fiction. One example is *warg*, which was taken from Old Norse, where it means "wolf", but also "outlaw", which would be the usual meaning of its Old English cognate *wearg* (*OED warg*, n.; Gilliver, Marshall and Weiner 206-207).

But there are also English words which were influenced in meaning by another language, a process called *semantic loan*. One example is *weapontake* (e.g. in *LotR* 778; Bk 5 ch. 2), which is more commonly spelled *wapentake* and refers to a subdivision of shires (*OED wapentake*, n.). Tolkien used it in its literal sense, as represented by its Old Norse cognate, and in order to clarify this particular meaning he also respelled it (Gilliver, Marshall and Weiner 209). The spelling of another English compound suggests a false etymology, namely *waybread* ("plantain"), the second element of which is actually derived from *broad* (*OED waybread*, n.1). Tolkien reinterpreted it as actual *bread* for his "translation" of *lembas* (*LotR* 369; Bk 2, ch. 8; *OED waybread*, n.2; Gilliver, Marshall and Weiner 208).

7 Tolkien's fascination with names: onomastics

Onomastics is concerned with the study of names for both persons (*anthroponymy*) and places (*toponymy*; Clark). Tolkien was particularly fascinated by this subject and even saw it as a basis for his fiction in his statement: "To me a name comes first and the story follows" (*L* 219; no. 165). It is therefore not surprising that there is generally a deeper meaning to the names encountered in Middle-earth, as has already been shown by the example of *orthanc* (see ch. 6 above; also cf. Tober, this volume). Even *Middle-earth* itself is characterised in this way: "It is just a use of Middle English *middle-erde* (or *erthe*), altered from Old English *Middangeard*: the name for the inhabited lands of Men 'between the seas'" (*L* 220; no. 165; cf. also Gilliver, Marshall and Weiner 162-164). Tolkien also compiled a list of names which explains many of their origins and has served as an indispensable guide to translators of his fiction ("Nomenclature").[25] If and how names should be translated is generally a problematic question and in Tolkien's case it is even more difficult due to their significance within his works, which is why a proper understanding of his intentions is crucial (Nagel, "Treatment").

Just by looking at the names of the main Hobbit protagonists, one is struck by the range of influences entailed (Nagel, *Hobbit* 43-54). Old English served as an inspiration for *Frodo* (< *frōd* "wise"). When used as a weak adjective, for example after the definite article *se*, its form would be *frōda* ("the wise one"); Tolkien explains the ending *-a* as the usual masculine ending for Hobbit names, which, just like others, has been changed to *-o* to bring it closer to modern and more familiar conventions (*LotR* 1135; App. F).[26] Significantly, *Frōda* with its Old English *a*-ending occurs also as a name in *Beowulf* (Klaeber 69, l. 2025) as well as in Tolkien's *The Homecoming of Beorhtnoth Beorhthelm's Son* (6, l. 45). Similarly, Samwise consists of two Old English elements, namely the prefix *sam-* ("half"; *OED sam-*, prefix) and the adjective *wīs* ("wise"; *OED wise*, adj.). This combination is also attested in Old English, and Tolkien merely modernised its second element for his naming of Frodo's companion.

---

25 A discussion of many personal names is provided by Allen, while the place names of the Shire are covered in detail in Nagel, *Hobbit*.
26 In other West Germanic languages, the ending *-o* is also generally used for the nominative singular of nouns belonging to the n-declension (Insley 295).

It is uncertain if *Bilbo* contains any Old English, but there is a word *bil(l)* meaning "sword" (*OED bill*, n.1) which would provide a well-suited link to Bilbo's sword *Sting*. Due to its power of glowing in the vicinity of Orcs, the element *-bo* might be seen as a shortened form of Old English *beorht* meaning "bright" (*OED bright*, adj. and n.), but this view may merely be an over-interpretation. A connection to the Spanish city of *Bilbao*, which was once famous for its sword production, has also been suggested (Marmor 184). The names of the other two main Hobbit protagonists have been created from different sources. *Peregrin* is derived from Latin *peregrinus* ("wanderer"), while *Pippin*, his nickname, appears several times within the Carolingian dynasty, most prominently referring to Charlemagne's father. Tolkien's choosing the name of a ruler may even allude to the fact that Pippin ultimately becomes Thain of the Shire. A mythical figure seems to be behind Merry's full first name *Meriadoc*: a character by the name of Conan Meriadoc, whose origins may go back to the fourth century, is considered to be both the legendary founder of Brittany and ancestor of the House of Rohan (Merdrignac).

It may come as a surprise that a Breton, and thereby Celtic, region served as the name-giver for a kingdom in Middle-earth which contains so many names taken from Old English (cf. Tinkler). But since the Anglo-Saxons settled in Britain, a territory which was at the time inhabited by Celts and therefore had many Celtic place-names, the choice of *Rohan* may have been inspired by this historical parallel. Many Anglo-Saxon names consist of compounds (Clark), such as *Beowulf* ("bee-wolf", "bear") and *Alfred* ("elf-counsel"). The most prominent element in Rohirric onomastics is *Éo-*, which is derived from Old English *eoh* ("horse"). There it is also the name of the rune ᛖ, which represents the sounds /e/ and /e:/, as found, for example, in the signature of Cynewulf (cf. ch. 3 above). There are many examples for names that combine this element with another one inspired by Old English, such as *Éomer* (*mere* "mare"; *mearh* "horse"; *mǣre* "famous"), and *Éowyn* (*wynn* "joy"), the second element of which is also the name of a rune (cf. ch. 3 above). Even the name of the ancestral race of the Rohirrim begins with it, namely *Éothéod* (*þéod* "people"). The Rohirric term for themselves, *Eorlingas*, as used, for example in Théoden's "Call to Arms" (*LotR* 517; Bk 3, ch. 6), consists of three Old English elements, namely *eorl* (*OED earl*, n.), the patronymic suffix *-ing*, and the plural ending

-*as*.²⁷ The Rohirrim are therefore described as the descendants of *Eorl*, whose name also has a meaning ("nobleman", "warrior"). There are many examples for composite names in Rohan that can be explained by Old English, such as *Théodwyn* ("people-joy"), *Théodred* ("people-counsel"), *Elfwine* ("elf-friend"), and Éowyn's alias *Dernhelm* ("hidden protection/protector"). A particularly interesting example outside Rohan is *Saruman* ("skill-man"), where the Old English element *searu*, or *saru* in the Mercian dialect, can have either a positive or a negative connotation (Tolley 55-57). Tolkien also combined modern forms with extinct words, as seen, for example, in *Shelob*, which links the third person singular feminine pronoun *she* (Old English *hēo*) with the Middle English spelling of Old English *lobbe* ("spider"; *OED lob*, n.1). Similarly, *Shadowfax* consists of the modern spelling of Old English *sceadu* ("shadow"; *OED shadow*, n.) and extinct *fax* (*OED fax*, n.1), which in Old and Middle English meant "hair", but is used for "mane" in the Old Norse cognate ("Nomenclature" 762-763).

There is also ample evidence for many simplex names taken from Old English which characterise the nature of their bearers, for example *Gríma* ("mask"). Besides the aforementioned *Théoden* (see ch. 1 above) we find another word for "ruler", namely his father *Thengel*. Other words for "warrior" besides *Eorl* are *Freca* and *Haleth*, or *hæleþ* in its Old English spelling (*OED heleth*, n.). Outside Rohan we have *Beorn*, which could also denote "warrior" or simply "man" and which is etymologically related to *bear* (*OED berne*, n.). Another Old English word for "man" is *wer* (*OED were*, n.1), which is still found in modern compounds, most prominently in *werewolf*. It is possible that Tolkien chose another Old English word for "man" to indicate the shape-shifting nature of Beorn. Moreover, the Old Norse cognate *bjǫrn*, which means "bear", is also used as a personal name. *Sméagol* was partly inspired by Old English *smygel* ("burrow"), which itself was modernised into *smial* as a term for Hobbit holes (cf. ch. 6 above; Gilliver, Marshall and Weiner 190-191). Other likely sources for Sméagol were Old English *smēagan* ("scrutinize") and *smēah*, which could either be an adjective ("penetrating") or represent an inflected past form of *smūgan* ("creep"). The Old Norse cognate to this origin of *smēah* ("he crept") is *smaug*, which was the obvious inspiration for the dragon in *The Hobbit* (Gilliver,

---

27 This ending is also found in *Edoras*, which therefore represents the plural of Old English *eodor* ("enclosure").

Marshall and Weiner 190-191). There is also an Old English compound *smēah-wyrm* ("penetrating worm").

Besides choosing names because of their literal meaning Tolkien could also use them because he liked their sound (cf. Spachmann, this volume). In fact, the name of one of the first characters he created was taken from an Old English poem called *Christ I*, namely *Earendil*: "I was struck by the great beauty of this word (or name), entirely coherent with the normal style of A-S [i.e. Anglo-Saxon], but euphonic to a peculiar degree" (*L* 385; no. 297). In the Old English text, *ēarendel* refers to the Morning Star which announces the arrival of Christ (Tolley 57-59). The entire line *Ēalā ēarendel engla beorhtast* ("Behold Earendel [the Morning Star], brightest of angels"; Tolley 58) is even echoed in Quenya *Aiya Earendil Elenion Ancalima* ("Hail Earendil, brightest of stars"; *L* 385; no. 297; *LotR* 720; Bk 4, ch. 9).[28] There are also Germanic cognates to this name, such as Old Norse *Aurvandil*, which appears in the *Younger or Prose Edda* for a companion of Thor's (Shippey, *Author* 258). Another Old Norse text collection served as a particularly rich onomastic resource for Tolkien, namely the *Elder or Poetic Edda*: almost all names of his Dwarves are taken from stanzas 9-16 of the *Völuspá* ("The Sybil's Vision"), a section also known as *Dvergatal* ("Tally of Dwarves"; Lee and Solopova 122-135; Shippey, *Author* 15-17). In addition, it also contains the name *Gandálfr*, which can be translated as "staff-elf" and was adopted for the best-known wizard in Middle-earth, though originally intended for the chief dwarf in *The Hobbit* (Shippey, *Author* 17).

8 Conclusion

By taking a closer look at some linguistic inspirations for Tolkien's work(s), this article has shown that there is much more to them than is obvious at first sight. Several words appearing in his fiction were taken and adapted from English language history, which is particularly evident for but not restricted to names. There are also many words which the general reader will be familiar with, but which have undergone interesting developments and can only be fully appreciated if one delves into their origins. Thereby one may be faced with important

---

28 Perhaps significantly, the following line in the Old English text contains the word *middangeard*, which can be translated as "middle earth" (Tolley 58; cf. also above).

linguistic concepts like *etymology* or *semantic change*, which were not only dear to Tolkien's heart but can also increase our own understanding of the English language. Such knowledge may even be expanded beyond English, as Tolkien's fiction shows influence from a range of other languages, for example Finnish and Welsh, which inspired the Elvish varieties of Quenya and Sindarin respectively (*L* 176; no. 144). Names within these fictional languages also had meanings, as can be seen, for example, in *Legolas*, which in Sindarin means "green-leaves" (*L* 282; no. 211).

Finally, it needs to be pointed out that Tolkien saw an inseparable connection between language, literature and history. His interdisciplinary approach is reflected in an academic discipline called *philology*, which, as has been argued, "is indeed the only proper guide to a view of Middle-earth" (Shippey, *Road* 8-9). In fact, Tolkien's work(s) can teach us a great deal about some aspects of the real world and its heritage, as has been illustrated by the linguistic examples discussed in this article. However, these represent only a selective choice and one is encouraged to explore more with the help of lexicographical resources, in particular *Bosworth-Toller Anglo-Saxon Dictionary*, *A Concise Anglo-Saxon Dictionary*, *Dictionary of Old English*, *Middle English Dictionary* and *Oxford English Dictionary*, all of which are available in electronic form and can easily be accessed. Tolkien would certainly have appreciated any linguistic interest he may have created in his readers.

About the Author

OLIVER M. TRAXEL is Professor in English Language and Linguistics at the University of Stavanger. He habilitated in English Philology at the University of Münster in 2008. He also has a BA in Medieval Studies from the University of Manchester as well as an MPhil and a PhD in Anglo-Saxon, Norse and Celtic from the University of Cambridge. There he was supervised by Andy Orchard, who is now Rawlinson and Bosworth Professor of Anglo-Saxon at the University of Oxford and therefore Tolkien's indirect successor in this position. Oliver M. Traxel worked at various German universities (Darmstadt, Göttingen, Heidelberg, Munich, Münster, Saarbrücken and Würzburg) before he took up a permanent position in Norway in 2016.

Word in Middle-earth	Old English form	meaning
Attercop	attorcoppa	spider
Beorn	beorn	warrior, man
Bilbo	bil, bill + beorht?	sword + bright
daisy	dæges ēage	eye of the day
Dernhelm	derne + helm	hidden + protection, protector
Dwarf	dweorg, dweorh	dwarf
Earendil	ēarendel	Morning Star
Elf	ælf, ylf	elf
Elfwine	ælf, ylf + wine	elf + friend
Ent	ent	giant
Éomer	eoh + mere; mearh; mǣre	horse + mare; horse; famous
Eorl	eorl	nobleman, warrior
Eorlingas	eorlingas	descendants of a nobleman, warrior
Éothéod	eoh + þēod	horse + people
Éowyn	eoh + wynn	horse + joy
Etten(moors)	eoten	giant
Freca	freca	warrior
Frodo	frōd	wise
Gríma	grīma	mask
Haleth	hæleþ	warrior
Hobbit	hol + bytla?	hole + builder
lord	hlāford	loaf-keeper
Mark	mearc	boundary, frontier
mathom	maðm	treasure
Meduseld	meduseld	mead-hall
Middle-earth	Middangeard	middle region
Orald	orald, oreald	very ancient
Orc	orc	demon
Orthanc	orðanc	cunning mind

Word in Middle-earth	Old English form	meaning
ring	hring	ring
Saruman	saru, searu + man	skill + man
Shadowfax	sceadu + fax	shadow + hair, mane
Shelob	hēo + lobbe	she + spider
Sméagol	smygel; smēagan; smēah (adj.); smēah (v.)	burrow; scrutinize; penetrating; he crept
smial	smygel	burrow
Thengel	þengel	ruler
Théoden	þēoden	ruler
Théodred	þēod + ræd	people + counsel
Théodwyn	þēod + wynn	people + joy

List of Abbreviations

GPO   TOLKIEN, John Ronald Reuel. trans. *Sir Gawain and the Green Knight, Pearl and Sir Orfeo*. London: George Allen and Unwin, 1975.

H   TOLKIEN, John Ronald Reuel. *The Hobbit or There and Back and Again*. London: HarperCollins, 2013.

L   *The Letters of J.R.R. Tolkien*. Ed. Humphrey Carpenter with the assistance of Christopher Tolkien. London: George Allen and Unwin, 1981.

LotR   TOLKIEN, John Ronald Reuel. *The Lord of the Rings*. 50th Anniversary One-Volume Edition. London: HarperCollins, 2004.

LR   TOLKIEN, John Ronald Reuel. *The Lost Road and Other Writings*. Ed. Christopher Tolkien. The History of Middle-earth 5. London: HarperCollins, 1987.

MC   TOLKIEN, John Ronald Reuel. *The Monsters and the Critics and Other Essays*. Ed. Christopher Tolkien. London: George Allen and Unwin, 1983.

SME   TOLKIEN, John Ronald Reuel. *The Shaping of Middle-Earth*. Ed. Christopher Tolkien. The History of Middle-Earth 4. London: HarperCollins, 1986.

UT   TOLKIEN, John Ronald Reuel. *Unfinished Tales of Númenor and Middle-earth*. Ed. Christopher Tolkien. London: George Allen and Unwin, 1980.

References

Print publications

Agøy, Nils Ivar, trans. *J.R.R. Tolkien: Hobbiten eller Fram og tilbake igjen*. 9th ed. Oslo: Tiden Norsk, 2014.

Allen, Jim. "The Giving of Names." *An Introduction to Elvish and to Other Tongues and Proper Names and Writing Systems of the Third Age of the Western Land of Middle-Earth as Set Forth in the Published Writings of Professor John Ronald Reuel Tolkien*. Ed. Jim Allen. Hayes: Bran's Head, 1978. 185-228.

Artamanova, Maria. "Writing for an Anglo-Saxon Audience in the Twentieth Century: J.R.R. Tolkien's Old English Chronicles." *Anglo-Saxon Culture and the Modern Imagination*. Eds. David Clark and Nicholas Perkins. Cambridge: D.S. Brewer, 2010. 71-88.

Atherton, Mark. *There and Back Again: J.R.R. Tolkien and the Origins of 'The Hobbit'*. London and New York: I.B. Tauris, 2012.

"Old English." *A Companion to J.R.R. Tolkien*. Ed. Stuart D. Lee. Chichester: Wiley-Blackwell, 2014. 217-229.

Baugh, Albert C., and Thomas Cable. *A History of the English Language*. 6th ed. London and New York: Routledge, 2013.

Bolintineanu, Alexandra. "Old English." *J.R.R. Tolkien Encyclopedia: Scholarship and Critical Assessment*. Ed. Michael D. C. Drout. New York: Routledge, 2007. 465-467.

Boyens, Philippa, and David Salo. "The Funeral of Théodred Known as Lament for Théodred." *The Annotated Score: A Companion Piece to 'The Music of the Lord of the Rings Films Part II: The Two Towers' Packaged with 'The Lord of the Rings: The Two Towers. The Complete Recordings'*. Ed. Doug Adams. Los Angeles: New Line Productions, 2006. 32.

Clark, Cecily. "Onomastics." *The Cambridge History of the English Language Vol. 1: The Beginnings to 1066*. Ed. Richard M. Hogg. Cambridge: University Press, 1992. 452-489.

Donovan, Leslie A., ed. *Approaches to Teaching Tolkien's 'The Lord of the Rings' and Other Works*. New York: The Modern Language Association of America, 2015.

Durkin, Philip. *The Oxford Guide to Etymology*. Oxford: University Press, 2009.

Findell, Martin. *Runes*. London: British Museum, 2014.

Gilliver, Peter, Jeremy Marshall and Edmund Weiner. *Tolkien and the 'Oxford English Dictionary'*. Oxford: University Press, 2006.

GILSON, Christopher, ed. "Early Qenya Pronouns." *Parma Eldalamberon* 15 (2004): 41-58.

GORDON. E. V., ed. *Pearl*. Oxford: University Press, 1953.

HALL, Alaric. *Elves in Anglo-Saxon England: Matters of Belief, Health, Gender and Identity*. Anglo-Saxon Studies 8. Woodbridge: Boydell, 2007.

HONEGGER, Thomas. "The Rohirrim: 'Anglo-Saxons on Horseback'? An Inquiry into Tolkien's Use of Sources". *Tolkien and the Study of His Sources: Critical Essays*. Ed. Jason FISHER. Jefferson, NC, and London: McFarland, 2011. 116-132.

HOSTETTER, Carl F., ed. "*Sir Orfeo*: A Middle English version by J.R.R. Tolkien." *Tolkien Studies* 1 (2004): 85-123.

"Elvish As She Is Spoke." *The Lord of the Rings 1954-2004: Scholarship in Honor of Richard E. Blackwelder*. Eds. Wayne G. Hammond and Christina Scull. Milwaukee, WI: Marquette, 2006. 231-255.

INSLEY, John. "J.R.R. Tolkien and the Historical Study of English." *Recording English, Researching English, Transforming English*. Eds. Hans Sauer and Gaby Waxenberger. Frankfurt: Lang, 2013. 287-298.

IRVINE, Susan, ed. *The Anglo-Saxon Chronicle: A Collaborative Edition. Vol. 7: MS E*. Cambridge: D. S. Brewer, 2004.

JACKSON, Howard, and Etienne ZÉ AMVELA. *Words, Meaning and Vocabulary: An Introduction to Modern English Lexicology*. 2nd ed. London: Continuum, 2007.

KLAEBER, Frederick, ed. *Klaeber's Beowulf and the Fight at Finnsburg*. 4th ed. Eds. Robert D. Fulk, Robert E. Bjork, and John D. Niles. Toronto: University of Toronto Press, 2008.

KOTLARCZYK, Adam. "Teaching Tolkien: Language, Scholarship, and Creativity." *Illinois English Bulletin* 102.2 (2015): 23-38.

LEE, Stuart D., and Elizabeth SOLOPOVA. *The Keys of Middle-Earth: Discovering Medieval Literature through the Fiction of J.R.R. Tolkien*. 2nd ed. Basingstoke: Palgrave MacMillan, 2015.

MARMOR, Paula. "An Etymological Excursion among the Shire Folk." *An Introduction to Elvish and to Other Tongues and Proper Names and Writing Systems of the Third Age of the Western Land of Middle-Earth as Set Forth in the Published Writings of Professor John Ronald Reuel Tolkien*. Ed. Jim Allen. Hayes: Bran's Head, 1978. 181-184.

MERDRIGNAC, Bernard. "Conan Meriadoc." *The Celts: History, Life and Culture* Vol. 1: A-H. Eds. John T. Koch and Antone Minard. Santa Barbara, CA: ABC-CLIO, 2012. 218-219.

NAGEL, Rainer. "The Treatment of Proper Names in the German Edition(s) of *The Lord of the Rings* as an Example of Norms in Translation Practice." *Translating Tolkien: Text and Film*. 2nd ed. Eds. Thomas Honegger. Cormarë Series 6. Zurich and Jena: Walking Tree, 2011. 89-107.

Hobbit Place-Names: A Linguistic Excursion through the Shire. Cormarë Series 23. Zurich and Jena: Walking Tree, 2012.

PAGE, R. I. *An Introduction to English Runes*. 2nd ed. Woodbridge: Boydell, 1999.

RISDEN, E. L. *Tolkien's Intellectual Landscape*. Jefferson, NC: McFarland, 2015.

SCHRIJVER, Peter. *Language Contact and the Origins of the Germanic Languages*. London and New York: Routledge, 2014.

SHIPPEY, Tom. *J.R.R. Tolkien: Author of the Century*. London: HarperCollins, 2000.

The Road to Middle-Earth: How J.R.R. Tolkien Created a New Mythology. Third revised and expanded edition. London: HarperCollins, 2005.

SISAM, Kenneth, ed. *Fourteenth Century Verse and Prose*. Oxford: Clarendon Press, 1921.

SMITH, Arden R. "Certhas, Skirditaila, Futhark: A Feigned History of Runic Origins." *Tolkien's Legendarium: Essays on 'The History of Middle-Earth'*. Eds. Verlyn Flieger and Carl F. Hofstetter. Westport, CT: Greenwood, 2000. 105-112.

"Runes." *J.R.R. Tolkien Encyclopedia: Scholarship and Critical Assessment*. Ed. Michael D. C. Drout. New York: Routledge, 2007. 579-580.

SMITH, Ross. *Inside Language: Linguistic and Aesthetic Theory in Tolkien*. 2nd ed. Cormarë Series 12. Zurich and Jena: Walking Tree, 2011.

SOLOPOVA, Elizabeth. *Languages, Myths and History: An Introduction to the Linguistic and Literary Background of J. R. R. Tolkien's Fiction*. New York: North Landing, 2009.

"Middle English." *A Companion to J.R.R. Tolkien*. Ed. Stuart D. Lee. Chichester: Wiley-Blackwell, 2014. 230-243.

TINKLER, John. "Old English in Rohan." *Tolkien and the Critics*. Eds. Neil D. Isaacs and Rose A. Zimbardo. Notre Dame, IN: University Press, 1968. 164-169.

TOLKIEN. J.R.R. *A Middle English Vocabulary*. Oxford: Clarendon Press, 1922.

and E. V. GORDON, eds. *Sir Gawain and the Green Knight*. Oxford: Clarendon Press, 1925.

"Ancrene Wisse and Hali Meiðhad." *Essays and Studies by Members of the English Association* 14 (1929): 104-126.

"*Beowulf*: The Monsters and the Critics." *Proceedings of the British Academy* 22 (1936): 245-295.

ed. *Sir Orfeo*. Oxford: Academic Copying Office, 1944.

"The Homecoming of Beorhtnoth Beorhthelm's Son." *Essays and Studies* 6, 1953. 1-18.

trans. *Sir Gawain and the Green Knight, Pearl and Sir Orfeo*. Ed. Christopher Tolkien. London: George Allen and Unwin, 1975.

Unfinished Tales of Númenor and Middle-earth. Ed. Christopher Tolkien. London: George Allen and Unwin, 1980.

The Letters of J.R.R. Tolkien. Ed. Humphrey Carpenter with the assistance of Christopher Tolkien. London: George Allen and Unwin, 1981.

The Monsters and the Critics and Other Essays. Ed. Christopher Tolkien. London: George Allen and Unwin, 1983.

The Shaping of Middle-Earth. Ed. Christopher Tolkien. The History of Middle-Earth 4. London: HarperCollins, 1986.

The Lost Road and Other Writings. Ed. Christopher Tolkien. The History of Middle-Earth 5. London: HarperCollins, 1987.

The Lord of the Rings. 50th anniversary edition. London: HarperCollins, 2004.

"Nomenclature of *The Lord of the Rings*." *The Lord of the Rings: A Reader's Companion*. Eds. Wayne G. Hammond and Christina Scull. London: HarperCollins, 2005. 750-781.

The Fall of Arthur. Ed. Christopher Tolkien. London: HarperCollins, 2013.

The Hobbit or There and Back and Again. London: HarperCollins, 2013.

Beowulf: A Translation and Commentary Together with Sellic Spell. Ed. Christopher Tolkien. London: HarperCollins, 2014.

TOLLEY, Clive. "Old English Influence on *The Lord of the Rings*." *'Beowulf' and Other Stories*. 2nd ed. Eds. Richard North and Joe Allard. London and New York: Routledge, 2012. 38-62.

TRAXEL, Oliver M. "Altenglische Wörter in Mittelerde." *Der Flammifer von Westernis: Die offizielle Vereinszeitschrift der Deutschen Tolkien Gesellschaft e.V.* 53 (2015): 37-39.

"Old English in the Modern World: Its Didactic Value." *Old English Newsletter* 46:3 (2016). <http://www.oenewsletter.org/OEN/issue/46-3_traxel.php>.

VELTEN, Alexandra. "The Soundtrack Lyrics of Peter Jackson's *The Lord of the Rings*: A Legitimate 'Translation' of Tolkien." *Translating Tolkien: Text and Film*. 2nd ed. Ed. Thomas Honegger. Cormarë Series 6. Zurich and Jena: Walking Tree, 2011. 209-238.

Websites (all accessed 2 Feb. 2017)

Bosworth-Toller Anglo-Saxon Dictionary. Digital version of Joseph BOSWORTH and T. NORTHCOTE TOLLER, eds. *An Anglo-Saxon Dictionary*. Oxford: Clarendon, 1898; supplement ed. T. N. Toller. Oxford: Clarendon, 1921. <http://www.bosworthtoller.com>. (*BT*)

A Concise Anglo-Saxon Dictionary. Digital version of John R. CLARK HALL, ed. *A Concise Anglo-Saxon Dictionary*. 2nd ed. New York: Macmillan, 1916. <http://www.ling.upenn.edu/~kurisuto/germanic/oe_clarkhall_about.html>. (*CASD*)

Deutsches Wörterbuch von Jacob Grimm und Wilhelm Grimm auf CD-ROM und im Internet. Digital version of Jacob GRIMM and Wilhelm GRIMM, eds. *Deutsches Wörterbuch*. 33 vols. Leipzig: Hirzel, 1854-1971. <http://dwb.uni-trier.de/de/>. (*DWB*)

Dictionary of Old English. <http://doe.utoronto.ca>. (*DOE*)

Middle English Dictionary. Digital version of Hans KURATH et al., eds. *Middle English Dictionary*. 13 vols. Ann Arbor, MI: University of Michigan Press, 1954-2001. <http://quod.lib.umich.edu/m/med/>. (*MED*)

The Names of Tolkien's Universe Explained. 20 Dec 2016. <http://sciencenordic.com/names-tolkiens-universe-explained>.

Oxford English Dictionary. 3rd ed. <http://www.oed.com>. (*OED*)

Teaching Tolkien – The Tolkien Society. <https://web.archive.org/web/20161104105758/http://www.tolkiensociety.org/education/teaching-tolkien/>.

Christine Vogt-William

Tolkien's Green Man: The Racialised Cultural Other Within and Green Spaces in *The Lord of the Rings*

Abstract

The central impetus for this piece is my curiosity about how the pre-modern pagan mythological figure of the Green Man manifests itself in English literary genres that were very much pertinent to J.R.R. Tolkien's areas of scholarship. In my elucidations of the figure of the Green Man in the medieval Arthurian romance poem *Sir Gawain and the Green Knight* as translated by Tolkien as well as his fantasy cycle of *The Lord of the Rings*, I explore how the liminality of this figure in the English imagination can be used to reflect on discourses around literary representations of forms of Otherness.

The sets of relationships under examination consist of those between *Sir Gawain and the Green Knight*, Treebeard's dealings with the Hobbits and the specific interaction between the Druedain or the Woses represented by Ghân-buri-Ghân and the Men of Rohan, represented by Theoden on the eve of the War of the Ring. Informing my readings of these works is Verlyn Flieger's observation that "(t)he form and subject matter of J.R.R. Tolkien's major fiction clearly derive from the medieval genres of epic, romance and fairy tale", whereby he has reconceptualized many stock characters and reconfigured archetypal situations and contexts i.e. putting "a modern spin on many of his characters [...] while at the same time keeping faith with the medieval types from which they derive" (Flieger, "Green Knight" 115).

I read the figure of the Green Man as functioning as a palimpsestic device in these texts, in that it evokes pagan cultural sensibilities that connote natural forces as having considerable influence on more Christian worldviews that mark the English cultural contexts. Thus a pertinent question then would be: could the Green Man function as a transcultural contact zone (see Mary Louise Pratt 1992) in these texts to allow for ruminations on constructions of the Self and the Other? A salient component in my ruminations here on both these Tolkienian works will be an intersectional lens considering forms of masculinity, religious and cultural standpoints Christian and pagan positions as well as their accompanying forms of racialization.

1 Introduction

Tolkien's credentials as a tree-hugger are more than apparent in his works[1]; indeed in *Tree and Leaf*, he ruminates on one of his personal loves:

> a great tree – a huge poplar with vast limbs – visible through my window [...] I loved it. It was suddenly lopped and mutilated by its owner, I do not know why. It is cut down now, a less barbarous punishment for any crimes it may have been accused of, such as being large and alive. I do not think it had any friends, or any mourners, except myself and a pair of owls. (*TL* vi)

The hapless poplar standing round "being large and alive", on the edge of human activity, moved Tolkien to do something about what he perceived as a great environmental injustice whereby his preference for trees in the Primary World may be considered a valuable force in his own understanding of myth for his works. Tolkien's indignation here recalls Yavanna's ire in *The Silmarillion*, when she notes that her *olvar* and *kelvar* (flora and fauna) are endangered by the Children of Ilúvatar and those of Aulë ("Now let thy children beware! For there shall walk a power in the forests whose wrath they will arouse at their peril." *S* 45-46). Raising this green power in Middle-earth was one strategy with which Tolkien demonstrates his commitment to conferring forms of agency on entities otherwise perceived as helpless and exploited. Hence a race of sentient beings was created with combined anthropomorphic and arboreal features, who live in the borderlands of human and elvish contexts, occupying liminal spaces between myth and history in Middle-earth.

The figure that serves as a cultural model here for Tolkien is the vegetation myth of the Green Man[2] in the primary world of England. I read this figure as demonstrating a facet of Tolkien's scholarship and creative output that was concerned with marginalized groups (Chance 172). My conceptualisation of Tolkien's Green

---

1 See Tom Shippey's 2002 lecture. "Trees, Chainsaws and Visions of Paradise" presented at Arizona State University. Also cf. www.vimeo.com/2843553. http://www.tolkiendil.com/essais/tolkien_1892-2012/tom_shippey.

2 The term "Green Man" was coined in 1939 by Lady Raglan, who conjectured the existence of a pagan nature god: "[...] the man wears a beard as well as a beard of leaves [...] the leaves spring from his forehead, cheeks and lips [...]. [...] the figure [is] variously known as the Green Man, Jack-in-the-Green, Robin Hood, the King of May, and the Garland, [who] is the central figure in May-Day celebrations throughout Northern and Central Europe" (Raglan 45, 47, 50). See also William Anderson. *Green Man: The Archetype of Our Oneness with the Earth*, 1991; cited in Flieger "Green Knight", 219.

Men addresses the aspect of cultural Othering, where I see a distinct racialisation[3] of Treebeard the Ent and Ghân-buri-Ghân of the Drúedain, based on Tolkien's understanding of discourses concerning difference, both in medieval and modern contexts (i.e. the first half of the 20th century).

As an image and an idea, the Green Man operates as a symbol connecting humanity and nature, whereby Verlyn Flieger ("Green Knight" 219) notes: "[t]he image itself is the text and must be compared with other kinds of texts for clues to its meaning". Thus the Green Man has left his mark on medieval Christian sites not only in English literature, but in European architecture as images that acquire hybrid cultural connotations. The most obvious manifestations of the Green Man to be found today are in carvings on medieval cathedrals and churches, thus inscribing pre-modern pagan worldviews into Christian bastions of faith since the Middle Ages. Sculptured male faces with foliage sprouting from their mouths and noses (also known as foliate heads) can be found in many European cathedrals (e.g. Rosslyn Chapel, Scotland; Rochester Cathedral, Kent, England; Bamberg Cathedral, Germany; Le Mans Cathedral, Loire Valley, France), dating from the 12th century onwards. The construction of these huge edifices of Christian worship depended very much on the erosion of natural landscapes and reconfiguring these spaces in terms of civilization, marked by these cathedrals, which themselves often resembled stone forests with their great ornate pillars and high ceilings (Mathews 20-21). Hence this imagery – meant to commemorate nature deities and their powers – was smuggled into Christian iconographies and

---

3 Racialisation is predicated on readings of biological characteristics i.e. phenotypical markers, more commonly skin colour, facial features and hair textures. The concept of race has been implemented to categorise people according to groups to denote both physical and cultural difference. And yet, physical features which ostensibly confer racial membership on groups of people are subject to evaluation and interpretation, producing discourses that have shaped hegemonic perspectives on difference. Despite having little basis in scientific veracity, the concept of race was implemented by European race-conscious scholars of the 18th and 19th centuries (e.g. Kant (1724-1804), Blumenbach (1752-1840), Gobineau (1816-1882), Galton (1822-1911), among others) to produce epistemologies that allowed for the establishment of racial hierarchies, which served to subjugate certain groups. Paul Spickard and Jeffrey Burroughs have described the rationale behind such work: "Such racists arranged the 'races' hierarchically, with northwestern Europeans at the top and a rough hierarchy of color descending. Differences between peoples were deemed to be immutable, the inevitable product of their gene pools" (Spickard and Burroughs 4). Rooted in European Enlightenment, such discourses resulted in colonial epistemologies and activity which propagated systems of slavery and indentured labour, where people of colour were denigrated as objects of exploitation. While biological concepts of race are not viable in current discourses, the term 'race' is burdened with negative historical and political implications, which are still operational socially and politically today to the detriment of many, despite contemporary vehement but problematic neoliberal stances assuming that current global societies are postracial.

architecture, these Green Men sculptures might thus be considered palimpsestic texts written into the stone tablets of these spaces of transcultural contact.

A relative of the Green Man is the Wild Man,[4] a common trope in European medieval literary texts e.g. the Middle English Arthurian poem *Gawain and the Green Knight*, the French *Yvain* by Chréétien de Troye and the German *Iwein* by Hartmann von der Aue. Brandon Centerwall has pointed out that "[...] this mythical figure emerged in the medieval period as the iconic representation of Man *sans* God and therefore, *sans* civilisation" (Centerwall 28). The physical features found in representations of the Wild Man figure denote understandings of race and civilization in medieval texts:

> His proper title is Wild Man of the Woods. A refugee from civilization, he is a prowler lurking both actually and metaphorically on the borders of society. His home is the forest, the wilderness outside the boundaries set by civilization. [...] The Wild Man is the archetypal outsider, the prowler on the borderlands between the wild and the tame [...] (Flieger, "Green Knight" 115)

This description resonates with the medieval imagination of the Wild Man (and the Green Man) as a monstrous, often demonic representation of "heathen" or "pagan" positions outside the civilised Christian space of the medieval court (Krass et al., *Durchkreuzte Helden* 31). David Williams has observed that medieval monsters transgress boundaries and cross categories and thus may be read as signs of divine transcendence of human categories (1996 cited in McFadden, 162-163). The Wild Man approximates the Green Man, in that their physical appearances align them with untamed natural surroundings replete with vegetation and stone. Thus existing in the interstices of Christian imaginaries contingent with ideas of civilisation, these figures can be read as liminal, hybrid monstrous cultural Others, due to their arboreal-anthropomorphic features as well as their inhabiting of marginal unpredictable spaces of woods and forests. Despite evoking

---

[4] The Wild Man has been described thus: "A hairy man curiously compounded of Human and animal traits, without, however, sinking to the level of an ape. It exhibits upon its naked human anatomy a growth of fur, leaving bare only its face, feet, and hands [...] Frequently the creature is shown wielding a heavy club or mace, or the trunk of a tree; and since its body is usually naked except for a shaggy covering, it may hide its nudity under a strand of twisted foliage worn around the loins." See Richard Bernheimer. *Wild Men in the Middle Ages*. 1952. 1; cited in Flieger "Green Knight", 116. A rendering of Ghân-buri-Ghân by Ted Nasmith (https://www.faszination-tolkien.de/2011/08/menschen-in-mittelerde-dunedain-vs-druedain/) bears a striking resemblance to an image of the Wild Man found in the *Roxburghe Ballads* ('Wild Man'. *The Roxburghe Ballads* (1874, II: 40) http://www.gutenberg.org/files/45249/45249-h/45249-h.htm).

the monstrous and the uncanny, I point out that the Green Men figures in the Gawain poem and in *The Lord of The Rings* also challenge prejudices that confer epithets of monstrosity and deviance on these figures, as I will demonstrate in what follows.

2 Racialising and spatialising the Green Man

While the most obvious Tolkienian Green Man figure is Treebeard the Ent, the figure of the Wild Man is embodied by Ghân-buri-Ghân, headman of the Woses or the Drúedain, an indigenous folk resident in the Drúadan forest. Both figures, I observe, are devices to mark cultural Otherness, constructed as deviant from that which is understood to denote the human, the civilized and cultured – characteristics often aligned with a Christian worldview and propounded as such especially in colonizing discourses.[5] I observe that Tolkien has worked with European medieval understandings of difference linked to physical features such as skin colour, hair textures and facial characteristics: "Bodily features deviating from the aesthetic canons of the Western European analyst – such as a very dark complexion – were often held to be deformities signaling serious spiritual defects" (Sinex 178). In more contemporary modern discourses, such markers of difference are understood as linked to processes of racialisation, where whiteness is read as an unmarked and privileged corollary to racialized Others both in human (e.g. the Haradrim, the Easterlings, and the Drúedain) as well as the not-quite human Green Man contexts (i.e. the Ents). The human Drúedain and the not-quite human Ent are anthropomorphic representatives of the Green world, marginal to the history of Middle-earth; these figures step out of the mythical realm into the War of the Ring to fulfil

---

5 The notion of paganism – created by the early Christian Church – was conferred on non-Christian Others often in a derogatory fashion to set them apart from Christian practices of self-definition. The Christian / pagan binary has been instrumental in processes of racialisation by white colonising agents: "Given that race is a cultural construct, it should occasion little surprise that the dominant feature of western cultural life – Christianity – should have exerted an enormous influence on its articulation. […] Race is conceptualized alongside issues of status and class, and the social relations of power are, reasonably enough, accorded pride of place in interpretations of the rise of racism. That race is also a theological construct has hitherto attracted much less attention, […]" (Kidd 19). Thus implemented in the constructions of racial and class hierarchies, the embrace of Christianity by colonized peoples was deemed a move towards forms of civilization and literacy congruent with European standards of evaluation – a sentiment echoed in Rudyard Kipling's 1899 poem "The White Man's Burden".

certain functions. Tolkien depicts these Green Men figures as either being able to wield citizenship rights in their efforts to fight Sauron, or as having their citizenship status withheld by other members of Middle-earth. Thus, I see Tolkien implementing these figures both as actual characters as well as symbols for particular political agendas in the narrative. It is here that I detect resonances with the Green Knight in the Gawain poem, that other exemplary of "pre-modern" mythological tropes in the shaping of literary texts and cultural contexts, whereby perceptions of the modern can be read in relation to medieval frameworks in the imagined fantasy world of Middle-earth.

While it is generally understood that race is a social construct, I want to be clear that in examining the trope of racialisation in the figure of the Green Man in Tolkien's *The Lord of the Rings*, I am not invested in "re-ontologising" race. Indeed there may be objections to reading representations of race in Tolkien's work using a 21st century politicised lens, however I contend that the tensions raised by such reading strategies can prove productive in considering how cultural Othering takes place using vocabularies of difference based on power hierarchies and how the political economy of such vocabularies is either maintained or undergoes change over time.[6] One should keep in mind that Tolkien was born into a colonial society in South Africa, but lived in England – thus making *The Lord of the Rings* very much a product of his own English contexts and heritage, which include England's past conquests and imperialist projects. Thus while Tolkien was conversant with medieval representations of embodied difference and the evaluations thereof in European literary texts and contexts, he was also aware of the language of race and racism in his own time, working as an educator in England at the height of colonialism and during the Second

---

[6] The vehemence with which both defense and condemnation of Tolkien's use of such language has been mounted, demonstrates the ongoing engagement with the fraught category of race and the connected power hierarchies. Reacting to reproaches of racism leveled at Tolkien, Brian McFadden and others have emphasized Tolkien's abhorrence of Nazi philosophies on racial superiority (*L* 37-38; also cf. McFadden 164, Fimi 157-159, and Sinex 190. Michael Martinez's 2012 piece "Is It True There is Racism in *The Lord of the Rings*" provides some insightful views on the matter. The discomfort in these debates was all the more apparent when Peter Jackson's film adaptation of *The Lord of The Rings* came out, whereby criticisms were made of Jackson's actor choices especially for the Orcs. At the same time, I note that McFadden (165-166) has also pointed out the problematic racial representation of Orcs in Tolkien's work.

World War.⁷ At the same time, Tolkien's own sociocultural frame of reference encompassed a white, middle class, Roman Catholic, conservative, heterosexual context as a norm; indeed one might ask if Tolkien had envisioned non-white and non-Christian readers as consumers of his texts, and how such readers might receive his shaping of characters like the Haradrim, the Drúedain, and Orcs, using medieval racial stereotypes and the connotations they carry.⁸ As a non-white reader, researcher and teacher – and I might add lover – of Tolkien's works, I am invested in adding to the critical conversations around the politics of Tolkien's art, by engaging in an intersectional reading of Tolkien's staging of cultural Othering embodied by the Green Man, which might be read as the Other produced from within the English cultural imaginary. What purpose might such an Other from within serve in Tolkien's work? I implement a critical whiteness studies approach in my readings, which posits whiteness as an unmarked position that connotes power and privilege throughout history, following Richard Dyer (2): "The sense of whites as non-raced is most evident in the absence of reference to whiteness in the habitual speech and writing of white people in the West."⁹ In this light, Tolkien's works are produced in a framework that privileges whiteness, where he uses tropes denoting Otherness in Middle-earth that resonate with forms of colonial discourse (considered a modern phenomenon by most medieval scholars), which are also contingent

---

7   Tolkien has expressed his disapproval of colonial activity, stating "as I know nothing about British or American imperialism in the Far East that does not fill me with regret and disgust, I am afraid I am not even supported by a glimmer of patriotism in this remaining war" (*L* 115). Tolkien's letters do not however show if he had a particularly critical stance towards British colonial activity in Africa, the Caribbean and India, which had strong racial implications. I do note however that Tolkien has integrated Treebeard's and Ghân-buri-Ghân's perspectives which reverberate with forms of resistance and decoloniality as indigenous subjects invested in the lands from which they derive their being, epistemologies and sustenance.
8   For recent non-white identifying perspectives on Tolkien's works, I point out the works of Native American (Pawnee) tribal historian Roger Echo-Hawk's *Tolkien in Pawneeland: The Secret Sources of Middle-earth*, 2013. Echo-Hawk demonstrates in his work that Tolkien had access to the *Traditions of the Skidi Pawnee* (acquired by the Oxford University library in 1904) in his shaping of "The Ainulindalë" in *The Silmarillion* (18). Another seminal indigenous work is New Zealand Maori scholar Alison Te Punga Somerville's 2008 essay "Asking that mountain: an Indigenous reading of *LOTR*." Te Punga Somerville considers the relationships of Maori peoples to the land in New Zealand, which proffered the cinematic locations for Peter Jackson's epic film adaptations of Tolkien's work, based on the country's "clean and green image"(251).
9   Baldwin, Cameron and Kobayashi (5) have observed that "[o]ne of the operative assumptions in whiteness studies is that both forms of race thinking – race as biological difference or race as cultural difference – are conceptualized against some assumed white norm."

with his use of medieval constructions of the Other.[10] Allusions to wild and civilised spaces connected to representations of the Green Man and Wild Man figures are redolent with discourses of primitivism and civilisation which were operative during colonial periods (recorded from 1600s to the mid-20th century). In these contexts, indigenous and other colonised peoples in former European colonies were constructed by the colonisers as wild, debauched, uncivilized, child-like, savage, uneducable and illiterate – or in a more romantic vein, 'close to nature' as noble savages (cf. Boehmer 79-89). Discourses of Christianity are implicated in such hegemonic descriptions and labels, whereby physical appearances were aligned with such adjectives and evaluations, thus contributing to racialised constructions of the colonised. At the same time, such discourses served hegemonic constructions of a European self which embodied white privilege contiguous with civilisation, Christian virtue, technological progress, as well as aesthetic and political Enlightenment.

3 White and Green Englishmen: intersecting citizens

The Green Man figure might be considered "indigenous" to the English cultural imagination, whereby a certain construction of "Englishness" may be evoked by the nature imagery of "England's green and pleasant land",[11] which operates with a hegemonic understanding of the human as contingent on whiteness, as Dyer notes:

> For those in power in the West, as long as whiteness is felt to be the human condition, then it alone both defines normality and fully inhabits it. [...] the equation of being white with being human secures a position of power.[...]

---

10 Bruce Holsinger's 2002 article "Medieval Studies, Postcolonial Studies and the Genealogies of Critique" delivers useful insights as to how postcolonial theories and reading strategies are useful in exploring power structures and social hierarchies in medieval contexts (1197). Similarly, Jeffrey Jerome Cohen's introduction to his seminal edited volume *The Postcolonial Middle Ages* (2000) posits the questions: "How might postcolonial theory encourage an opening up of what the medieval signifies? And how might that unbounded 'middle space' then suggest possible futures for postcolonial theory?" (6). I contend that Tolkien has opened a space for just such a "possible future" with regard to his fantasy literary epic in that while he has implemented medieval tropes, images and their symbolisms, he has implemented these in ways that bear scrutiny using postcolonial reading strategies, such as those I use here. Here I would point out a recent postcolonial study of Tolkien's works by Louise Liebherr, entitled *Reimagining Tolkien: A Post-colonial Perspective on The Lord of the Rings*, 2012.
11 Cf. William Blake's (1757-1827) poem "And did those feet in ancient time" – written for his epic *Milton* (1810-1811); it has been cast as a romanticized reading of England as a bastion of Christian morality and civilization.

> white people create the dominant images of the world and don't quite see that they thus construct the world in their own image; white people set standards of humanity, by which they are bound to succeed and others are bound to fail. [...] there are enormous variations of power amongst white people, to do with class, gender and other factors; [...]. White power nonetheless reproduces itself regardless of intention, power differences and goodwill, and overwhelmingly because it is not seen as whiteness, but as normal. White people need to learn to see themselves as white, to see their particularity. In other words, whiteness needs to be made strange. (Dyer 9-10)

Considering *The Lord of the Rings* against this backdrop raises questions as to Tolkien's (un?)conscious reproduction of whiteness in his narrative frameworks. In considering Green Otherness in this light, it would be necessary to recognise the unmarked positions of power and privilege that particularly Elves, Men and Hobbits possess with regard to how social hierarchies are arranged in Middle-earth and how agency is claimed and individual and communal rights are asserted. One is conscious of the dire circumstances produced by Sauron's abuse of power in his plans to subjugate the Free Peoples of Middle-earth. However there are other structures of power and privilege evident in the relations among the Free Peoples themselves which cannot be ignored. These are contingent on the way differences are perceived and treated with, where certain cultural contexts marked as white in Tolkien's universe are "made strange" to each other e.g. the Hobbits' strangeness to the Rohirrim, the Gondorians and the Elves, the Elves' strangeness to the same Men and the Hobbits, the Dwarves' strangeness to Elves, Men and Hobbits and so on. How whiteness itself is also negotiated in relation to the Green and Wild Men will hence be a necessary element in my readings here. Thus I find that while it is not particularly productive to cursorily accuse Tolkien of racism in his works, it is imperative to consider the privileging of normative whiteness in his constructions of the different races of Men,[12] Hobbits, Dwarves and Elves, alongside other anthropomorphic

---

[12] Tolkien has been criticized for his use of fraught racial stereotypes in his depiction of Orcs and non-Rohirric and non-Gondorian Men ("[...] during the Third age of Middle-earth the men Allied to the good side were still fair-skinned and descendants of the same primordial races, while the evil Men were dark-skinned and came from a completely different background". Cf. Fimi 150). Despite the prejudices and tensions between Elves and Men (both races are notably marked as white), chiefly due to their eschatological destinies, Tolkien advocates the mingling of both races. While there have been examples of racist contempt from Elven lords (Thingol and Elrond) towards mortal Men (Beren and Aragorn) who dare to court Elven women (Lúthien and Arwen), at least three such unions have been sanctioned, whereby their Half-Elven offspring acquire significant roles in driving the fate of Middle-earth (Fimi 151-154; McFadden 161-164).

non-human entities like Orcs, Ents, Trolls. Rather one should explore the frameworks and vocabularies used by Tolkien as a writer whose works cannot be decontextualised neither from his timeframe, nor from the medieval or Old English contexts he deploys in the shaping of his secondary world. Similarly it is not feasible to expect (white and non-white) readers to decontextualize themselves completely in approaching *The Lord of the Rings* and its other attendant works. I read Tolkien's representation of the Green Other in his works using an intersectional[13] lens that questions homogeneous categories and subjects by locating them in networks of relations that complicate their social situations. Hence I investigate how the Ents and the Drúedain occupy complex positionalities in the social hierarchies of Middle-earth.[14] Cordelia Beattie and Kirsten Fenton have observed, that while the main intersectional categories focused on in the modern period are race, class and gender, "[...] taking the approach into the medieval realm helps to shed a different light because these categories are not as apparently self-evident (socially or analytically) in the pre-modern world" (Beattie and Fenton 3). The arboreal figures of the Green Man and the Wild Man are read against masculinities (both hegemonic and subordinate) in human societies of Middle-earth, whereby a particularly medieval sensibility constructs masculinity as the idealized context of citizenship.[15] Here then Tolkien implements the Green Man as a racialised medieval trope to depict the cultural Other from within a particular English framework, incorporating

---

13 Intersectionality theory analyses how social and cultural categories and relations (re)produce hegemonic structures. These are formed through intersections and interactions of race, gender, class, sexuality, religion, nationality, ethnicity, literacy etc. Thus intersectionality theory is used to investigate power relations and imbalances based on the categories, i.e. intersectionality elucidates strategies of discrimination and disadvantage in socio-cultural hierarchies within diverse discourses and institutions. Cf. Crenshaw 93-118.

14 For a more recent comprehensive treatment of intersectionality in German medieval literature, see Krass et al. *Durchkreuzte Helden*, 2014. Krass cautions that one should be aware that such categories (civilized/uncivilized, Christian/pagan, natural/unnatural, white/black) are cultural constructions that fulfill certain strategic purposes and are not ontological characteristics. The strategic uses of such categories consist of the establishment of hierarchical systems of preference and disadvantage informed by ideology. Care should be taken not to uncritically implement similar strategies in analysis and thus render invisible once again, that which should be made visible through a critical lens (13).

15 Andreas Krass reads medieval and early modern concepts of male friendship set out by Aristoteles, Cicero, Aelred of Rievaulx and Michel de Montaigne, against each other and finally subjects these readings to a 20th-century critical analysis using Jacques Derrida's gender criticism of these models of citizenship which set up power differentials and excludes women and foreigners from the purview of citizenship. (Krass, "Im Namen des Bruders" 4-22; also cf. Carpenter, *Inklings*, 167). In this understanding of gender pertaining to citizenship, I note that there is no mention of "Wild Women" among the Drúedain, while the Entwives are absent during the Siege of Isengard and in the War of the Ring – and as such are depicted as not having much stake in Middle-earth citizenship.

masculinity, race, and cultural epistemologies that are both connotative of the Self and the Other in English cultural space. The *Gawain* poem provides a salient point of departure, whereby it is notable that Tolkien derives his own Green Man figure Treebeard in direct descent from the Green Knight (Flieger, "Green Knight" 215).

4 "The figures of elder myth": raising (and racing) the Green Knight

Flieger (215-215) observes that Tolkien was quite aware of "the tradition of the Green world, [...] celebrated to this day in folk-festivals and mummers' plays whose origins pre-date Christianity." In his 1953 W.P. Ker lecture at the University of Glasgow, Tolkien alludes to such a tradition that might be considered "hybrid" in its combination of the natural and the supernatural (or perhaps he would have preferred the binary "encyclopedic / faerie"?):

> Behind our poem stalk the figures of elder myth, and through the lines are heard the echoes of ancient cults, beliefs and symbols remote from the consciousness of an educated moralist (but also a poet) of the late fourteenth century. His story is not about those old things, but it receives part of its life, its vividness, its tension from them. [...] As the author of *Sir Gawain*, it would seem, perceived; or felt instinctively, rather than consciously: for being a man of the fourteenth century, a serious, didactic, encyclopedic, not to say pedantic century, he inherited 'faerie', rather than turned deliberately to it. (*MC* 73)

He aligns "the figures of elder myth" – i.e. the Green Man for my purposes – with the principle of 'faerie' as being part of the cultural inheritance of the medieval *Gawain* poet. 'Faerie' then is implicated in shaping the figure of the Green Knight, as a supernatural arboreal being of ambiguous origins and motivations.[16] Tolkien notes that the figure occupied a marked niche in the English cultural imagination, where it operates as a literary tradition that English

---

16 See also Verlyn Flieger's reading of *Sir Gawain and the Green Knight* against Tolkien's Treebeard in her seminal essay "The Green Knight, The Green Man and Treebeard: Scholarship and Invention in Tolkien's Fiction", 2012. Flieger observes that "the power of his [the Green Knight's] presence transcends the didacticism of the text to evoke an ancient archetypal response" (215). I read this response as based on the construction of the Green Knight as an uncanny Other.

writers and poets have inherited.[17] In Tolkien's translation of the *Gawain* poem, one notes the element of "faerie" foregrounded in the description of the Green Knight, as "a fay man", "mightiest on Middle-earth", and who, despite his rich knightly apparel, is "green all over":

> [T]here passed through the portals a perilous horseman
> The mightiest on Middle-earth in measure of height, [...]
> That half a troll upon earth I trow that he was. [...]
> And yet the seemliest for his size that could sit on a horse, [...]
> For at the hue men gaped aghast
> In his face and form showed;
> As a fay-man fell he passed,
> And green all over glowed. [...] (*GPO* 21-23)

Both familiarity and strangeness are evoked in this figure, who on the one hand is recognizably human, but is defamiliarised to the Arthurian (read: English) perspective by the hue of his skin, his apparel and his horse[18] on the other. We learn later that all these are attributed to the workings of "faerie", more precisely the machinations of Morgan le Fay. While the Green Knight is conversant with the Christian chivalrous contexts of Arthur's court, he is more aligned with the world of "faerie", marked as unpredictable, ambivalent, pagan and subject to the natural laws of the Green world. What is apparent in the course of the story is the Green Knight's intention to test the rumoured masculine perfection embodied by Arthur and his Knights of the Round Table. As a racialised cultural Other, the Green Knight is provided with "faerie" agency to queer these hegemonic constructions of masculinity, where Arthur, Gawain and their brother knights are set up as representatives of a normative English model of citizenship to be

---

17 One contemporary narrative is *The Green Man* (1969), a darkly comedic ghost story by Sir Kingsley William Amis (1922-1995), a notable satirical British author. Amis' novel, dealing with death, desire and the supernatural, is set in more modern contexts of 1950s Hertfordshire, England. In contrast to Tolkien's Treebeard and the Gawain poet's Green Knight, Amis' Green Man is simultaneously connected with sexual desire, vitality and death, exhibiting a malign disregard for human dignity and moral principle.

18 The Green Knight is recognizable as a knight, a nobleman as well as an example of warrior masculinity by virtue of his horse (aside from his axe), which was as green as he. This adds to the uncanniness of seeing a familiar instance rendered ambiguous through the green hue, which seemed to occupy a liminal conceptual space in the medieval imagination. In his 2004 essay "Dilatatio Materiae", Franz-Josef Worstbrock considers the extraordinary colouring of a piebald horse in Hartmann von Aue's description of the nobility of this horse, which has bearing on the construction of the masculinity of the knight Erec. The zone of melding of both colours white and black, which comes out as green – thence with regard to skin color, alludes to the major marker of racial difference (217-218). This lends itself to a reading of green as a form of hybridity, a conceptual space of liminality, whereby putative forms of mixed racial and cultural belonging between the natural world and civilization are symbolized by the color green.

aspired to – contingent notably on the exclusion of women, foreigners, disabled and queer Others. I observe however that this Other is intrinsically connected to England's actual geophysical natural environment; this Other's actual bodily substance derives from the Green world – and is read against a putative human and civilized English self. The observation from Andrew Baldwin et al., that geography and geographical imaginaries are integral to the reinforcement and circulation of white normativity, bears some reflection here: "[…] if whiteness is above all else a complex system of contradictory and converging values, then the stability of such values is not pre-given, but is instead guaranteed through some corresponding 'discourse upon social space'" (6). It becomes obvious then in my reading of the *Gawain* poem, that while the English Self is marked as normative space through whiteness, the presence of the Green Other destabilizes the space (and the self) of hegemonic masculine citizenship.

While these green spaces inhabited by the Green Other gain significance when reflecting on the porosity of the borders between legend and history in Middle-earth,[19] one notes that the body acting in such space, is itself a space of negotiating difference. The sets of binaries that Tolkien would have been familiar with: good/evil, saved/damned, light/dark, are intrinsically informed by the colour coding of white/black. Colour especially was salient in the visual arts and literature in the Middle Ages to guide viewers' responses to characters. Here the aspect of racialisation comes into play when skin, facial features and hair are allocated moral connotations (aside from aesthetic values), alongside other bodily features, clothing and cosmetic practices, as well as spoken language variations. These are evaluated according to arbitrary measures of civilization and intellectual capacity: "Tolkien's own choices demonstrate that he was well aware of this color-coding as part of the negative visual vocabulary used for the target races in the medieval period" (Sinex 185). Very often the cultural Other is described as having dark skin and giant body proportions which are often a combination of human and bestial elements as seen in both the *Iwein* and *Yvain* poems – resulting in a monstrous hybrid entity that denotes the strange, the

---

19 Siewers remarks that the term Middle-earth "relates to the Old Icelandic or Old Norse term *miðgarðr*, part of a belief system involving a sense of multiple worlds with our Earth in the center, terminology from an Old Norse culture whose worldview Tolkien felt was analogous in important ways to that of the Anglo-Saxons. The name could be read in both pagan and Christian terms ("middle" Earth being also between chaos and the realm of the gods, or Hades and heaven in later medieval Christian cosmology) […]" (142).

fearful, the uncanny, the deviant, the different. One might ask: different from what? Thus in this vein, it would be imperative to define a putative cultural norm against which this Other is measured – and found wanting.

Constructions of the Other as monstrous and deviant from normative standards of human forms and behavior show a form of racialising in Tolkien's shaping of Ents and the Woses. Here the lack of conventional clothing, natural living spaces and unusual speech patterns and tones contribute to setting these figures apart from normative constructions of human men like the Rohirrim and the Hobbits (who were conceived of as men).[20] Skin colour too is a pertinent aspect implemented in different ways by Tolkien in his representations of the Green Man and the Wild Man figures in his works – this will be discussed shortly in what follows. Thus bodily strangeness marks the Green and Wild cultural Other; the body of the Green Man is also a discursive site, where embodied subjects encounter each other and negotiate power relations through forms of social contact (Krass et al., *Durchkreuzte Helden* 17).

While the Green Knight's humanity presents an element of familiarity, Treebeard is quite the hybrid being – "Man-like, almost Troll-like" in appearance, thus also aligning him with the Green Knight described as "half a troll upon earth". The Green Knight's beard and hair, not only reminiscent of the foliate heads found in the aforementioned cathedrals, also resonate in Treebeard's facial features. The physical appearance of the Ent is described from the Hobbits' perspective at their first encounter:

> They found that they were looking at a most extraordinary face. It belonged to a large Man-like, almost Troll-like, figure, at least fourteen foot high [...] Whether it was clad in stuff like green bark and grey bark, or whether that was its hide was difficult to say. At any rate the arms, at a short distance from the trunk, were not wrinkled, but covered with brown smooth skin. [...] The lower part of the long face was covered with a sweeping gray beard, bushy, almost twiggy at the roots, thin and mossy at the ends. (*LotR* 452)

---

20 Tolkien (*L* 158) was clearly of the opinion that Hobbits belong to the human race: "The Hobbits are of course, really meant to be a branch of the specifically human race (not Elves nor Dwarves) – hence the two kinds can dwell together (as at Bree), and are called just the Big Folk and the Little Folk. They are entirely without non-human powers, but rather represented as being more in touch with 'nature' (the soil and other living things, plants and animals), and abnormally for humans, free from ambition or greed of wealth. They are made small (little more than half human stature, but dwindling as years pass) partly to exhibit the pettiness of man, plain unimaginative parochial man [...] and mostly to show up, in creatures of very small physical power, the amazing and unexpected heroism of ordinary men 'at a pinch'."

The mention of the brown skin alongside Treebeard's verdant features allows for a reading of the Ent as the racially constructed Other reminiscent of the description of the Green Knight in the *Gawain* poem, whereby the Knight's green skin excites much comment. Tolkien's construction of Treebeard may not immediately lead one to read the Ent as a racialised and monstrous being, especially since he is capable of human and Elvish speech, albeit with Entish inflections. Treebeard is a loremaster of Middle-earth with his own close historical associations with Elves and the Valar, which allows him to inhabit both mythical and historical time in Middle-earth. Treebeard is a cultural Other for the Hobbits and the Men who encounter him and his fellow Ents at the Siege of Isengard, "walking out of legends" (Basney 194).

5 Liminal Green "Othered" spaces

In my reading of the Green Man as a cultural Other rooted in the English natural space complicated through the discourses of Christianity and paganism, geophysical space is a salient aspect of the interaction of the Green Men figures with normative white constructions of Englishness in *The Lord of the Rings*. Considering the spaces where the green world interacts with humanity would merit some rumination in the sense that Michel de Certeau advocates:

> In our examination of daily practices that articulate that experience, the opposition between "place" and "space" will rather refer to two sorts of determinations in stories: the first, a determination through objects ultimately reducible to the being-there […], the law of the "place" […] the second, a determination through operations which, when they are attributed to a stone, tree or human being, specify "spaces" by the actions of the historical subjects (a movement always seems to condition the production of a space and to associate it with a history). […] the awakening of inert objects ([…] a forest, a person who plays a role in a certain environment which emerging from their stability, transform[s] the place where they lay motionless into the foreignness of their own space. Stories thus carry out a labor that constantly transforms places into spaces or spaces into places. They also organize the play of changing relationships between places and spaces. (118)

And indeed the Green Man figures of *Sir Gawain and the Green Knight* and *The Lord of The Rings* live in the natural environs of forests, inscribing and prescribing meanings for such spaces through their presence (often conceived of as inert and motionless – trees and stone). These presences produce signs or are signs in themselves that are then read and interpreted by the human characters who intrude or are invited into these spaces and interact with these entities. The Green Knight, Treebeard and Ghân-buri-Ghân all occupy positions that are marginal to the spaces of human civilization. It is notable that the meanings generated by these Green Men are constitutive of their histories and cultural epistemologies as nature entities and as citizens of these spaces, despite – or perhaps because of – their liminality.

In engaging with the roles of greenery in Tolkien's work, Tom Shippey has addressed the importance of forest spaces in medieval English literature, and the ambiguity of these (Shippey n.p.). As a significant traditional trope in the English literary imagination, especially for the genre of romance, the forest not only offers a backdrop for human action in stories but also has specific functions. The literary function of this green space is that the story's acteurs get lost in it and then find their way out, whereby the forest is an allegorical space of error, of moral and physical disability, of the sense of despair and hopelessness (Shippey n. p.). And indeed the Old Forest, Fangorn Forest and Drúadan Forest all present challenges to Men and Hobbits alike, where getting lost is an ever-present obstacle on the journeys undertaken to fulfill their quests. Treebeard meets the Hobbits Merry and Pippin in Fangorn Forest, after they have escaped the Orcs. Both the Ent and the Hobbits, who are figures from myth in the eyes of the Men of Middle-earth,[21] become acquainted with each other, engendering an alliance to resist Saruman's colonizing infringements on the natural spaces and its denizens that Treebeard and his fellow Ents protect. Ghân-buri-Ghân is approached by the Rohirrim on their journey to Gondor: they benefit from the Drúedain's knowledge of the forest. This uneasy cooperation is even more significant when Ghân-buri-Ghân demands that the Rohirrim stop hunting the Drúedain. Both stories perform the labour of transforming the natural spaces where these encounters take place, into sites where hegemonic contexts are questioned in order to reflect on uneven power structures in which a normative privileged masculine English human civilized self is interrogated.

---

21 Hobbits and Men do however live in close proximity to each other in the town of Bree (cf. *LotR* 146-151).

Flieger points out that despite his love of trees, Tolkien does not always present his natural spaces and their arboreal entities as benign agents (Flieger, "Taking the Part of Trees" 263-267). The Old Forest's hostility towards Hobbits is attributed to its "hatred of things that go free upon the earth, gnawing, biting, breaking, hacking, burning: destroyers and usurpers", which motivates Old Man Willow to attack Frodo and his fellow Hobbits (*LotR* 127).[22] In this episode, the Hobbits are saved by Tom Bombadil, an enigmatic character closely aligned with the Green world and its nature spirits (his wife is a river nymph) – but who does not fit in with the Green Man model[23] (*LotR* 121-131). What is notable is that Old Man Willow, representing the Old Forest's desire for revenge is depicted as evil, while Treebeard and his fellow Ents are considered well within their rights to destroy the Orcs decimating Fangorn's trees. In both instances, both the Old Forest and the Ents are shown to be not quite tame, but wild and unpredictable and located literally on the edges of human knowledge and comprehension.

This binary of wild and civilized spaces, often read contiguously with Christianity and paganism, can be found once again in "the figures of elder myth". *Sir Gawain and the Green Knight* provides Tolkien with such an 'elder myth' template, where the Green Knight is set in opposition to Arthur's Knights of the Round Table who are representatives of Christianity (masculinity is an important corollary here). The Green world is implicated in such interpretations of wild pagan space in the Green Knight's domicile of the Green Chapel. He arranges a meeting with Gawain, a year after Gawain

---

22 The Hobbits however have their own history of committing violence on the forest itself which threatened at one point to encroach on Hobbit Shireland, in ways similar to the Orcish activities instigated by Saruman in Fangorn Forest. Flieger points out ruefully that it is not just Sauron's and Saruman's minions – the axe-wielding Orcs – who posit danger to the denizens of the natural world but also entites represented as good – the Entwives and the human and Hobbit agricultural communities – who also encroach on natural wilderness landscapes and cause alterations thereof (274).

23 Bombadil lives in a house exhibiting recognizably human architecture, wears human clothing and shoes; he is conversant in history and political events in the world despite his choice to live in an isolated marginal forest space, over which he wields power. He is very obviously humanoid if not human i.e. he is not aligned with natural plant foliage with regard to his biological body composition. While living in a natural environment in the middle of the Old Forest, he lives in conjugal bliss with his river nymph wife Goldberry – hence he is still aligned with civilized heteronormative human contexts, despite his affinity with natural enchantments and some overlaps with the lifestyles and spaces of the other Green Men figures.

answers the Knight's challenge to behead him at Arthur's Christmas feast in Camelot – an engagement that Gawain keeps:

> Then he halted and held in his horse for a time,
> and changed oft his front the Chapel to find.
> Such on no side he saw, […],
> Save a mound as it might be near the marge of a green,
>
> A worn barrow on a brae by the brink of a water, […].
> Then he went to the barrow and about it he walked, […].
> It had a hole at the end and at either side,
> and with grass in green patches grown all over,
> And was hollow within […].
> 'Can this be the Chapel Green, o Lord? said the gentle knight.
> 'Here the Devil might say, I ween,
> His matins about midnight!'
>
> 'On my word,' quoth Wawain, 'tis a wilderness here!
> This oratory looks evil. With herbs overgrown
> it fits well that fellow transformed into green
> to follow here his devotions in the Devil's fashion!' (*GPO* 81-82)

The space of the Green Chapel is by virtue of the very term evocative of a Christian architectural space of worship reminiscent of the medieval cathedrals mentioned earlier – but it turns out to be a most contradictory and ambivalent space, which does not resemble a church or the like in the least. Rather it resembles a burial mound or a barrow, redolent of ghostly presences which evoke death – which Gawain may have to face given the purpose of his tryst with the Green Knight. The unusual appearance of the Green Chapel leads Gawain to interpret the Green Knight as an unholy entity, by reading the space in which the Green Knight ostensibly resided as wild, uncivilized – and deadly. Here Gawain perceives the natural verdure of the mound as exuding a devilish atmosphere in keeping with the Green Knight's "deviant" physical appearance, whereby the space itself seems in Gawain's eyes to be reinforced in its uncanniness through its green resident's presumed devilish "devotions".

Given Alfred K. Siewers's observation that Tolkien drew upon "views of nature that emerged before the formative 'Twelfth Century Renaissance' of Western Europe in constructing his own ecocentric Middle-earth" (140), it is notable that the colour green occupies an ambivalent position in the medieval imaginary, as observed by Michel Pastoreau (78, 89):

> Beginning in the mid-twelfth century and until well into the thirteenth century, chivalry and courtesy went hand in glove. [...] The colors are vivid and clear, creating strong contrasts in which red and green dominate, [...] Poets and romancers gave green a large place in their descriptions of tournaments. [...] At the end of the Middle Ages, green, so admired in the time of chivalry and courtesy began to lose standing. As a chemically unstable color, both in painting and dyeing, it was henceforth associated symbolically with all that was changeable or capricious [...] By the same token it tended to have a split personality. On the one hand, there was good green, associated with gaiety, beauty and hope, which had not disappeared but had become more subdued; on the other there was bad green, associated with the Devil and his creatures [...]

Thus this changeability or "split personality" of the colour green marks ambivalence and in-betweenness, evoking the Green Man's own liminal half human, half arboreal form. Greenness then could be read as a form of physical and cultural hybridity, aligning the Green Man closely with natural spaces and contexts but also with the marginal (and monstrous?) borderlands of humanity. Umberto Eco alludes to green as "halfway between white and black" (46), where, given the racial connotations of white and black skin colours both in medieval and contemporary discourses, green could be interpreted as a liminal racialized position. Here again I am mindful of the normative whiteness evoked in the construction of both the Arthurian and the Middle-earth worlds, where the Green Man embodies ambiguity and unpredictability, indeed unknowability as the Other, whose origin is rooted in myth, in faerie. Siewers has noted that the fantasy space of Middle-earth was the real earthy space of England for Tolkien, whereby this view of Middle-earth as a place integrating mythical and physical realms, is implied in an exchange between a Rider of Rohan and Aragorn:

> 'Do we walk in legends or on the green earth in the daylight?'
> 'A man may do both,' said Aragorn. 'For not we but those who come after will make legends of our time. The green earth, say you? That is a mighty matter of legend, though you tread it under the light of day!' (*LotR* 424)

While this exchange alludes to the emergence of the Hobbits into the ken of Men, Aragorn's reply can also pertain to other inhabitants who are even more evocative of the fabric of myth, as well as the substance of the green earth – the Ents and the Drúedain – considered just as unknown and unknowable to Men. The Green Man of Middle-earth is not necessarily contained by the Christian/pagan binary as the Green Knight of the *Gawain* poem is. Indeed Tolkien has stated: "I don't feel under any obligation to make my story fit with formalized Christian theology, though I actually intended it to be consonant with Christian thought and belief [...]" (*L* 355). In his conception of Treebeard, Tolkien seems to have rendered porous the boundary between the natural and the supernatural, the definitions of which are contingent on discussions of paganism and Christianity. Here Tolkien works with the medieval idea of a being that might be conceived of as monstrous since it transcends human categories, yet marvellous in its reflection of the mythic realm (till Pippin and Merry actually meet Treebeard).[24]

In keeping with de Certeau's ideas of a being acting on its space and thus generating story, Tolkien inscribes the Ents into Fangorn forest space, providing a description of Treebeard's home Wellinghall from the Hobbits' perspective:

> Suddenly before them the hobbits saw a wide opening. Two great trees stood there, one on either side, like living gate-posts; but there was no gate save their crossing and interwoven boughs. As the old Ent approached, the trees lifted up their branches and all their leaves quivered and rustled. [...] Beyond them was a wide level space, as though the floor of a great hall had been cut in the side of the hill. On the other hand the walls sloped upwards, until they were fifty feet high or more, and along each wall stood an aisle of trees that also increased in height as they marched inwards. At the far end, the rock-wall was sheer, but at the bottom it had been hollowed back into a shallow bay with an arched roof: the only roof of the hall, save the branches of the trees, which at the inner end overshadowed all the ground leaving only a broad open path in the middle. A little stream escaped from the springs above, and leaving the main water, fell tinkling down the sheer face of the wall, pouring in silver drops, like a fine curtain in front of the arched bay. The water was gathered again into a stone basin in the floor between the trees, and thence it spilled and flowed away beside the open path, out to join the Entwash in its journey through the forest. (*LotR* 458-459)

This description of Wellinghall in the deeps of Fangorn Forest incorporates the natural elements of wood, water and stone, used by Ents to shape their living spaces, at once familiar and marvellously strange to the Hobbits.

---

24 The Hobbits had only ever heard of the Tree-Shepherds and had merely seen strange landscape formations caused by them, but had never actually interacted with Ents (cf. *LotR* 108).

This resonates with the aforementioned palimpsestic reading of Green Man sculptures inscribed in medieval cathedral architectures, atmospheres and dimensions, which are congruent with Tolkien's reading of "the ancient work of giants", where he notes:

> [...] looking back analytically I should say the Ents are composed of philology, literature and life. They owe their name to the *eald enta geweorc* [old creations of giants] of Anglo-Saxon, and their connection with stone. (*L* 211-212)

This allusion to the work of ancient giants in shaping the natural world is based in Tolkien's own philological investment in resurrecting the "figures of elder myth"; an exercise that Flieger notes "had not just a generative or resurrective role, but a nominative and philosophical one" (213). While Tolkien observes that something should be done about "the peculiar Anglo-Saxon word *ent* for "'giant' or mighty person of a long ago" (*L* 208), Flieger cites the Bosworth-Toller definition of *ent* as "giant", and the *OED*'s definition as "the ent, or existent" (213). Besides Tolkien's agenda of resurrecting "a society long since vanished" (Shippey 37, cited in Flieger, "Green Knight" 213), i.e. a race of giants from mythical time whose activities shaped natural landscapes, I would venture two other terms: "sentient" and "entity" – both containing the word "ent". With these, I attribute a form of citizenship to the Ents, encompassing cultural epistemes, history, identity and belonging in Middle-earth. Occupying marginalized spaces in Middle-earth and having experienced violence at the hands of Men and Orcs, the Ents prefer segregation from human contexts, thus exacerbating their own Otherness. At the same time, they are divided along gender lines, showing discrepancies in worldviews amongst themselves (*LotR* 464-466). Corey Olsen considers the Ents as actual characters rather than just mere symbols of the Green world. Entish culture has different and incommensurate sensibilities towards their living space: the Ents embrace a less intrusive and contemplative appreciation of the natural world, while the Entwives are more active in their desire to domesticate nature. In his analysis of the duet between the Ent and the Entwife, Olsen demonstrates how Tolkien produces an Entish narrative that runs counter to "traditional gender concepts that characterize the feminine as the passive principle and the masculine as the active" (42). Despite this subversion, the Entwives are not Green Woman figures who have the privilege of citizenship in the manner of the Ents. Rather the Entwives vacate the forests and fields – and recede into myth.[25]

Despite living in isolation, mourning his decimated trees and the missing Entwives and Entings, having the Hobbits Merry and Pippin in his home moves Treebeard to hospitality by providing them with drink and shelter after their harrowing experiences with the Orcs – indeed he welcomes them into his own inner forest sanctuary where his Green Self is at home. The Hobbits witness a peculiarly Entish form of "grace before meals" which evokes Treebeard's great age and his connections to mythological contexts:

> A great stone table stood there [...] Treebeard lifted two great vessels and stood them on the table. They seemed to be filled with water; but he held his hands over them and immediately they began to glow, one with a golden light and the other with a rich green light; and the blending of the two lights lit the bay as if the sun of summer were shining through a roof of young leaves. Looking back the hobbits saw that the trees [...] had also begun to glow, faintly at first, but steadily quickening [...]; while the tree-trunks looked like pillars molded out of luminous stone. (*LotR* 459)

The ancientness and the "faerie" knowledge of the Elder Days that Treebeard transports with him, has its origins in the making of Arda in *The Silmarillion*, before the coming of Elves and Men. The mysticism and faerie of the Green world are again evoked through natural elements of water, light and verdure; Treebeard's blessing of the liquid in the stone vessels and its resultant glow is reminiscent of the lights of the Two Trees of Valinor that Yavanna had created before the Sun and Moon were made. The Ent-draught that the Hobbits are given to drink is at once familiar as a water-like liquid, but also contains the taste of the strange:

> The drink was like water [...] and yet, there was some scent or savour in it which they could not describe; [...] it reminded them of the smell of a distant wood borne from afar by a cool breeze at night. The effect of the draught began at the toes, and rose readily through every limb, bringing refreshment and vigour as it coursed upwards [...] Indeed the hobbits felt that the hair on their heads was actually standing up, waving and curling and growing. (*LotR* 460)

---

25 Here male privilege and female resistance to patriarchal authority are staged, when the Ents and the Entwives disagree about where they should set up home (Chance 180). The Ents' inability to consider the needs and positions of the gendered Other has led to a decrease in offspring and total estrangement from the Entwives, who had chosen to roam further afield and teach agricultural skills to Men in the earlier ages.

It is not clear if the Entdraught contained any of the liquid light that Treebeard had sanctified – if this is the case, this could be read as a form of "Holy Communion" that the Hobbits receive from the Ent, who may have taken on a priestly role as a nature deity. The sense of vigour, well-being and growth resulting from the Hobbits' consumption of the Ent-draught is the result of a voluntary ingestion and integration of the Other's substance into the Self. Indeed the words "waving, curling and growing" allude to the Hobbits' new self-perceptions as plants or young trees putting out new growth. Merry's and Pippin's actual increase in physical size (making them Entish Hobbits) can also be read as their psychological and social growth that allows them to meet subsequent challenges they encounter as knights of Gondor and Rohan in the War of the Ring.

Thus where difference might once have been considered threatening due to physical strangeness and discrepancies in knowledge of each other, this acceptance of the Other into the Self demonstrates positive cultural interaction between those who had once been strangers; knowledges have been exchanged, hospitality and trust have been demonstrated, both parties have benefitted in the encounter. A similar encounter in Drúadan Forest between the Rohirrim and the Drúedain will be the next site of interrogation between yet another English Self and the Wild Other.

6 Tolkien's wild man: the decolonial indigenous Green Other

Ghân-buri-Ghân is described as the "typically medieval Wild Man [...] one of the aboriginal Drúadan" (Flieger 120). Like the Ents, the Drúedain, are depicted as close to nature and marginal in relation to the Elvish and human peoples of Middle-earth. They are considered by the Rohirrim, at least, to be pre-historic figures "of an older time [...] wild and wary as beasts" (*LotR* 813). Such discourse Others the Drúedain, as occupying a conceptual space between human and animal; this resonates with racialising discourses contingent on colonial anthropological attitudes to indigenous peoples in Africa, Australia, New Zealand, India, the Caribbean and the North American continent. That the Drúedain might have something approximating a "culture" (in the sense of producing works of art depicting cultural standpoints and marking certain spaces to claim them) may be instantiated in the "primitive" stone figures of the Pukelmen on the road to Dunharrow. It is however not clear if these are the works of Drúedain artists themselves or sculptors from other cultural groups, who may have created these statues from memories or actual encounters. Merry, the Hobbit from whose perspective this indigenous folk is described, remembers these figures: "Here was one of those images brought to life, or maybe a creature descended in true line through endless years from the models used by the forgotten craftsmen of long ago" (*LotR* 813-814). Given that the Drúedain are the aboriginals connected to the land of Drúadan Forest at the foot of the White Mountains to the north of Minas Tirith, it follows that they are invested in their rights to that land and how they can live in that space.[26] Tolkien notes:

> But in Rohan, the identity of the statues of Dunharrow called 'Pukelmen' with the 'Wild Men' of the Drúadan Forest was not recognized, neither was their humanity: hence the reference by Ghân-buri-Ghân to persecution of the 'Wild Men' by the Rohirrim in the past [...]. Since Ghân-buri-Ghân was attempting to use the Common Speech he called his people 'Wild Men' (not without irony); but this was not of course their own name for themselves. (*UT* 496)

Tolkien evidently was invested in representing the Drúedain as a people bent on resisting oppression from the Rohirrim; so while he has used medieval and modern colonial images of the primitive savage to mark this Wild Man figure, he manipulates these in certain ways. I do note that in having Ghân-buri-Ghân act as a spokesman for his people, Tolkien represents the Drúedain as a homogenous people, with an essentialised cultural identity that is based on a patriarchal and masculine value system. Concerning the trope of the primitive, Pawnee historian Roger Echo-Hawk has observed that Tolkien "yearned for an English mythology that had more of what he termed 'primi-

---

26 See Bob Hodge and Vijay Mishra's 1991 essay, which considers forms of Australian Aboriginal art and epistemologies, which "express a twin sense of alienation and belonging", whereby the strategies used by Aboriginal artists are demonstrations of adapting traditional knowledge forms to map "broad stretches of space and time, to give meaning and perspective, direction and hope on the bewildering journey of the life of themselves and their people" (417). I contend that the Druedain's sense of rootedness in their land is fraught with a sense of virulent Othering when they are hunted by the Rohirrim in the environs of their forest, making this place both home, but also an unhoming ("unheimlich") space – hence the "twin sense of alienation and belonging" ascribed to indigenous folk in the Primary World can also be extrapolated from Tolkien's literary representation of Middle-earth's indigenous people.

tive undergrowth'" and he wished "we had more of it left...something that belonged to the English" (148).²⁷ Hence like the Ents, the Drúedain could be read (conceptually and literally) as "primitive undergrowth" then, denoting a form of pre-modern Englishness integrated into Middle-earth landscapes, embodying epistemologies and ontologies lost to more civilized communities like the Rohirrim and the Gondorians. The Drúedain are however categorized as Men (unlike Ents) – who remain unknowable and marginalized compared to the Hobbits and other groups of Men.

While the Drúadan's physical appearance resembles stone and vegetation, the implication is that his skin colour is of a familiar tint that does not require remark from Merry – in contrast to the Hobbits' description of Treebeard's brown skin. Does that mean that Ghân-buri-Ghân was to be understood as white,²⁸ like the Hobbit and the Rohirrim? Could this form of whiteness be understood as racialised through the trope of primitiveness, the inhabitation of wild forest spaces, the difference in language, "uncivilised" behaviour and lack of literacy in the normative sense? Was Ghân-buri-Ghân's racial difference then encoded in his gnarled "unlovely" body shape and guttural "uncouth" words? I see Tolkien navigating the slippery terrain of racialising discourse here, while working with a medieval world view that constructed Wild Men as uncivilised. Indeed a kind of primitive citizenship may be conferred on the Drúedain, when one considers Tolkien's philological explanation of the word "wose":

---

27 Tolkien thus gives this mythic "primitive undergrowth" form and voice in the figures of the Ents and the Drúedain, constructing natural "roots" evocative of England's cultural and geophysical substance. Cf. Tolkien, "The Story of Kullervo" 264; cf. also Scull and Hammond 441.
28 As ensconced as Middle-earth is in Tolkien's imagination for his mythological idea of England, the cultural imaginary evoked is inherently white and seen as "normal". Richard Dyer (45) notes: "Whites must be seen to be white, yet whiteness as race resides in invisible properties and whiteness as power is maintained by being unseen. To be seen as white is to have one's corporeality registered, yet true whiteness resides in the non-corporeal. The paradox and dynamic of this are expressed in the very choice of white to characterize us." This paradox set out by Dyer can be seen in the way Merry does not remark on the Wild Man's skin colour; Ghân-buri-Ghân's unremarked whiteness marks him as familiar to the Hobbit – whereby his whiteness is both invisible and hypervisible. However this familiarity is dubious, considering how Ghân-buri-Ghân is Othered by the Hobbit (and other Men) as deviant with regard to received understandings of civilized humanity, which then contributes to racialising the Wild Man as an unknowable objectified savage who merits a curious and dehumanizing gaze.

> *Wose* is a modernization [...] of an Anglo-Saxon word *wása* which is actually found only in the compound *wudu-wása* 'wild man of the woods'. [...] The actual word employed by the Rohirrim (of which 'wose' is a translation [...]) It seems that the term 'Pukel-men' (again a translation: it represents Anglo-Saxon *púcel* 'goblin, demon', a relative of the word *púca* [...]) was only used in Rohan of the images of Dunharrow. (*UT* 500-501)

In this philological exercise, Tolkien implies that the Drúedain are demonized by the Rohirrim in their use of the word "Pukel-men", whereby the stone sculptures are read as akin to the actual people, who are described as "gnarled as old stone". While the Hobbits are described as child-like, like the Drúedain, one notes that the Hobbits are depicted in terms that are recognizably human, "cultured" and capable of speech – they are familiar to Men in ways that the Drúedain are not (cf. *L* 158). The Hobbits too are marked as white (despite their tanned brown skins marking them as an outdoors people) – a commonality shared with Elves, Gondorians and the Rohirrim in Middle-earth. A significant point is that Merry gains information about the Drúedain and the planned meeting with their headman from a Rohirric soldier, who himself likens Merry to a tree-root when he unexpectedly comes upon him, thus underscoring the Hobbit's own likeness to the Drúedain as small, and bound to the land (*LotR* 813). Merry however does not note such similarities between Hobbits and the Woses; rather his gaze directed on Ghân-buri-Ghân is just as Othering as that of the Rohirrim:

> There sat Theoden and Eomer, and before them on the ground sat a strange, squat shape of a man, gnarled as an old stone, and the hairs of his scanty beard straggled on his lumpy chin like dry moss. He was short-legged and fat-armed, thick and stumpy, and clad only with grass about his waist. Merry felt that he had seen him before somewhere, and suddenly he remembered the Pukel-men of Dunharrow. Here was one of the old images brought to life [...] the Wild Man began to speak, in answer to some question [...] His voice was deep and guttural [...] he spoke the Common Speech, [...] and uncouth words were mingled with it. [...] The old man's flat face and dark eyes showed nothing, but his voice was sullen with displeasure. 'Wild Men are wild, free, but not children,' he answered. 'I am great headman, Ghân-buri-Ghân. I count many things: stars in sky, leaves on trees, men in the dark. [...] But if you live after the Darkness, then leave Wild Men alone in the woods and do not hunt them like beasts anymore.' (*LotR* 813-815)

This parley scene between the Rohirrim and the Drúedain resonates with museum dioramas depicting negotiation scenes between colonising agents and colonised peoples.[29] The gaze directed on the Drúedain chief is an anthropological one that serves to objectify and name his strangeness, marking him and his people as the Other. Keeping in mind Faramir's classification of the Wild Men as belonging to the group "Men of Darkness" (*LotR* 663), I observe Ghân-buri-Ghân displaces the trope of darkness onto Sauron's oppression of Middle-earth, pointing out that both the Rohirrim and the Drúedain alike face a common enemy. At the same time, the headman points out that he is aware of the kinds of prejudices used by the Rohirrim to justify their persecution of the Drúedain and refutes and rejects these firmly, by asserting Drúedain worldviews. In his astute negotiations with Théoden, where he offers to help move the Rohirrim forces towards Gondor through the Stonewain valley, to avoid the Orc troops on the main approach to the city, Ghân-buri-Ghân demonstrates diplomatic savvy, asserting a form of political agency born of necessity in the war against the greater threat of Sauron. He offers the knowledge that he and his people possess of Drúadan forest, based on their ability to navigate natural environs. Theoden and his people had evidently disregarded the rights of the Wild Men, deeming them inferior in intelligence, because their cultural epistemologies were not considered civilised enough. Here then, I read Ghân-buri-Ghân's act of negotiation and demand of rights as a decolonial gesture, in the sense that Walter Mignolo describes:

> 'Decolonial gestures' would be any and every gesture that directly or indirectly engages in disobeying the dictates of the colonial matrix and contributes to building of the human species on the planet in harmony with the life in/of the planet of which the human species is only a minimal part and of which it depends. And that would contribute to planetary re-emergence, re-surgence, and re-existence of people whose values, ways of being, languages, thoughts and stories were degraded in order to be dominated. (no pagination)

Here the dominated Wild Men assert their ways of being and their knowledges in order to claim their citizenship rights, for their lives and living spaces. This is contingent on the other races of Men resisting Sauron's thralldom. In their acceptance of Ghân-buri-Ghân's offer of help, there is a significant change in attitude on the part of the Rohirrim towards the Wild Men – "Yet to no

---

29 This is borne out by a painting by the Hildebrandt brothers (*Ghân-buri-Ghân*, August 1977); Cf. Greg and Tim Hildebrandt 67.

heart in all the host came any fear that the Wild Men were unfaithful, strange and unlovely though they might appear" (*LotR* 817) – whereby the moral integrity of the Wild Men is dissociated from the evaluation of their strange appearance. The implication here is that there are forms of whiteness that are racialised images of primitiveness, evoking the monstrosity of the medieval Wild Man and resonating with colonial language depicting the strangeness of indigenous peoples in the Primary World. At the same time, the stereotypes which justified the Rohirrim's persecution of the Drúedain are subverted.[30] This is a particularly decolonizing instance, where a marginalized and disenfranchised people reclaim their rights and their living spaces from a formerly oppressive adversary who had dehumanized them. This watershed moment would be a step towards reinstating Drúedain ontologies and epistemologies thus conferring citizenship on these human denizens of the Green world.

7 Concluding remarks

I have attempted to show above how Tolkien uses the Green Man figure to illustrate the proximity of the cultural Other within the concept of Englishness. It is in the wild forest spaces that Men and Hobbits meet residents of the Green world and acquire assistance from them, although these human agents have been complicit in the exploitation and erosion of these natural spaces and by extension, the exploitation and abuse of the Green Men figures themselves. Thus Tolkien's racialised descriptions of these Green Men, and the connotations of wildness accompanying them have been instrumental in demonstrating how the behaviours of these figures are contingent on Christian value systems typically ascribed to humankind. At the same time these Green Men figures underscore a strong decolonising element in Tolkien's work, where they reclaim their spaces and forms of citizenship. The Hobbits learn from Treebeard respect for the forest and its inhabitants

---

30 Margaret Sinex notes that Aragorn and Frodo exercise love and forgiveness towards their former enemies – the Haradrim and others who had been seduced by Sauron into fighting for him, and Saruman who had attempted to take over the Shire, respectively (Sinex 190). These are virtues closely aligned with a Christian worldview that Tolkien clearly espoused through his Catholicism. I note however that the entities constructed according to medieval conceptions of monstrosity and wildness, as uncivilized, unknowable and "uncouth", demonstrate considerable forms of forgiveness and cooperation despite Men's and Hobbits' exploitation of them and the living resources that they embody and represent.

and accrue valuable knowledge that will stand them in good stead to fight for the Shire. Treebeard learns about the Hobbits and includes them in his "Lore of Living Creatures" – a historical record of Middle-earth's beings. This oldest of beings, who at one time might have held a privileged position in terms of knowledge and wisdom demonstrates humility and generosity in his communications with creatures heretofore unknown to him, despite their child-like appearance; he demonstrates hospitality to these cultural Others. The Rohirrim learn that they need to depend on the knowledge and goodwill of those they had once indiscriminately persecuted, while the Drúedain make their demands for dignity and sovereignty heard with their offers of help to defeat a common enemy.

Working with the self-other paradigm of the medieval texts he was conversant with, Tolkien has doubtless implemented certain types of racialising discourse in the shaping of his world, using binary oppositions (good-evil, light-dark, beauty-ugliness, wild-civilised). At the same time, the liminality of these Green Men figures – attributed to their oscillations within the narrative along the boundaries between Middle-earth myth and history, both within and outside the purview of Men and Hobbits – serves to destabilise such rigid binary structures. Hence while Tolkien has racialised his Green Men figures, he does subvert to certain extents these very same perceptions and prejudices regarding the qualities of civilisation, wisdom, justice and knowledge inherent to these binaries that have been traditionally inscribed with normative masculine scripts that dictate forms of citizenship.

Yes, Tolkien should be recognized as a representative of English colonial power and privilege by virtue of his own hegemonic position as a white male Oxford professor invested in procuring and preserving forms of Englishness in his mythic *magnum opus* – there is no getting round that fact. But there is reason to believe that he was intent on some level, in recuperating the racialised, dehumanised, marginalised and monsterised in medieval and modern colonial traditions that are contiguous with each other. Here I note Jane Chance and Alfred Siewers' standpoint:

> [Tolkien's] medievalized fantasy illustrates how texts and stories (ultimately fictions) work in our cultural history to produce complex signifying systems of mythology, ideology and history, and how we ourselves use these systems

> to produce theories of meaning. In the process, reading Tolkien with fresh scholarly views, we can understand better how traditions themselves can, paradoxically, subvert. (Chance and Siewers 11)

In this vein, I would say that Tolkien himself performs a decolonial subversive gesture in that he provides the Drúedain and the Ents with powerful voices to articulate their resistance against objectification and abjectification, to express their cultural epistemologies which inhere with their specific ontologies. However it bears thinking that these Green and Wild Men were not to share in the forms of citizenship envisioned in the Fourth Age of Middle-earth – the Age of Men. While the Wild Men are bequeathed the Drúadan Forest at the end of the War of the Ring by King Elessar as a reward for their loyal efforts and generosity to their erstwhile enemies, they elect to remain hidden in the Wild, isolated and free – they disappear into the realm of myth (*LotR* 954). In a last decolonial move on my part, I ask if the Drúadan forest had belonged to King Elessar in the first place, which he then chooses to bestow on the Drúedain – considering that the Drúedain are the indigenous inhabitants of that space. The Ents will recede into the forest space, into myth ("the willow-meads of Tasarinan"), much like the Elves (*LotR* 958-959); loss marks the Ents in the resolution of the narrative. Thus the Green Man figures walk out of legend and into Middle-earth, at least for a while to underscore how constructions of English selfhood must needs consider recognising this same self, mirrored (perhaps in fractured or refracted ways) in the Other. Temporary sojourns in such metaphorical forests would be then a necessary part of the journey to a more inclusive and diverse cultural sensibility.

About the Author

Originally from Singapore, CHRISTINE VOGT-WILLIAM studied English, German and Psychology at the University of Essen, Germany. She completed her doctoral thesis at the Centre for Women's Studies at the University of York, England, as a Marie Curie Gender Graduate Fellow. Besides publications on South Asian diasporic literature from the US, Canada, England and the Caribbean, she is co-editor of *Disturbing Bodies* (2008), an essay collection on artistic and literary representations of deviant bodies. She is also the author of *Bridges, Borders and Bodies: Transgressive Transculturality in Contemporary South Asian Diasporic Women's Novels* (2014). Vogt-William was a Visiting Scholar at the Department of Women's Studies at Emory University, Atlanta, Georgia, USA from 2008 to 2010. On returning to Germany, she taught in the Postcolonial and Media Studies Department at the University of Münster, as well as in the North American Studies department at the University of Freiburg. Vogt-William was Interim Professor for Postcolonial and Gender Studies at the English and American Studies Department, at Humboldt University, Berlin, where she taught in the fields of literary and cultural studies for the past three years. She is currently working on her second book on biological twinship in Anglophone literatures and is adjunct faculty at the Universities of Erlangen-Nuremberg and Augsburg. Other current research interests include transnational and transracial adoption narratives, and representations of womb surrogacy in contemporary women's fiction.

List of Abbreviations

GPO TOLKIEN, J.R.R. (transl.) *Sir Gawain and the Green Knight, Pearl and Sir Orfeo*. Ed. Christopher Tolkien. London: HarperCollins, 2006.

L CARPENTER, Humphrey, ed. with the assistance of Christopher Tolkien. *The Letters of J.R.R. Tolkien*. London: HarperCollins, 1995.

LotR TOLKIEN, J.R.R. *The Lord of The Rings*. London: HarperCollins, 1994.

MC TOLKIEN, J.R.R. *The Monsters and the Critics and Other Essays*. Ed. Christopher Tolkien. London: HarperCollins, 1997.

S TOLKIEN, J.R.R. *The Silmarillion*. Ed. Christopher Tolkien. London: HarperCollins, 1998.

TL TOLKIEN, J.R.R. *Tree and Leaf*. London: HarperCollins, 2001.

UT TOLKIEN, J.R.R. *Unfinished Tales of Numénor and Middle-earth*. Ed. Christopher Tolkien. London: HarperCollins, 1998.

Bibliography

BALDWIN, Andrew, Laura CAMERON, and Audrey KOBAYASHI. *Rethinking the Great White North: Race, Nature and the Historical Geographies of Whiteness in Canada*. Vancouver, Toronto: University of British Columbia Press, 2011.

BASNEY, Lionel. "Myth, History and Time in *The Lord of The Rings*." *Understanding The Lord of the Rings: The Best of Tolkien Criticism*. Eds. Rose Zimbardo and Neil D. Isaacs. Boston and New York: Houghton and Mifflin, 2004. 183-194.

BEATTIE, Cordelia and Kirsten FENTON. *Intersections of Gender, Religion and Ethnicity in the Middle Ages*. Basingstoke: Palgrave MacMillan, 2011.

BOEHMER, Elleke. *Colonial and Postcolonial Literature*. Oxford University Press, 1995.

CARPENTER, Humphrey, ed. with the assistance of Christopher TOLKIEN. *The Letters of J.R.R. Tolkien*. London: HarperCollins, 1995.

The Inklings: C.S: Lewis, J.R.R. Tolkien, Charles Williams and Their Friends. London: HarperCollins, 2006.

CENTERWALL, Brandon S. "The Name of the Green Man." *Folklore*, 108 (1997): 25-33.

CHANCE, Jane. "Tolkien and the Other: Race and Gender in Middle-earth." *Tolkien's Modern Middle Ages*. Eds. Jane Chance and Alfred K. Siewers. New York: Palgrave MacMillan, 2005. 171-186.

and Alfred K. SIEWERS. "Introduction: Tolkien's Modern Medievalism." *Tolkien's Modern Middle Ages*. Eds. Jane Chance and Alfred K. Siewers. New York: Palgrave MacMillan, 2005. 1-13.

COHEN, Jeffrey Jerome, ed. *The Postcolonial Middle Ages*. New York: Palgrave MacMillan. 2000.

CRENSHAW, Kimberlé Williams. "Mapping the Margins: Intersectionality, Identity Politics, and Violence Against Women of Color." *The Public Nature of Private Violence*. Eds. Martha Albertson Fineman and Rixanne Mykitiuk. New York: Routledge, 1994. 93-118.

DE CERTEAU, Michel. *The Practice of Everyday Life*. Berkeley and Los Angeles, California: University of California Press, 1984.

DYER, Richard. *White*. London and New York: Routledge, 1997.

ECO, Umberto. *Art and Beauty in the Middle Ages*. (Transl. Hugh Bredin). New Haven, CT: Yale University Press, 2002.

ECHO-HAWK, Roger. *Tolkien in Pawneeland: The Secret Sources of Middle-earth.* CreateSpace Independent Publishing Platform, 2013.

FIMI, Dmitra. *Tolkien, Race and Cultural History: From Fairies to Hobbits.* New York: Palgrave MacMillan, 2010.

FLIEGER, Verlyn. "The Green Knight, The Green Man and Treebeard: Scholarship and Invention in Tolkien's Fiction." *Green Suns and Faerie: Essays on J.R.R. Tolkien.* Kent, OH: Kent State University Press, 2012. 211-222.

"Taking the Part of Trees: Eco-Conflict in Middle-earth." *Green Suns and Faerie: Essays on J.R.R. Tolkien.* Kent, OH: Kent State University Press, 2012. 262-274.

"Tolkien's Wild Men from Medieval to Modern." *Green Suns and Faerie: Essays on J.R.R. Tolkien.* Kent, OH: Kent State University Press, 2012. 115-126.

HILDEBRANDT, Greg and Tim. *The Tolkien Years.* New York: Watson and Guptill Publications, 2001.

HODGE, Bob and Vijay MISHRA. "Aboriginal Place." *The Postcolonial Studies Reader.* Eds. Bill Ashcroft, Gareth Griffiths, and Helen Tiffin. London and New York: Routledge, 1995. 412-417.

HOLSINGER, Bruce. "Medieval Studies, Postcolonial Studies and the Genealogies of Critique." *Speculum* 77.4 (2002): 1195-1227.

KIDD, Colin. *The Forging of Races: Race and Scripture in the Protestant Atlantic World, 1600-2000.* Cambridge: Cambridge University Press. 2006.

KRASS, Andreas, Natasa BEDEKOVIC, and Astrid LEMBKE, eds. *Durchkreuzte Helden. Das "Nibelungenlied" und Fritz Langs "Die Nibelungen" im Licht der Intersektionalitaetsforschung.* Bielefeld: Transcript Verlag, 2014.

KRASS, Andreas. "Im Namen des Bruders: Fraternalität in Freundschaftsdiskursen der Antike, des Mittelalters und der Frühen Neuzeit.". *Behemoth: A Journal on Civilisation* 4.3 (2011): 4-22.

LIEBHERR, Louise. *Reimagining Tolkien: A Post-colonial Perspective on The Lord of the Rings.* PhD Thesis. University of Limerick. 2012. Online Publication. https://dspace.mic.ul.ie/xmlui/handle/10395/1526

MATHEWS, John. *The Green Man: Spirit of Nature.* London: Connections, 2002.

McFADDEN, Brian. "Fear of Difference, Fear of Death: The Sigelwara, Tolkien's Swertings and Racial Difference." *Tolkien's Modern Middle Ages.* Eds. Jane Chance and Alfred K. Siewers. London: Palgrave MacMillan, 2005. 155-169.

MIGNOLO, Walter. "Looking for the Meaning of Decolonial Gesture". *E-misferica Gesto Decolonial* 11.1 (2014). No pagination. Web. http://hemisphericinstitute.org/hemi/pt/e-misferica-111-gesto-decolonial/mignolo.

OLSEN, Corey. "The Myth of the Ent and the Entwife." *Tolkien Studies* 5 (2008): 39-53.

PASTOUREAU, Michel. *Green: The History of a Color*. Princeton, N.J.: Princeton University Press, 2014.

RAGLAN, Lady. "The 'Green Man' in Church Architecture." *Folklore* 50.1 (1939): 45-57.

SCULL, Christina and Wayne HAMMOND. *The J.R.R. Tolkien Companion and Reader's Guide*. Boston and New York: Houghton Mifflin, 2006.

SHIPPEY, Tom. "Trees, Chainsaws and Visions of Paradise." 2012. On http://www.tolkiendil.com/essais/tolkien_1892-2012/tom_shippey. No pagination.

SIEWERS, Alfred K. "Tolkien's Cosmic-Christian Ecology: The Medieval Underpinnings." *Tolkien's Modern Middle Ages*. Eds. Jane Chance and Alfred K. Siewers. New York: Palgrave MacMillan, 2005. 139-153.

SINEX, Margaret. "'Monsterized Saracens'. Tolkien's Haradrim, and Other Medieval 'Fantasy Products'." *Tolkien Studies* 7 (2005): 175-196.

SOMERVILLE, Alison Te Punga. "Asking that mountain: an Indigenous reading of LOTR?" *Studying the Film-Event: The Lord of the Rings*. Eds. Sean Cubitt, Thierry Jutel, Barry King, and Harriet Margolis. Manchester: Manchester University Press, 2008. 249-258.

SPICKARD, Paul, and Jeffrey BURROUGHS, eds. *We Are A People: Narrative and Multiplicity in Constructing Ethnic Identity*. Philadelphia: Temple University Press, 2000.

TOLKIEN, J.R.R. *The Lord of The Rings*. London: HarperCollins, 1994.

The Silmarillion. Ed. Christopher Tolkien. London: HarperCollins, 1998.

"Sir Gawain and the Green Knight." *The Monsters and the Critics and Other Essays*. Ed. Christopher Tolkien. London: HarperCollins, 1997. 73-108.

(transl.) *Sir Gawain and the Green Knight, Pearl and Sir Orfeo*. Ed. Christopher Tolkien. London: HarperCollins, 2006.

"'The Story of Kullervo' and Essays on Kalevala." Edited and transcribed by Verlyn Flieger. *Tolkien Studies* 7 (2010): 211-278.

Tree and Leaf. London: HarperCollins, 2001.

Unfinished Tales of Númenor and Middle-earth. Ed. Christopher Tolkien. HarperCollins, 1998.

WORSTBROCK, Franz-Josef. "Dilatatio Materiae: Zur Poetik des *Erec* Hartmanns von Aue." *Ausgewaehlte Schriften. Band 1: Schriften zur Literatur des Mittelalters.* Stuttgart, 2004. 197-228.

Walking Tree Publishers
Zurich and Jena

Walking Tree Publishers was founded in 1997 as a forum for publication of material (books, videos, CDs, etc.) related to Tolkien and Middle-earth studies.

http://www.walking-tree.org

Cormarë Series

The *Cormarë Series* collects papers and studies dedicated exclusively to the exploration of Tolkien's work. It comprises monographs, thematic collections of essays, conference volumes, and reprints of important yet no longer (easily) accessible papers by leading scholars in the field. Manuscripts and project proposals are evaluated by members of an independent board of advisors who support the series editors in their endeavour to provide the readers with qualitatively superior yet accessible studies on Tolkien and his work.

News from the Shire and Beyond. Studies on Tolkien
Peter Buchs and Thomas Honegger (eds.), Zurich and Berne 2004, Reprint, First edition 1997 (Cormarë Series 1), ISBN 978-3-9521424-5-5

Root and Branch. Approaches Towards Understanding Tolkien
Thomas Honegger (ed.), Zurich and Berne 2005, Reprint, First edition 1999 (Cormarë Series 2), ISBN 978-3-905703-01-6

Richard Sturch, *Four Christian Fantasists. A Study of the Fantastic Writings of George MacDonald, Charles Williams, C.S. Lewis and J.R.R. Tolkien*
Zurich and Berne 2007, Reprint, First edition 2001 (Cormarë Series 3), ISBN 978-3-905703-04-7

Tolkien in Translation
Thomas Honegger (ed.), Zurich and Jena 2011, Reprint, First edition 2003 (Cormarë Series 4), ISBN 978-3-905703-15-3

Mark T. Hooker, *Tolkien Through Russian Eyes*
Zurich and Berne 2003 (Cormarë Series 5), ISBN 978-3-9521424-7-9

Translating Tolkien: Text and Film
Thomas Honegger (ed.), Zurich and Jena 2011, Reprint, First edition 2004 (Cormarë Series 6), ISBN 978-3-905703-16-0

Christopher Garbowski, *Recovery and Transcendence for the Contemporary Mythmaker. The Spiritual Dimension in the Works of J.R.R. Tolkien*
Zurich and Berne 2004, Reprint, First Edition by Marie Curie Sklodowska, University Press, Lublin 2000, (Cormarë Series 7), ISBN 978-3-9521424-8-6

Reconsidering Tolkien
Thomas Honegger (ed.), Zurich and Berne 2005 (Cormarë Series 8), ISBN 978-3-905703-00-9

Tolkien and Modernity 1
Frank Weinreich and Thomas Honegger (eds.), Zurich and Berne 2006 (Cormarë Series 9), ISBN 978-3-905703-02-3

Tolkien and Modernity 2
Thomas Honegger and Frank Weinreich (eds.), Zurich and Berne 2006 (Cormarë Series 10), ISBN 978-3-905703-03-0

Tom Shippey, *Roots and Branches. Selected Papers on Tolkien by Tom Shippey*
Zurich and Berne 2007 (Cormarë Series 11), ISBN 978-3-905703-05-4

Ross Smith, *Inside Language. Linguistic and Aesthetic Theory in Tolkien*
Zurich and Jena 2011, Reprint, First edition 2007 (Cormarë Series 12), ISBN 978-3-905703-20-7

How We Became Middle-earth. A Collection of Essays on The Lord of the Rings
Adam Lam and Nataliya Oryshchuk (eds.), Zurich and Berne 2007 (Cormarë Series 13), ISBN 978-3-905703-07-8

Myth and Magic. Art According to the Inklings
Eduardo Segura and Thomas Honegger (eds.), Zurich and Berne 2007 (Cormarë Series 14), ISBN 978-3-905703-08-5

The Silmarillion - Thirty Years On
Allan Turner (ed.), Zurich and Berne 2007 (Cormarë Series 15), ISBN 978-3-905703-10-8

Martin Simonson, *The Lord of the Rings and the Western Narrative Tradition*
Zurich and Jena 2008 (Cormarë Series 16), ISBN 978-3-905703-09-2

Tolkien's Shorter Works. Proceedings of the 4th Seminar of the Deutsche Tolkien Gesellschaft & Walking Tree Publishers Decennial Conference
Margaret Hiley and Frank Weinreich (eds.), Zurich and Jena 2008 (Cormarë Series 17), ISBN 978-3-905703-11-5

Tolkien's The Lord of the Rings: Sources of Inspiration
Stratford Caldecott and Thomas Honegger (eds.), Zurich and Jena 2008 (Cormarë Series 18), ISBN 978-3-905703-12-2

J.S. Ryan, *Tolkien's View: Windows into his World*
Zurich and Jena 2009 (Cormarë Series 19), ISBN 978-3-905703-13-9

Music in Middle-earth
Heidi Steimel and Friedhelm Schneidewind (eds.), Zurich and Jena 2010 (Cormarë Series 20), ISBN 978-3-905703-14-6

Liam Campbell, *The Ecological Augury in the Works of JRR Tolkien*
Zurich and Jena 2011 (Cormarë Series 21), ISBN 978-3-905703-18-4

Margaret Hiley, *The Loss and the Silence. Aspects of Modernism in the Works of C.S. Lewis, J.R.R. Tolkien and Charles Williams*
Zurich and Jena 2011 (Cormarë Series 22), ISBN 978-3-905703-19-1

Rainer Nagel, *Hobbit Place-names. A Linguistic Excursion through the Shire*
Zurich and Jena 2012 (Cormarë Series 23), ISBN 978-3-905703-22-1

Christopher MacLachlan, *Tolkien and Wagner: The Ring and Der Ring*
Zurich and Jena 2012 (Cormarë Series 24), ISBN 978-3-905703-21-4

Renée Vink, *Wagner and Tolkien: Mythmakers*
Zurich and Jena 2012 (Cormarë Series 25), ISBN 978-3-905703-25-2

The Broken Scythe. Death and Immortality in the Works of J.R.R. Tolkien
Roberto Arduini and Claudio A. Testi (eds.), Zurich and Jena 2012 (Cormarë Series 26), ISBN 978-3-905703-26-9

Sub-creating Middle-earth: Constructions of Authorship and the Works of J.R.R. Tolkien
Judith Klinger (ed.), Zurich and Jena 2012 (Cormarë Series 27),
ISBN 978-3-905703-27-6

Tolkien's Poetry
Julian Eilmann and Allan Turner (eds.), Zurich and Jena 2013
(Cormarë Series 28), ISBN 978-3-905703-28-3

O, What a Tangled Web. Tolkien and Medieval Literature. A View from Poland
Barbara Kowalik (ed.), Zurich and Jena 2013 (Cormarë Series 29),
ISBN 978-3-905703-29-0

J.S. Ryan, *In the Nameless Wood*
Zurich and Jena 2013 (Cormarë Series 30), ISBN 978-3-905703-30-6

From Peterborough to Faëry; The Poetics and Mechanics of Secondary Worlds
Thomas Honegger & Dirk Vanderbeke (eds.), Zurich and Jena 2014
(Cormarë Series 31), ISBN 978-3-905703-31-3

Tolkien and Philosophy
Roberto Arduini and Claudio A. Testi (eds.), Zurich and Jena 2014
(Cormarë Series 32), ISBN 978-3-905703-32-0

Patrick Curry, *Deep Roots in a Time of Frost. Essays on Tolkien*
Zurich and Jena 2014 (Cormarë Series 33), ISBN 978-3-905703-33-7

Representations of Nature in Middle-earth
Martin Simonson (ed.), Zurich and Jena 2015, (Cormarë Series 34),
ISBN 978-3-905703-34-4

Laughter in Middle-earth
Thomas Honegger and Maureen F. Mann (eds.), Zurich and Jena 2016
(Cormarë Series 35), ISBN 978-3-905703-35-1

Julian Eilmann, *J.R.R. Tolkien – Romanticist and Poet*
Zurich and Jena 2017 (Cormarë Series 36), ISBN 978-3-905703-36-8

One Ring to Bind Them All.
Interdisciplinary Perspectives on J.R.R. Tolkien and his Works
Monika Kirner-Ludwig, Stephan Köser, Sebastian Streitberger (eds.),
Zurich and Jena 2017 (Cormarë Series 37), ISBN 978-3-905703-37-5

Claudio A. Testi, *Pagan Saints in Middle-earth*, forthcoming

Tolkien and Literary Worldbuilding
Dimitra Fimi and Thomas Honegger (eds.), forthcoming

Middle-earth, or There and Back Again
Łukasz Neubauer (ed.), forthcoming

Music in Tolkien's Work and Beyond
Julian Eilmann and Friedhelm Schneidewind (eds.), forthcoming

Beowulf and the Dragon

The original Old English text of the 'Dragon Episode' of *Beowulf* is set in an authentic font and bound in hardback as a high quality art book. Illustrated by Anke Eissmann and accompanied by John Porter's translation. Introduction by Tom Shippey. Limited first edition of 500 copies. 84 pages. Selected pages can be previewed on: www.walking-tree.org/beowulf
Zurich and Jena 2009, ISBN 978-3-905703-17-7

Tales of Yore Series

The *Tales of Yore Series* provides a platform for qualitatively superior fiction that will appeal to readers familiar with Tolkien's world:

The Monster Specialist

Sir Severus le Brewse, among the least known of King Arthur's Round Table knights, is preferred by nature, disposition, and training to fight against monsters rather than other knights. After youthful adventures of errantry with dragons, trolls, vampires, and assorted beasts, Severus joins the brilliant sorceress Lilava to face the Chimaera in The Greatest Monster Battle of All Time to free her folk from an age-old curse. But their adventures don't end there; together they meet elves and magicians, friends and foes; they join in the fight to save Camelot and even walk the Grey Paths of the Dead. With a mix of Malory, a touch of Tolkien, and a hint of humor, The Monster Specialist chronicles a tale of courage, tenacity, honor, and love.

The Monster Specialist is illustrated by Anke Eissmann.

Edward S. Louis, *The Monster Specialist*
Zurich and Jena 2014 (Tales of Yore Series No. 3), ISBN 978-3-905703-23-8

Tales of Yore Series (earlier books)

Kay Woollard, *The Terror of Tatty Walk. A Frightener*
CD and Booklet, Zurich and Berne 2000, ISBN 978-3-9521424-2-4

Kay Woollard, *Wilmot's Very Strange Stone or What came of building "snobbits"*
CD and booklet, Zurich and Berne 2001, ISBN 978-3-9521424-4-8

Information for authors

Authors interested in contributing to our publications can learn more about the services we offer by reading the "services for authors" section of our web pages.

http://www.walking-tree.org/authors

e-mail: info@walking-tree.org

www.ingramcontent.com/pod-product-compliance
Lightning Source LLC
Chambersburg PA
CBHW050846240426
43667CB00022B/2936